Critical Dialogues of Urban Governance, Development and Activism

Critical Dialogues of Urban Governance, Development and Activism

London & Toronto

Edited by

Susannah Bunce, Nicola Livingstone, Loren March,
Susan Moore and Alan Walks

First published in 2020 by
UCL Press
University College London
Gower Street
London WC1E 6BT

Available to download free: www.uclpress.co.uk

ISBN: 978-1-78735-681-8 (Hbk.)
ISBN: 978-1-78735-680-1 (Pbk.)
ISBN: 978-1-78735-679-5 (PDF)
ISBN: 978-1-78735-682-5 (epub)
ISBN: 978-1-78735-683-2 (mobi)
DOI: https://doi.org/10.14324/111.9781787356795

Contents

List of figures

List of tables

List of acronyms

AONB	Area of Outstanding Natural Beauty
AST	Assured Shorthold Tenancy (London)
BC	British Columbia
BID	Business Improvement District (London)
BOST	Bankside Open Spaces Trust (London)
CAPREIT	Canadian Apartment Properties REIT
CIL	Community Infrastructure Levy (London)
CLHL	Community-Led Housing London
CLSA	Conditional Land Sale Agreement (London)
CLT	Community Land Trust
CMA	Census metropolitan area (Toronto)
CMHC	Canada Mortgage and Housing Corporation
CSCB	Coin Street Community Builders (London)
CTRL	Channel Tunnel Rail Link (London, see also HS1)
DCLG	Department for Communities and Local Government (London)
DEFRA	Department for the Environment, Farming and Rural Affairs
DfT	Department for Transport (London)
DIY	Do-it-yourself
ELCLT	East London Community Land Trust, now London CLT
EiP	Examination in Public (London)
GDP	Gross domestic product
GFC	Global Financial Crisis
GLA	Greater London Authority
GLC	Greater London Council
GTA	Greater Toronto Area
HCA	Homes and Communities Agency (London)
HDV	Haringey Development Vehicle (London)
HMO	Houses in Multiple Occupation (London)
HNWI	High net-worth individuals
HPI	House price index
HRA	Housing Revenue Account (London)
HS1 and HS2	High Speed One and High Speed Two (London)
ICT	Information and communications technology

IFC	International financial centre
ILEO	Inclusive Local Economic Opportunity
JSEP	Just Space Economy and Planning (London)
KMCLT	Kensington Market Community Land Trust
LP	London Plan
LPDM	London Plan density matrix (London)
LQ	location quotient
LTV	Loan-to-value ratio
LVC	Land value capture
NLT	Neighbourhood Land Trust
OMB	Ontario Municipal Board (Toronto)
PARC	Parkdale Activity Recreation Centre (Toronto)
PCED	Parkdale Community Economic Development, also Parkdale People's Economy Community Planning (Toronto)
PNLT	Parkdale Neighbourhood Land Trust (Toronto)
POPS	Privately owned public spaces
PRS	Private rented sector
PTAL	Public transport accessibility level (London)
REIT	Real estate investment trust
RTP	Regional Transport Plan (Toronto)
SE	Shared equity
SO	Shared ownership
SPD	Supplementary planning documents
SPV	Special purpose vehicle
SRQ	Sustainable residential quality (London)
TfL	Transport for London
TOD	Transit-oriented development
TSNS	Toronto Strong Neighbourhoods Strategy
TTC	Toronto Transit Commission
TTSSG	Thames Tideway Strategic Study Group
WECH	Walterton and Elgin Community Homes
WKGGCH	West Ken and Gibbs Green Community Housing (London)

List of contributors

Editors

Susannah Bunce is Associate Professor in the Department of Human Geography and City Studies Program at the University of Toronto Scarborough. Her research focuses on the relationships between spatial, social and environmental processes in urban neighbourhoods and urban community-based development. She has researched community land trusts, as a model for collective and de-commodified land ownership, in cities in the UK, US and Canada for the past 10 years. In addition to articles in international peer-reviewed journals, Bunce is the author of *Sustainability Policy, Planning, and Gentrification in Cities* (2018).

Nicola Livingstone is Associate Professor in Real Estate at the Bartlett School of Planning, UCL. Before joining UCL she worked as a lecturer at Heriot-Watt University, where she completed her PhD. Her background is in real estate and urban studies. She has published widely on these topics and has recently been working on projects examining real estate investment trends, the evolution of the retail market, the impacts of changes to the planning system on cities, the political economy of charity and food insecurity. Recent co-authored publications include *Understanding the Impacts of Deregulation in Planning* (2020) and *New Money in Rural Areas* (2019). She has completed funded research work for both the RICS and the British Academy/Leverhulme and is currently working on a collaborative ORA-ESRC-funded project on investment flows and residential development in London, Paris and Amsterdam named WHIG: What is Governed in Cities.

Loren March is a PhD candidate in Human Geography at the University of Toronto's Department of Geography and Planning. Their research centres around complex processes and experiences of change in altered urban environments and has critically examined gentrification, redevelopment and creative place-making practices. Their most recent work specifically examines questions of environmental gentrification and the more-than-human implications of capitalist urbanisation processes in Toronto.

Susan Moore is Associate Professor in Urban Development and Planning at the Bartlett School of Planning, UCL. Her research has focused on relational geographies of urban and suburban development, with a particular focus on development cultures in context. She has written extensively on New Urbanism in Toronto and is currently co-authoring a book on the international reach and mainstreaming of New Urbanism with Dan Trudeau (Macalester College), to be published by University of Toronto Press as part of the Global Suburbanisms Book Series. Her other work has looked at urban development and governance models and the formation and circulation of so-called best practices. Most recently, she has collaborated with geography and media colleagues from Birkbeck, University of London in examining the use of social media platforms in relation to processes of local urban change in east London. She is also co-author of several papers and book chapters on the phenomenologies of Platform Urbanism and a co-researcher in a collaborative, international UNECE-supported project on Urban Data Cultures.

Alan Walks is Professor of Urban Planning and Geography at the University of Toronto. His work examines the causes and consequences of different forms of urban inequality, including those related to housing policies and housing markets, financial markets, gentrification, automobility, gated communities and neighbourhood segregation processes. In addition to publishing his research in numerous international peer-reviewed journals, he is the editor of the book *The Political Economy and Ecology of Automobility: Driving Cities, Driving Inequality, Driving Politics* (2015), and co-editor of the books *The Political Ecology of the Metropolis* (2013) and *Changing Neighbourhoods: Social and Spatial Polarization in Canadian Cities* (2020).

Authors

Jeff Biggar is an urban planning professional and adjunct professor. His research focuses on planning and urban governance, with a focus on land use conflict in neighbourhood-level urban redevelopment. His current research assesses the implications of smart city schemes for innovation and governance in the public sector. He has taught courses in urban studies, geography and planning and he has extensive experience consulting on planning and policy projects. He holds a PhD in Planning from the University of Toronto.

Shauna Brail is Associate Professor in the Institute for Management and Innovation at the University of Toronto. As an urban planner and economic geographer, Brail's research focuses on the transformation of cities as a result of economic, social and cultural change.

Daniel Durrant is Lecturer in Infrastructure Planning at UCL's Bartlett School of Planning and currently a Humboldt Fellow at the Humboldt-Universität zu Berlin. His interests are in the issues surrounding large infrastructure projects and new infrastructures, how they are planned, how they function as socio-technical systems and the politics of infrastructure. He has a long-standing interest in the role of civil society in shaping the built environment and the provision of public goods.

Beyond this he is interested in the political economy of the built environment, which has also led him to conduct research into the development industry and housing.

Theresa Enright is Associate Professor of Political Science at the University of Toronto. Her research examines urban and regional politics with a focus on transport and mobility. She is the author of *The Making of Grand Paris: Metropolitan Urbanism in the Twenty-first Century* (2016) and editor (with Ugo Rossi) of *The Urban Political: Ambivalent Spaces of Late Neoliberalism* (2017). She is currently working on a book titled *Art in Transit: The Cultural Politics of Mobility.*

Jessica Ferm is Associate Professor at the Bartlett School of Planning, UCL. She is a practice-focused academic with research interests in spatial planning, economic development and social justice, with a particular interest in land use conflicts between industry and housing. She has published widely on these topics in the journals *Urban Studies, European Planning Studies, Planning Practice and Research* and *Journal of Corporate Real Estate.* She is co-editor of a book on planning practice in the UK and co-author of *Understanding the Impacts of Deregulation in Planning: Turning Offices into Homes* (2019). She has worked on research projects for the RICS Research Trust and is currently a Co-Investigator on the ESRC project WHIG: What is Governed in Cities, which compares residential investment landscapes and the governance and regulation of housing production in London, Amsterdam and Paris. She is active in planning practice and policy in London and is a member of Just Space Economy and Planning, the London Planning and Development Forum, the Economics Roundtable for London and the Commission for Economic Renewal. Prior to academia, she worked for 10 years as a planning consultant and in public practice for a north London planning authority.

Daniel Fitzpatrick is a Teaching Fellow at the Bartlett School of Planning, UCL, where he finished his PhD in Planning Studies in 2017, investigating mutual housing models in London and their governance. His current research is around community-led planning, housing and governance issues and he has co-authored the book *Community-led Regeneration* (2020) with Pablo Sendra.

Tommaso Gabrieli is Associate Professor in Real Estate at UCL's Bartlett School of Planning. His research focuses on the economic analysis of urban policy issues and his major area of contribution is currently in the interface between urban planning/design and real estate/urban economics. His expertise encompasses the economic modelling of real estate markets, the analysis of the financial viability of major urban projects, multidimensional value measurement and value capture, as well as urban policy issues related to segregation, poverty and deprivation. He employs interdisciplinary methods merging behavioural economics, game theory and real option analysis, as well as qualitative empirical methods, and he is one of very few economists in the UK actively collaborating with scholars in urban planning and urban design. He has authored research reports, book chapters and journal articles across various fields, including *Urban Studies*, *Progress in Planning* and *Journal of Economic Asymmetries*. He is currently Co-Investigator in the UCL team for the 'Urban Maestro' Horizon 2020 project.

Sean Grisdale is a PhD candidate in Human Geography at the University of Toronto. His research on the political economy of urban development focuses on how digital technologies and platforms are increasingly centred as solutions to problems of sustainability and affordable housing, particularly in post-industrial, global city contexts such as Toronto. His most recent projects have considered the politics of short-term rental platforms and the 'smart city' as expressions of the ongoing but shifting dynamics of urban planning and governance under capitalism.

Emily Hawes is a PhD candidate in Human Geography at the University of Toronto. Her research on urban and economic life is concerned with the interactions between large-scale processes and everyday lived experiences. Her most recent projects have considered financialisation, inequality, household debt, FinTech and rental housing.

Claudio De Magalhães is Professor in Urban Regeneration and Management at the Bartlett School of Planning, UCL, with a background in architecture and urban planning. His interests have been in planning and the governance of the built environment at various levels, looking at property development processes and urban regeneration policy, the management of urban quarters and the provision and governance of public space. He has conducted research for UK Research Councils, professional bodies such as the RICS, CABE, UK government departments and local authorities and published widely on property markets and globalisation; capacity-building for urban governance; the relationship between urban governance, the built environment and property markets; business improvement districts; and the provision and management of public spaces. His most recent research looks at the relationship between planning policies and perceptions of risk in the housebuilding industry. His most recent books include *Design Governance: The CABE Experiment* (2017) and *Planning, Risk and Property Development: Urban Regeneration in England, France and the Netherlands* (2013). He is currently working on a book comparing the governance and management regimes for public spaces in London and Hong Kong.

Tatiana Moreira de Souza is a Research Fellow in Urban Planning and Property Markets at Oxford Brookes University. Her research interests include urban regeneration and neighbourhood change, urban diversity and social mix, housing policy and the links between housing tenure, housing conditions and well-being. She was educated in Brazil and in the UK, with a first degree in Architecture and Urbanism from the University of São Paulo, Brazil, an MSc in Urban Regeneration and a PhD in Planning Studies from UCL's Bartlett School of Planning.

Elena Ostanel holds a PhD in Urban Planning. She is now running a Marie Skłodowska-Curie research project at Iuav University of Venice in partnership with University of Toronto and TU Delft. At Iuav she is based at the Department of

Architecture and Arts, where she collaborates with the UNESCO Chair on Social and Spatial Inclusion of International Migrants. She teaches courses in community planning and innovation in local governments. Among her recent publications is '(In)visibilising Vulnerable Community Members: Processes of Urban Inclusion and Exclusion in Parkdale, Toronto'.

Joe Penny is Lecturer in Economic Geography at Queen Mary University of London. He is interested in the local state, the governance of austerity and the financialisation of housing.

Mike Raco is Professor of Urban Governance and Development at the Bartlett School of Planning, UCL. He has published widely on the topics of urban governance and regeneration, urban sustainability, social diversity, and the politics of urban and regional economic development. He is currently leading a team at UCL that is working on a collaborative ORA-ESRC-funded project on investment flows and residential development in London, Paris and Amsterdam named WHIG: What is Governed in Cities. Recent works include *The Future of Sustainable Cities: Critical Reflections* (2011, with John Flint), *State-led Privatisation and the Demise of the Democratic State: Welfare Reform and Localism in an Era of Regulatory Capitalism* and *Regenerating London: Governance, Sustainability and Community in a Global City* (2013, with Rob Imrie and Loretta Lees).

Pablo Sendra is Lecturer in Planning and Urban Design at the Bartlett School of Planning, UCL. He combines his academic career with professional practice in urban design. He is co-founder of the urban design practice Lugadero, which has recently facilitated a co-design process for two public spaces in Wimbledon, London. He is also co-founder of Civicwise, a network that works on civic engagement and collaborative urbanism. He develops action research projects and radical teaching in collaboration with community groups and activists in London. At UCL, he is Acting Director of the MSc in Urban Design and City Planning programme, coordinator of the Civic Design CPD Course and Deputy Leader of the Urban Design Research Group. He is co-author of *Designing Disorder* (2020, with Richard Sennett) and *Community-Led Regeneration* (2020, with Daniel Fitzpatrick) and co-editor of *Civic Practices* (2017, with Maria J. Pita and Civicwise).

Michael Short is Principal Teaching Fellow in Planning and Urban Conservation, Bartlett School of Planning, UCL. He is an urbanist and conservator interested in issues of design quality in the historic environment. He undertakes practice-based projects, teaching and research in three main areas. The first area is how design issues are negotiated through the planning process and how they are implemented on site; the second is the conservation of buildings of the recent past and the challenges this presents for conservation and planning practice; and the third is debates about increased building height and density in environments where the historic environment and character of place are relevant. At the heart of all three areas of research is an interest in the negotiation of a higher-quality built environment.

Matti Siemiatycki is Canada Research Chair in Infrastructure Planning and Finance and the Interim Director of the School of Cities at the University of Toronto. His work focuses on delivering large-scale infrastructure projects, public–private partnerships and the effective integration of infrastructure into the fabric of cities. His recent studies explore the value for money of delivering infrastructure megaprojects through public–private partnerships, the causes of and cures for cost overruns on large infrastructure projects, the development of innovative mixed-use buildings and the diversity gap in the infrastructure industry workforce.

Tara Vinodrai is Associate Professor in the Institute for Management and Innovation at the University of Toronto. She holds a graduate appointment to the Department of Geography and Planning and is a Senior Associate at the Innovation Policy Lab at the Munk School of Global Affairs and Public Policy. Her research focuses on the dynamics of urban economies, including issues related to the cultural and creative economy of cities; local and regional economic development; clusters, innovation and technological change; and local labour market dynamics.

Acknowledgements

We would like to first extend our gratitude to the Global Engagement Office at UCL and the Office of the Vice-President, International Partnerships at the University of Toronto (UofT), which have provided significant and important funding to foster urban research collaboration between the two universities. The offices provided administrative support and funding for workshops held in London (in June 2017) and Toronto (in April 2018) that were integral for building discussions between contributors to this book and in the development of the book themes. Funding by the Global Engagement Office at UCL also supported an additional editorial meeting for the book, held in Toronto in June 2019.

We also wish to thank Professor Mark Fox, Associate Director of Research at the School of Cities, University of Toronto, and Professor Mike Raco, Bartlett School of Planning, UCL, who brought together UofT and UCL urban researchers for the first joint collaborative workshop in London in June 2017. Without their foresight, this book would not have been possible. It was at this first workshop in London that a commitment to pursuing a book was decided upon and an editorial team was formed. We are also grateful for the assistance of Tatiana Moreira de Souza and Dimitris Panayotopoulos-Tsiros at the Bartlett School of Planning, UCL, who were instrumental in creating a literature review and for helping to compile a database of London-focused literature, respectively. On the Toronto side, we would like to extend our thanks to Ewa Modlinska, PhD candidate in Planning at the UofT, who provided assistance in compiling Toronto-based literature and was key to the successful organisation of the second workshop held in Toronto in April 2018. Two cities, London and Toronto, have made the contents of this book possible. They are cities that are dynamic, fascinating, complex and never lacking in excitement. London and Toronto are close to our hearts as cities in which we live and work on an everyday basis, and as places that are constantly transforming in multiple ways.

Introduction: Critical dialogues of urban governance, development and activism in London and Toronto

Susan Moore, Susannah Bunce, Nicola Livingstone, Loren March and Alan Walks

Cities and urban change have been among the most visible manifestations of the evolution of processes of globalisation, neoliberalisation and population expansion. Global cities, in particular, are at the cutting edge of such changes and are often the first to experience policy experimentation and to spur a host of community political actions in response. This book examines changes in governance, property development and urban political change and community activism, in two key global cities – London and Toronto.

Why Toronto and London?

Taking these two cities as empirical cases, this edited volume engages in constructive dialogues about the contested and variegated built forms, formal and informal governmental mechanisms and practices, and policy and community-based responses to contemporary urban concerns in London and Toronto. But why *these* two cities? Colonial history, politics and path dependencies might evoke part of the answer, but there is more to the contemporary condition of urban existence, and the governance of such existence, in these two cities that seems to bind them as mirrored reflections onto one another. To be sure, certain symmetries exist between Toronto and London – both are considered amongst the most multicultural cities in the world, both are the dominant economic powerhouses in their national contexts and both have highly diversified knowledge economies, exhibited in recent years by the development of major tech-driven or -oriented urban quarters (e.g. King's Cross London and now shelved Sidewalk Labs in Toronto). But there are also significant asymmetries. The City of Toronto is roughly 2.8 million people and the population of the Greater Toronto Area (GTA) hovers at approximately 6.1 million, making it the fifth largest metropolis in North America.

London as a city has a population of 8 million, and Greater London approximately 10 million. Toronto was/is known as Tkaranto by the Mohawk First Nations and was formerly named York in 1790, after being colonised as a military and political outpost of British expansion into Canada and based upon oppressive processes of taking Indigenous land for colonial settlement. Toronto was incorporated as a city in 1834 and since that time has reproduced its colonial ties to Britain through the adoption of similar forms of governance, planning and architecture, cultural norms and waves of immigration from the UK. In many ways, Toronto can be viewed as a puritanical version of London. The history of British colonial settlement in the city was one led by an austere and religious 'family compact' of British lawyers, military leaders and politicians, who shaped periods of temperance, norms of social obedience and its long-lasting moniker of 'Toronto the Good', in spite of Toronto's problematic colonialism. London, by contrast, is over 2,000 years old, receiving its first Royal Charter in 1067 and becoming the capital seat of England in the twelfth century. London has entrenched its role as a centre of politics and commerce over centuries. Much more recently, and as we note in more detail in this Introduction, London and Toronto have emerged as comparable global cities, with both cities acting as key financial entrepôts, political capitals, social and cultural centres, and places for large and diverse waves of transnational migration and settlement.

This is the space in which our conversation began, initiated admittedly more pragmatically than deliberately, via a choreographed academic workshop. In early summer of 2017 a group of urban scholars from the University of Toronto (UofT) visited UCL to take part in a workshop to discuss and debate issues of 'affordable housing' in London and Toronto. The workshop demonstrated the seemingly near-universal urban problematics affecting policy and governance in both cities, including a lack of affordable housing, the increasing financialisation of real estate development and investment, unsustainable urban growth and sprawl, austerity and the rolling back of the welfare state, social inequality, and uneven public engagement in urban regeneration and development processes, to name but a few. Despite many similarities in vocabularies, laws and policy frameworks, we identified key differences in the practices of engagement and operational cultures of urban development and governance in Toronto and London.

None of us on that first day could have anticipated what was to unfold the following morning, which would put our academically oriented discussion into stark contrast with the lived realities of the urban condition in our respective contemporary cities. On 14 June 2017, the world awoke to scenes of horror and disbelief as Grenfell Tower, a 24-storey residential block situated on a recently 'refurbished' housing estate in the affluent Royal Borough of Kensington and Chelsea in London, burned uncontrollably, killing 72 people and leaving hundreds dispossessed. The poignancy of this event coinciding with the coming together of scholars who do research on urban housing financialisation, neoliberal governance, gentrification, social infrastructure provision and distributive justice in cities was not lost on us.

In the weeks, months and years following the blaze, evidence of the multiple failings of governance and the vagaries of the dominant models of urban regeneration in cities has not just infiltrated the psyche of urban sociologists, geographers and planners, but has also awakened a renewal of broad-based urban activism and civically engaged academe too. Resistance to rampant displacement via state-led gentrification in the guise of large estate regeneration or the new urban quarters in the post-industrial parts of many cities has altered the degree, scale and nature of opposition to neoliberal capitalism and austerity politics. London and Toronto are at the palpable centre of this new urban reality. This volume seeks to unpack the contested governmental rationalities, development and planning 'cultures', and the local and neighbourhood-based politics of both cities, and to bring them into critical dialogue with each other with the aim of generating new spaces for debate, learning and possibilities for reform in both contexts.

Critical dialogues as part of the comparative gesture

The book is inherently comparative, albeit not in the traditional sense. It does not seek to deliver a like-for-like comparison of the legal, administrative and political 'systems', contrasting the complexities of the English centralised, discretionary, non-constitutional system with that of the regulatory system enacted through the power of provincial legislation in Canada. Nor is it a descriptive journey through research projects from each city. Rather it seeks to draw out critical lines of urban reflection from the trans-disciplinary perspectives of planning, real estate and urban geography research emerging from the work of leading urban scholars from the UofT and the Bartlett School of Planning, UCL.

Our analytical framework draws on recent calls for nuanced approaches to comparative urbanism prompted by the work of Robinson (2016), Ward (2010), Healey (2012), Friedmann (2005) and others. Such approaches privilege the relational contexts of geographical, social and material assemblages in enabling understandings of urban transformation and governance in a diversity of locales and scales (McFarlane 2011). Studies of urban assemblages identify key patterns and trends in what Robinson refers to as the 'strongly interconnected genesis of often repeated urban phenomena' (2016, 6). By focusing on London and Toronto independently and in contrasting narratives of reflection, the result is a 'generative' (Robinson 2016) dialogue that prompts international debate on existing and emergent theorisations of these repeated phenomena of global significance and concern (e.g. the neoliberalisation of urban governance and policy). We seek to build on the idea of understanding cities 'as sharing diversity, differentiation and contestation' (Minnery et al. 2012, 861). As such, each chapter of the book engages critically with the dominant discourses fuelling urban transformation in London and/or Toronto, but also crucially reflects on the wider implications for comparative urbanism, some more explicitly than others.

The aim of the book is to provide an original intervention focused on the comparative understanding of the transformative processes incited by urban development and governance rationalities and the formal and informal political response to them. This dialogue traverses the contested terrains of housing and real estate, the impacts of governance and regulation and the mobilisation of community-based action and activism in the contemporary period. The less traditional approach to comparative framing seeks to understand London and Toronto from a nuanced perspective. It promotes critical reflection on the experiences and evaluative critiques of each urban context, providing insight into each city's urban trajectory and engaging critically with wider phenomena and influences on urban governance challenges beyond these two cities. Composing comparative dialogues of two cities in the global north interrogates the degree of speculated convergence in the type and nature of urban challenges affecting and affected by the built environment and its governance. The ways in which such challenges are both manifest and mediated at the urban level are complex, fluid and variegated. This book draws attention to the contextual specificity of each city, the varied scope and scale of formal and informal governmental responses and the spectrums of influence and power enacting the dominant development rationalities.

We see the contribution as part of the 'comparative gesture', following Robinson (2011), albeit not one that fills the gap in comparative work on cities across the north–south divide, nor indeed that spans the poor–rich divide. Robinson provokes us to consider how much this book, or similar edited volumes which 'take care to juxtapose case studies from different parts of the world', still fall short of 'allowing them to engage either with each other or with more general or theoretical understandings of cities' (2011, 2). We have attempted to enliven a space for critical dialogue on three 'big' issues in contemporary urban studies – governance, real estate and housing, and community, activism and engagement – but theorising the comparative tropes (strategies and causalities) is indeed more challenging. In short, this comparative project must be seen to extend beyond the pages of this book. We are making no claims for the definitive value of our comparative investigation of two already independently well-researched urban metropolises, but we are pointing to a lack of contemporary comparative studies of these two cities. In fact we struggled to find *any* contemporary urban studies book titles looking comparatively at Toronto and London when proposing this volume. Despite the tendency for comparative studies to coalesce around cities with shared or common economic and political national contexts, it still broadly means a restricted number of cities tend to get compared.

Universities as part of the community of city builders

Entering into a productive dialogue with what was initially a small group of scholars who attended the original workshops was only the start of something much larger and much more fulfilling. So, yes, UofT and UCL may have prioritised a strategic link between the two institutions, but this alone of course did not prompt us to write this book. It is perhaps illustrative to pause for a moment to reflect on why our institutions were so keen to partner. In short, each sees the other as its reputable equal – as an international hub of research and higher learning in a global city; both attract thousands of international students each year; both publish influential and acclaimed research; both have esteemed faculty; and both are situated centrally in the core of their respective cities, experiencing rapid growth and urban transformation. It is this last point that is most significant to us as editors of this volume, a key facet of why these critical dialogues matter so much *now*.

UCL and UofT are both well placed to consider themselves as genuinely 'urban' learning laboratories. And indeed both institutions have endeavoured to embody this positionality through establishing vehicles for improving outreach and knowledge production and circulation beyond the disciplinary silos of academia. The UCL Urban Laboratory was established in 2005 as the university's first urban-focused cross-disciplinary research centre, and more recently the UofT established the School of Cities in 2018 as a hub for urban research and outreach for multi-disciplinary urban faculty. But the so-called laboratorising of cities is not without ethical, methodological and pedagogical complexities – the drawing of boundaries around what is part of the 'laboratory' can indirectly reinforce the 'divide between the knowledge community and the surrounding neighbourhoods rather than integrate these in new ways' (Karvonen and Evans 2014, 415). Ultimately this can lead to instances of distrust of universities by local stakeholders (Melhuish 2015).

Being a 'living lab', or part of one, means more than teaching 'about' cities by default of being located in one. Increasingly, universities and other institutes of higher education globally are called to account for their role in the local community and the wider impact of their presence in place-making and the social sustainability of the towns and cities where they are located. Universities are often promoted as agents of urban regeneration 'because they are seen to generate economic activity and produce skilled localised workforces to power the knowledge economy, while offering stability and "sticky capital" as anchors of development with a long-term commitment to place and community participation' (Melhuish 2015, 13). These debates intensify when the institutions decide they need to expand their campuses in order to remain competitive or project a new or improved globalised, modernised image. Often substantial landowners in cities, universities and college campuses tend to occupy separated precincts, districts or contiguous parcels of land in cities and towns (Bromley 2006), set apart from 'the rest of the city', often both physically and symbolically. For a long time this meant that city politics happened *to* the city and that academics in their 'ivory towers' merely responded when approached by media, industry or government, or encouraged their students to go out and 'engage' in ethnographic case studies of the experiences of those directly 'affected'. In part this was normalised through the twinned pursuits of higher education – teaching and research – goals which much of the time have relatively little to do with local contexts and needs (Fernandez-Esquinas and Pinto 2014; Addie et al. 2015). But as universities are increasingly pitched at the forefront of debates regarding their role as cultural 'anchors' of urban regeneration schemes or tech hubs linked to enterprise zones (Melhuish 2015), and as speculative developers of new academic buildings or student housing complexes, the politics of gentrification, displacement and financialisation cannot be seen as external to our academic (and economic development) pursuits.

Toronto and London have both dealt with the expansion plans of universities in their administrative borders and both have had to reckon with an increased scrutiny of their plans and their potential impact within the wider neighbourhood or community. Some of these plans have been controversial and the public response to establishing a new campus or demolishing existing buildings and constructing new ones has been hotly contested. UCL was at the centre of such a debate beginning in 2011 with its eastward expansion into a new campus located in Stratford, east London (known as UCL East), a site within the Queen Elizabeth Olympic Park. The University of Toronto has faced criticism since the 1970s of its development plans around its downtown campus (leading to efforts by the then-Toronto City council to downzone university-owned land and prevent the university from demolishing old housing), while its two 'suburban' campuses, in Scarborough to the east and Mississauga in the west, have been viewed by some as having a 'concrete curtain' (referring to their modernist concrete buildings) between campus activities and the experiences of neighbouring communities. This has changed in the 2000s, with an increasingly concerted effort on all three campuses to engage with their surrounding areas through teaching and research with and in local communities.

Acknowledging the university as a 'local stakeholder' involves, as Bromley (2006) puts it, 'enlightened self-interest not only in improving their own campuses, but also in improving the neighbourhoods around their campuses and in strengthening the economy and image of their municipalities and regions' (11). Meaningful outreach and engagement with community groups, industry and governmental bodies is a critical endeavour for universities to fulfil their role as political stakeholders and part of the community-building apparatus of contemporary cities. Building civic engagement into all aspects of academic life is now a primary goal for most urban institutions. Part of this deliberate recasting of higher education institutions is obviously a function of them being more visible as major speculative urban developers, alongside which emerges a complex array of new partnerships and 'a gradual blurring of public/private and for-profit/not-for-profit distinctions' (Bromley 2006, 20). The challenge for both UofT and UCL is to counterbalance the trajectory of their own branding and marketing, for as an institution becomes 'more globally oriented, the more detached it can be from the local context' (Fernandez-Esquinas and Pinto 2014, 1467).

Though not explicitly a theme of this edited volume, the role of universities and other institutions of higher education as political stakeholders in community building underpins the origins of our initial discussions. Some of the chapters of this book directly relate to the experiences of scholar-activists in Toronto and London. Chapters 1, 8, 13 and 16 all engage to varying degrees with the work of JustSpace, an informal alliance of academics (UCL), community groups, campaigns and concerned independent organisations which formed as a grassroots voice in response to major planning strategy processes in London. Chapters 15, 17 and 19 (in Part III) likewise demonstrate varying degrees of academic activism occurring in and with Toronto's hidden, under-represented communities and displaced groups. This book is not exhaustive in its coverage of the action-oriented and community-engaged scholarly work being undertaken by urban researchers in Toronto and London – our colleagues in other departments, universities, urban laboratories and institutes in both cities (and beyond) also need to be acknowledged. But what we do hope is that this book will be a catalyst for readers to gain an insight into what are the driving concerns in each city and to investigate the variety of progressive research emerging simultaneously from both urban contexts. The comparative gesture is again here positioned as a generative one, 'enabled by the bringing together of different singularities, or cases, into conversation' (Robinson 2016, 18), inspired in this instance by problems associated with urban governance, property and activism. This is a primer for an enduring critical dialogue between Toronto and London. We start with three dialogic lenses for better understanding the comparative urban condition in Toronto and London as we work towards concluding on the implications for richer conceptualisation of the comparative imagination of global cities.

Dialogic lenses of the comparative urban condition in Toronto and London

Governance in the global city

Among the myriad issues besetting global cities such as London and Toronto, questions around the changing forms, processes and outcomes of governance are of utmost importance. Global cities are at the cutting edge of what Allen Scott (2011) calls 'third wave urbanization', that is, post-Fordist forms of urban change in which industry has largely decanted to developing nations and low-wage regions, while processes of financialisation, globalisation and neoliberalisation direct development pressures on the largest, most globally connected cities, especially their inner cores. As the 'command and control' centres of a global economy, global cities such as London and Toronto concentrate the headquarters of transnational firms as well as financial firms, while also maintaining competitive advantages in key specialised services that attract labour of varying skills from around the world (Sassen 2001). As a result, London and Toronto are among the most diverse cities on the planet, with high levels of immigration, concentrations of racialised communities and high levels of income and wealth inequality. Demand pressures from those with high incomes, coupled with high levels of in-migration, lead to high housing costs, especially in the inner cores where the financial sector is concentrated, promoting gentrification and displacement. And because of the need to remain connected to other global cities, but within a context of severe land pressures which promote high-density residential and employment development, global cities contain unique challenges related to the governing of infrastructure development. Although other cities also face a number of similar pressures, their intensity and combination in global cities such as London and Toronto require a number of simultaneous interventions, and these present their own unique challenges to governance.

As scholars have noted (Raco 2016), the neoliberalisation of public policy has involved a shift from government to governance. Instead of accountable state activity directed by public bodies responsible to elected representatives and funded by taxes (government), states have increasingly contracted out functions and responsibilities for service delivery, monitoring, financing and even policy-making to a diverse and fragmented ecology of quasi-public and private actors/firms with varying levels of direct public accountability (governance). This has been implemented on ideological grounds – to encourage market-based solutions to public policy problems and to promote the private sector as the key driver of economic growth – as well as for pragmatic reasons – as national and especially local state budgets come under strain, the impetus to search for solutions requiring less direct expenditure rises. It has led to the so-called post-political city (Swyngedouw 2009), in which political issues of access and accountability are depoliticised and rendered as technical issues of efficiency. Governance is the result of both 'roll-back' forms of neoliberalisation (the attack on the welfare state and the privatisation of public resources and services), and 'roll-out' forms of neoliberalisation (the promotion of market-based models of service delivery and access) (Peck and Tickell 2002). Governance includes not only the normal (and increasingly residual) state functions of government, but also the activities and interests of the many quasi-public and private firms that are involved in organising and influencing firm and resident behaviour, development and everyday life.

The shift from government to governance presents its own challenges, not least because it becomes more difficult to understand what each actor is doing and how they relate to other actors and to stated public policy objectives. The rise of governance is associated with both increasing policy innovation and greater potential for chaos and unintended consequences. Furthermore, as Peck (2010) notes, under neoliberalism the tendency is to 'fail forward' – that is, to point to failures of governance, including those resulting from market-based models, as justification for further and deeper neoliberalisation and privatisation. Because of this the neoliberal shift away from government to governance has been characterised by a forward momentum under positive feedback loops in which deeper and more fragmented governance is seen as the only solution to the challenges besetting fragmented governance. In this context, many states – even those ruled by left-leaning political parties – have adopted hybrid 'roll-with-it' forms of neoliberalisation (Keil

2009) in which some aspects of marketisation have been added into the larger governance mix, producing assemblages of policy experimentation and innovation that overlap with established institutions and political cultures.

London and Toronto have been at the vanguard of such policy experimentation and governance innovation. In addition to facing the most extreme pressures from development, rising inequalities, financialisation, gentrification and economic change, global cities are also often the national (or sub-national) capital cities. As the seats of power, they are highly visible to policy-makers and have a disproportionate concentration of political actors, parties and groups, as well as media outlets, universities, think tanks and other 'knowledge producers'. Global cities are therefore often the first to be targeted for governance reforms and experiments by upper levels of the state, and because of the myriad challenges they face, they are often the first to innovate their own policy solutions at the municipal level, including in the realm of land use planning. Both London and Toronto, for instance, had their well-respected regional governments (the Greater London Council, and the Municipality of Metropolitan Toronto) disbanded by Conservative-led governments elected to upper levels of the state (by Margaret Thatcher's Conservatives in the case of Greater London in 1986, and by the Mike Harris-led Ontario Conservatives in the case of Metropolitan Toronto in 1998). However, with the dynamic economies resulting from their connections to global processes, global cities often have more resources and higher tax bases with which to experiment and to monitor the outcomes of such policy innovation. In both London and Toronto, the central cities have pursued policy innovations with the intention of dealing with, and partly making up for, the political whims of upper levels of the state, although municipalities in London retain more autonomy than do municipalities in Toronto, where according to the Canadian constitution, municipalities are always 'creatures of the Province'. Global cities appear as the 'natural' test sites for the neoliberalisation of urban policy.

London and Toronto, as the pre-eminent global cities of the UK and Canada respectively, thus make for a compelling, and telling, comparison in governance. As the chapters in Part I of this volume attest, both urban regions have been at the forefront of targeted policy experimentation in planning and governance, both those that pre-date (by decades) the rise of neoliberalisation and those that were (often unwillingly) the result of neoliberal shifts in ideology. Both urban regions exhibit the highest levels of immigration, diversity and racialisation in their respective nations, and both have witnessed extreme development pressures and pressures on their housing markets in recent decades. Furthermore, interestingly, both cities have witnessed major fluctuations in the ideological approach of their elected municipal regimes, at roughly the same times, and municipal politics in both cities have acted as realms for political experimentation among neoliberal politicians who then moved on to lead upper levels of the state where the power really lies. For instance, London went from electing one of the most left-leaning mayors in the UK (Ken Livingstone) to one of the more eccentric and controversial Conservatives

(Boris Johnson in 2008), and the latter went on to become Prime Minister in 2019. Toronto, similarly, went from the equally left-leaning mayorship of David Miller to the equally eccentric and controversial Conservative Rob Ford (in 2010) (see Walks 2015). Although Rob Ford passed away in 2014, in 2018 his older brother Doug Ford, who was a municipal councillor during Rob's mayoral tenure, became Premier of the Province of Ontario (the province where Toronto is located) in 2018.

Yet it is also notable that cities in the UK are often seen as poster-children for the kinds of fragmented forms of private governance noted by scholars (Raco 2016), whereas Toronto has acted as a model of the 'public metropolis' in historically avoiding the delegation of political decisions to unaccountable bodies and instead maintaining strong democratic institutions and levels of public accountability, even at the risk of policy inefficiency (Frisken 2007). Although Toronto has also witnessed the shift from democratic government to governance, usually as a result of initiatives of the Province of Ontario attempting to make the political process more 'efficient' (such as the amalgamation of six former boroughs into the new City of Toronto in 1998, and the Doug Ford government's reforms of the City Council in 2019; see Boudreau 2000; Boudreau et al. 2009; Rider and Kopun 2019), cities all over Canada still often look to Toronto for guidance on ways of maintaining democratic input. These two metropolises thus constitute an excellent comparison for examination and discussion of the evolution of governance in contemporary global cities.

Real estate and housing

Since the Global Financial Crisis (GFC), the overriding trajectory of the real estate and housing markets in both London and Toronto has been one of 'growth', as both cities are key financial centres with diverse and increasing populations. This growth has been founded on neoliberal approaches to governance, with each city ever more reliant on market-led, profit-driven private sector actors to reproduce the real estate and housing markets. The real estate and housing markets in both London and Toronto illustrate the tensions that are currently emerging across both cities in their commercial and residential markets, tensions and antagonisms which are dynamic, transformative and constantly in flux, and it is clear that the narratives of positive growth are not always beneficial to everyone.

Since the last decades of the twentieth century, the real estate and housing markets of established global cities pursuing an agenda based on growth have become increasingly accessible, transparent and attractive propositions to both investors and developers in search of lucrative financial opportunities. Capital flowing into global cities can now be distributed across a varied spectrum of investment vehicles, as the real estate and housing markets have become increasingly financialised under neoliberalism in order to accommodate the 'wall of money' (Aalbers 2016) moving across markets in pursuit of maximum profits and strong returns. Investment into commercial and residential real estate can now be carried

out in myriad ways, in addition to the traditional approach of direct property ownership. Listed vehicles such as real estate investment trusts (REITs) and unlisted
property funds provide contemporary methods of investing indirectly into commercial and residential real estate as assets becoming increasingly subject to processes of financialisation, where 'the increasing dominance of financial actors,
markets, practices, measurements and narratives, at various scales, [is] resulting
in a structural transformation of economics, firms, states and households' (Aalbers
2017, 544). Real estate offers an investor exposure into unfamiliar markets with
risk-based returns, and in the last decade global REITs have achieved returns of
11 per cent, outperforming other asset classes (JLL 2019).

Although direct and indirect real estate investments differ in terms of characteristics, there are clear reasons for investing in real estate and housing as asset
classes: real estate is typically seen as a sound hedge against inflation, with attractive risk and return profiles and diversification benefits, especially if considering
investing or developing internationally (Baum and Hartzell 2012). Driven by
London, the United Kingdom's commercial real estate market is ranked at number
one for global real estate transparency, which is ranked via six measures relating
to sustainability, performance, transaction processes, market fundamentals, regulatory and legal systems and governance (JLL 2018). Canada sits at fifth position
in the transparency index out of 100 global markets (JLL 2018): both cities have
strong underlying economic fundamentals and performance potential. In 2019,
London was the fourth most liquid real estate market globally, with $22.3 billion
of real estate transacted, and real estate sales volumes in Canada increased by 9
per cent, with Toronto one of the key performers (JLL 2019). The governance and
policy frameworks active within the London and Toronto markets have facilitated
processes of financialisation and actively encouraged continued investment into
the real estate and housing markets, from both domestic and international actors,
where locally distinctive practices and outcomes are mediated by global practices
of investment, development and cycles of capital flows.

As the London and Toronto markets have become increasingly attractive and
viable propositions for investors and developers, land values have escalated due
to factors such as market competition and demand economies, exacerbated by the
spatial boundaries within each city, restricting supply. As a consequence of these
influences, both London and Toronto have experienced increasing deindustrialisation as industrial/employment land is sacrificed for the purpose of housing, to the
detriment of the local economy, even though demand for such space is increasing
(CAG 2017; Toronto City Planning 2019). Although additional housing may be created, negative impacts of the loss of industrial land include loss of employment
spaces, which no longer contribute to the local economy, and the prioritisation of
other uses over industrial spaces. The prioritisation of housing may not be a surprising market trend, as both cities are experiencing ongoing housing crises due to
varied reasons ranging from the economic to the political and the social: examples
of these include supply and demand imbalances, increasing spatial and income

inequalities, the assetisation and financialisation of housing and challenges in land supply. Politics, at a local, regional and national level, clearly impacts the demand and supply of housing and the funding for its provision, as elected mayors and political representatives struggle to balance out challenges with social and public housing provision in an era of austerity and budget cuts for local authorities. Policy mechanisms, such as those included in the London Plan and Section 37 of the Planning Act in Toronto, have related to the systems by which planning gain and financial contributions can be captured by the local authorities when housing is being developed. However, questions arise over the financial viability of such developments and whether sufficient value is being extracted through these policies by local government: often developers will argue over the viability and profitability of particular sites, and due to the discretionary planning systems in operation, the private sector often develops housing that has minimal affordable units. The housing crisis is one of access and affordability, and both the London and Toronto markets have seen substantial rises in rental values concomitant with the growth of the private rented sector (PRS) and burgeoning gentrification processes in each market. Although densification debates point to ways in which housing provision can be increased in effective and progressive ways, there are political vulnerabilities to approaches that rely on densification, a situation made even more salient by the COVID-19 pandemic, which has disproportionately affected dense areas of interconnected cities such as London and Toronto – in particular those that are home to usually racialised and lower-income residents who continue to work on various front lines of the pandemic, are at greater risk of exposure and are often more likely to suffer from serious illness.

Synergies of near-universal urban problematics emerge through the real estate and housing markets in our two study cities, which demonstrate how city form and urban environments are perpetuated and consistently reconstituted through interactions and interconnections both between and within markets. The processes occurring in London and Toronto demonstrate how fluid global processes have impacts at local levels: generally, the commercial markets of each city are well established and exhibit strong performance fundamentals in terms of investment and development. However, the negative impacts of growth can be seen in the crisis-ridden housing market, dominated by questions relating to financial viability, the politics and policies of planning obligations and development, and social issues relating to affordability and increasing spatial inequalities.

Community, activism and engagement

London and Toronto are cities of neighbourhoods; indeed, most of the everyday life that occurs in both cities happens at the neighbourhood scale and is set within the unique terrains of, and place attachments to, the very local. London's neighbourhoods and communities have emerged and been shaped over centuries, with distinctive urban dialects, social, cultural and spatial geographies, and an understanding of their often-changing position in relation to the landscape of the city. London's East End has historically been socially separated by class, culture and politics from the city's West End (Glynn 2005), although over the past few decades the East End of London has become a place of rapid gentrification, drawing influxes of people attracted by relatively cheaper rents and housing and expectations of a grittier urban 'authenticity'. Toronto is officially called a 'city of neighbourhoods' by its local government, which has demarcated 140 neighbourhoods across the city as socio-cultural units and in turn has used these areas to highlight and market the city's social history and diversity, as well as the uniqueness of these particular areas. As is the case in London, Toronto's more affluent neighbourhoods exist primarily in the central, west and north of the city, with very small areas of the centre and pockets of the north-west and the east being home to residents with lower incomes as well as a higher proportion of immigrants (Hulchanski 2010, 2015).

London and Toronto have been key receptor cities for immigrants from across the globe, which has added to the dynamism and cultural make-up of different communities and neighbourhoods in both cities. Indeed, immigration (and internal migration) has added a great deal to the social and economic infrastructure of both cities. Nearly half (47 per cent) of Toronto's residents were born outside Canada and thus arrived as immigrants or refugees (City of Toronto 2017), while 35 per cent of Londoners were born outside the UK, with this figure including migrants from EU countries (Migration Observatory 2020). Patterns of immigration are clearly experienced in the social life of communities and neighbourhoods, in working life and in the different socio-cultural practices that permeate everyday spaces in both cities. In these ways, Toronto and London are constituted by transnational communities that are intricately woven across each city and are closely connected with diverse countries of origin. Interestingly, in both cities the colonial and postcolonial ties to places across the globe are readily apparent, with Toronto, as a colonial city, attracting immigrant communities from former and current British colonies in the Caribbean, South Asia and Africa in a similar way to London. This has produced complex associations between colonial histories and current de-/postcolonial contexts. London's and Toronto's thriving Jamaican communities, for example, have intrinsically contributed to and shaped the cultural dynamism and social fabric of both cities. Yet these communities also bear the problematic outcomes of a history of colonial racism that is evident in spatialisation processes and income disparities across both cities, where racism is embedded in the cities' uneven development and impacts the equitable location of housing and communities, access to services and political agency, among other issues (see Dwyer and Bressey 2008; Hulchanski 2010, 2015; Gilroy 1991; Paradis et al. 2008). London and Toronto are cities that, while reliant on immigration, have yet to effectively grapple with and find real solutions to the multiple and entwined issues of socio-spatial inequity and racialisation.

Historical and emergent activist practices have sought to address these issues, however, and both cities have long histories of anti-racist and social justice activism.

In London, the Notting Hill Riots that first started in 1958 and continued at different times into the 1980s, and the Brixton Riot in 1981, were significant events that brought anti-Black racism to the forefront of public discourse and underlined the connections between racial discrimination and issues such as targeted policing, social cutbacks and inadequate housing. These events became inscribed in the social imaginaries of different communities: in community solidarity, in art and music and in possibilities for activism that would bring together issues of race and class. The legacies of these events are noticeable in contemporary community-based activism in London, through the efforts of organisations such as Focus E15, who represent diverse racialised and newcomer residents to fight against eviction and displacement in east London, and those that explicitly work against racist policies, such as Lewisham Anti-Racist Action Group. Never ones to be afraid of taking to the streets in protest, Londoners tend to leave indelible prints of activism in the form of rallies and direct actions that now increasingly connect issues of racial, social and environmental injustice together. The climate action protests by Extinction Rebellion in 2019 that closed down London streets, railway stations and Thames river bridges raised awareness about the interrelationships between these injustices and articulated calls for an emergent community-based and global climate justice activism.

Similarly, in Toronto, activism is increasingly shaped by a focus on the multiple forms and scales of injustice and calls for justice as a praxis-based and aspirational process. As in London, activism for social, environmental and racial justice is emerging as a vital force for change in Toronto, with organisations working together and across more specific mandates. Toronto's activist history has laid the groundwork for this intersectional activist approach through the coming together of different organisations to protest singular issues since the 1960s, with the city being a key place in Canada (and globally) for anti-nuclear, anti-apartheid and anti-poverty rallies and other actions. While specific and targeted activism is certainly an integral part of activist culture in Toronto, as in the work of groups such as the Ontario Coalition against Poverty and Parkdale Organize in relation to issues of housing injustice, homelessness and evictions in the city, this is noticeably set within a larger conversation about injustice and the need for equity and justice more broadly. In Toronto, this is also placed within an important and necessary public discussion and activism for Indigenous rights to land, political agency and environmental protection, among other issues. Emergent activism for climate justice is closely linked with Indigenous activism in Toronto, with both issues being important to Toronto's communities and across Canada. This has been noticeable in the recent joining together of multiple activists and organisations across Toronto neighbourhoods to protest against plans for a gas pipeline on Indigenous (Wet'suwet'en) territory in western Canada.

London and Toronto share similar characteristics as cities with long, interesting and dynamic histories of activism and engagement and with vibrant and diverse communities and neighbourhoods, although the types of activism and engagement may differ according to localised contexts and issues in each city. In both places, emergent and hopeful actions are occurring in response to the problems that face each city, including the defining urban moment of the twenty-first century – the COVID-19 global pandemic; at the time of press we had yet to see the other side of post-peak outbreak urban governance reforms, development recovery plans and neighbourhood resilience and self-sufficiency agendas. Scholars and journalists have already speculated that the legacy of the coronavirus may well be a digital one (see Safi 2020), imprinted on collective ideas of privacy and surveillance. It is likely too, perhaps, to be similar to the post-2008 global economic recession period, when activists and lobbyists as well as politicians and the general public started to ask whether or not it is a moment to do things differently, an opportunity to rethink the sustainability of dominant regeneration, development and governance models. High-profile, controversial projects, such as Sidewalk Labs in Toronto's industrial waterfront, have already collapsed in the wake of COVID-19. Toronto-based urban scholar Roger Keil was recently quoted in *The Guardian* as saying: 'there is no one path for all great cities to follow … this is a negotiated process. It's one we have some agency in' (Safi 2020). It is perhaps too early to speculate on the reality of a post-pandemic urbanism, but there is scope for optimism, in no small part evidenced by the neighbourhood-level activism and improvisational support network formations emerging in the absence of clear government guidance and policy.

Structure of the book

The book is organised into three parts, drawing on recent work of the contributing authors, with chapters from both London and Toronto included in each part, followed by a commentary written collaboratively by one London-based scholar and one Toronto-based scholar from the editorial team. The purpose of the commentaries is to enhance the 'dialogue effect' we are intending to achieve through joint consideration of the key narratives, lessons and generative directions for further research and theorisation.

The seven chapters in Part I, *Perspectives on governance*, deliver a conceptual engagement with the key themes of governmental imaginations and political networks of development influence and power, unequal urban outcomes in the built environment, ambiguities in property regulation and questionable policy shifts. The commentary by Raco and Walks draws attention to the challenges associated with integrating changes in the global political economy into national and local governance during periods of austerity and variegated urban pressures, as they consider Toronto and London as global cities.

Both cities are the focus of the financial services industries and are seen as key to sustaining global economic competitiveness and advantages, which are also important to the local and national scale and predicated on neoliberal policies and reforms. The role of the planning system in governance, and its varied mechanisms for addressing tensions across the two cities, is to find a (somewhat precarious) balance between supporting neoliberal, private, market-led actors in the market and public and community interests. Chapters 4 and 6 discuss pressures on city infrastructure and transit-oriented developments, accounting for the influence that political perspectives have on their development and the uneven impacts of such developments across London and Toronto. Certain parts of the city become more accessible to some, enhancing connectivity and accessibility, while other parts of the city fail to benefit from such infrastructure – exacerbating social injustice, polarisation and inequality in terms of transport and accessibility, and compounding other issues such as the challenges in housing provision. Another issue relating to accessibility in the city is discussed in Chapter 5, which considers the governance of formerly public parks. As management of these spaces has become quasi-privatised and is no longer the responsibility of local authorities, these spaces are now differentiated in terms of their governance and their multiple understandings of 'publicness'.

Chapter 1 discusses the political rhetoric and ambiguities surrounding the planning and delivery of housing in London, where private developers are increasingly influential and ambiguities emerge in regulatory and political approaches. Further questions are raised over the capacity for local governments to provide affordable and accessible housing, which is both effectively produced and regulated (Chapters 1, 2 and 3). Moreira de Souza's Chapter 3 reflects on the disjointed approaches to governing the PRS through inconsistent licensing across boroughs, and Brail and Vinodrai incorporate similar discussions relating to 'ghost' regimes for market sectors in Chapter 2 on Toronto. Their chapter raises questions about the inclusivity of Toronto, as although the city's technology and innovation sectors are booming, and the labour market supports a diverse economic base, spatial inequalities persist in relation to the governance of housing, infrastructure and community benefit agreements.

Part II, *Real estate and housing*, develops the empirical foundation for critical debate on the drivers and outcomes of various governmental mechanisms employed to address the crisis of affordable housing (and related concerns) in London and Toronto. The six chapters discuss the challenges of competing land uses, the public benefit derived from land value capture mechanisms, the institutional drivers of the housing crisis and the implications of urban densification agendas. Bunce and Livingstone's commentary (Chapter 14) reflects on the key themes emerging from the chapters in line with market-led developments, the de/re-regulation of the state and the relational practices which form the cities.

As both London and Toronto are financial centres, with continually growing populations and ever increasing pressure on the housing and real estate markets, a number of chapters in Part II (Chapters 9 and 11) discuss the impacts of neoliberalism, financialisation and assetisation processes. Such processes can be demonstrated by the growth of investment vehicles whose values are underpinned by housing and real estate assets, assets that have been securitised and exchanged on global markets which are becoming increasingly deregulated. Practices of deregulation and the 'rolling back of the state' contribute to the urban development and transformation of London and Toronto, and Chapters 8, 12 and 13 illustrate how these processes are embedded at city level through changes in policies which influence investment practices and how the planning systems operate at a national and local scale. The outcomes of these practices for the real estate and housing markets are relational and emerge across diverse scales, from challenges relating to small-scale 'soft' densification processes (Chapter 12), the integration of mixed-use housing and industrial property (Chapter 8), differentiated experiences of short-term rentals and the growth of Airbnb (Chapter 11), to large-scale, longitudinal issues of the creation of 'housing bubbles' (Chapter 9) and the inconsistencies in the capacities of planning mechanisms to successfully capture benefits from developments (Chapters 8, 12 and 13).

One of the key issues interwoven through all the chapters in Part II relates to the affordability, or lack of affordability, currently being experienced in the London and Toronto housing markets. Walks (Chapter 9) discusses the causes of the housing bubble and affordability concerns in Toronto, coupled with the decline in social housing provision, and Gabrieli (Chapter 10) concentrates on the significant affordability differences between London boroughs, reflecting on the impact of house price growth for first-time buyers. These housing challenges are considered in line with the growth of the PRS and concepts such as 'affordable rent', coupled with the continual escalation of land 'values' and the ways in which developments are assessed for financial viability and planning obligations. Policies at play in the markets which are inherently connected to the cities' housing markets include those related to density bonusing in Toronto (Chapter 13 by Biggar and Siemiatycki), the current consideration of the London Plan's density matrix for housing (Chapter 12) and the 'no net loss' approaches to London's industrial land in the newest iteration of the London Plan (Chapter 8).

Part III, *Community, activism and engagement*, shifts attention to the actions and actual existing practices of non-state actors engaged in urban transformations, often via local initiatives that critically respond to governmental reforms and urban development processes. The prevalence of community-based activism in opposition to 'top-down' public urban regeneration efforts, the retraction of funding for neighbourhood-level programmes and the challenges of social and environmental injustices in both cities are explored. Trends such as the emergence of community land trusts, do-it-yourself (DIY) communities of social change and ambient forms of public engagement are critically presented and evaluated in the chapters and further debated in the commentary written by March and Moore (Chapter 20), which asks, 'Who is activist now?'

Again, as in Parts I and II, the question of housing, and how it could be better provided, is interwoven into the discussions across a number of chapters. Penny (Chapter 16) focuses on ideas around the financialisation of housing in a period of 'austerity urbanism' in London and evaluates how local boroughs are becoming ever more entrepreneurial and creative in their provision of housing (by forming public–private partnerships for example). Activist responses to displacement, dispossession and associated negative impacts relating to housing under austerity urbanism in London are explored by Sendra and Fitzpatrick (Chapter 18), which demonstrates how empowered local communities can shape decision-making processes, political agendas and policies. Other approaches to revitalising neighbourhoods and counterbalancing gentrification impacts in local areas in a move away from 'top-down' urban regeneration are discussed in Bunce's Chapter 19 on activist-oriented community land trusts in Toronto and London, recognising the opportunities this approach offers local communities to act collectively towards effective land stewardship. Responses from communities are also explored in chapters by both March and Ostanel (Chapters 15 and 17), with the former exploring how a culture of organisational collaboration has developed in Parkdale, Toronto, and the latter considering ideas around creative place-making and the important role of DIY workspaces in the city. Both Ostanel and March focus on how activism and social change can be spatially and temporally particular to specific areas of a city, while remaining connected to (and often in conflict with) broader agendas of institutional and market-led changes.

In the conclusion to the book, we reflect on the patterns that have emerged through our collaborative work and about what the comparisons between our two urban regions tell us about urban governance, real estate and housing processes, and communities, engagement and activism in contemporary global cities, at least as they have evolved up to the time the COVID-19 pandemic hit. The dialogic approach taken within this book has helped us identify three key conclusions, which contribute to a more nuanced understanding of contemporary urban development processes, not only in London and Toronto but in cities more generally, and to a conceptualisation of the comparative imagination of global cities.

References

Aalbers, Manuel. 2016. *The Financialization of Housing: A Political Economy Approach*. Abingdon: Routledge.
Aalbers, Manuel. 2017. 'The Variegated Financialization of Housing'. *International Journal of Urban and Regional Research* 41(4):542–54. https://doi.org/10.1111/1468-2427.12522.
Addie, Jean-Paul, Keil, Roger and Olds, Kris. 2015. 'Beyond Town and Gown: Higher Education Institutions, Territoriality and the Mobilization of New Urban Structures'. *Territory, Politics, Governance* 3(1):27–50. https://doi.org/10.1080/21622671.2014.924875.
Baum, Andrew and Hartzell, David. 2012. *Global Property Investment: Strategies, Structures, Decisions*. Chichester: Wiley-Blackwell.
Boudreau, Julie-Anne. 2000. *The Mega-City Saga: Democracy and Citizenship in this Global Age*. Montreal: Black Rose Books.
Boudreau, Julie-Anne, Young, Douglas and Keil, Roger. 2009. *Changing Toronto: Governing Urban Neoliberalism*. Toronto: University of Toronto Press.
Bromley, Ray. 2006. 'On and Off Campus: Colleges and Universities as Local Stakeholders'. *Planning, Practice & Research* 21(1):1–24. https://doi.org/10.1080/02697450600901400.
CAG Consultants. 2017. London Industrial Land Demand. June. Accessed 18 September 2019. https://www.london.gov.uk/sites/default/files/ilds_revised_final_report_october_2017.pdf.
City of Toronto. 2017. *2016 Census: Housing, Immigration and Ethnocultural Diversity, Aboriginal Peoples*. Toronto: City of Toronto.

Dwyer, Claire and Bressey, Caroline (eds). 2008. *New Geographies of Race and Racism*. London: Routledge.

Fernandez-Esquinas, Manuel and Pinto, Hugo. 2014. 'The Role of Universities in Urban Regeneration: Reframing the Analytical Approach'. *European Planning Studies* 22(7):1462–83. https://doi.org/10.1080/09654313.2013.791967.

Friedmann, John. 2005. 'Globalization and the Emerging Culture of Planning'. *Progress in Planning* 64(3):183–234. https://doi.org/10.1016/j.progress.2005.05.001.

Frisken, Frances. 2007. *The Public Metropolis: The Political Dynamics of Urban Expansion in the Toronto Region, 1924–2003*. Toronto: Canadian Scholars' Press.

Gilroy, Paul. 1991. *There Ain't No Black in the Union Jack*. Chicago: University of Chicago Press.

Healey, Patsy. 2012. 'The Universal and the Contingent: Some Reflections on the Transnational Flow of Planning Ideas and Practices'. *Planning Theory* 11(2):188–207. https://doi.org/10.1177/1473095211419333.

Hulchanski, David. 2010. *The Three Cities within Toronto: Income Polarization among Toronto's Neighbourhoods, 1970–2005*. Toronto: Cities Centre Press.

Hulchanski, David. 2015. *Toronto's Social Divide – Update on 3 Cities*. Toronto: City Planning Department. Accessed 22 July 2020. http://neighbourhoodchange.ca/documents/2015/11/toronto-social-divide-update-on-3-cities.pdf.

JLL. 2018. *Global Capital Flows*. London: JLL Research.

JLL. 2019. *Global Capital Flows*. London: JLL Research.

Karvonen, Andrew and Evans, James. 2014. '"Give Me a Laboratory and I Will Lower Your Carbon Footprint!" Urban Laboratories and the Governance of Low Carbon Futures'. *International Journal of Urban and Regional Research* 38(2):413–30. https://doi.org/10.1111/1468-2427.12077.

Keil, Roger. 2009. 'The Urban Politics of Roll-with-it Neoliberalization'. *City* 13(2–3):230–45. https://doi.org/10.1080/13604810902986848.

McFarlane, C. 2011. *Learning the City: Knowledge and Translocal Assemblage*. Chichester: Wiley-Blackwell.

Melhuish, Clare. 2015. *Case Studies in University-led Urban Regeneration*. London: UCL Urban Laboratory.

Migration Observatory. 2020. University of Oxford. Accessed 22 July 2020. https://migrationobservatory.ox.ac.uk/resources/briefings/migrants-in-the-uk-an-overview.

Minnery, John, Storey, Donovan and Setyono, Jawoto. 2012. 'Lost in Translation? Comparing Planning Responses to Urban Growth in the Global North and South'. *Urban Geography* 33(6):850–65. https://doi.org/10.2747/0272-3638.33.6.850.

Paradis, Emily, Novak, Sylvia, Sarty, Monica and Hulchanski, David. 2008. *Better Off in a Shelter? A Year of Homelessness and Housing among Status Immigrant, Non-Status Migrant, and Canadian Born Families*. Toronto: Cities Centre, University of Toronto.

Peck, Jamie. 2010. *Constructions of Neoliberal Reason*. Oxford: Oxford University Press.

Peck, Jamie and Tickell, Adam. 2002. 'Neoliberalizing Space'. *Antipode* 34(3):380–404. https://doi.org/10.1111/1467-8330.00247.

Raco, Michael. 2016. *State-led Privatisation and the Demise of the Democratic State*. London: Routledge.

Rider, David and Kopun, Francine. 2019. 'Ford Government's Cut to the Size of Toronto City Council Can Stand, Appeal Court Rules'. *Toronto Star*, 19 September. Accessed 22 July 2020. https://www.thestar.com/news/city_hall/2019/09/19/ford-governments-cut-to-the-size-of-toronto-city-council-can-stand-appeal-court-rules.html.

Robinson, Jennifer. 2011. 'Cities in a World of Cities: The Comparative Gesture'. *International Journal of Urban and Regional Research* 35(1):1–23.

Robinson, Jennifer. 2016. 'Thinking Cities through Elsewhere: Comparative Tactics for a More Global Urban Studies'. *Progress in Human Geography* 40(1):3–29. https://doi.org/10.1177/0309132515598025.

Safi, Michael. 2020. 'Coronavirus Will Reshape Our Cities – We Just Don't Know How Yet'. *The Guardian*, 22 May. Accessed 26 May 2020. https://www.theguardian.com/world/2020/may/22/coronavirus-will-reshape-our-cities-we-just-dont-know-how-yet.

Sassen, Saskia. 2001. *The Global City: New York, London, Tokyo* (2nd edition). Princeton, NJ: Princeton University Press.

Scott, Allen J. 2011. 'A World in Emergence: Notes toward a Resynthesis of Urban-economic Geography for the 21st Century'. *Urban Geography* 32:845–70. https://doi.org/10.2747/0272-3638.32.6.845.

Swyngedouw, Eric. 2009. 'The Antinomies of the Postpolitical City: In Search of a Democratic Politics of Environmental Production'. *International Journal of Urban and Regional Research* 33:601–20.

Toronto City Planning. 2019. *Toronto Employment Survey 2018*. City of Toronto. Accessed 19 September 2020. https://www.toronto.ca/wp-content/uploads/2019/03/8fd3-Toronto-Employment-Survey-2018-Bulletin.pdf.

Walks, Alan. 2015. 'Driving the Vote? Automobility, Ideology, and Political Partisanship'. In *The Political Economy and Ecology of Automobility: Driving Cities, Driving Inequality, Driving Politics*, edited by Alan Walks, 199–220. London: Routledge.

Ward, Kevin. 2010. 'Towards a Relational Comparative Approach to the Study of Cities'. *Progress in Human Geography* 334(4):471–87.

Part I
Perspectives on governance

1

Capital flows in the capital: Contemporary governmental imaginations in London's urban development

Mike Raco and Nicola Livingstone

Introducing systematic ambiguities: Questioning the planning, politics and perceptions of London's real estate market

Much of the critical literature on neoliberal urban development, and many of the policy frameworks that shape planning systems, characterise the real estate and investment sectors in a relatively simplified way. They are often presented, implicitly or explicitly, as a unified interest with a clear subjectivity built around fast returns from investment decisions, a lack of consideration for broader public interests, outlooks dominated by the conversion of places into profit-maximising investment spaces and counterproductive approaches towards citizens and government authorities who potentially seek to disrupt their programmes and projects. Such characterisations are becoming increasingly important as regulators in major cities such as London and Toronto are calling for the introduction of new policy technologies and techniques to try to exert greater territorial control over increasingly fluid investment flows, real estate actors and other institutions within cities. Through this chapter we will challenge these preconceived notions relating to real estate actor behaviour and demonstrate their more nuanced, integrated and essential role within London's politics of planning. Just as the urban form is a social product (Harvey 1979, 196), we need to better understand how the creation and ongoing dynamics of our built environment are impacted by the social (and not purely economic) form of market actors and regulators actively mediating the commercial and residential landscapes of the city.

This chapter draws on a content and discourse analysis of contemporary planning documents, political statements and speeches in London to examine the *conceptions* and *imaginations* of the development and investment sectors that exist within policy-making processes, and their apparent manifestations in the real estate market in reality. We argue that it is important to reflect on the active networks of real estate and planning actors who are mediating the flows of capital into London's commercial and residential market, demonstrating that there is a process (often asymmetrical but symbiotic) at play through the 'rules of the game' present within the local market context, policy environment and political perspective. The chapter will assess dominant understandings and diverse interconnections between market actors who are actively creating and mediating London's urban environment, and the analysis will demonstrate that systematic *ambiguities* lie at the heart of the political narratives and the planning system's characterisations and imaginations of the real estate and housing sectors.

On the one hand, they are infused with a critical view that portrays large developers and investors as overly powerful actors whose activities need to be tamed and restricted in order to meet a broader public interest. These actors are often presented as prioritising economic impacts of their behaviour over the social implications, whose actions can only be regulated through the deployment of hard financial incentives and regulations rather than through negotiated forms of softer regulation that could seek to establish more ethical and/or more community-oriented forms of intervention. There are also calls for a broadening of the diversity of investor and developer typologies, with smaller firms viewed as being more publicly oriented and socially progressive than the larger firms that disproportionately dominate the building of new housing, real estate and infrastructure; the latter are often perceived as purely driven by the prospect of financial benefits. There are also conflicting perspectives at play in relation to the scale of internationalisation in London as an investment and development market, as questions arise relating to the global nature of real estate actors and their potential (or lack of) connections to the city.

On the other hand, the chapter will illustrate how the rolling out of a market-led planning system means that the implementation of broader objectives requires the active and privileged cooperation of major private sector actors and their skills, expertise and resources. In planning fields ranging from the provision of affordable housing to energy and infrastructure management, private actors are increasingly called upon to work in harmony with the planning system and governing agencies to deliver public policy priorities. In the core strategic planning blueprint, the London Plan (LP) (GLA 2018), developers wishing to implement projects are expected to draw up proposals to (amongst other things): boost training and employment for young people; ensure that heritage standards are maintained; mitigate the impacts of developments on local urban environments; ensure the provision of green spaces; develop local utility infrastructure networks; and develop recycling and waste management systems. Market-led policies thus generate new forms of dependence on private sector resources and this, in turn, limits the scope and scale of regulation and political interventions.

The analysis will also show that there exists a clear knowledge gap that helps to generate and institutionalise these ambiguities. There is a relatively weak understanding of the investment landscapes that now shape urban environments and the systematic changes that have been underway in the form, character and structure of the real estate sector in recent decades, particularly in the wake of the Global Financial Crisis of 2008 (Baum and Hartzell 2012). We draw attention to the lack of knowledge and the contradictions active within the London market, by evaluating the antagonistic characterisations of institutional real estate actors, the lack of reflexivity in the governance and regulation of such actors through the planning system, and the importance of knowledge-laden networks in producing the city's built form. The chapter begins by unpacking some of the relevant literature relating to the planning system, real estate and housing markets, before presenting an analysis of these ambiguities. A concluding section outlines some of the implications of current trends for the (effective) regulation of the real estate sector in global cities such as London and Toronto, and the directions for further research in the future.

Dominant representations of real estate developers and investors in planning

Within much of the critical urban studies and planning literature, contemporary real estate developers and investors are represented as a relatively undifferentiated group of capitalist institutions. As Rachel Weber (2015) argues, much of this work has been dominated, on the one hand, by neoclassical framings of market systems and corporate practices and, on the other hand, by critical economy approaches. Weber maintains that both approaches are 'debilitated by their lack of attention to the action of actors and institutions that mediate between demand and supply' (2015, 30). The latter are found within 'urban political economy, cultural studies and geography traditions [in which] capital is often characterised as perpetually dynamic and naturally expansionary while the actors and institutions that make capital mobile are deemed irrelevant and unexamined' (Weber 2015, 30). Influential writings and models that draw on neoclassical interpretations suffer from similar limitations, with their focus on idealised and abstract models of action and practice of the management and ownership of urban land and real estate assets. Both real estate developers and investors are often represented as seeking fast returns from investment decisions, lacking an ethical concern with the impacts their development may have on broader public interests and/or the sustainability of places and communities. Since the beginning of the twenty-first century, writings on financialisation of the city have reinforced some of these inscriptions and it is an approach that stands in stark contrast to studies of social movements and non-governmental organisations, many of which highlight the variegated and place-specific nature of organisational structures and outlooks. Part of this explanation arises from the globalisation and/or internationalisation of the real estate sector and a degree of convergence and monopolistic behaviour between firms (Theurillat et al. 2015). Simplifications are especially evident in planning documents and policy frameworks, with Adams et al. showing that planning frameworks often 'reveal only scant awareness of both the structure of the development industry and the varied characteristics of individual developers' (2012, 2593; see also Campbell et al. 2014). Too often plans are built on simple assumptions about the practices of private firms, their outlooks, their ethical frameworks and their views of planning and regulation (see Imrie 2010).

There is only a basic understanding of the internal structures of investment and development companies, the tensions that exist between different types of private sector institutions, the greater importance given to knowledge production within the private sector, and the reflexive nature of actor subjectivities, networks, systems and practices. Ownership structures and models also vary, along with managerial practices and systems, firm traditions and outlooks towards investment ethics and attitudes to sustainable urbanism. This knowledge gap, the chapter argues, has under-researched implications for both the effectiveness of planning interventions and understandings of the types of investment that are now shaping London's built environments. Such knowledge gaps are becoming ever more significant as, under conditions of contemporary globalisation, we are also seeing the emergence of new investment landscapes underpinned by a plurality of institutions and actors. Projects are now funded by complex investment vehicles with finance sourced through foundations, charities or even public sector authorities (including local governments and quangos) and representing non-traditional real estate investors. Neither developers nor investors can be easily defined or categorised, due to their diverse strategies, motivations, scale, size and capital structures.

The previous section emphasised how the perceptions of complex real estate actors are limited in planning and (to an extent) urban studies literature. Relatively little attention is paid to the institutional organisation of the sector and/ or the extent to which the real estate processes of developing and investing possess specific difficulties and challenges vis-à-vis other forms of investment. Property trading is also a resource- and capital-intensive process when compared with, for instance, the buying and selling of stocks and shares. Development itself is also inelastic in the short term, requiring a highly regulated and lengthy production process, and its position as an asset is always shifting in terms of governance landscapes. As Baum and Hartzell (2012) note, direct property as an investment asset is relatively illiquid, entirely heterogenic and fixed to a location, making it difficult to diversify without the invention of financial vectors and innovations, combined with significant amounts of capital. The high degree of 'spatial fixity' in real estate assets means that investments are particularly place dependent and vulnerable to market shifts that are outside the control of site owners, encapsulating both systematic and specific types of risk.

However, how this is manifest and expressed is contingent on the investor's perception of risk as well as the particular real estate asset being considered, and it is reflected through its specific physical characteristics, its security of income and wider economic influences (such as interest rates). For example, large-scale residential investment was often seen as an unattractive real estate proposition in the UK market; however, with the emergence of the niche student accommodation sector and built-to-rent markets, institutional investors are becoming increasingly interested in diversifying into the housing market due to attractive longer-term returns and the opportunity to concentrate capital. All real estate is a constantly deteriorating asset that needs to be maintained, again creating longer-term uncertainties and risks (Graham and Thrift 2007) which need to be managed by investors. Data within the real estate market is always seen as weakly developed in comparison with other investment fields (such as the stock market), but information accuracy and accessibility continues to improve in mature markets. Irrespective of the challenges associated with direct property as an asset generally, investment and development continue to boom in London as there are clear benefits to being an active presence within the city's real estate market. As well as being perceived as a 'safe haven' for capital (Fernandez et al. 2016), offering attractive and consistent returns to investors, London is also the most transparent city market globally (JLL 2018a), with knowledge-rich, networked actors contributing to improving liquidity through efficient transaction and brokerage processes (Devaney et al. 2017).

Investment landscapes themselves are also becoming increasingly complex with the emergence of new investment players, including public sector actors and new types of investment funds, adding to market uncertainties and complexities. Some English local authorities, for instance, are now major property speculators and investors, as are publicly owned organisations with land assets such as Transport for London (TfL) and Network Rail (Findeisen 2016). The Global Financial Crisis of 2008 has also led to a wide-scale restructuring of the sector itself and the growth in importance of international hedge funds. In many instances there has been greater specialisation within the property sector and the emergence of clear distinctions between housebuilder developers, commercial property developers, landowners of different types and multiple forms of investor. As Beauregard notes, these specialised sectors possess 'different micro-logics' (2005, 2431), with authors such as Coiacetto (2001) identifying six types of firm: passive local property-owning developers, 'means to a mission' developers, specialised client developers, showpiece developers, value-adding opportunity developers and, finally, eye on the street builder-developers. To these (and more non-traditional investors) we can add specialist real estate investors and actors, such as listed Real Estate Investment Trusts, unlisted private equity funds, property investment companies, Property Authorised Investment Funds (PAIFs), Property Unit Trusts, family offices, Sovereign Wealth Funds and pension funds. There is significant granularity within the real estate investment and development sectors; however, this is underpinned by institutional processes which reflect spatially and temporally concentrated relations of networked knowledge, connections and interpretations actively shaping the increasingly international London market.

Both the London and Toronto markets can be viewed as a constellation of systems which broadly reflect 'interaction characterized by a specific institutional framework, that is, by a set of rules defining certain restrictions on the behaviour of market participants' (Vanberg 1986, 75), as defined by the planning and regulatory systems as well as the motivations of market actors themselves. Such 'rules of the game' are reflected through a response 'or action of some prevalence and permanence, which is embedded in the habits of a group' (Hamilton 1932, 84) and cannot be viewed from a purely economic or one-dimensional perspective. Although institutional behaviour and expert knowledge can become both established and embedded as market functions are fulfilled within the realms of the law, the 'rules of the game' through which such processes are expressed are nuanced, dynamic and particular to real estate (be it commercial, residential or infrastructure assets). The behaviour of networked real estate market actors, although habitual and locally embedded, is not static and is central to the emergence of these complex new investment landscapes, contingent on governance mechanisms and planning systems in global cities. Within the UK there is an apparent and potentially ever-increasing disconnect between the complex embedded knowledge, strategic subjectivities and dynamic market processes guiding real estate investor/developer decision-making, and current policy and planning frameworks.

Capital flows in London: Embedded knowledge, challenges and market trends

Recent decades have seen ever increasing flows of capital into London's commercial real estate markets, as both domestic and international actors seek to capitalise on property investment and development opportunities across such an internationalised, highly desirable global market. Transaction volumes were up 14 per cent in London year-on-year in 2018 to $36.3 billion, and the city was the largest recipient of cross-border investment globally (JLL 2018b). Within the commercial and residential real estate market, private service providers (such as real estate agents, valuers and planners working for JLL, CBRE and Cushman & Wakefield) have become increasingly important in terms of the diverse skill sets they offer and have concomitantly become globalised (De Magalhães 2001). In addition to increased transparency and improved brokerage practices globally, there are 'more robust and better-governed investment platforms covering most of the world's real estate markets' (Aussant et al. 2014, 3). Such platforms are mediated not just by the investors, developers and policy-makers, but also by those with specialist local knowledge working within private sector providers who contribute to the creation, interpretation and perpetuation of institutional processes and networks.

The professional companies that support the investment and divestment of domestic and international capital into and out of London can be considered to be a type of institution themselves and are part of a global network which enables actors to 'move capital through the built environment, articulating arguments for its free passage' (Weber 2016, 587). Although investment flows have been somewhat dampened by the political uncertainty due to Brexit, the commercial real estate sector within London remains resilient and relatively buoyant, reinforcing the perspective of London as a safe haven and one of the key global markets, as investment opportunities are still sought constantly. As previously mentioned, post-2008 the residential/housing sector within the UK has become a much more attractive proposition, not just to smaller retail investors but also to global institutions that have turned their attention to purchasing housing and entering the private rented sector (PRS). Although the UK has historically embraced owner-occupation of housing, the growth of institutional and international investors ploughing capital into new residential development and investment opportunities, coupled with the costs to buyers of accessing mortgage finance, limited supply pipelines and the decline of socially provided housing, has resulted in the emergence of 'generation rent', which further exacerbates the ongoing housing crisis of affordability in the capital (Minton 2017; Edwards 2016; Beswick et al. 2016; Whitehead and Williams 2011; see Chapter 10 by Gabrieli for more on London and Chapter 9 by Walks for a Toronto perspective).

As of 2018, the house price index (HPI), which relates the median house price to gross annual resident-based earnings, sat at 18.43 in the London local authority of Camden, 33.44 in Westminster and 14.88 in Wandsworth (ONS 2018). This cannot remotely compare to an average HPI in England of 8.0 (ONS 2018), and although house prices showed signs of declining or stabilising in 2019–20, rents are rising (GLA 2019). Global investors, especially those at smaller-scale level, are often perceived negatively as dominant networked elites, with London's residential sector in particular 'being made for money, and the monied' (Atkinson et al. 2017, 2443). However, less critique has been levied at the institutional investment flows into housing in the city's PRS market (e.g. Sigma Capital, M&G, Legal & General), although Gallent (2019) argues that the fixing of both institutional and smaller-scale capital into London's residential markets has been fostered by the withdrawal of the state from housing production and the deregulation of the market. This chapter argues that it is the latter and other governance mechanisms, coupled with the misunderstanding of the complexities of real estate processes within the planning and policy frameworks, which creates systematic ambiguities between market actors who are actively mediating the urban landscape across the capital. How such ambiguities and disconnects find expression in London is explored in the following section.

Contemporary governmental imaginations and the realities of real estate in London: Narratives and the politics of crisis

From a planning perspective, the lack of available housing to buy and rent in London and the city's affordability crisis have become the most significant issues facing the mayor and the 32 local boroughs. The victory in the 2016 mayoral election of Labour's Sadiq Khan was in part down to his proposals to tackle the city's housing problems and to challenge the perceived hegemony of international investors and developers. As he claimed during his campaign:

> There is no point in building homes if they are bought by investors in the Middle East and Asia ... I don't want homes being left empty. I don't want us to be the world's capital for money laundering. I want to give first dibs to Londoners. (Khan 2016, 1)

Such statements set a clear tone for 'Londoners' and against international investors shoring up their capital in the city's residential market. This prioritising of London residents has been institutionalised through new arrangements and partnership agreements that include larger-scale housebuilders, such as Berkeley Homes and other major builders and housing associations. Under the agreement, London and UK residents have first option to purchase homes under £350,000, at the lower end of the market (however, whether this is affordable considering current levels of the HPI remains questionable). Housebuilders have agreed not to market their properties internationally or sell them to non-UK residents for three months after completion (Mayor of London 2018b). Although such steps can be construed as a clear and constructive effort to influence the market-led housing market, even without international marketing the capacity of global real estate investors to operationalise the complex vehicles and channels available to them to ensure purchase of assets cannot be underestimated.

The complexities of investment structures, which can potentially provide alternative routes to investment, could still meet the criteria of the mayor and the housebuilders depending on their form and structure. Indeed, the mayor's criticisms raise not insubstantial concerns about market transparency, especially in relation to foreign buyers, and he goes further, as the rhetoric and tone of planning politics has become hostile to major developers, particularly international developers and investors:

> 44% of all the UK properties owned by overseas registered companies are located in London ... [the mayor] has long believed the legal and beneficial ownership of companies and other entities that own UK property should be more transparent, to help prevent offences such as tax evasion, theft and terrorist activities ... (Khan 2018, 1)

There is a clear territorial narrative that makes simple connections between international developers and investors through overseas-registered companies and these illegal practices. International investors, rather than domestic regulations, are being blamed for the fact that 'Londoners born and raised in our great capital have struggled to rent and stood little or no chance of owning a home in their own city' (Khan 2017, 1). Housing in this context is presented as a right that it is the planning system's obligation to meet (Madden and Marcuse 2017), but one which is being restrained due to the presence and potentially dubious activities of international investors, even if those investors are acting within the realms of the law and in response to the deregulated, market-led system of governance in the UK. Ambiguities emerge in interpreting the current crisis and where the apparent liability for such a crisis lies.

These ambiguities are reinforced through a set of additional simplifications over the *size* of firms and how the promotion of more diversity would make a difference to the form and character of residential development in London. It is claimed that building is too concentrated in the hands of a small number of larger firms. A number of piecemeal approaches have been proposed; for example, under a 'Small Sites Small Builders' programme the mayor is prioritising development on 10 small sites owned by TfL with the aim of completing only 111 homes (Mayor of London 2018c), a tiny impact on the proposed target of 65,000 new homes per year.

Reductions in local government finance mean that the mayor, as with local governments across England, is increasingly reliant on business rates drawn from the commercial real estate sector and other forms of finance to generate revenue. One initiative, launched in February 2018, saw the mayor negotiating an arrangement with central government under which 100 per cent of the growth of business rates would be allocated to the Greater London Authority, raising an additional £114 million. It was announced that this would help underpin a £140 million investment programme to boost London's economy. The scheme has a particular focus on support for a diversity of uses and acknowledges the continual erosion of spaces for small businesses and 'alternative' activities in the wake of recent development projects, a direct critique of the impacts of projects by large developers on the city and its residents (Mayor of London 2018a). While such initiatives clearly depend on the generation of more activity, they also represent an attempt to establish some autonomy and develop planning agendas for a broader range of needs and interests.

The mayor has been promoting greater liberalisation of planning to allow for an expansion of supply, an agenda that mirrors that of major housebuilders in the city. At the same time, after coming to power, the mayor also claimed that planning rules that prevented development were a significant barrier to new development and pledged that he would be:

> ripping up existing planning rules and calling on homebuilders to develop sites at higher housing densities to substantially increase capacity in the capital. … the Mayor has set out how he will ask homebuilders to maximise the use of valuable land in the city – and that means developing sites with more homes on them than existing developments nearby that would have had to follow previous guidelines. (Mayor of London 2017a)

While such plans impose additional demands on developers, the call for increased densities and more flexibility in design reflects the broader dependence of the public sector on market-led forms of planning gain and value capture, while also increasing opportunities for profit maximisation by developers (for more on densification in London's housing market see Chapter 12 by Short and Livingstone). Therefore, in some respects, the needs of the market, and private actors within it, are being equated with the needs of the public sector and to an extent can be considered mutually beneficial. But at the same time as there is something of a reification of the 'diversity' of the private sector and actors within it (even in the light of the negative connotations discussed earlier), the form and character of an entrepreneurial planning system *structurally privileges* the role and resources of major developers through four key dynamics.

Firstly, planning arrangements are systematically seeking out the development of *major sites* as the basis for tackling the housing crisis and boosting supply. This focus, in turn, privileges those developers and investors with the resources to bring complex and large-scale sites to fruition. The mayor's transport agency, TfL, for instance, has launched a Property Partnerships Framework that has brought into the pipeline six major development sites, all to be delivered by major housebuilders. The construction of the major cross-London Crossrail project provides sites for 12 'major property developments over and around the new stations along the railway and other key locations' (TfL 2016, 1). Francis Salway, Chairman of TfL's Commercial Development Advisory Group, has pointed out that 'TfL has some of the best assets in London and over the coming years we will be working together with these developers to ensure that we are delivering for Londoners' (TfL 2016, 1). TfL is now an active player in the 'identification of development opportunities' and has submitted some of London's largest planning applications in partnership with international investors and housebuilders for major sites such as Nine Elms, Northwood and Parsons Green. As TfL (2016, 1) states:

> it is anticipated that the three sites will generate over £100m for reinvestment in London's transport network as well as delivering more than 600 new homes, a new step-free London Underground station at Northwood, new workspaces, retail units and high-quality public spaces. The three sites will also support the creation of more than 500 new jobs.

While promoting new arrangements for smaller firms and developers, the biggest projects are being implemented through partnerships with large developers, as listed in Table 1.1.

Secondly, this drive to develop partnerships with major national and international firms is de facto, if not de jure, reinforced by the weight of the LP's obligations on real estate developers. Applicants will only be granted planning permission for their proposals if they contribute directly to a growing array of planning objectives – in line with the broader restructuring of the planning system towards entrepreneurialism and local self-sufficiency (see Table 1.2). Many of these obligations,

Table 1.1 Firms signed up as TfL property development partners

Balfour Beatty PLC
Barratt Development PLC/London and Quadrant Housing Association (Consortium)
Berkeley Group PLC
The British Land Company PLC
Canary Wharf Group PLC
Capital and Counties PLC
U+I/Notting Hill Housing Group (Consortium)
Land Securities Group PLC
Mace Ltd/Peabody Trust/DV4 Ltd (Consortium)
Mount Anvil Group Ltd/Hyde Housing Association Ltd
Redrow Homes Ltd
Stanhope PLC/Mitsui Fudosan Company Ltd
Taylor Wimpey UK Ltd

Source: TfL (2016)

Table 1.2 Key planning objectives that proposals must meet in the London Plan

- Public transport improvements
- Enhancements to public places
- Mixed-use developments and affordable housing
- Sustainable development programmes for Opportunity Areas
- Heritage planning
- Training and skills development
- Urban greening
- Noise reduction and the building of quality infrastructure
- Primary care infrastructure
- Helping to tackle climate change

Source: Information synthesised from GLA (2018)

particularly in fields such as education and training or investments in the creation of new urban spaces, would traditionally be undertaken by public agencies. Instead, under austerity cuts and planning gain-led arrangements, it is anticipated that developers and their funders will meet these objectives on behalf of the state. For instance, the LP calls on local boroughs 'to investigate with developers the possibility of providing local businesses and residents the opportunity to apply for employment during the construction of developments and in the resultant end use' (GLA 2018, 173). In relation to public transport, 'appropriate developer contributions are also needed to deliver public transport improvements to support the proposed intensification of residential use' (GLA 2018, 358). The implication, as with the more ambitious planning projects across the city, is that larger (possibly international) developers and investors who possess the expertise, knowledge and financial resources to meet these obligations will be in a stronger position to obtain planning permission than the 'smaller' and 'more diverse' firms that the LP and the mayor ostensibly want to support and nurture.

Thirdly, there is relatively little understanding given in the new planning frameworks of the differentiations within and between different types of house-builder, investor and developer and this also counts against smaller firms. Unnamed and ill-defined 'institutional investors' and 'greater institutional involvement' will help to solve shortages of rented property in the city as they will bring 'more professional and less fragmented management, greater stability, high quality standards and, potentially, longer term rental periods and affordable homes for rent', thereby helping to create more stable neighbourhoods across the city (Mayor of London 2018, 115). Real estate developers and landowners are expected to 'partner' with local authorities to protect town centres across London and ensure that any proposals they submit are 'closely integrated with investment in supporting social, environmental and physical infrastructure' (GLA 2018, 75). At the same time as mainstream housing developers are criticised in public and political discourse, the DLP makes it clear that major companies are the only ones able to help the mayor meet objectives such as the provision of residential environments for older residents, and planners are required to 'encourage mainstream housing developers to extend their product range to meet specialist needs' (GLA 2018, 112). It is anticipated that smaller developers will be unable to deliver on these social objectives to the same extent.

Most significantly in the context of London's housing crisis, the LP and the London Housing Strategy see real estate developers as key to delivering social and affordable housing and suggest they must 'provide development appraisals to demonstrate that each scheme provides the maximum reasonable amount of affordable housing output' (GLA 2018, 123). It is in relation to housing that some of the ambiguities are at their most evident. Underpinning the mayor's reforms is a critical challenge to the private sector to build more housing units that will help meet the city's crisis of affordability. The focus is mainly on the category of 'developers', with occasional references to a more generic group termed the 'development industry' and 'landowners', although it is not always clear if these are the same institutions or what their capacities might be to meet extra planning obligations. The Housing Special Planning Guidance (Mayor of London 2017b, 20) warns developers that

the requirement to deliver investment in other infrastructure will generally be set out in the development plan, relevant planning frameworks and CIL [Community Infrastructure Levy (London)] charging schedules. It should be taken into account by the applicant and the land owner, and should not necessarily lead to a reduction in affordable housing.

However, the mechanisms through which to meet these multiple priorities remain ill-defined.

Yet at the same time, the requirement to deliver development and for this to be implemented by private companies is structurally inscribed into the city's planning frameworks. The plans expose the financial weaknesses on the part of state institutions – and how they are structurally dependent on the resources and practices of private companies – yet they show little awareness or understanding of how private companies operate, what their priorities are, or their capacities to deliver financial resources to public projects and budgets. There is a constant tension between the mayor's threat to 'call in' and challenge development proposals if he is 'not satisfied with the viability information submitted by the applicant, the assumptions that underpin the information, or the level of scrutiny given by the local planning authority' (Mayor of London 2017b, 12), and the political reality that in order to deliver on election pledges, too many of these challenges might result in fewer successful applications and a clear public governance failure.

The fourth dimension of the representations made of private firms is that they are perceived to be economic agents responding to economic incentives and priorities. Firms are not viewed as reflexive social organisations or as a differentiated sector. Thus there is a tension between, on the one hand, seeing developers as 'co-producers' of the urban landscape who are willing and ready to use their resources to contribute to planning objectives and (indirectly) defined public interests, while on the other hand opening up opportunities for them to 'fast-track' investments to generate profits and giving 'good developers' the opportunity to limit obligations if they meet their housing targets (of 35 per cent affordable housing). If they are unwilling to contribute to broader policy objectives, then it is unclear how they will be policed given the reliance on market dynamics to deliver on policy objectives.

Conclusions

Future research on urban planning should focus less attention on the stated intentions, aims and objectives of public policy fields, and give more weight to the analysis of the frames of reference and types of knowledge that shape governmental imaginations and perspectives. Regulatory structures in cities such as London are, in part, built on these imaginations and specific understandings of how social and economic processes operate. Yet there is little evidence that policy-makers and regulators understand the institutional structures that shape real estate development and investment practices, and such lack of understanding has emerged as one of the key weaknesses of a market-led system. Deregulation in the UK market has encouraged global capital flows into the London real estate market, which is a dynamic and constantly evolving network of actors and vehicles producing knowledge in a complex system.

However, this burgeoning knowledge is not sufficiently integrated into governance, planning and regulatory framings, which are slow to understand and process real estate market knowledge even though there is an opportunity for greater connectivity between the public and private sectors to foster positive outcomes for the city. Rather than viewing the actions of real estate investors and developers with scepticism laced with purely economic assumptions, the planning system in particular could improve its functionality by facilitating burgeoning and positive relationships between public and private sector actors, so that actors have both abstract knowledge and concrete connections to the processes at play in London's markets: market actors should strive to learn each other's 'rules of the game'. Such efforts could be developed in other global cities, considering the significant flows of capital into real estate assets across the world. International developers and investors cannot and should not be considered as separate entities to local or national actors, due to the blurred lines between definitions of 'overseas' and 'domestic', as our understandings move towards eradicating notions that may demonise international actors. Efforts to 'incentivise' the right types of activity or to generate different forms of subjectivity among investors and developers need to be founded on a broader and deeper knowledge base and a recognition of the types of diversity that exist across the real estate sector. Regulatory powers and interventions would be significantly strengthened by a deeper understanding of the role that property, land use and other assets play in the portfolios of different types of investment actor.

Acknowledgements

This chapter is based on research funded by the ORA/ESRC project 'What Is Governed in Cities: Residential Landscapes and the Governance and Regulation of Housing Production' (2019–22).

References

Adams, David, Croudace, Robert and Tiesdell, Steve. 2012. 'Exploring the "Notional Property Developer" as a Policy Construct'. *Urban Studies* 49(12):2577–96. https://doi.org/10.1177/0042098011431283.

Atkinson, Rowland, Parker, Simon and Burrows, Roger. 2017. 'Elite Formation, Power and Space in Contemporary London'. *Theory, Culture & Society* 34(5–6):179–200. https://doi.org/10.1177/0263276417717792.

Aussant, Jean-Martin, Hobbes, Per, Yang, Liu and Shepard, Peter. 2014. *The Erosion of Real Estate Home Country Bias*. London: MSCI IPD Research.

Baum, Andrew E. and Hartzell, David. 2012. *Global Property Investment: Strategies, Structures, Decisions*. Oxford: Wiley-Blackwell.

Beauregard, Robert. 2005. 'The Textures of Property Markets: Downtown Housing and Office Conversions in New York City'. *Urban Studies* 42(13):2431–45. https://doi.org/10.1080/00420980500380345.

Beswick, Joe, Alexandri, Georgia, Byrne, Michael, Vives-Miró, Sònia, Fields, Desiree, Hodkinson, Stuart and Janoschka, Michael. 2016. 'Speculating on London's Housing Future'. *City* 20(2):321–41. https://doi.org/10.1080/13604813.2016.1145946.

Campbell, Heather, Tait, Malcolm and Watkins, Craig. 2014. 'Is There Space for *Better* Planning in a Neoliberal World? Implications for Planning Practice and Theory'. *Journal of Planning Education and Research* 34(1):45–59. https://doi.org/10.1177/0739456x13514614.

Coiacetto, Eddo. 2001. 'Diversity in Real Estate Developer Behaviour: A Case for Research'. *Urban Policy and Research* 19(1):43–59. https://doi.org/10.1080/08111140108727862.

De Magalhães, Claudio. 2001. 'International Property Consultants and the Transformation of Local Markets'. *Journal of Property Research* 18:99–121. https://doi.org/10.1080/09599910110014156.

Devaney, Steven, Livingstone, Nicola D., McAllister, Pat and Nanda, Anupam. 2017. 'Institutional Convergence in Real Estate Markets: A Comparative Study of Brokerage Models and Transaction Costs'. *Journal of Real Estate Literature* 25(1):169–88. https://doi.org/10.15396/eres2017_174.

Edwards, Michael. 2016. 'The Housing Crisis and London'. *City* 20(2):222–37. https://doi.org/10.1080/13604813.2016.1145947.

Fernandez, Rodrigo, Hoffman, Annelore and Aalbers, Manuel. 2016. 'London and New York as a Safe Deposit Box for the Transnational Wealth Elite'. *Environment and Planning A, Economy and Space* 48(12):2443–61. https://doi.org/10.1177/0308518x16659479.

Findeisen, Francesco. 2016. 'Financing Urban Infrastructure in London after the Financial Crisis'. In *Britain For Sale: Perspectives on the Costs and Benefits of Foreign Ownership*, edited by Mike Raco, 68–74. London: Smith Institute.

Gallent, Nick. 2019. *Whose Housing Crisis? Assets and Homes in a Changing Economy*. Bristol: Policy Press.

GLA (Greater London Authority). 2018. *Draft London Plan*. London: GLA.

GLA (Greater London Authority). 2019. *Quarterly Housing Market Report, November 2019*. London: GLA Housing and Land.

Graham, Stephen and Thrift, Nigel. 2007. 'Out of Order: Understanding Repair and Maintenance'. *Theory, Culture and Society* 24:1–25. https://doi.org/10.1177/0263276407075954.

Hamilton, Walton. 1932. 'Institutions'. In *Encyclopaedia of the Social Sciences*, edited by Edwin R. A. Seligman and Alvin Johnson, 84–9. New York: Macmillan.

Harvey, David. 1979. *Social Justice and the City*. London: Edward Arnold.

Imrie, Rob. 2010. 'An Exemplar for a Sustainable World City: Progressive Urban Change and the Redevelopment of King's Cross'. In *Regenerating London: Governance, Sustainability and Community in a Global City*, edited by Rob Imrie, Loretta Lees and Mike Raco, 93–111. London: Routledge.

Khan, Sadiq. 2016. 'Sadiq Khan Warns "Greedy" Developers as He Outlines Housing Plan'. *The Guardian*, 16 May. Accessed 10 June 2019. https://www.theguardian.com/politics/2016/may/16/sadiq-khan-developers-housing-plan-london-mayor-affordable.

Khan, Sadiq. 2017. 'Mayor Strikes Landmark Deal for 20,000 New Homes'. Press Release, Mayor of London, 6 April.

Khan, Sadiq. 2018. 'Speed Up Transparency of Foreign Property Ownership, Says Mayor'. Press Release, Mayor of London, 27 February.

JLL. 2018a. *Global Real Estate Transparency Index 2018*. London: JLL. Accessed 25 April 2019. http://greti.jll.com/greti.

JLL. 2018b. *Global Capital Flows: JLL Research Report, Q4 2018*. London: JLL. Accessed 25 April 2019. https://www.theinvestor.jll/gcf.

Madden, David and Marcuse, Peter. 2017. *In Defense of Housing*. London: Verso Books.

Mayor of London. 2017a. 'Mayor Rips Up Old Planning Rules to Get London Building'. Press Release, 29 November.

Mayor of London. 2017b. *Special Planning Guidance: Homes for Londoners*. London: Greater London Authority.

Mayor of London. 2018a. 'Mayor Announces £140million Investment to Boost London Economy'. Press Release, 15 February.

Mayor of London. 2018b. 'Mayor Reveals Landmark Step to Offer Londoners First Dibs on New Homes'. Press Release, 5 February.

Mayor of London. 2018c. 'Mayor Launches Small Home Builders Programme with TFL Pilot Sites'. Press Release, 9 February.

Minton, Anna. 2017. *Big Capital: Who Is London For?* London: Penguin Random House.

ONS (Office for National Statistics). 2018. *House Price to Residence-based Earnings Ratio*. London: Office for National Statistics.

TfL (Transport for London). 2016. 'TfL Selects 13 Property Partners to Help it Deliver Thousands of Homes for London'. Press Release, 3 February.

Theurillat, Thierry, Rerat, Patrick and Crevoisier, Olivier. 2015. 'The Real Estate Market: Players, Institutions and Territories'. *Urban Studies* 52(8):1414–33. https://doi.org/10.1177/0042098014536238.

Vanberg, Viktor. 1986. 'Spontaneous Market Order and Social Rules'. *Economics and Philosophy* 2:5–100.

Weber, Rachel. 2015. *From Boom to Bubble: How Finance Built the New Chicago*. Chicago: University of Chicago Press.

Weber, Rachel. 2016. 'Performing Property Cycles'. *Journal of Cultural Economy* 9(6):587–603. https://doi.org/10.1080/17530350.2016.1212085.

Whitehead, Christine and Williams, Peter. 2011. 'Causes and Consequences? Exploring the Shape and Direction of the Housing System in the UK Post the Financial Crisis'. *Housing Studies* 2(7–8):1157–69. https://doi.org/10.1080/02673037.2011.618974.

2
The elusive, inclusive city: Toronto at a crossroads

Shauna Brail and Tara Vinodrai

Introduction

We have entered an urban era where the combination of heightened concentration of innovation-based economic activity and best-practice urbanism is leading to increasingly polarised and unequal cities, especially within global cities. This relatively small number of globally oriented, so-called superstar cities benefit disproportionately from employment and income growth when measured against national counterparts (Sassen 2001; Manyika et al. 2018; Kemeny and Storper 2020). However, within global cities, the clustering effects that drive growth are also leading to deep intra-urban inequality and do not benefit all workers equally (Marcuse and van Kempen 2000; Brenner and Keil 2006; Lee and Clarke 2019). By examining an emerging urban narrative in which a growing number of thriving, economically vibrant cities are experiencing dual, connected challenges that align economic growth with socio-economic and spatial polarisation, this chapter explores the urban dynamics characteristic of prominent cities in the early twenty-first century.

Emblematic of twenty-first-century urbanism, global cities in advanced economies face significant challenges. In these cities, a lack of affordable housing, growth in homelessness and food insecurity, poor transit access for low-income residents and weak employment prospects particularly for racialised groups exist side by side with prominent city centres characterised by expansive real estate valuations, investments in downtown properties and even entire neighbourhoods by multinational firms, and a rising concentration of wealthy households. This form of winner-take-all urbanism presents serious challenges for civic and business leaders, politicians and community activists who care deeply about the prospects for inclusive city building. Toronto and London are no exception, and these cities face similar challenges and opportunities (cf. Sassen 2001; Walks 2001, 2011; Boudreau et al. 2009). Hunter (2019) suggests that increasing concentrations of poverty in outer London are in deep contrast to economic development strategies that prioritise investment attraction to central London. Likewise in Toronto, income inequality is expressed geographically. This is particularly acute in the City of Toronto, with high-income neighbourhoods closer to the core and transit corridors surrounded by middle- and low-income neighbourhoods (Hulchanski 2015). Over time, the middle-income portions of the city have shrunk, while the high-income areas concentrated in the urban core and close to the subway have grown, as have the low-income areas in which access to transport, employment and life opportunities is limited (see map in Figure 2.1). The disparities between wealth and poverty in Toronto have continued to grow over the past several decades and threaten the city's and the region's future.

A long-standing literature on global cities identifies the challenges of multinational investment and the pursuit of economic competitiveness (see Sassen 2001; Marcuse and van Kempen 2000; Brenner and Keil 2006; Boudreau et al. 2009). More recently, observers have articulated concerns that the urban inequalities identified in places such as London and Toronto are heightened in an era of tech-based urban development, driven by the investments and activities of global technology firms (Florida 2018; Zukin 2019). Indeed, as Berridge (2019, 141) notes, 'global digital companies are now major forces in the modern city, and cities have not figured out how to deal with them'. These firms, including Amazon, Apple, Facebook and Google, have extraordinary market valuations that enable real estate dominance wherever they choose to invest (Langley and Leyshon 2017). Therefore, technology firms in particular have an impact on urban land use and

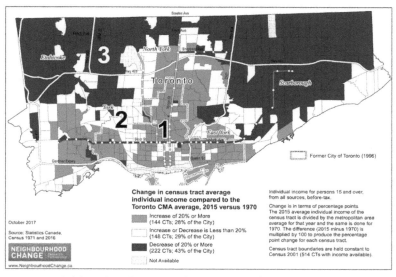

Figure 2.1 Neighbourhood income change: City of Toronto, 2015 vs 1970 (Hulchanski 2017)

exclusion. Zukin (2019) identifies the phenomenon of the 'urban tech landscape' – an environment in which the physical presence of technology firms in world cities is increasingly evident. While such tech investment generates benefits to cities, there are also disadvantages, which accrue unevenly to local residents in the reordering of urban space associated with the expansion of multinational technology firms. Juxtaposing the reality of oftentimes unrealised economic development promises associated with large-scale tech investment against the displacement of low-income and racialised populations in urban spaces, Zukin (2019) laments the lack of equity and sharing of local benefits from the growth of global tech firms (see also Ash et al. 2019; Grisdale 2019).

As cities such as Toronto and London become increasingly desirable places in which to invest, live, work, learn and play, this chapter examines whether there are public policies and collaborative strategies that can better address unequal urban outcomes. To do so, this chapter explores the potential for inclusive development in Toronto at a time when growth and investment in the city may be exacerbating inequality and increasing socio-economic divides. The chapter identifies initiatives that address inclusion, broadly defined as any initiative that reduces barriers to access or attempts to make opportunities available to a wider population, especially those in marginalised groups. Initiatives related to housing, transport and economic development are examined vis-à-vis their capacity and potential to result in a city that is both thriving and inclusive. None of these efforts are led by municipal government alone. Rather, and as is increasingly common, the role of partnerships among government, civil society and industry feature prominently in efforts to address each challenge.

Toronto: Canada's largest city

As Canada's largest city and metropolitan region,[1] Toronto plays an important role in the national economy and acts as a global financial hub. Toronto houses the Toronto Stock Exchange and has the largest concentration of lenders and financial headquarters in the country, including all the major Canadian banks. It is the second largest financial centre in North America, and, with almost 275,000 workers, it has a higher proportion of employment in the financial services industry than other global financial epicentres such as London and New York (Edenhoffer 2018) and the sector has grown faster than in other global financial hubs, with the exception of Shanghai and Beijing (Edenhoffer 2018). Data on gross domestic product (GDP), investment attraction and jobs underscore Toronto's position in the Canadian economy. In 2013, Toronto's census metropolitan area (CMA) contributed nearly one-fifth (18.6 per cent) of Canada's GDP (Statistics Canada 2017b). Between 2015 and 2018, firms located in the Toronto region received just over $3.5 billion in venture capital investment, making it the highest-ranked Canadian city for venture capital investment. In the first three-quarters of 2019, Toronto had

119 deals amounting to $1.4 billion (CVCA 2019). Toronto is also the employment capital of the country, with approximately 18 per cent of all Canadian jobs located in Toronto.

Economic activity, including activity related to the global financial industry, is highly concentrated in the downtown core of the city proper, which accounts for just 3 per cent of the city's land area yet represents one-third of the city's jobs, one-quarter of the tax base and is also home to 240,000 residents (City of Toronto 2014a). The concentration of population and economic activity in a small area within the regional economy means that planners and city builders are challenged to find appropriate local policies, including land use policy and zoning, that balance economic growth and development goals alongside provisions that ensure housing affordability and broader liveability and social inclusion. Such interventions are made more challenging, since local-level decision-making is constrained by senior levels of government. Notably, provincial governments in Canada have the authority to override municipal powers.

A diverse regional economy

The Toronto regional economy is highly diversified. After the end of the Second World War, the region established itself as a major manufacturing hub and subsequently evolved to become a centre for high-order business and financial services, as well as a dynamic hub for cultural and creative industries, advanced manufacturing, the tech sector and other research-intensive activities. This economic diversity has helped the city weather economic shocks and downturns over time (Bourne et al. 2011; Wolfe and Bramwell 2016).

While the Toronto regional economy is diverse, the region has developed a number of strong sectoral specialisations. The City of Toronto's economic development plans and strategies have consistently identified a series of globally competitive high-value economic sectors that are important drivers of growth and innovation. These include: biotechnology; culture; design; education and training; film and digital media; financial services; food and beverage; green/renewable energy; information and communications technology (ICT); and professional and business services (City of Toronto 2013).

The dynamism of Toronto's industrial clusters can be measured quantitatively. Figure 2.2 shows the relative economic performance of selected clusters in the Toronto CMA by measuring specialisation (location quotient, or LQ, on the x-axis), 10-year compound annual employment growth rates (y-axis) and employment (the size of each point).[2] Figure 2.2 emphasises the growing importance of activities related to high-order business services and the creative economy. The clusters located in the top right quadrant have high levels of specialisation (LQs greater than 1) and positive compound annual employment growth rates between 2006 and 2016. Clusters that are growing include those related to the construction, higher education, ICT services, food and beverage, business services, biomedical

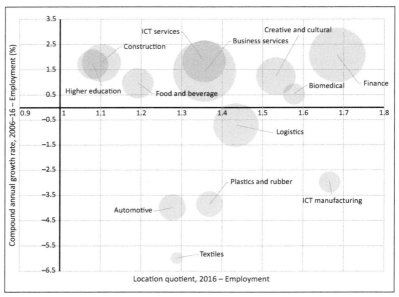

Figure 2.2 Economic performance of clusters in the Toronto CMA (authors' calculations based on Statistics Canada, Census of Population, 2006 and 2016, custom tabulations)

and life sciences, creative and cultural, and finance industries. Indeed, growth in the finance industry, which accounts for 8.3 per cent of Toronto's employment and 13.6 per cent of Toronto's GDP (Edenhoffer 2018), underscores Toronto's position as a global hub. In contrast, clusters located in the bottom right quadrant, while demonstrating regional specialisation (LQs greater than 1), have negative growth rates, meaning that employment declined between 2006 and 2016. These include clusters related to the automotive, plastics and rubber, textiles, ICT manufacturing and logistics industries. With the exception of logistics, these industries reflect the traditional and legacy industries that have historically been an important part of Toronto's economic base. While the logistics cluster continues to be important since Toronto acts as a key distribution centre for the broader region, it is possible that employment decline is related to automation in these industries.

While exploring the intra-regional geography of these activities in the Toronto region, Blais (2018) corroborates these patterns, showing the hyper-concentration and growth of economic activity in the downtown area, especially in knowledge- and design-intensive industries. Downtown Toronto contains concentrations of financial services firms, healthcare and educational institutions, government, retail, and arts and cultural activities (City of Toronto 2014b).

This sectoral and spatial distribution of jobs is influenced and supported by both the city's economic development strategy and city policy on employment lands. The city's employment lands policy encourages the preservation of employment land, the separation of incompatible uses in a way that protects employment areas and the development of higher-density office uses in proximity to public transit infrastructure, and it supports the growth of retail and institutional land uses serving the regional population (Blais 2018; City of Toronto 2018).

Within the Toronto region, policy related to the development and preservation of employment lands remains a contentious issue tied to shifts in the structure of the regional economy and desires to increase the supply of housing. Given that the proportion of manufacturing activity in the city has declined and that the remaining manufacturing activities are 'cleaner' and less noxious, there is a sense that many employment uses in areas zoned for manufacturing do not require full separation from other types of land uses. Thus, there are calls for the city to relax employment lands zoning policies to enable or encourage greater opportunities for mixed-use redevelopment, including housing, in these areas. Proposed shifts in land use policy are connected not only to economic change and employment restructuring, but also contribute to addressing the city's housing affordability challenges that are tied to housing supply, and the desire to better utilise transport infrastructure, especially public transit (Boudreau et al. 2009; Greenberg 2017).

The desire to convert employment lands raises tensions. City planners are tasked with ensuring that the city has sufficient land designated for a diversity of employment types over the long term. Making physical changes to the urban landscape can be slow due to the local planning process, and also such changes have permanence. Decisions to reduce employment capacity by changing land use designations can have detrimental long-term impacts. It is difficult to imagine how land rezoned to residential or mixed use could be returned to manufacturing uses in a timely manner, should economic restructuring necessitate different and unplanned land uses. Nevertheless, there was almost a 10 per cent reduction in the proportion of land zoned exclusively for employment between 2006 and 2018 in Toronto (Dingman 2018). Moreover, city planners assume that designating land for mixed use will result in a mix of housing types, prices and social characteristics. However, recent evidence in Toronto suggests that these lands are more likely to be converted to owner-occupied condos targeted at a narrow demographic (Rosen and Walks 2014) and that mixed use may not lead to greater access across the income spectrum (Moos et al. 2018). As the city's population continues to grow alongside shifts in industry, the subject of protecting employment lands exclusively for industry is likely to persist.

A global tech 'superstar' city?

Toronto has long been home to a concentration (or cluster) of ICT firms; Toronto's ICT cluster is consistently identified as one of the largest in North America (Denney et al. 2018). While defining the tech industry can be challenging, recent estimates suggest that Toronto's tech labour force accounts for over 400,000 jobs (Tech

Toronto 2016). This concentration of tech-based activity can be attributed to a variety of factors, including the large talent base generated by publicly funded universities and colleges, other public investments in knowledge infrastructure and the presence of a number of anchor firms and other institutions (Wolfe 2018; CBRE 2018b).

Tech sector employment and investment is also on the rise. Toronto has been identified as the fastest-growing tech market in both 2017 and 2018, adding 28,900 jobs in 2017 (CBRE 2018a). There are both venture capital-based investments in start-up firms and inbound investment from major global players. For example, ride-hailing firm Uber has made the city a key site of investment and employment in its global network (Brail 2020). In 2017, Sidewalk Labs (owned by Alphabet, the parent company of Google) was named the winning partner on a $1 billion bid for a smart city development along Toronto's waterfront; Amazon shortlisted Toronto as one of 20 North American cities for a second headquarters (HQ2) site slated to employ 50,000 high-skilled workers and invest $5 billion in capital expenditures; and the launch of the Vector Institute, a $150 million partnership between the University of Toronto, federal and provincial governments and private corporations including Google and Shopify, highlighted Toronto's role as a leading centre of artificial intelligence. While the Sidewalk Labs project was subsequently cancelled and Amazon did not select Toronto for HQ2, there were other substantial international tech investments in Toronto, including over $1.4 billion by Microsoft, Uber and Shopify (Sheppard 2018).

These recent tech investments have solidified Toronto's position as a global technology hub, bringing additional investment, profile, jobs and talent to the region. Moreover, these investments coincide with the rapid development and expansion of the local tech start-up scene. There is evidence that some of these home-grown firms are becoming globally competitive and scaling in size (Denney et al. 2018). One challenge for locations benefiting from the investment and growth of global technology firms is the emergence of 'techlash', the backlash against powerful technology firms. This has included growing frustration with large, multinational technology firms due to their influence on labour markets and a number of high-profile cases citing privacy breaches and unethical behaviour. This extends to how technology firms are shaping cities. Technology firms are increasingly choosing central city locations. A US-based study found that start-ups prioritise locations in proximity to transit, regardless of their industry (Credit 2019). While the allure of the city is celebrated by some, the urban location preferences of technology firms along with above-average salaries for high-skilled workers are credited with driving up real estate prices, promoting gentrification and negatively impacting housing affordability (CBRE 2018b; Florida 2018; Grisdale 2019). This raises an important question regarding tech-led urban development: can cities benefit from the growth of firms and the ensuing investments in talent and place while also ensuring equitable, inclusive access to housing, transport and jobs for those who do not benefit directly from this growth and change?

Challenges facing Canada's largest city: Inequality and governance

As the above discussion makes clear, Toronto has a dynamic regional economy and has been a beneficiary of the global shift towards a knowledge-based, cognitive-cultural economy. The City of Toronto's primacy both regionally and nationally contributes to its increasing desirability as a place to live and work. However, this status as a desired location for businesses and talent is accompanied by challenges. The Toronto region continues to struggle with questions of equity, affordability, accessibility and how to share the benefits of the city-region's success more broadly (Walks 2001, 2011; Boudreau et al. 2009; Bourne et al. 2011). And in turn, this situation has led to a housing affordability crisis that pushes people to make suboptimal housing decisions. The City of Toronto is the inequality capital of the country, its neighbourhoods are increasingly divided based on measures of income and race and the region's transport infrastructure is inadequate. Moreover, inequality is deepening in the surrounding suburban municipalities in the region.

Addressing these challenges is by no means straightforward and they are compounded by existing urban and regional governance structures. The Toronto region is composed of many municipalities, each with its own government, elected city council and mayor. According to the Canadian constitution, written in 1867 when the country was overwhelmingly rural, municipalities are considered 'creatures of the province'. Provincial governments have authority over essentially all elements of municipal power, including municipal boundaries, revenue tools and council size. New meaning was brought to this statement in 2018 when the provincial government introduced legislation to reduce the number of councillors in the City of Toronto from 44 to 25, in the midst of the 2018 municipal election campaign and without prior consultation. The lack of autonomy and inability to make decisions without the threat of being overridden by the provincial government is one example of the fragmented environment in which decision-making and governance operates. Fragmentation and weak decision-making powers are compounded by the politics and challenges of cooperation and coordination across a large number of local governments in the region (Boudreau et al. 2009; Wolfe and Bramwell 2016). Various initiatives have evolved to work around these challenges, such as the creation of arm's-length agencies or independent organisations dedicated to coordinating a particular dimension of urban development, such as investment attraction or newcomer workforce development.

The city proper has fewer financial constraints compared with other municipalities in the region due to the City of Toronto Act (2006). The Act allows the city to generate revenue through financial tools, such as vehicle registration or land transfer taxes, yet these have been controversial and underutilised. For example, a vehicle registration tax introduced in 2007 was cancelled in 2010 with a change in local government. The city's inability or unwillingness to raise revenue beyond property taxes creates additional barriers and limits in terms of amassing the financial resources needed to, for example, provide sufficient, high-quality subsidised hous-ing or provide economic and social supports to help integrate newcomers.

Overall, the Toronto city-region faces a serious conundrum. On the one hand, the city is a dynamic hotbed for innovation and economic development, attracting both highly skilled talent and investment. Yet these very activities are exacerbating underlying social issues and threaten the very foundations of this prosperity. These challenges are compounded by existing municipal finance structures, political choices and urban and regional governance structures. Herein lies the great chal-lenge for Toronto: what policies and actions can governments and other stakehold-ers implement to ensure that cities can be both economically vibrant and socially inclusive?

Questions about how best to address the wicked urban challenges associated with inequality are among the most vexing problems faced by municipal govern-ments worldwide. It is commonly understood that governing a twenty-first-century city requires a rethinking of the role of government and the ways in which it oper-ates. With this in mind, the remainder of the chapter examines urban experiments and pilot projects primarily located within the City of Toronto that offer potential solutions to address some of the most pressing questions related to inequality. This is not to suggest that pilots do not exist in the suburban communities in the rest of the Greater Toronto Area. We focus on initiatives that are well developed and that address issues that are congruent with the challenges faced by global cities else-where. Initiatives in the realms of housing affordability, transport equity and eco-nomic opportunity are highlighted to explore the possibility of a more inclusive city.

Piloting the possibilities for the inclusive city

Government, business and civic leaders in the Toronto region have experimented with mechanisms to address the very challenges that test the balance of prosper-ity and inclusion. Despite complications associated with systems and structures of governance and seemingly rapid and threatening urban change, cities have dem-onstrated an ability to respond to shifts relatively quickly, often through the use of pilot projects. Pilots (or trials) are an increasingly popular way for governments to test out whether and how an idea might work in practice, in a low-threat envi-ronment. They can be limited in terms of geography, and also can have a limited period of time in which testing is conducted. Over the past decade, cities have piloted programmes as a means to regulate emerging sectors, increase the supply and quality of affordable housing, improve public transport, spur redevelopment of post-industrial land and reorient streets and other public spaces. In cities includ-ing New York, London, Paris and Toronto, initiatives first launched as pilots have been the testing ground needed to create more significant, scalable, lasting change. Below, we identify and discuss a series of pilots and experiments that primarily focus on the City of Toronto, where the challenges of urban development are acute.

Increasing the supply and quality of affordable housing in Toronto

Toronto is far from alone in facing the challenges of an affordable housing crisis, precipitated in part by increases in housing prices that exceed increases in household income, and combined with years of inaction and disinvestment. Access to affordable housing is crucial to a city's ability to ensure that its residents can thrive, and also critical to ensuring that cities can continue to function. Other high-cost, global cities have sought to address the challenges of housing provision and affordability with some success. For example, Paris – one of the world's most expensive cities – has used funding and regulatory mechanisms and has leveraged land values in a financialised real estate market to increase housing production and affordability. Since 2015, the Paris metropolitan area has doubled annual housing production to 70,000 units/year. This was accomplished through reforms led by multiple levels of government and involved new funding, utilisation of public land, zoning amendments and a requirement that municipalities ensure more affordable housing for low- and moderate-income households (Freemark 2019).

In Toronto, housing affordability has reached a crisis point. While more than 180,000 new residential units were added between 2009 and 2018, housing affordability challenges, previously concentrated in lower-income households, have grown to encompass both low- and middle-income households in the city (Kalinowski 2019). One study found that nearly 90 per cent of renter households with annual incomes lower than $30,000 spend more than 30 per cent of their income on housing (CCEA and CUI 2018). In 2019, the average monthly rent (a figure used to calculate eligibility for affordable housing) for a two-bedroom apartment in the Greater Toronto Area reached $1,492 – 21.7 per cent higher than five years previously (City of Toronto 2019c); two-bedroom condo rentals reached an average of $2,868 per month (TREB 2020). Homeownership, either in the form of a single-family home or in a multi-unit building, was assessed to be unaffordable for most households in a majority of the city's neighbourhoods (Winsa and Bailey 2019). Two pilot initiatives that improve and expand the supply of affordable housing are underway, each focused solely on the City of Toronto rather than the surrounding suburban municipalities.

As the second largest provider of public housing in North America, the City of Toronto holds responsibility for the provision of deeply subsidised public housing. Through the Toronto Community Housing Corporation (TCHC), the City owns real estate valued at over $10 billion and houses over 110,000 residents in nearly 60,000 units (TCHC 2019). TCHC is reorienting towards an entrepreneurial approach to public housing redevelopment. TCHC is engaged in a number of large-scale, public–private partnership redevelopment schemes to revitalise public housing in Toronto. Their largest project is the redevelopment of Regent Park, a 69-acre neighbourhood in Toronto's downtown core. From the 1950s to the early 2000s, Regent Park was home exclusively to low-income residents living in public housing, leading to a neighbourhood of concentrated poverty (August 2014). Since 2006,

Regent Park has been undergoing a wholesale transformation, which will take nearly 20 years to complete. Once finished, the neighbourhood will include 1800 public housing units, 5400 market units and 200 affordable housing units (Brail and Kumar 2017). Similar to the approach in Paris, TCHC, in partnership with the City of Toronto and a private development partner, has leveraged land values to finance redevelopment in Regent Park. While the Regent Park redevelopment has encountered challenges, including resident displacement during construction and tensions regarding resident access to new neighbourhood amenities such as the aquatic centre, it is now a model for redeveloping other public housing sites in Toronto and globally. For example, the United Nations recently announced the opening of a UN Urban Pavilion in Toronto, which will serve as a hub that informs similar housing revitalisation initiatives globally.

Repairing and replacing dilapidated public housing units is insufficient to address the city's affordable housing needs. Another pilot, aimed at increasing the number of affordable rental housing units in the city, is being led by CreateTO, a city agency that manages over 8000 city-owned properties. CreateTO is leading an effort, Housing Now, to identify city-owned properties that can be redeveloped to accommodate affordable housing for a range of income groups. Support for Housing Now is embedded in the city's HousingTO 2020–2030 Action Plan and – if fully realised – will facilitate the addition of more than 10,000 new residential units in the city. The city and agency are currently in the early stages of planning, with 11 sites activated (City of Toronto 2019b). Some critics have charged that to succeed, Housing Now requires not only publicly owned land but also the relaxation of existing planning regulations (Bozikovic 2019). While it is too soon to evaluate the impact of this effort, both the phased pilot approach and Housing Now's contribution to the range of housing initiatives being undertaken by the city hold some promise.

Transport

'The best transportation plan is a good land use plan' has become an accepted truism among urban planning and economic development professionals. Current best practice in land use and transport planning is to connect development plans with transit planning. In 2018, 88 per cent of residential units and 77 per cent of non-residential units proposed or under development were within 500 metres of higher-order transit in the City of Toronto (City of Toronto 2019a). Research on Toronto's changing neighbourhoods indicates that in 1970, most neighbourhoods in the central city with subway access were characterised as low- and middle-income neighbourhoods. By 2010, however, an inversion occurred and most central city Toronto neighbourhoods with strong transit access had become high-income neighbourhoods (Hulchanski 2015). Low- and moderate-income households in Toronto have been forced to move away from the core, which is served by subway and light rail, as real estate prices rise.

Toronto has an extensive suburban bus network, with frequent service times that are far superior in comparison with its US counterparts (English 2019). Although the city has struggled to achieve political agreement on efforts to expand its subway system, it is beginning to invest smaller sums of money and political capital to improve bus travel. In autumn 2017, the city launched a streetcar rapid transit project on a 2.6-kilometre stretch of the city's busiest surface transit route. Limiting cars and privileging transit sped up peak hour commute times by 33 per cent for morning commuters travelling eastbound and by 44 per cent for afternoon commuters travelling westbound (Toronto Transit Commission 2019). Within eight months of making the downtown transit pilot permanent, the Toronto Transit Commission (TTC) announced that it would explore the potential of adding five new priority bus routes, all located in the city proper's suburban neighbourhoods serving lower-income residents (Toronto Transit Commission 2019). The TTC acknowledges that equity considerations in transit planning can positively impact individuals' access to economic opportunity and employment. New infrastructure development is underway, including a new light rail service which will serve residents living in low-income neighbourhoods, reducing travel times and improving service levels.

Economic development

While many of Toronto's economic development initiatives have raised controversy because of their potential downsides (e.g. Amazon HQ2 bid), city planners and other actors have also actively considered strategies that support and preserve industries traditionally offering a supply of middle- or high-skill jobs with strong wage prospects and that create (or minimise displacement of) jobs across the skill and income spectrum.

Toronto has historically been a centre for manufacturing (Bourne et al. 2011; Wolfe and Bramwell 2016). Yet industrial restructuring leading to manufacturing disinvestment alongside pressures to release land for housing development has led to a situation where employment lands have been rezoned for condominium development (see above). In some areas, especially those within the city's boundaries, this repurposing of land has raised serious concerns about the loss of production space for artisanal, craft and other manufacturing. In some areas of the city, these issues are also tied to concerns around the outcomes of gentrification. For example, in the City of Toronto's Queen West neighbourhood, low-rise light industrial buildings and warehouses have been converted into condominium developments, reflective of a broader trend towards condo-ism in the city (Rosen and Walks 2014). However, a recent development in this same neighbourhood indicates a potential shift towards more inclusive forms of economic development.

A site at 440 Dufferin Street became the source of controversy as it was slated for redevelopment, leading to the displacement of many artists, makers and craft manufacturers. City planners brokered a deal with the developer to create a mixed-use development that preserved 60,000 square feet for light manufacturing, including a 14,000 square foot light manufacturing incubator and rental apartment housing. This marks a departure from previous neighbourhood developments, which were exclusively oriented towards owner-occupied condominium development. City staff tendered the incubator space; the winning bid is organised around a partnership between George Brown College, MaRS Discovery District, Refined Manufacturing Acceleration Process and the City of Toronto. While mixed-use zoning for individual land parcels may lead to unintended outcomes that do not promote mixed-income or occupational communities (Moos et al. 2018), the project represents a small step towards more inclusive development.

Elsewhere, initiatives have addressed some of the most pressing issues related to inclusive economic development more directly. For example, Inclusive Local Economic Opportunity (ILEO) is a Toronto-based partnership led by the CEOs of United Way and the Bank of Montreal. By bringing together corporate, city and community leaders, ILEO is working to develop a model that prioritises community economic inclusion in low-income neighbourhoods undergoing large-scale redevelopment across the Toronto region. ILEO is piloting a model of corporate–city–community collaboration in the Golden Mile neighbourhood, working to ensure that the area's upcoming redevelopment (preceded in part by new transit infrastructure investment) provides economic benefit and opportunity for existing residents and community-based businesses. It remains too early to evaluate ILEO's impact. However, the purpose is directly connected to the acknowledgement that growth and investment can facilitate displacement, but that intentional planning, action and collaboration may result in improved economic outcomes for more people.

Realising the inclusive city?

This chapter has explored the economic dynamics of the Toronto region and has identified some of the serious challenges that the region faces. Building on the extensive body of scholarship on Toronto and other global cities, we have suggested that, without deliberate intervention, the pursuit of economic development and competitiveness in the Toronto region does not lead to shared, inclusive prosperity. However, with intentional policy change and collaboration between government, the private sector, the community and civil society organisations, it may be possible to support growth while also redistributing the benefits of growth. The pilots and experiments outlined above provide examples of how this might be achieved, although it is too early to evaluate the extent to which they will have a long-standing impact on inclusive development and outcomes. Moreover, many of these projects sidestep the governance issues associated with scaling such efforts beyond a single municipality. Yet all involve complex, cross-sectoral partnerships representing a range of actors and interests.

The inclusive city remains elusive. This chapter demonstrates that addressing cities' most complex challenges requires a new approach. It is incumbent on public, private and non-profit actors to work collaboratively towards identifying and understanding change – whether in Toronto, London or other global cities. Cities need to continue to find effective and just ways to redirect opportunity.

Notes

1. The Toronto region can be defined in a number of ways. This chapter focuses on the Toronto census metropolitan area with a population of 5.92 million (Statistics Canada 2017a). The CMA includes the City of Toronto and 23 adjacent municipalities, including Mississauga (the sixth largest city in Canada with a population of 721,599), Brampton (the ninth largest Canadian city with 593,638 residents), Markham (the sixteenth largest) and Vaughan (the seventeenth largest).
2. Clusters are defined using a method developed by Spencer et al. (2010).

References

Ash, James, Kitchin, Rob and Leszczynski, Agnieszka. 2018. 'Digital Turn, Digital Geographies?'. *Progress in Human Geography* 42(1):25–43. https://doi.org/10.1177/0309132516664800.

August, Martine. 2014. 'Challenging the Rhetoric of Stigmatization: The Benefits of Concentrated Poverty in Toronto's Regent Park'. *Environment and Planning A* 46(6):1317–33. https://doi.org/10.1068/a45635.

Berridge, Joe. 2019. *Perfect City*. Toronto: Sutherland House.

Blais, Pamela. 2018. *Planning the Next GGH*. Metropole Consultants and the Neptis Foundation. Accessed 17 March 2019. http://www.neptis.org/sites/default/files/planning_the_next_ggh/neptis_planningthenextggh_report_dec4_2018.pdf.

Boudreau, Julie-Anne, Keil, Roger and Young, Douglas. 2009. *Changing Toronto: Governing Urban Neoliberalism*. Toronto: University of Toronto Press.

Bourne, Larry S., Britton, John N. H. and Leslie, Deborah. 2011. 'The Greater Toronto Region: The Challenges of Economic Restructuring, Social Diversity and Globalization'. In *Canadian Urban Regions: Trajectories of Growth and Change*, edited by Larry Bourne, Tom Hutton, Richard Shearmur and Jim Simmons, 236–68. Toronto: Oxford University Press.

Bozikovic, Alex. 2019. 'Toronto Needs Housing Now – and the Planning to Match'. *The Globe and Mail*, 23 November. Accessed 22 July 2020. https://www.theglobeandmail.com/canada/toronto/article-toronto-needs-housing-now-and-the-planning-to-match/.

Brail, Shauna and Kumar, Nishi. 2017. 'Community Leadership and Engagement after the Mix: The Transformation of Toronto's Regent Park'. *Urban Studies* 54(16):3772–3788. https://doi.org/10.1177/0042098016683122.

Brail, Shauna. 2020. 'World cities of ride-hailing'. *Urban Geography*, 1–22. https://doi.org/10.1080/02723638.2020.1775030.

Brenner, Neil and Keil, Roger (eds). 2006. *The Global Cities Reader*. New York: Routledge.

CCEA (Canadian Centre of Economic Analysis) and CUI (Canadian Urban Institute). 2018. *Toronto Housing Market Analysis: From Insight to Action*. Accessed 22 July 2020.https://www.toronto.ca/legdocs/mmis/2019/ph/bgrd/backgroundfile-124480.pdf.

CBRE. 2018a. *Scoring Tech Talent in North America 2018*. CBRE Research. Accessed 22 July 2020. https://www.cbre.com/research-and-reports/Scoring-Tech-Talent-in-North-America-2018.

CBRE. 2018b. *2018 Tech 30 – Measuring Tech Industry Impact on North American Office Markets*. CBRE Research. Accessed 22 July 2020. http://hightech.cbrevancouver.com/wp-content/uploads/2018/10/CBRE-Tech-30-Report-2018.pdf.

City of Toronto. 2013. *Collaborating for Competitiveness: A Strategic Plan for Accelerating Economic Growth and Job Creation in Toronto*. Accessed 22 July 2020. https://www.toronto.ca/legdocs/mmis/2013/ed/bgrd/backgroundfile-55511.pdf.

City of Toronto. 2014a. *Comprehensive to the Core: Planning Toronto's Downtown*. Accessed 31 July 2020. https://www.toronto.ca/legdocs/mmis/2014/te/bgrd/backgroundfile-69191.pdf.

City of Toronto. 2014b. *Downtown Toronto: Trends, Issues, Intensification.* Accessed 1 August 2020. https://www.toronto.ca/legdocs/mmis/2014/te/bgrd/backgroundfile-69192.pdf.

City of Toronto. 2018. *City of Toronto Official Plan Indicators, Attachment 1.* Accessed 22 July 2020. https://www.toronto.ca/legdocs/mmis/2018/pg/bgrd/backgroundfile-117549.pdf.

City of Toronto. 2019a. *Annual Report, City Planning.* City of Toronto. Accessed 22 July 2020. https://storymaps.arcgis.com/stories/5b01fbd4f14548ca8749553201c1c861.

City of Toronto. 2019b. *Implementing the 'Housing Now' Initiative.* Accessed 22 July 2020. https://www.toronto.ca/legdocs/mmis/2019/ex/bgrd/backgroundfile-123663.pdf.

City of Toronto. 2019c. *Current City of Toronto Average Market Rents & Utility Allowances.* Accessed 22 July 2020. https://www.toronto.ca/community-people/community-partners/social-housing-providers/affordable-housing-operators/current-city-of-toronto-average-market-rents-and-utility-allowances.

Credit, Kevin. 2019. 'Transitive Properties: A Spatial Econometric Analysis of New Business Creation around Transit'. *Spatial Economic Analysis* 14(1):26–52. https://doi.org/10.1080/17421772.2019.1523548.

CVCA. 2019. *Venture Capital Canadian Market Overview: YTD Q3 2019.* Accessed 22 July 2020. https://central.cvca.ca/wp-content/uploads/2019/12/CVCA_EN_Canada_VC_Q3-2019_Final2.pdf.

Denney, Steven, Southin, Travis and Wolfe, David. 2018. *The Evolution of Toronto's ICT Cluster: Breakthroughs and Challenges.* CDO Partnership Meetings, Vancouver, Canada. Accessed 22 July 2020. https://munkschool.utoronto.ca/ipl/files/2018/04/S2-Denney_Wolfe_Southin_Toronto-ICT_Final_AP2018.pdf.

Dingman, S. 2018. 'Toronto Land Zoned for Employment Use Is Shrinking'. *The Globe and Mail,* 25 September. Accessed 1 August 2020. https://www.theglobeandmail.com/real-estate/article-toronto-land-zoned-for-employment-use-is-shrinking.

Edenhoffer, Klaus. 2018. *Toronto on the Global Stage: 2018 Report Card on Canada and Toronto's Financial Services Sector.* Ottawa: Conference Board of Canada. Accessed 22 July 2020. https://cdn2.hubspot.net/hubfs/4372260/Toronto%20on%20the%20Global%20Stage%20-%20for%20TFI.pdf.

English, Jonathan. 2019. 'Toronto's Secret Success: Suburban Buses'. *The Globe and Mail,* 25 October. Accessed 22 July 2020. https://www.theglobeandmail.com/opinion/article-torontos-secret-success-suburban-buses.

Florida, Richard. 2018. *The New Urban Crisis.* New York: Basic Books.

Freemark, Yonah. 2019. 'Doubling Housing Production in the Paris Region: A Multi-policy, Multi-jurisdictional Response'. *International Journal of Housing Policy.* http://doi.org/10.1080/19491247.2019.1682233.

Greenberg, Ken. 2017. *More than a Desk and a Parking Spot: Tapping into the Region's Employment Lands.* CBI Policy Paper, Ryerson City Building Institute.

Grisdale, Sean. 2019. 'Displacement by Disruption: Short-term Rentals and the Political Economy of "Belonging Anywhere" in Toronto'. *Urban Geography.* http://doi.org/10.1080/02723638.2019.1642714.

Hulchanski, Davis. 2015. *Toronto's Social Divide – Update on 3 Cities.* Accessed 22 July 2020. http://neighbourhoodchange.ca/documents/2015/11/toronto-social-divide-update-on-3-cities.pdf.

Hulchanski, Davis. 2017. *Neighbourhood Income Change: City of Toronto, 2015 vs. 1970.* Neighbourhood Change Research Partnership. Toronto: University of Toronto.

Hunter, Paul. 2019. *The Unspoken Decline of Outer London: Why Is Poverty and Inequality Increasing in Outer London and What Needs to Change?* Smith Institute. Accessed 22 July 2020. http://www.smith-institute.org.uk/book/the-unspoken-decline-of-outer-london-why-is-poverty-and-inequality-increasing-in-outer-london-and-what-needs-to-change.

Kalinowski, Tess. 2019. 'Toronto Has Seen Huge Growth in the Last Decade. The Challenges Ahead Are Just as Huge'. *Toronto Star,* 27 December. Accessed 22 July 2020. https://www.thestar.com/news/gta/2019/12/27/toronto-has-seen-huge-growth-in-the-last-decade-the-challenges-ahead-are-just-as-huge.html.

Kemeny, Thomas and Storper, Michael. 2020. *Superstar Cities and Left-behind Places: Disruptive Innovation, Labor Demand, and Interregional Inequality.* Working Paper 41, International Inequalities Institute. London: London School of Economics and Political Science.

Langley, Paul and Leyshon, Andrew. 2017. 'Platform Capitalism: The Intermediation and Capitalization of Digital Economic Circulation'. *Finance and Society* 3(1):11–31. https://doi.org/10.2218/finsoc.v3i1.1936.

Lee, Neil and Clarke, Stephen. 2019. 'Do Low-skilled Workers Gain from High-tech Employment Growth? High-technology Multipliers, Employment and Wages in Britain'. *Research Policy* 48(9). https://doi.org/10.1016/j.respol.2019.05.012.

Manyika, James, Ramaswamy, Sree and Birshan, Michael. 2018. 'What's Driving Superstar Companies, Industries and Cities'. *Harvard Business Review,* 25 October. Accessed 22 July 2020. https://hbr.org/2018/10/whats-driving-superstar-companies-industries-and-cities.

Marcuse, Peter and van Kempen, Ronald (eds). 2000. *Globalizing Cities: A New Spatial Order?* Malden, MA: Blackwell.

Moos, Markus, Vinodrai, Tara, Revington, Nick and Seasons, Michael. 2018. 'Planning for Mixed Use: Affordable for Whom?' *Journal of the American Planning Association* 84(1):7–20. https://doi.org/10.1080/01944363.2017.1406315.

Rosen, Gillad and Walks, Alan. 2014. 'Castles in Toronto's Sky: Condo-ism as Urban Transformation'. *Journal of Urban Affairs* 37(3):289–310. http://doi.org/10.1111/juaf.12140.

Sassen, Saskia. 2001. *The Global City: New York, London, Tokyo* (2nd edition). Princeton, NJ: Princeton University Press.

Sheppard, Veronica. 2018. 'September Brought over $1.4 Billion in International Investment for Toronto's Tech Ecosystem'. *MaRS*, 1 October. Accessed 22 July 2020. https://www.marsdd.com/news-and-insights/september-brought-over-1-4-billion-in-international-investment-for-torontos-tech-ecosystem.

Spencer, Gregory M., Vinodrai, Tara, Gertler, Meric S. and Wolfe, David A. 2010. 'Do Clusters Make a Difference? Defining and Assessing their Economic Performance'. *Regional Studies* 44(6):697–715. https://doi.org/10.1080/00343400903107736.

Statistics Canada. 2006. *Census of Population: Custom Tabulations*. Ottawa: Statistics Canada.

Statistics Canada. 2016. *Census of Population: Custom Tabulations*. Ottawa: Statistics Canada.

Statistics Canada. 2017a. *Focus on Geography Series, 2016 Census*. Ottawa: Statistics Canada.

Statistics Canada. 2017b. 'Gross Domestic Product at Basic Prices, by Census Metropolitan Area, 2009 to 2013'. *The Daily*, 27 January. Accessed 22 July 2020. https://www150.statcan.gc.ca/n1/en/daily-quotidien/170127/dq170127b-eng.pdf?st=hWzdw0oe.

TCHC (Toronto Community Housing Corporation). 2019. *2018 Annual Report – Investing in Our Future (Draft)*. Accessed 22 July 2020. https://www.torontohousing.ca/events/Documents/GCHRCC/April%2015%202019/Item%203%20-%202018%20Annual%20Report-Letter%20to%20SH.pdf.

Tech Toronto. 2016. *How Technology Is Changing Toronto Employment*. Accessed 1 August 2020. https://munk-school.utoronto.ca/wp-content/uploads/2016/10/TechTO_Report2016.pdf.

TREB (Toronto Regional Real Estate Board). 2020. *TREB Releases Q4 2019 Condo Rental Market Stats*. Accessed 22 July 2020. http://www.trebhome.com/index.php/market-news/rental-market-report.

TTC (Toronto Transit Commission). 2019. *Next Stop, Even Better: 2020–2024 and Beyond*. Accessed 22 July 2020. https://www.ttc.ca/About_the_TTC/Commission_reports_and_information/Commission_meetings/2019/December_12/Reports/Attachment%201%20TTC_5_year_SP_web.pdf.

Walks, R. Alan. 2001. 'The Social Ecology of the Post-Fordist/Global City? Economic Restructuring and Socio-spatial Polarisation in the Toronto Urban Region'. *Urban Studies* 38(3):407–47.

Walks, R. Alan. 2011. 'Economic Restructuring and Trajectories of Socio-spatial Polarization in the Twenty-first-century Canadian City'. In *Canadian Urban Regions: Trajectories of Growth and Change*, edited by Larry Bourne, Tom Hutton, Richard Shearmur and Jim Simmons, 236–68. Toronto: Oxford University Press.

Winsa, Patty and Bailey, Andrew. 2019. 'Here's What You'd Need to Buy a Mid Priced Home in Your Toronto Neighbourhood'. *Toronto Star*, 5 July. Accessed 22 July 2020. https://www.thestar.com/news/gta/2019/07/05/heres-what-youd-need-to-earn-to-buy-a-mid-priced-home-in-your-toronto-neighbourhood-and-what-a-typical-family-there-earns-hint-not-nearly-enough.html.

Wolfe, David. 2018. *Creating Digital Opportunity for Canada*. Brookfield Institute on Innovation and Entrepreneurship and the Munk School of Global Affairs and Public Policy. Accessed 22 July 2020. https://munkschool.utoronto.ca/ipl/files/2018/04/UTMK028-Digital-Opps_V6.pdf.

Wolfe, David and Bramwell, Alison. 2016. 'Toronto's Fourth Era: An Emerging Cognitive-cultural Economy'. In *Growing Urban Economies: Innovation, Creativity, and Governance in Canadian City-Regions*, edited by David A. Wolfe and Meric S. Gertler, 51–81. Toronto: University of Toronto Press.

Zukin, Sharon. 2019. 'The Origins and Perils of Development in the Urban Tech Landscape'. *The Architect's Newspaper*, 8 May. Accessed 22 July 2020. https://archpaper.com/2019/05/urban-tech-landscape.

3
Regulating property conditions in the private rented sector: The complex geography of property licensing in London

Tatiana Moreira de Souza

Introduction

Since the turn of the milennium, the UK housing market has been shaped by a resurgence in private renting. During the 1980s and 1990s the proportion of households renting from a private landlord in England hovered around 9–10 per cent, but since 2013–14 this proportion has increased to approximately 19 per cent of all households in the country (MHCLG 2019a). Today, the private rented sector (PRS) is the second largest housing tenure in England, accounting for 4.5 million households (MHCLG 2019a). In London, the proportion of renters is even higher. The latest figures show that approximately 29 per cent of households rent from a private landlord and it is forecast that one in three households will be renting privately by 2025.

The recent growth of the PRS is not unique to London or England. Since the 2008–9 Global Financial Crisis (GFC), many global north countries have witnessed a rise in private renting, with this rise being more pronounced in Anglo-Saxon countries with liberal markets (Kemp 2015; Crook and Kemp 2014a). Explanations extend beyond current trends in household formation and the weakening of the economic position of working populations. They reflect a multitude of factors, such as reduced accessibility to mortgage finance, austerity politics in response to the GFC – which have also negatively impacted the production of subsidised housing – the financialisation of the residential sector, rent liberalisation and reduced tenant protections (Pawson et al. 2017; Hochstenbach 2017; August and Walks 2012).

In many countries, notably those in which the sector is loosely regulated, there is substantial variability in the quality of housing and management of privately rented properties, with substandard accommodation commonly being found at the lower end of the sector. The impacts of poor housing on health have been widely researched (Roys et al. 2010; Marsh et al. 1999) and studies have shown how some landlords take advantage of reduced tenant protections and the precarious situation of some tenants – such as recipients of housing benefits, ethnic minority groups and undocumented immigrants – to reduce spending on repairs and property maintenance (Desmond et al. 2015; Grineski and Hernández 2010). Others have highlighted the lack of interest from landlords in investing in property maintenance in areas of high housing demand (Ambrose 2015), and recent studies in the United States, Canada and Germany have connected the growing financialisation of rental housing to reduced spending from investors on property maintenance as part of a wider strategy to reduce costs and increase tenant turnover in order to raise rents (August and Walks 2018; Fields and Uffer 2016).

Issues related to poor property conditions have generally been tackled through the provision of direct subsidies for housing improvement and through a regulatory approach. This is generally done through the prescription of minimum standards for privately rented housing and/or through the requirement that landlords register or license their rental properties. Examples range from national landlord registration schemes, such as in Scotland and Wales, to legislation introduced by city, state or regional governments, such as in the case of Toronto, where a by-law passed in 2017 introduced minimum property maintenance standards and the requirement for registration of certain types of purpose-built rental properties. In England, there is no minimum standard of housing condition in the PRS. Instead, property conditions are assessed by a system of risk assessment that identifies hazards to occupants. Local authorities are responsible for enforcing housing standards. They have a duty to license certain types of private rental accommodation and they also have discretionary powers to implement licensing schemes for other types of rental properties under certain conditions. This approach to licensing, however, due to its targeted focus, results in considerable variability in terms of regulation and of enforcement activity when local authorities are compared with one another.

This chapter explores the complex and fragmented regulatory landscape that is forming in London as a result of the various discretionary licensing schemes operating in Greater London's 32 boroughs. The study draws from the analysis of licensing schemes currently in place in each local authority, the analysis of two parliamentary inquiries into the sector and interviews conducted between September 2017 and February 2018 with eight enforcement officers and policy-makers in charge of private sector housing and enforcement in 11 of these local authorities. The chapter reveals that this fragmentation results from the combination of central government's aversion to regulation, austerity politics and differing local political willingness to implement licensing schemes. This results in substantial variation across London in the amount of intelligence held about the sector and in significant disparities in the terms and conditions of schemes as well as in enforcement, affecting both tenants and landlords, with wider impacts to the local community. Finally, it considers how this inconsistent regulatory landscape interacts with the current mayor's plans of introducing rent controls based on information gathered from a London-wide landlord register.

The chapter starts with an overview of the PRS in England and in London, followed by an overview of the regulatory framework that governs property conditions and landlord management and of how the PRS is problematised by different levels of government (central and local). It then gives an overview of the licensing schemes operating in London and discusses the wider implications of these different licensing approaches and capacities. It concludes with a discussion of the views expressed by local authority enforcement officers on the Mayor's proposal for a London-wide register, which highlighted the need to reduce regulatory complexity in order to increase compliance.

A brief overview of the PRS in England and in London

The PRS in England has been growing since the late 1990s due to a combination of deregulatory policies introduced by the 1988 and 1994 Housing Acts which removed rent controls and introduced shorter tenancy agreements, and new financial products that have allowed homeowners to buy additional properties to let (Buy-to-Let mortgages). Much of the sector's growth has been due to tenure change rather than to new housing construction (Crook and Kemp 2014b), with estimates that over 500,000 privately rented dwellings were originally social housing properties sold under 'right to buy' (Rugg and Rhodes 2018). Decades of undersupply in housing markets, coupled with easy availability of credit, contributed to house prices rising, while the decline of the social housing stock has resulted in social housing being allocated to those most in need. Since the onset of the GFC, the PRS has rapidly changed from being a marginal tenure – housing mainly students, young professionals, recently arrived migrants and newly formed households (Rugg and Rhodes 2008) – to becoming 'the new normal' (Reynolds and de Santos 2013). This has led to the phenomenon of 'Generation Rent', as many more people are renting for longer in their lives and see no prospects of ever changing their housing tenure status (Hoolachan et al. 2017; McKee et al. 2017). In London, where the housing crisis is most acute (see Penny, Chapter 16), rents have been rising substantially faster than earnings, surpassing the average mortgage payment. Londoners already spend on average 42 per cent of their income on rent (MHCLG 2019b) – with 25 per cent of them paying more than half of their wages (GLA 2018) – and welfare reforms introduced by central government have significantly impacted the ability of low-income families to afford rents in the capital.

Differently from countries such as Canada, which has a long history of institutional and corporate investment in purpose-built privately rented housing, the PRS in England has a larger share of older properties and is dominated by small-scale landlordism. Ninety-four per cent of landlords are private individuals, with 45 per cent owning one property and only 17 per cent owning more than five (MHCLG 2019b, 5). Despite active support from central government for institutional investment in the sector – through subsidies for purpose-built developments solely for private renting, called 'build to rent' – this segment of the PRS is still in its infancy. As of 2019, approximately 32,000 units had been built and another 111,000 are under construction or in planning across the UK (Savills 2019). This predominance of private individual landlords has been associated with great variability in the quality of PRS properties and standards in property management being endemically poor, due to a large proportion of landlords being unaware of their responsibilities (Rhodes and Rugg 2018; Faulkner and Saxena 2016).

Thus, compared with the owner-occupied and social rented sectors, the PRS in England has the highest proportion of housing in poor condition. The latest figures show that over a quarter of PRS homes fail to meet the Decent Homes Standard,[1] a proportion that is well above what is found in the owner-occupied and social rented sectors (19 per cent and 13 per cent respectively) (MHCLG 2019a). Although the proportion of non-decent housing has reduced over time – from almost 47.7 per cent in 2006 (MHCLG 2018) to 25 per cent in 2018 – in absolute terms this figure has increased from 1.29 million to 1.35 million (Rugg and Rhodes 2018, 139). In London, the proportion of non-decent homes in the sector also stands at 25 per cent. Between 2015 and 2016, almost 4,000 serious health and safety hazards in privately rented dwellings were identified by local authorities (Pidgeon 2016). A study by Rhodes and Rugg (2018) showed that almost all vulnerable households living in PRS accommodation in the capital experience problems of unaffordability or overcrowding (living without a sufficient number of bedrooms) due to living in a non-decent home.

The deregulatory measures introduced in the 1980s and 1990s are also partly to blame for property standards and management being poor, because they significantly weakened the position of tenants. The standard tenancy agreement in England usually lasts six months to one year, after which the landlord has the right to repossess the property at two months' notice by serving a Section 21 eviction notice – which allows landlords to evict tenants without a reason once a fixed-term tenancy agreement expires. Over the years, cases of landlords evicting tenants who complain about housing conditions have been widely documented by housing charities and the media. In response, the Deregulation Act 2015 introduced protection for tenants by prohibiting landlords from serving such notices for a period of six months after receiving an improvement notice from a local authority.[2] Although this has been seen as an improvement, it reveals that tenants are highly dependent on the quality of enforcement provided by local authorities once they make a complaint.

The power imbalance between central and local government and its impacts on London

The main tools available to local authorities for enforcing housing conditions in both the PRS and the owner-occupied sector were introduced by the New Labour government (1997–2010) in the Housing Act 2004. New Labour endorsed the earlier deregulation of the sector initiated by the Conservative Party and created regulation targeting only the underperforming portion of the PRS (Lowe 2007), after it was acknowledged that the sector contained a disproportionate amount of housing in poor condition and a sizeable portion of landlords providing poor management and profiteering from tenants (DETR 2000). This new regulatory framework comprised a system for assessing housing conditions – the Housing Health and Safety Rating System, a risk-based assessment that identifies 29 categories of hazards attributable to property conditions and the degree to which they can affect the health and safety of any potential occupier and visitor – and a new licensing model comprising three forms of licensing. The first is *mandatory licensing* for large Houses in Multiple Occupation (HMOs),[3] which then applied to HMOs with three or more storeys (including cellars, basements and loft conversions) and occupied by five or more people forming at least two households.[4] The other two forms of licensing are *discretionary* and include (i) *additional licensing*, which applies to smaller HMOs, and (ii) *selective licensing*, which initially applied to all privately rented properties located in areas of low housing demand but currently includes areas with high rates of properties in poor conditions or that are experiencing a rapid increase in PRS properties, inward migration or high levels of deprivation or crime.

However, it is widely known that decision-making and the systems in place for funding public services and local government in England are highly centralised. It has been argued that this high level of centralisation impacts on local democracy, as local authorities are generally seen by ministers as 'agencies for the provision of services in accordance with national policies rather than as local government meeting the needs and aspirations of local communities and citizens' (Stewart 2014, 846). Despite central government's signalling to devolve more powers to local government through the Localism Act (2011) and through legislation that will allow local authorities to retain business rates and council tax, in reality, the latter often have to abide by rigid terms and conditions which limit their ability to take initiatives and innovate. Their situation is exacerbated by the fact that since 2010 they have been severely impacted by austerity measures implemented by central government which have resulted in cuts of nearly 50 per cent to local authorities' budgets without any reduction in their statutory obligations to provide services (NAO 2018). The enforcement of housing standards is funded by local authorities' environmental health budgets and these have been reduced by an average of 30 per cent despite the rapid growth of the PRS (LGA 2018). Consequently, many local authority enforcement teams have been reduced to a handful of officers and have just enough resources to provide basic statutory service, thus lacking capacity to take complex cases to court, particularly given the often protracted nature of the enforcement process.

The discretionary powers given to local authorities were not free from rigid conditions. On the contrary, they can only implement discretionary licensing schemes if they provide evidence that licensing is the most appropriate response to problems in the PRS and conduct extensive public consultation. Once implemented, discretionary schemes can only run for a maximum period of five years during which their need must be occasionally reviewed. In 2010, the need for additional and selective licensing schemes to be reviewed by the Secretary of State was abolished. However, in 2015, in a move that resembles Stoker's (1991, 150) description of the Thatcher government 'setting for local authorities arbitrary and non-negotiated goals and targets', central government reintroduced this requirement for selective licensing designations covering more than 20 per cent of a local authority geographical area or more than 20 per cent of its privately rented housing stock. This change was in response to four London boroughs and Liverpool City Council rolling out district-wide selective licensing schemes. Despite much criticism for interfering in local democracy, central government defended its position, stating that:

> as its name implies, selective licensing should be targeted to deal with specific local problems. Blanket licensing of all landlords may impose unnecessary costs on responsible landlords, which would be passed on to tenants in the form of higher rents. (MHCLG 2018b, para. 72)

This change in legislation has particularly affected London as some boroughs have attempted to either implement or continue with large or borough-wide selective licensing schemes to deal with a rapid increase in private renting in their areas. Soon after the legislation was passed, Redbridge Council was barred from introducing a borough-wide selective licensing scheme despite it arguing that licensing would allow it to respond more effectively to significant and persistent problems with anti-social behaviour in the PRS, crime and inward migration (Phillipson and Baker 2016). In 2017, the London Borough of Newham's application to continue with its borough-wide selective licensing scheme was approved with modifications by the Secretary of State.[5] Despite the outcome being considered a success because Newham's new selective licensing designation still covers 97 per cent of the borough, the decision-making process was severely criticised by the borough mayor, who stated that 'local people showed their overwhelming support for a borough-wide scheme and these decisions should be taken on the ground by local authorities who know their local area rather than ministers sitting in Whitehall' (Hopps 2017).[6]

The examples discussed above highlight the importance of examining the effects on Greater London of the different approaches to property licensing taken by London boroughs as these create spatial disparities in terms of housing quality, enforcement response and landlord obligations. Despite the mayor having little power over housing and no statutory powers over the PRS,[7] the housing crisis is London-wide, as evidenced by the fact that housing increasingly plays a central part in mayoral elections. London-wide measures to improve housing conditions in the PRS have been proposed since the 2012 elections, when it was acknowledged that private renting had risen by 75 per cent between the 2001 and 2011 censuses. Although these initially relied on voluntary action by landlords – such as Labour Party mayoral candidate Ken Livingstone's proposal to set up a not-for-profit London Lettings Agency (Mulholland 2011), and former mayor Boris Johnson (Conservative Party) creating the 'London Rental Standard', a voluntary set of rental standards which was severely criticised for accrediting only 1,800 landlords in the capital – in the 2016 mayoral election, some candidates (particularly from the Labour and Green parties) pledged to take a more interventionist approach towards the sector. The winner and current mayor, Sadiq Khan, has so far fulfilled his pledge to create a London-wide database of criminal landlords,[8] has been playing a coordinating role with London boroughs to share best practice in terms of enforcement of housing standards and, most importantly, has been lobbying central government for more powers to introduce rent controls and increase tenant security. These were unveiled in his blueprint for reform of the PRS (GLA 2018) which calls for devolution on the basis that 'London's housing market self-evidently presents particular challenges', and in other global cities such as 'Paris, Berlin, and New York, it is common for these powers to be devolved to a city, state or regional level to allow for appropriate local decision-making' (33).

Mayor Sadiq Khan's strategy revolves around the introduction of rent controls informed by a light-touch universal register of landlords intended to collect accurate data about PRS properties and rent prices. The register is supposed to work in tandem with licensing, as explained by the Mayor's Housing Strategy: 'landlord registration helps to ensure landlords are fulfilling their legal duties, while property licensing ensures the homes themselves meet relevant legal requirements' (GLA 2019, para. 6.25). By doing this, it is clear that the mayor wants to tip the power balance towards the metropolitan level without interfering with local authority autonomy over licensing schemes. It is to these schemes that the chapter will now turn.

The complex geography of licensing in London

There are multiple property licensing schemes operating across London and when these are seen together, a complex and fragmented regulatory landscape emerges. Overall, three situations are found across the capital: (i) local authorities that do not run any discretionary licensing scheme, (ii) local authorities that run either additional HMO or selective licensing schemes and (iii) local authorities that run both additional HMO and selective licensing schemes (see Figure 3.1). This fragmentation is also materialised by differing prices and the way fees are calculated,[9] terms and conditions, types of HMOs that qualify for additional licensing, dates that licences start and cease to operate and, most importantly, their spatial coverage. While some licensing schemes cover entire boroughs, others cover wards, portions of wards or a certain number of streets. For example, Islington Council's

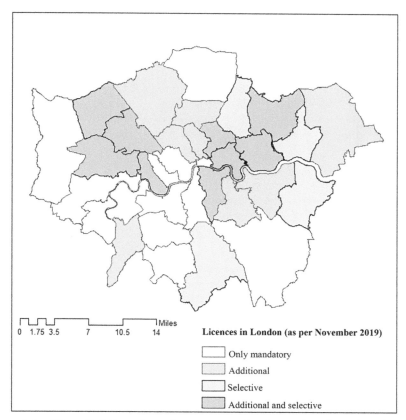

Figure 3.1 Map of all licensing schemes operating in London (based on data from London Datastore 2017)

additional licensing scheme covers only two main roads in the borough while the London Borough of Tower Hamlets' additional and selective licensing designations cover three wards. The complexity of this regulatory geography is evidenced by the large amount of online forum discussion and advice on the topic, as well as the existence of a website,[10] 'London Property Licensing', solely created for those looking into, as its slogan puts it, 'making sense of property licensing in London'.

The interviews revealed that this fragmented licensing landscape reflects substantial disparities in the amount of intelligence held about the sector across London. Currently, licensing is the only instrument that allows local authorities to directly gather detailed information about the location of private rented properties and those in charge of managing them (landlords or managing agents). Without it, local authorities have to rely on stock condition surveys produced from aggregated data obtained from council tax returns, housing benefits and other sources to estimate the size of the sector and location of properties. At the time of the interviews, some of these surveys – which are commissioned to external consultancies – were over three years old and did not capture recent fluctuations in the sector. These disparities were also reflected in the human, financial and technical capacities of private sector housing teams as the local authorities that operated schemes – especially of the selective type – were able to hire staff to work on matters related to licence registration and data analysis with the income generated from licensing, which is ring-fenced to its function only.

Regarding enforcement, the findings bear a resemblance to the results of a survey conducted by London Assembly member Caroline Pidgeon (Pidgeon 2016) which showed significant variation in enforcement activity across London, with much more vigorous work taking place in local authorities that ran borough-wide selective licensing schemes, such as the London Borough of Newham, responsible for more than two-thirds of all prosecutions in London. The interviews with officers working for local authorities that did not run discretionary schemes revealed that their teams were generally only able to carry out their statutory duty of responding to complaints: 'they've been a very reactionary team. They are just about keeping their heads above water.' Conversely, those working for local authorities that ran licensing schemes, particularly selective licensing, were able to conduct enforcement in a proactive manner as they were able to more easily identify non-compliant landlords, as noted by one officer: 'everyone that didn't license became conspicuous by their absence'.

Thus it can be argued that this fragmented licensing landscape is also creating a 'postcode lottery' in London in terms of tenant protection, landlord obligations and the overall quality of neighbourhoods. Landlords, particularly those who have more than one property, might have to license their property and adhere to certain conditions in one borough, or in one area within a borough, but not in another, and they might be fined or face prosecution if they fail to license a property in an area that requires a licence. Besides improved housing standards, tenants living in areas subject to licensing will be better protected against unfair use of a Section 21 eviction notice as these are invalidated if the landlord does not have a licence in such areas. Lastly, since licensing allows local authorities to impose certain conditions related to property standards, management, use and occupation,[11] officers spoke of a noticeable improvement to certain neighbourhoods due to a reduction in overcrowding, criminal activity in the PRS and fly-tipping as a result of more active enforcement in areas where licensing schemes, particularly selective licensing, are in operation.

What would the future of licensing be if the mayor's plans come to fruition? In the interviews, local politics played a significant role in local authorities' responses to the increase in private renting in their areas. In certain local authorities, officers reported that some councillors believed in 'not burdening landlords' with any type of discretionary licensing despite being aware of problems related to poor housing conditions and management in their areas. Conversely, interviews with officers working in two local authorities that had borough-wide licensing schemes revealed that there was 'a push from the top', referring to local councillors reaching a consensus over the need to improve conditions in the PRS and setting aside a considerable amount of funding to initiate the licensing process despite cuts to their budgets. For this reason, there was strong support from officers for a system of compulsory registration of landlords with a universal set of terms and conditions, which most officers believed should be nationwide rather than London-wide.[12] In the absence of a national system, many supported the idea of a London-wide approach, with the responsibility of registration falling to the Greater London Authority and enforcement being conducted by local authorities. The removal of regulatory complexity – rather than the introduction of regulation – was seen as crucial to increase compliance and produce more effective enforcement. The view was that a system of landlord registration would render licensing redundant, exactly because of the fragmentation of rights and obligations that it currently produces as a result of central government legislation and the different terms and conditions imposed by local authorities. However, since the proposal for a register is not accompanied by a minimum standard for property conditions and management, some of the improvements to PRS properties found in licensing designation areas – which also have spillover effects to the wider community – could be potentially lost.

Conclusion

This chapter has given an overview of the regulations governing property standards in the PRS in England and its impacts on London, where the housing crisis is most acute and where one in three households are renting privately. It argues that central government's targeted approach to regulation – focused on regulating accommodation either at the bottom end of the sector or in problematic areas – is producing a patchy licensing landscape in London. This is producing a complex geography of rights and obligations and creating disparities in the intelligence held by local authorities on the sector and their enforcement activities, with wider implications for the mayor's ability to implement his rent control policy.

The interviews also highlighted that local politics as well as austerity play an important role in local authorities' decisions to use their discretionary powers over licensing schemes – whether or not to roll them out, as well as their type and reach. If the system continues as it is, with time, the already noted disparities in terms of data and enforcement activities might become even more accentuated, as local authorities that run licensing schemes can build more capacity since the income from both licensing registration and civil penalties are ring-fenced to their respective departments.

Although one could argue that this loose and disjointed licensing landscape can be found elsewhere in England, the challenges imposed by the London housing market and the rapid increase in private renting in the capital undoubtedly call for a more London-focused response. If this response comes in the form of more powers to the mayor to introduce rent control and increase security of tenure, it is important that property and management standards and their enforcement are also consistent across the capital in order to reduce possibilities of disinvestment in maintenance.

Notes

1. The Decent Homes Standard was introduced in 2000 to provide a minimum standard of housing conditions in the social rented sector. In 2006, it was updated to include the Housing Health and Safety Rating System, introduced by the Housing Act 2004. The Standard only applies to the social rented sector but is used to compare property conditions in all tenures.
2. Central government recently carried out consultation on abolishing Section 21 eviction notices after it was announced that the end of a tenancy through Section 21 notices is one of the biggest causes of homelessness.
3. HMOs are residential properties where facilities such as toilets, kitchens and bathrooms are shared by more than one household. These generally fall under the category of bedsits, shared flats or houses and households with lodgers (Lowe 2007).
4. In 2018 the three-storey condition was scrapped, and requirements were added for minimum room sizes for sleeping accommodation and for the provision of refuse disposal.
5. Newham was the first council in England to implement such a scheme and it has been highly successful in disrupting criminal operation, reducing overcrowding and anti-social behaviour, and increasing tax collections from landlords' rental income (Collinson 2017).
6. Whitehall is a street in London where many government departments are located and thus is a metonym for the UK government.
7. The mayor's role is mostly confined to setting the overall amount, type and location of new housing across London in their Housing Strategy, to distributing some funding for affordable homes and to calling in planning applications that are of potential strategic importance to London – generally those with 150 residential units or more.
8. The Rogue Landlord and Agent Checker (https://www.london.gov.uk/rogue-landlord-checker) was launched in December 2017 and shows information from all London councils about private landlords and letting agents who have been prosecuted or fined.
9. This calculation is based on the costs of operating licensing schemes, which vary according to borough. For example, while the London Borough of Enfield charges a flat fee of £650 for mandatory licences, Bromley charges £185 per unit of accommodation at the time an application is submitted, followed by £75 per unit of accommodation once a licence is granted. This means that a mandatory licence for a five-bedroom HMO in the borough would cost £1300 ((185 x 5) +(75 x 5)).
10. See http://www.londonpropertylicensing.co.uk.
11. Examples include the imposition of limits on the number of occupants in a dwelling, and the requirement for the licence holder to provide details of the arrangements in place to prevent or reduce anti-social behaviour and for repairs and property management.
12. Many officers drew parallels to drivers being required to have a driving licence or business owners needing to register their businesses.

References

Ambrose, Aimee R. 2015. 'Improving Energy Efficiency in Private Rented Housing: Why Don't Landlords Act?'. *Indoor and Built Environment* 24(7):913–24. https://doi.org/10.1177/1420326X15598821.

August, Martine and Walks, Alan. 2012. 'From Social Mix to Political Marginalization? The Redevelopment of Toronto's Public Housing and the Dilution of Tenant Organisational Power'. In *Mixed Communities: Gentrification by Stealth?*, edited by Gary Bridge, Tim Butler and Loretta Lees, 273–98. Bristol: Policy Press.

August, Martine and Walks, Alan. 2018. 'Gentrification, Suburban Decline, and the Financialization of Multi-Family Rental Housing: The Case of Toronto'. *Geoforum* 89:124–36. Accessed 9 September 2019. http://www.sciencedirect.com/science/article/pii/S0016718517300982.

Crook, Tony and Kemp, Peter A. (eds). 2014a. *Private Rental Housing: Comparative Perspectives*. Cheltenham: Edward Elgar.

Crook, Tony and Kemp, Peter A. 2014b. 'England'. In *Private Rental Housing: Comparative Perspectives*, edited by Tony Crook and Peter A. Kemp, 224–46. Cheltenham: Edward Elgar.

Desmond, Matthew, Gershenson, Carl and Kiviat, Barbara. 2015. 'Forced Relocation and Residential Instability among Urban Renters'. *Social Service Review* 89(2):227–62. https://doi.org/10.1086/681091.

DETR (Department of Environment, Transport and the Regions). 2000. *Quality and Choice: A Decent Home for All*. Housing Green Paper. London: HMSO.

Faulkner, Kate and Saxena, Akansha. 2016. *The Impact of Accidental Landlords on the Private Rented Sector*. Hemel Hempstead: TDS Charitable Foundation.

Fields, Desiree and Uffer, Sabina. 2016. 'The Financialisation of Rental Housing: A Comparative Analysis of New York City and Berlin'. *Urban Studies* 53(7):1486–502. Accessed 29 June 2017. http://journals.sage-pub.com/doi/abs/10.1177/0042098014543704.

GLA (Greater London Authority). 2018. *London Housing Strategy*. London. Accessed 17 June 2018. https://www.london.gov.uk/sites/default/files/2018_lhs_london_housing_strategy.pdf.

GLA (Greater London Authority). 2019. *Reforming Private Renting: The Mayor of London's Blueprint. A Proposal for Reforming Tenure and Rents*. London: GLA.

Grineski, Sara E. and Hernández, Alma Angelica. 2010. 'Landlords, Fear, and Children's Respiratory Health: An Untold Story of Environmental Injustice in the Central City'. *Local Environment* 15(3):199–216. https://doi.org/10.1080/13549830903575562.

Hochstenbach, Cody. 2017. 'State-led Gentrification and the Changing Geography of Market-oriented Housing Policies'. *Housing, Theory and Society* 34(4):399–419. https://doi.org/10.1080/14036096.2016.1271825.

Hoolachan, Jennifer, McKee, Kim, Moore, Tom and Soaita, Adriana Mihaela. 2017. '"Generation Rent" and the Ability to "Settle Down": Economic and Geographical Variation in Young People's Housing Transitions'. *Journal of Youth Studies* 20(1):63–78. http://dx.doi.org/10.1080/13676261.2016.1184241.

Hopps, Kat. 2017. 'Newham Council Property Licensing Scheme Renewed except for East Village, Stratford'. *Newham Recorder* 17 December. Accessed 12 October 2020. https://www.newhamrecorder.co.uk/news/newham-council-property-licensing-scheme-renewed-except-for-east-village-stratford-1-5303494.

Kemp, Peter A. 2015. 'Private Renting After the Global Financial Crisis'. *Housing Studies* 30(4):601–20. https://doi.org/10.1080/02673037.2015.1027671.

LGA (Local Government Association). 2018. *Local Government Association Briefing Debate on the Housing, Communities and Local Government Report: Private Rented Sector*. Accessed 19 January 2019. https://www.local.gov.uk/sites/default/files/documents/LGA%20briefing%20-%20debate%20on%20private%20rented%20sector%20report%20-%20HC%20291118.pdf.

London Datastore. 2017. 'Statistical GIS Boundary Files for London'. Contains National Statistics data © Crown copyright and database right [2015] and Contains Ordnance Survey data © Crown copyright and database right [2015]. Accessed 12 August 2017. https://data.london.gov.uk/dataset/statistical-gis-boundary-files-london.

Lowe, Stuart. 2007. 'The New Private Rented Sector – Regulation in a Deregulated Market'. In *The Private Rented Housing Market: Regulation or Deregulation?*, edited by David Hughes and Stuart Lowe, 1–14. Aldershot and Burlington, VT: Ashgate.

McKee, Kim, Muir, Jenny and Moore, Tom. 2017. 'Housing Policy in the UK: The Importance of Spatial Nuance'. *Housing Studies* 32(1):60–72. https://doi.org/10.1080/02673037.2016.1181722.

Marsh, Alex, Gordon, David, Pantazis, Christina and Heslop, Pauline (eds). 1999. *Home Sweet Home? The Impact of Poor Housing on Health*. Bristol: Policy Press, University of Bristol.

MHCLG (Ministry of Housing, Communities and Local Government). 2018. *English Housing Survey. Headline Report, 2016–17*. London: MHCLG. Accessed 9 October 2018. https://assets.publishing.service.gov.uk/government/uploads/system/uploads/attachment_data/file/705821/2016-17_EHS_Headline_Report.pdf.

MHCLG (Ministry of Housing, Communities and Local Government). 2019a. *English Housing Survey. Headline Report, 2017–18*. London: MHCLG.

MHCLG (Ministry of Housing, Communities and Local Government). 2019b. *English Housing Survey. Private Rented Sector, 2017–18*. London: MHCLG. Accessed 20 August 2019. https://assets.publishing.service.gov.uk/government/uploads/system/uploads/attachment_data/file/817630/EHS_2017-18_PRS_Report.pdf?_ga=2.234517399.847729822.1566579768-982615184.1561459799.

Mulholland, Hélène. 2011. 'Ken Livingstone Promises to Tackle Soaring London Rents If Elected'. *The Guardian*, 13 December. Accessed 8 May 2019. https://www.theguardian.com/politics/2011/dec/13/ken-livingstone-tackle-london-rent.

NAO (National Audit Office). 2018. *Financial Sustainability of Local Authorities 2018*. N.p.: National Audit Office.

Pawson, Hal, Hulse, Kath and Morris, Alan. 2017. 'Interpreting the Rise of Long-term Private Renting in a Liberal Welfare Regime Context'. *Housing Studies* 32(8):1062–84. https://doi.org/10.1080/02673037.2017.1301400.

Phillipson, John and Baker, Edward. 2016. *Redbridge Selective Licensing, Evidence Base*. London: Borough of Redbridge. Accessed 22 July 2020. https://www.redbridge.gov.uk/media/3396/redbridge-property-licensing-proposal-supporting-evidence-base-1.pdf.

Pidgeon, Caroline. 2016. *A Survey of Local Authority Enforcement in the Private Rented Sector*. London: Greater London Assembly. Accessed 12 September 2017. https://www.london.gov.uk/sites/default/files/rogue_landlords_in_london_-_a_survey_of_local_authority_enforcement_in_the_private_rented_sector.pdf.

Reynolds, Liam and de Santos, Robbie. 2013. *The Rent Trap and the Fading Dream of Owning a Home*. London: Shelter England. Accessed 22 July 2020. https://england.shelter.org.uk/__data/assets/pdf_file/0007/624391/Rent_trap_v4.pdf.

Rhodes, David and Rugg, Julie. 2018. *Vulnerability amongst Low-income Households in the Private Rented Sector in England*. York: Centre for Housing Policy, University of York.

Roys, Mike, Davidson, Maggie, Nicol, Simon, Ormandy, David and Ambrose, Peter. 2010. *The Real Cost of Poor Housing*. Bracknell: IHS BRE Press.

Rugg, Julie and Rhodes, David. 2008. *The Private Rented Sector: Its Contribution and Potential*. York: Centre for Housing Policy, University of York.

Rugg, Julie and Rhodes, David. 2018. *The Evolving Private Rented Sector: Its Contribution and Potential*. York: Centre for Housing Policy, University of York.

Savills. 2019. *Build to Rent Market Update Q2 2019*. Accessed 9 September 2019. https://www.savills.co.uk/research_articles/229130/286997-0/uk-build-to-rent-market-update---q2-2019.

Stewart, John. 2014. 'An Era of Continuing Change: Reflections on Local Government in England 1974–2014'. *Local Government Studies* 40(6):835–50. https://doi.org/10.1080/03003930.2014.959842.

Stoker, Gerry. 1991. *The Politics of Local Government*. Basingstoke: Palgrave Macmillan.

4

Metromobility and transit-led urbanisation in London and Toronto

Theresa Enright

Mass transit systems have long played multiple roles in urban development. This trend is captured by the concept of metromobility, a reference both to the social systems of metro rail and to the metropolises they bring about (Enright 2016).[1] A key socio-technical institution shaping modern cities, mass transit indelibly shapes regional space and is an important vehicle in the transformation of the built environment, land use and governance. In this chapter, I consider various dimensions of metromobility in London and Toronto with a focus on mass transit's capacity to render cities global. Not only do urban rail systems influence local territories and populations, but increasingly they are vectors of global engagement, providing the material and symbolic supports for extra-local connections and flows. Through this analysis of the 'worlding' practices (Roy and Ong 2011) enacted on and through mobility systems, I identify transit as a key institution of contemporary urbanism.

London and Toronto represent two different pathways of globalising cities. Whereas London has long been an imperial power and its contemporary authorities have explicitly developed urban strategies to assert and maintain global dominance, Toronto is better understood as a settler-colonial city turned 'accidental metropolis' (Berridge 2019) where global integration has proceeded in an incremental and haphazard manner. In both of these cases, however, mass transit is central to these development trajectories and is a pivot upon which recent worldly ambitions turn. In London, transit was explicitly leveraged in pursuit of global competitiveness and was a driver of post-industrial urban transformations. In Toronto, in contrast, transit frequently lagged behind massive spatial reform, which remained wedded to the automobile, and only recently has been envisioned as a necessary precondition for new capital projects. Examining recent trends of transit-led urbanisation in each city reveals transit as a key institution of urban reform, and it clarifies how global pathways and networks rely upon distinct and contingent patterns of engagement and connection.

This chapter has two main aims. First, it identifies the various practices through which urban rail transit systems are tied up in global city pursuits. Second, it compares the experiences of London and Toronto in order to suggest that the global repertoires of transit-led urbanisation are best understood as place- and space-specific. Understanding the contingent political economic dynamics of metromobility clarifies some of the ways in which contemporary global cities are being built and reordered.

Global regimes of metromobility

The provision of mass urban transit has become a key policy agenda in large urban regions around the world based on the widespread consensus that passenger rail is a vehicle of development and prosperity. Improving transport through the construction of new or extension of existing urban rail systems is one of the primary means for cities to manage growth, organise vast and diverse spaces, integrate populations, enhance economic productivity, facilitate intergovernmental coordination and improve quality of life (Dittmar and Ohland 2004; Grescoe 2012). In response to the now well-established woes of automobility, transit-oriented development (TOD) has become a best practice (though by no means universally accepted practice) of contemporary planning. The intensified promotion and investment in rapid urban rail projects around the world is testament to their rising importance across a range of cities (Cervero 1998; see also http://www.urbanrail.net).

In comparison with other emerging modes of urban mobility (e.g. bicycle, scooter, tram, gondola), urban rail has an unprecedented capacity to dramatically reconfigure metropolitan space. Beyond their most immediate function to meet local commuter travel demands, urban rail networks are vast socio-technical complexes that bring together multiple economic sectors and political institutions at various scales (Dupuy 2008). They are, as Wiig and Silver (2019, 913) argue of infrastructure networks in general, 'where globalized circulations – people, goods, and information – enter and reconfigure urban spaces, creating, facilitating or exacerbating spatial figurations and cities integrated into global capitalism'. Just as the metropole invokes local urban territory as well as the place of a city in world-spanning networks, metromobility, as a set of political, economic, cultural and social relations, has this dual character. In this chapter I look to the practices through which cities articulate global ambitions and to the processes by which deterritorialised global flows become territorialised and embedded in local urban contexts (Peck and Tickell 2002; Sassen 2001). As transit plays an active role in local and global circuits, it is a particularly useful site from which to understand these power-laden worlding engagements (Roy and Ong 2011).[2]

Broadly speaking, rapid urban rail is frequently used as a tool to deal with urban expansion and to manage the economic and social contradictions of rapidly transforming city-regions (Kantor et al. 2012). Urban rail also plays more active roles in generating growth, acting as a map to guide investment and to signal priority areas for development. In the context of competitive global urbanisation, many urban authorities are seeking priority investment in select infrastructure – such as rapid urban rail – as a means to enhance the attractiveness of regional territory, to anchor investment and to integrate into transnational value chains (Brenner 2004; Enright 2016). Through explicit TOD, or through more implicit growth imperatives or tax incentives, urban rail systems are essential to infrastructure-driven economic and territorial restructuring.

In a world of neoliberal imperatives, transit is particularly prized for its ability to produce urban rent. Urban transport schemes seeking global city status unabashedly aim to unlock potentials and to raise the value of land in underperforming regional territories through targeted developments. Most prominently, major transit initiatives seek to link international airports with regional hubs of the new economy, thereby projecting the city into global networks at the same time that they dramatically transform metropolitan space. In these spatial and social restructurings, transit is a vehicle of uneven development, the 'splintering' of urban space (Graham and Marvin 2001) and the entrenchment – and even heightening – of existing class hierarchies and relations of domination. Tied to the physical and normative models of financialisation, transit is implicated in the gentrification, spatial polarity and racialised inequality that are hallmarks of the global city (Enright 2016; Hulchanski 2018; Massey 2007; Sassen 2001).[3]

In terms of its concrete geographies, it is notable that this uneven production of global city space occurs not only in central areas but also through complex dynamics of polycentric and post-suburban territorial restructuring (Soja 2000; Phelps and Wood 2011). Keil (2018, 84), for example, emphasises the importance of suburbs in these processes, stressing that peripheries play a key role in 'defining globalization both through their importance to globalizing economies and due to their socio-demographic diversification'. It is also in these suburban spaces – where transit is not well integrated – that conflicts over transit, and the urban values it represents, become most pronounced.

Processes of suburban and regional transit planning and policy-making also offer a particularly useful lens onto the reconfiguration of governance because they necessarily involve the interaction of diverse stakeholders traversing multiple administrative boundaries. In this sense, the emergence of metromobility is inextricable from shifts in urban politics beyond the state and beyond the traditional territorial borders of the city. Preliminarily, these shifts in politics and governance include development models based on megaprojects and public–private partnerships (Flyvbjerg et al. 2003; Siemiatycki 2009), multilevel and collaborative governance arrangements (Brenner 2004; Pinson 2009), multi-scalar and multi-sectoral 'networked' urbanisms (Dupuy 2008), new transit-led regionalisms and nationalisms (Enright 2016; Wachsmuth 2017) and diffuse patterns of contentious politics (Attoh 2012; Caldeira 2013). This leads to new experiments in collective action as well as inter-institutional and civil society battles over who controls, manages, finances, owns, operates and uses transit systems.

If in its economic, spatial and political functions urban rail forges physical connections between and among territories, the extra-material dynamics of transit networks concretise cities' ideological commitments to globality and globalism. Underground transit networks, as much as vertical skyscrapers, are gleaming icons to progress and modernity. The messages, stories and aesthetics of metro-mobility convey collective dreams and desires, sometimes in line with, but often at odds with, a transit network's technical functioning (Easterling 2014; Siemiatycki 2006). Metros are a permanent stamp of urban legitimacy, and the integrity of a city's urban rail system is a metric of its arrival to 'true' city-dom. Real or proposed transit systems thus frequently function as tools to present and project utopian images of a better society and an improved future on which current plans are to be based. A transit network is a particularly salient tool for inward- and outward-facing rebrandings as it promises to solve economic, social and environmental problems simultaneously. Even when they fail – and the tangible benefits of transit-led development are unpredictable – urban rail projects do important work in articulating global and regional development and sparking territorial transformation.

The influence of metro systems on urban development can be seen globally, but individual metropolises and metro networks are rendered global very particularly. Mass transit moves people, places, ideas and capital in ambivalent, contested and contingent ways. What results from the growing prominence of metromobility is not a smooth frictionless world, or the same patterns of mobility everywhere, but a variegated and uneven global urban landscape. An analysis of London's and Toronto's respective trajectories reveals the contextual nature of these general trends.

Mobilising London as a global city

London's historical development has long been shaped by its transport and infrastructure systems. Its iconic bridges, docklands, railways, airports and highways have responded to London's evolution and have transformed the city's role within the United Kingdom and in the world. From the construction of the Metropolitan Railway in 1863 through to the extensive multimodal rail networks of Transport for London (TfL), rapid urban rail has been central to London's development from imperial metropole to alpha global city.

If the Underground rail network has indelibly shaped London's development (Bownes et al. 2012), the planning of the global city as it relates to mass transit emerged in 1996 with a document by the central public authority, London Transport, titled *Planning London's Transport to Win as a Global City*. Claiming that London's 'greatest strength' is its status as a world city (London Transport 1996, 1), the report analyses how transport can best support and enhance this position in the years ahead to help London adapt to changing conditions and maximise its comparative advantage. The central claim of the report is that 'in order to maintain its status as a world city London requires a modern efficient transport system which meets the needs of its residents, businesses and visitors while respecting and improving the environment' (1). While the report aims at all transport modes, particular attention is given to the promises and shortcomings of London's Underground and urban rail networks in meeting existing and future travel demands.

The spatial strategy outlined by London Transport relies on a number of interconnected goals. These include connecting downtown and suburbs, linking the centre of the city to international corridors and amenities and enhancing the quality of travel conditions 'serving increasingly affluent and discriminating passengers' (London Transport 1996, 27). In these changes, transit should facilitate four priority world city sectors: creative and cultural industries, finance and business services, tourism, and power and influence (15). The report emphasises mass transit's role in generating regional coherence, promoting international rail and airport links, attracting elite users and growing priority sectors of a post-industrial economy. Maintaining and improving mass transit, and urban rail in particular, was identified as an imperative and urgent need. 'Promoting the competitive position of London as a world city is the top priority for this transport strategy, because the future of London depends on it and because of the importance of London's invisible earnings to the economy of the UK as a whole' (23).

The desire and seeming requirement to become global by following this market-oriented development path was further supported by the 'Four World Cities Transport Study' in 1999, which put London in comparison with New York, Tokyo and Paris in order to identify comparative advantages of London as well as best practices to be learned from perceived competitors (London Research Centre 1999). Comparing London with other similarly positioned cities vying for global influence, the report found that London's main weaknesses lay in the overcrowding of the current system and in a lack of long-term vision and investment. This concretised the priorities and values that would set the path for transit planning into the twenty-first century.

In 2000, as part of the institution of the regional Greater London Authority (GLA) (replacing the Greater London Council), responsibility for urban-regional transit was shuffled from the central government agency London Transport to the new Transport for London corporation. London's transport system was named as one of the Mayor of London's four key policy areas and was seen by Ken Livingstone (and his successors Boris Johnson and Sadiq Khan) as key to realising sucess for London as a whole (GLA 2001; Johnson 2013). Indeed, as a regional body the GLA has responsibility over transport, land use and economic development and the three are considered interdependent. Since its origin, the mandate for TfL's transport and transit planning is to 'unlock' development potentials in regional sites while responding to the city's growth needs. At the same time, then, that the state was rescaled to the regional level, the GLA and Department of Communities and Local Government adopted a narrative about development and globalism seeing world market integration as the solution to the problems plaguing the city at the turn of the century. Successive London Plans (see especially Mayor of London 2004) would later provide the broad development framework for the city based on these values.

Transit was absolutely essential to the various post-industrial strategies employed by London's governing elites to create the world city. The immense project to revitalise Canary Wharf and the London Docklands, for example, would have been impossible politically and materially without the extension of the Jubilee line of the London Underground and the construction of Docklands Light Rail. While the Docklands held a central position in local and national debates over strategic development priorities, debates over what kind of transit should be built, where and for what purposes were at the heart of virulent struggles over the city's future more generally (Massey 2007). New transit links were imperative in the transformation of the fading imperial city into a new centre of international finance (Massey 2007) and they invariably contributed to the devastating social and spatial problems inherent in such a transition.

Throughout the early 2000s, notions of transit's world-class potential were closely aligned with the British urban policy of 'urban regeneration', a normative concept to deal with urban decline, decay and transformation through territorial restructuring and welfare provision (Cochrane 2007; Couch et al. 2003; Imrie et al. 2009). Regeneration was a local social and spatial policy, but it was also embedded within 'the broadcloth of international relations and transnational processes relating to the capital's position as a global city and as a pre-eminent player in the global economy' (Imrie et al. 2009, 4). Transit solidified regeneration by assuring the capital's economic competitiveness at key economic hubs and through jump-starting land and property markets. In addition to Canary Wharf, twenty-first-century regeneration megaprojects such as Paddington Basin, King's Cross, Thames Gateway and Stratford Olympic Park have been achieved through vast investments in new and improved urban rail. Transit was thus a significant, if often unacknowledged, participant in the neoliberal deregulation, commercialisation and financialisation of urban life that has defined the recent history of London.

The Crossrail, London's newest railway, is the latest project to cement the city's growth-first regional and national development priorities (see Cochrane 2007). The vast network (renamed the Elizabeth Line) is expanding the scale of the city while bringing Heathrow and other international infrastructure hubs (including the Royal Albert Docks, also the new site of China's Belt and Road network; see Wiig and Silver 2019) in connection with each other and with major employment hubs. Crossrail promises to completely transform movement throughout London by providing a high-speed east–west link and by increasing the capacity of London's rail transit by 10 per cent (Crossrail 2018). Even more impressively, the Crossrail is exemplary of property-led transit regeneration, characterised by the stimulation of regional office parks, retail centres and telecommunications districts along the network. It has been a major catalyst for large-scale gentrification across London and the South East. Building on this rent and realty focus of the Crossrail, TfL (which will eventually take over operations of the line) has recently launched a much broader programme to leverage its land assets in financial markets and to offset shortfalls in public revenue (*Financial Times* 2018).

Not merely a technical megaproject, the Crossrail has 'world-class design' at its heart (Crossrail 2020) and investment in this immense infrastructure has been paired with notable programmes of heritage, arts and culture. From impressive starchitecture to blue-chip arts installations along the central portion of the railway known as 'the Culture Line', the railway is generating support for metromobility while reworking what Asher Ghertner (2015) calls 'world class' aesthetics. This yoking of culture and infrastructure, along with the cultivation of the Underground 'superbrand' (Bownes et al. 2012, 227), exemplifies how imaginative changes are essential to transit's role in development. A highly cultivated imaginary network supports ideals of transit urbanity, while also consolidating urban identities and selling the physical network abroad. Building on its brand recognition and prestige, TfL has also vastly expanded its international consultancy wing and is becoming an influential global policy actor in its own right (Transport for London 2018).

Toronto

Not unlike London, Toronto's history can be written through its infrastructures of transport. Yet in contrast to the rich historical legacy of London's railways and Underground, Toronto's mass transit system has a more modest history. Urban dynamics remain dominated by automobility (Filion 2003, 2010; Walks 2014, 2015). While a recent consumer-led civic renewal in the city has created a market for Toronto Transit Commission (TTC) paraphernalia and sparked nostalgia for the city's beloved streetcars, transit – and, in some cases, its absence – is more often than not seen as an obstacle to Toronto's global ambitions and not its wellspring (OECD 2010; Toronto Board of Trade 2009). Nevertheless, metromobility has not been absent from Toronto's recent development and it is useful to understand transit's role in what J. P. Addie (2013, 198) calls 'Toronto's growth from provincial city to global metropolis'.

The TTC subway network emerged in the 1950s following citywide battles over transport that cut across urban–suburban and partisan viewpoints on how the city should develop. In its early days, the TTC rail network was used by reformist politicians to support infrastructure-led growth through a Fordist-Keynesian regime of growth and collective consumption. In contrast to many North American cities where planning was sacrificed to the car, Toronto at this time gained a favourable reputation for visionary planning that emphasised mass transit alongside, if not in place of, the private automobile. The TTC's early planning was driven by social reproduction as much as by economic rationales. By the late 1980s, however, the system had not kept pace with the population or the sprawling urbanisation of the Greater Toronto region and began to be seen as a hindrance both to daily travel and to sustained growth.

The dynamics of the city's mobility systems – and in particular contests between auto- and metromobility – would prove central to Toronto's post-Fordist transition and entry into the twenty-first century (see especially Walks 2015). In Toronto, urban neoliberalisation originally featured a disinvestment in mass transit in favour of continued support for the automobile and automobile manufacturing. When Mike Harris was elected Premier of Ontario in 1995, for example, his 'Common Sense Revolution' viewed transit as an unnecessary service cost. Rather than positioning mass transit as a lever to restore growth to the province and support his large-scale state restructuring, and with a decidedly anti-urban bias, mass transit was downloaded from the province onto the City of Toronto, effectively halting the roll-out of ambitious capital projects and regional schemes.

Through what Julie Anne Boudreau and co-authors (2009, 61) call a 'reluctant global city strategy', Harris and his Progressive Conservative government were antagonistic toward urban issues yet 'consistently pushed Toronto as a location for international capital accumulation'. Transit was not part of the framework for urban boosterism that otherwise fuelled commitment to large-scale development and regeneration activity. As Toronto's version of neoliberalism had been ideologically and politically expressed along the lines of automobility (Walks 2015), entrepreneurial and global regimes of metromobility did not have a strong pull. The somewhat paradoxical strategy of emphasising regional and global competitiveness, while disinvesting in infrastructure, however, eventually proved untenable.

Following the Harris reforms, business leaders as well as reformist politicians responded to the lack of investment, the poorly integrated network and the drawbacks of intergovernmental conflict. Although they differed in aim and approach, repeated attempts by business and progressive city-politicians to implement comprehensive overhauls of the transit system cohered around the need to build new rapid links, especially to the underserved suburbs. The Toronto Board of Trade (2001) wrote a publication outlining their 'Strategy for Rail Based Transit in the GTA' in which they saw mass transit as a way to project the wealthy city-region onto the world stage and into world markets. The Board of Trade had an ambitious regional vision for transport, with an emphasis on rail over bus service, stressing the importance of connections between supra-local circuits of transport rather than local transit in its own right. They also demanded a governing body at the metropolitan scale that would be capable of arranging such a service. Transit, write Keil and Young (2008), had become 'a bottleneck to the very economic competitiveness that largely drives public policy in the region' (181).

At the same time, progressives under Mayor David Miller put forward a holistic plan in 2006 called Transit City that also sought to use transit as a lever for radical urban transformation. Featuring 120 kilometres of Light Rail Transit (with a rapid route to Pearson International Airport), Transit City aimed primarily to weave a dense mesh of local links, with priority given to underserved areas of the city, especially the inner suburbs. Transit City did have extra-local connections, but its main purpose was to equalise territory within the existing City of Toronto. This plan, however, never received funding and was overturned in 2010 when Rob Ford became mayor. With this stalling, a lack of adequate transit provision is a central element in Toronto's entrenched urban social spatial inequity (Boudreau et al. 2009; Hertel et al. 2015; TTCriders 2012).

For its part, in its 'Ridership Growth Strategy' the TTC (2003) also did not seek to create a new global network or lead the global city charge. Rather, it adopted a 'defensive strategy' of service improvements, fare initiatives and small-scale improvements (Keil and Young 2008, 741). Strikingly, in the last two decades of TTC annual reports, there is almost no mention of worldly ambition, global vision or international competitiveness.

The discourses of competitive metromobility, however, did rise in prominence and influence after the provincial government of Dalton McGuinty established a new regional body with significant powers for planning and management of transport in the Greater Toronto region in 2008. This authority, later to become Metrolinx, explicitly sought to build Toronto's regional competitiveness. With the speculative development and the creation of regional growth poles guiding their 'Big Move' Regional Transport Plan (RTP), Metrolinx crystallised mass transit's role as a driver of urban development and verified the link between Toronto's regional transformation and global ambition. 'The RTP will not only reclaim our region's traditional transport advantage, but also bolster our global competitiveness, protect the environment and improve quality of life. For the first time, like so many of our competitors, we are truly thinking like a single region' (Metrolinx 2008, i). While Metrolinx frequently mentions international connections, competitiveness and regional prosperity in the same breath, the discourses of the global city are far less developed than they are in London and competition is only one of a number of other priorities and goals.

Overall, a less reluctant global city strategy began to take shape through infrastructure-led growth coalitions. All three levels of government used signature projects – both 'soft' cultural initiatives such as arts and cultural investments, and 'hard' endeavours such as waterfront restructuring – to drive renewal and regeneration projects in Toronto. The revitalisation of Union Station (the keystone of the regional Metrolinx Big Move initiative) is particularly notable here on both of these fronts. These renovations were leveraged as a selling point in advance of the Pan American Games in 2015 and as a launching pad for a potential 2024 Olympic bid. With extensive design and cultural programming associated with the rebuild, a major aspect of upgrading the station is to convince residents of Toronto as well as investors and tourists that the city's transit network is a state-of-the-art amenity fit for the world-class city it aspires to become (Enright 2018).

The creation of a new privately operated airport connection, the Union Pearson Express (UP Express), also exemplifies an emerging globalising rationality – and its limits. The UP Express was created to provide high-speed connections between Pearson International Airport, located in the suburb of Mississauga, and Union Station in the centre of Toronto. It opened in 2015, but from the outset plans for the link were plagued with controversy. Residents along the proposed route, for example, were concerned about the environmental impact of the link and questioned the choice of diesel over electric rail cars. Community organisations in Weston village were also concerned about how the line would cut through their neighbourhood. Residents in Weston – home to many airport workers – were eventually given a new station along the line as a compromise. Despite this, many were not able to use the new 'premium' train as the fares were priced out of their reach. Indeed, due to its exorbitantly high fares (especially when compared with other TTC options), the UP Express ran well below capacity throughout its first years of operation. The debacle over UP Express shows the continued disconnections from the world, despite global world-class imaginaries and marketing.

Nevertheless, a more explicit – if tenuous – political consensus on the importance of urban rail to urban prosperity and global urbanisation after 2010 facilitated the completion of transit projects, such as the TTC's Spadina subway extension and Metrolinx's Eglinton Crosstown Express, and it prompted new leadership, including the appointment of Andy Byford (formerly of TfL) as CEO of the TTC in 2011. New flagship stations along the Spadina extension and elite art, architectural and design features announced an era defined by ambitious vision. Despite ongoing obstacles to long-term renovations and growth of the network, these changes appeared to be a bold new direction for a city that is repeatedly criticised for lack of ambition and action (Levine 2014; Lorinc 2012).

The provincial government of Doug Ford has also recently embraced a very particular variant of metromobility, mobilising subways to 'open up' Ontario for business. Through a re-upload of the subway system from the City of Toronto in 2019, they have proposed an aggressive strategy of attempting to take back control over Toronto's key infrastructure network and use it as a scaffolding for massive new private developments. Transit in Toronto thus continues to be a highly contested point of convergence for many aspects of Toronto's development.[4] Competing plans to balance metromobility and automobility, and to determine the guiding values of these mobility systems, are at the heart of ongoing struggles between various levels of government and between civil society actors.

Conclusion

Mass urban transit is today a crucial aspect of spatial and economic planning. This chapter has considered the emergence of metromobility systems in London and Toronto and the way that mass transit is bound up with worlding practices. Through attention to urban rail infrastructures as complex social systems, it has argued that transit mediates global and local connections and is the structure whereby internal space comes to align with the role of cities in the global economy. Moreover, as metromobility systems are extensive and topological, these cities cannot be thought of as isolated from one another but must be seen as part of the same networks of personnel, corporations and ideological agendas. The comparison between Toronto and London is not a story of standardisation, nor is it offered to claim either city as a 'success' or 'failure' along a given pathway to global city status. Rather, these cases demonstrate the varied and ambivalent functions of transit in global urban development.

Notes

1. By metromobility I refer primarily to mobility systems (Urry 2007) centred on metros (or subways) and rapid passenger urban rail (including commuter trains and light rail transit). In the North Atlantic, metromobility is emerging alongside and often in competition with the dominant system of automobility.
2. Urban rail systems are involved in worlding processes insofar as they comprise what Roy and Ong (2011, 312) describe as 'practice[s] of centering, of generating and harnessing global regimes of value'. The focus in this chapter is primarily on the meso-level political economy of transit-led urbanisation, but this is understood to be embedded within a broader range of world-making practices that occur in and through transit networks (see e.g. Chattopadhyay 2012; Datta 2012).
3. Mass transit today is also, of course, a key tool of liberation, redistribution and democratisation. It is integral to a city's quality of life, essential for collective urban access and can be mobilised in the pursuit of universal social welfare and collective spatial justice. Due to the networked importance of transit infrastructures, as well as their significance in everyday life, growth-maximising economic imperatives often dovetail with more social and environmentally oriented city building practices.
4. Doug Ford's subway upload goes against previous conservative policies of service downloading. Yet it gives the province unprecedented control over regional governance and land use planning. The precise futures of this plan and his proposed 'Ontario Line', however, remain uncertain and embroiled in controversy.

References

Addie, Jean-Paul D. 2013. 'Metropolitics in Motion: The Dynamics of Transportation and State Reterritorialization in the Chicago and Toronto City-regions'. *Urban Geography* 34(2):188–217.

Attoh, Kafui Abolde. 2012. 'The Transportation Disadvantaged and the Right to the City in Syracuse, New York'. *Geographical Bulletin* 53(1):1–13.

Berridge, Joe. 2019. *Perfect City: An Urban Fixer's Global Search for Magic in the Modern Metropolis*. Toronto: Southerland House.

Boudreau, Julie-Anne, Keil, Roger and Young, Douglas. 2009. *Changing Toronto: Governing Urban Neoliberalism*. Toronto: University of Toronto Press.

Bownes, David, Green, Oliver and Mullins, Sam. 2012. *Underground: How the Tube Shaped London*. London: Allen Lane.

Brenner, Neil. 2004. *New State Spaces: Urban Governance and the Rescaling of Statehood*. New York: Oxford University Press.

Caldeira, Teresa. 2013. 'São Paulo: The City and its Protests', 11 July. Accessed 27 July 2020. https://www.opendemocracy.net/en/opensecurity/sao-paulo-city-and-its-protest.

Cervero, Robert. 1998. *The Transit Metropolis: A Global Inquiry*. Washington, DC: Island Press.

Chattopadhyay, Swati. 2012. *Unlearning the City: Infrastructure in a New Optical Field*. Minneapolis: University of Minnesota Press.

Cochrane, Allan. 2007. *Understanding Urban Policy: A Critical Approach*. Oxford: Blackwell.

Couch, Chris, Fraser, Charles and Percy, Susan (eds). 2003. *Urban Regeneration in Europe*. Cambridge, UK: John Wiley & Sons.

Crossrail. 2018. 'Crossrail in numbers'. Accessed 19 August 2020. https://www.crossrail.co.uk/news/crossrail-in-numbers.

Crossrail. 2020. 'Crossrail's approach to design: stations, art and public space'. Accessed 14 August 2020. https://www.crossrail.co.uk/route/design.

Datta, Ayona. 2012. '"Where Is the Global City?" Visual Narratives of London among East European Migrants'. *Urban Studies* 49(8):1725–40. https://doi.org/10.1177/0042098011417906.

Dittmar, Hank and Ohland, Gloria. 2004. *The New Transit Town: Best Practices in Transit-oriented Development*. Washington, DC: Island Press.

Dupuy, Gabriel. 2008. *Urban Networks—Network Urbanism*. Amsterdam: Techne Press.

Easterling, Keller. 2014. *Extrastatecraft: The Power of Infrastructure Space*. New York: Verso Books.

Enright, Theresa. 2016. *The Making of Grand Paris: Metropolitan Urbanism in the Twenty-first Century*. Cambridge, MA: MIT Press.

Enright, Theresa. 2018. 'Mobile Futures: Urban Revitalisation and the Aesthetics of Transportation'. In *Handbook on Spaces of Urban Politics*, edited by Andy Jonas et al., 577–88. London: Routledge.

Filion, Pierre. 2003. 'Towards Smart Growth? The Difficult Implementation of Alternatives to Urban Dispersion'. *Canadian Journal of Urban Research* 12(1):48–70.

Filion, Pierre. 2010. 'Reorienting Urban Development? Structural Obstruction to New Urban Forms'. *International Journal of Urban and Regional Research* 31(1):1–19. https://doi.org/10.1111/j.1468-2427.2009.00896.x.

Financial Times. 2018. 'TfL's Commercial Arm Eases Pain of £1bn Deficit'. *Financial Times*, 22 July. Accessed 20 August 2019. https://www.ft.com/content/1a804da2-8c27-11e8-b18d-0181731a0340.

Flyvbjerg, Bent, Bruzelius, Nils and Rothengatter, Werner. 2003. *Megaprojects and Risk: An Anatomy of Ambition*. New York: Cambridge University Press.

Ghertner, Asher. 2015. *Rule by Aesthetics: World-class City Making in Delhi*. Oxford: Oxford University Press.

Graham, Stephen and Marvin, Simon. 2001. *Splintering Urbanism*. London: Routledge.

GLA (Greater London Authority). 2001. *The Mayor's Transport Strategy*. London: Greater London Authority.

Grescoe, Taras. 2012. *Straphanger: Saving our Cities and Ourselves from the Automobile*. New York: Times Books.

Hertel, Sean, Keil, Roger and Collens, Michael. 2015. *Next Stop Equity: Routes to Fairer Transit Access in the Greater Toronto and Hamilton Area*. Accessed 20 August 2019. https://city.apps01.yorku.ca/wp-content/uploads/2016/02/Transit-Equity_Reduced_020216.pdf.

Hulchanski, J. D. 2010. *The Three Cities within Toronto*. Toronto: Cities Centre.

Imrie, Rob, Lees, Loretta and Raco, Mike (eds). 2009. *Regenerating London: Governance, Sustainability and Community in a Global City*. London: Routledge.

Johnson, Boris. 2013. *2020 Vision – The Greatest City on Earth*. London: Greater London Authority. Accessed 20 August 2019. https://www.london.gov.uk/sites/default/files/2020_vision_web.pdf.

Kantor, Paul, Lefèvre, Christian, Saito, Asato, Savitch, H. V. and Thornley, Andy. 2012. *Struggling Giants: City-region Governance in London, New York, Paris, and Tokyo*. Minneapolis: University of Minnesota Press.

Keil, Roger. 2018. *Suburban Planet: Making the World Urban from the Outside in*. Cambridge: Polity.

Keil, Roger and Young, Douglas. 2008. 'Transportation: The Bottleneck of Regional Competitiveness in Toronto'. *Environment and Planning C: Governance and Policy* 26(4):728–51. https://doi.org/10.1068/c68m.

Levine, Allan. 2014. *Toronto: Biography of a City*. Toronto: Douglas & McIntyre.

London Research Centre. 1999. *Four World Cities Transport Study: London, New York, Paris, Tokyo*. London: London Research Centre.

London Transport. 1996. *Planning London's Transport to Win as a World City*. London: London Transport.

Lorinc, John. 2012. 'How Toronto Lost its Groove'. *The Walrus*, 12 September. Accessed 20 August 2019. http://thewalrus.ca/how-toronto-lost-its-groove/.

Massey, Doreen. 2007. *World City*. London: John Wiley and Sons.

Mayor of London. 2004. *The London Plan: Spatial Development Strategy for Greater London*. Accessed 20 August 2019. https://www.london.gov.uk/sites/default/files/the_london_plan_2004.pdf.

Metrolinx. 2008. *The Big Move: Greater Toronto Transportation Authority*. Accessed 20 August 2019. http://www.metrolinx.com/thebigmove/en/default.aspx.

OECD (Organisation for Economic Development and Co-operation). 2010. *Territorial Reviews: Toronto, Canada*. Geneva: OECD.

Peck, Jamie and Tickell, Adam. 2002. 'Neoliberalizing Space'. *Antipode* 34(3):380–404. https://doi.org/10.1111/1467-8330.00247.

Phelps, Nicholas A. and Wood, Andrew M. 2011. 'The New Post-Suburban Politics?' *Urban Studies* 48(12):2591–610. https://doi.org/10.1177/0042098011411944.

Pinson, Gilles. 2009. *Gouverner la ville par projet: urbanisme et gouvernance des villes européennes*. Paris: Presses de Sciences Po.

Roy, Ananya and Ong, Aihwa. 2011. *Worlding Cities: Asian Experiments and the Art of Being Global*. London: Wiley.

Sassen, Saskia. 2001. *The Global City: New York, London, Tokyo* (2nd edition). Princeton, NJ: Princeton University Press.

Siemiatycki, Matti. 2006. 'Message in a Metro: Building Urban Rail Infrastructure and Image in Delhi, India'. *International Journal of Urban and Regional Research* 30(2):277–92. https://doi.org/10.1111/j.1468-2427.2006.00664.x.

Siemiatycki, Matti. 2009. 'Delivering Transportation Infrastructure through Public–Private Partnerships: Planning Concerns'. *Journal of the American Planning Association* 76(1):43–58. https://doi.org/10.1080/01944360903329295.

Soja, Edward W. 2000. *Postmetropolis: Critical Studies of Cities and Regions*. Malden, MA: Wiley-Blackwell.

Toronto Board of Trade. 2001. *A Strategy for Rail-based Transit in the GTA*. Toronto: Toronto Board of Trade.

Toronto Board of Trade. 2009. *From World-class to World Leader: An Action Plan for the Toronto Region*. Toronto: Toronto Board of Trade.

Transport for London. 2018. *TfL Consulting and International Operations*. Accessed 20 August 2019. http://content.tfl.gov.uk/fc-20180704-pt1-item12-tfl-consulting.pdf.

TTC (Toronto Transit Commission). 2003. *Ridership Growth Strategy*. Toronto: Toronto Transit Commission. Accessed 20 August 2019. https://www.ttc.ca/PDF/Transit_Planning/ridership_growth_strategy_2003.pdf.

TTCriders. 2012. *The State of Public Transit in Toronto*. Accessed 20 August 2019. http://www.ttcriders.ca/wp-content/uploads/2012/07/The-State-of-Public-Transit-in-Toronto-July-2012.pdf.

Urry, John. 2007. *Mobilities*. Cambridge, UK: Polity.

Wachsmuth, David. 2017. 'Competitive Multi-city Regionalism: Growth Politics beyond the Growth Machine'. *Regional Studies* 51(4): 643–653.

Walks, Alan. 2014. *The Urban Political Economy and Ecology of Automobility: Driving Cities, Driving Inequality, Driving Politics*. London: Routledge.

Walks, Alan. 2015. 'Stopping the "War on the Car": Neoliberalism, Fordism, and the Politics of Automobility in Toronto'. *Mobilities* 10(3):402–22. https://doi.org/10.1080/17450101.2014.880563.

Wiig, Alan and Silver, Jonathan. 2019. 'Turbulent Presents, Precarious Futures: Urbanization and the Deployment of Global Infrastructure'. *Regional Studies* 53(6):1–12. http://doi.org/10.1080/00343404.2019.1566703.

5

The governance of urban public spaces in London: In the public interest or in the interest of local stakeholders?

Claudio De Magalhães

Introduction

This chapter discusses forms of urban public spaces governance that are emerging in London out of a rearrangement of governance responsibilities between local government, communities and private interests. Beyond the so-called privately owned public spaces (POPS)[1] – the privately owned and managed parts of the physical public realm – there has been an increasing takeover of the management of parks and other public areas by not-for-profit organisations from the voluntary, community and private sectors, as well as the emergence and multiplication of Business Improvement Districts (BIDs).[2]

This is not a phenomenon peculiar to London. However, the city's size, its history of private and voluntary involvement in public space provision and management, and the multiplicity of stakes in those spaces make it a laboratory in which to observe how public space governance has responded to pressures on existing governance systems and to try to understand the full implications of those responses.

Should we be concerned about the transfer of public space governance from elected local governments to organised groups of stakeholders? Does this make those spaces more private than public? What are the aggregate consequences of transferring public space governance to third parties for the city?

For some, direct stakeholder involvement in governance represents a more effective way of ensuring that towns and cities remain viable and competitive, with potentially more efficient, demand-sensitive and differentiated ways of delivering services and managing public spaces. Added to this is the access to resources of various kinds beyond those of declining public sector budgets (Audit Commission 2002). For others, the transfer of public realm governance functions from the state to other social agents, and especially to the private sector, constitutes privatisation. As such, it entails the expansion of market and commodity imperatives into the public realm and their prevalence over more communal ones (see Low and Smith 2006; Kohn 2004).

This chapter discusses the implications of governance transfer processes in public spaces with evidence from London. It deploys an analytical framework based on the notion of rights over public goods (Blomley 2014; Ostrom 2003) to reflect on how those arrangements shape the attributes that make up the public essence of those spaces – their publicness. In doing that, the chapter explores the point highlighted by Boydell and Searle (2014), of cities made up of constellations of spaces with fine-grained differences in publicness making up the public realm.

In its look at emerging forms of public space management in London through the lens of allocation and appropriation of rights, the chapter also examines the emerging tensions between the active participation of those with a recognised stake in a public space and the protection of other legitimate interests, including those of the wider society. In its conclusion, the chapter discusses the implications of its findings for local democracy, for London and for other global cities.

The context: Declining public space budgets and increasingly diverse demands

The offloading of governance and management responsibility over public goods in general and public spaces in particular in the UK has a long history, with its fair share of controversy and opposition. The background has been the long process of redesign of the role of the state under a powerful mix of ideological aspirations for a reduced state and the move to adapt the economy and society to a globalised economy. It has been at play from the late 1970s, since the early years of Margaret Thatcher's Conservative government, and its latest incarnation has taken the shape of 'devolution of power' from government to regional, local government and civil society, and goes hand in hand with a search for alternative ways to fund public services (Lowndes and Pratchett 2012). This process has been given a considerable push with the recent financial crisis and the austerity measures that have come to dominate many western economies (see e.g. Raco 2013; Hastings et al. 2015; Peck 2012). Local authorities have used this devolution of power framework to transfer in part, or as a whole, governance and management responsibilities for local public services to interested parties in civil society, under what some have termed contractual governance (Peel et al. 2009; Vincent-Jones 2000). For public spaces, this has been substantiated in many forms: in the proliferation of long leases to allow the transfer of public land containing, or designated to contain, parks and green space to not-for-profit trusts; in the increasing use of the 2002 right-to-manage legislation to transfer the management of local authority housing estates and their grounds to resident-led bodies; and in the use of public–private partnerships and private finance initiative mechanisms in build–operate–transfer contracts to secure private capital investment for redeveloping and managing public facilities. This is in addition to the wide use of simpler contracting-out instruments transferring all or some public space governance responsibilities to a contractor and the multiplication of less formal arrangements incorporating stakeholders in governance decision-making. The implications of this process for the nature of public spaces can be significant.

There is considerable academic literature on the withdrawal of the state from the provision and management of public spaces (see Low and Smith 2006; Law 2002; Minton 2006, 2009; Németh and Schmidt 2011; Langstraat and van Melik 2013). It draws on long-standing, predominantly US debates about the changing nature of the state and of the relationship between state and markets, the public and the private, and the extension of forms of commodification into social life. In most of the pre-financial crisis literature, the decreasing presence of the public sector in the provision and management of public spaces is associated with a more assertive role of market forces in urban governance in the 1980s and 1990s (see Kohn 2004; Sorkin 1992). This shift would be a corollary of the dominance of 'neoliberal' or pro-market approaches to politics and to policy-making and the emergence of the 'entrepreneurial' city.

Overall, the literature suggests a gradual process of privatisation, with corporate interests taking over public spaces. This would be exemplified either in direct provision in the context of privately led urban regeneration projects and the multiplication of privately owned public spaces (Hayden 2006), or through the business-led management of publicly owned spaces, as in the case of BIDs (Minton 2009; Ward 2006). Some have even suggested the 'death of public space' (Sorkin 1992) as the outcome of this commodification and privatisation process, with adverse consequences for an inclusive democratic polity.

The post-financial crisis literature has emphasised the impacts of austerity policies and the search for resources outside the public sector to provide and manage public goods. Privatisation is still the main theme, as a cash-starved public sector sells off its assets to the highest bidder in order to obtain the necessary resources to invest in underfunded public services (see Raco 2013; Whitfield 2012). Some, however, have focused on the potential for a new citizen–state relationship that process might facilitate (see e.g. Pestoff and Brandsen 2010). Difficulties in progressing with capital-intense redevelopment operations might create a challenge to the 'neoliberal order' and offer opportunities for the temporary takeover of public spaces by activists and community groups in the name of an alternative, more democratic publicness. This would represent a form of resistance urbanism, creating a new 'commons' and suggesting embryonic forms of citizen empowerment (Kohn 2013; Lubin 2012; Gursozlu 2015; Eizenberg 2011).

Is that what we see in London? A visit to most of its public spaces would not give the impression that they are in immediate danger of becoming corporatised spaces, and the 'end of public space' still seems far off. On the contrary, there is evidence that old and new public spaces in London under different regimes have flourished (see e.g. Carmona and Wunderlich 2012). At the same time, the few, occasional and temporary acts of radical takeover – such as those of the Occupy London movement – have so far not succeeded in bringing about new types of state–citizen relationship. Not that there are not examples of both, but, more numerous than corporatised public private spaces and their opposite, the protest takeover spaces – and arguably more significant for the daily life of the majority of citizens – are those in which governance and management regimes have become hybridised. As they seek ways to cope with austerity, while often under pressure to respond to historical demands from pressure groups, local governments and communities have been devising ways to ensure that existing and new public spaces somehow meet their aspirations and fulfil the functions expected of them. This has taken place in some planned and some ad hoc fashions, through various forms of transfer of governance and management responsibility from the public sector to a plethora of other actors from the private, voluntary and community sectors, as indicated earlier. Whereas those governance transfers might not be as dramatic as corporate or activist takeover, they raise fundamental questions about the very nature of publicness, of what public spaces are or should be.

Assessing publicness

There is good evidence of an increasing number of public spaces in London governed through arrangements that diverge from the norm (De Magalhães and Freire Trigo 2017a, 2017b). This has led to questions about how public they really are, manifest in recent policy concerns with the consequences of the proliferation of public spaces outside direct local government control (see e.g. London Assembly 2011). This is reflected in turn in the popular press and informs the debate around a potential loss of 'publicness' caused by those governance arrangements.

However, assessing 'publicness' is not a straightforward matter. Most of the literature on the subject adopts a normative stance, centred on ideal models of publicness, against which individual spaces could be measured. The criteria defining those models vary considerably, from ownership to the nature and range of the users, to the type of relationships public spaces should foster between them, to the nature of the practices that take place there, to design elements, and to a combination of those in varying proportions (see e.g. Ellin 1996; Varna 2014; Low and Smith 2006; Mitchell and Staeheli 2006; Benn and Gauss 1983; Németh and Schmidt 2011). Implicit in most formulations is the view of publicness as an objective and absolute concept with a measurable dimension, with spaces being more or less public the closer to or further away from the norm they are. Any progressive policy agenda should therefore be concerned with making as many public spaces as possible come closer to that norm and with changing those that diverge from it.

The problem is that cities are made up of a vast array of public spaces performing different functions for different groups of people, with varying practical and symbolic meaning and significance, creating different stakes in those spaces and giving rise to a myriad of potential conflicts. There is only a weak rationale for the idea that a place such as Trafalgar Square in central London, with its central location, easy accessibility, large symbolic appeal and tradition of events and large demonstrations, should have its publicness measured with the same gauge as a small local park, used primarily by local elderly people, dog walkers and young mothers and their children. Moreover, whereas there are spaces that might be easily classified as fully public or fully private, for many more this is far more nuanced, and most will have attributes that might exhibit different degrees of publicness or privateness. The case for a spectrum of publicness rather than a more simplistic public/private dichotomy is not new (see e.g. Carmona 2015).

Understanding what different types of public space governance arrangements mean requires a relational, non-normative conceptualisation of publicness. This should take into account the context in which a space is located, the manifold stakes that people and groups of people might have in it and the ways through which these stakes are negotiated and the priorities defined by those arrangements.

Publicness is about the rights people have over the attributes of a space – what they can and cannot do with them. The literature on property rights and the commons suggests the basis for a non-normative view of publicness, understanding it as the result of the allocation of rights and responsibilities over those attributes (Ostrom 2003; Colding et al. 2013; Lee and Webster, 2006; Németh 2012; Boydell and Searle 2014). Whereas the list of material and immaterial attributes of a public space will be extensive, the chapter focuses on the rights associated with the most basic and defining elements of publicness: the degree of openness of access and use of the space and its attributes and the power to have a say on them (De Magalhães and Freire Trigo 2017a).

Firstly, then, is the right of *access*: the most basic expectation is that a public space should be provided and managed in a way that secures relatively open access to most members of society. This formulation accepts Webster's (2002) point that very few urban public goods – public spaces included – are public in the sense of absolute openness to access. Rights of access encompass rules and mechanisms that regulate whatever restrictions there might be on how individuals access the attributes they value in a particular public space, be they physical access to the site or the access to a facility or activity.

Secondly, the expectation is that people who have access to that space would be able to use it and enjoy its attributes – that is, the right of *use* – without other restrictions than those dictated by broadly accepted social norms of behaviour and rights of other users. Rights of use refer to the rules and codes of behaviour, and to enforcement mechanisms that regulate how individuals that have access to a public space can enjoy its attributes, be they physical or the confirmation of a symbolic function.

Thirdly, people would expect that users of a public space, the public, would have the right to a say on key decisions regarding its management and future, including the setting of rules about access and use. This would represent a third basic right, the right to *accountability*. Rights to accountability refer to the rules and mechanisms through which the different stakes in a particular public space are heard and recognised in its governance and management, and through which conflicts and disputes between them are solved.

Drawing on Ostrom's (2003) conceptualisation of the governance of common pool resources, distribution and exercise of rights to access, use and accountability is itself shaped by a negotiation process that involves the allocation of rights to manage, regulate, exclude, dispose and so forth, which make up public space governance (see also Foster 2011; Garnet 2012). In other words, the negotiation process through which these rights are defined, bundled up, unbundled and allocated defines public space governance, which in turn affects how the rights that characterise publicness are themselves allocated and exercised.

Using that analytical framework, the chapter turns to four cases in London in which local authorities and other public bodies have reallocated the governance rights that shape publicness to different stakeholders.

Devolved publicness and stakeholders' rights

A cursory look at the main public spaces in many areas of London will show a collection of public space governance regimes, replicated in various degrees elsewhere. This chapter focuses on those cases in which the transfer of governance rights away from the public sector has been more extensive, and the rights transferred more significant in their impacts on publicness. The chapter looks at four cases within walking distance of each other, in the South Bank area of London, across the Thames from the West End (Figure 5.1). This leaves aside the more obvious cases of privately

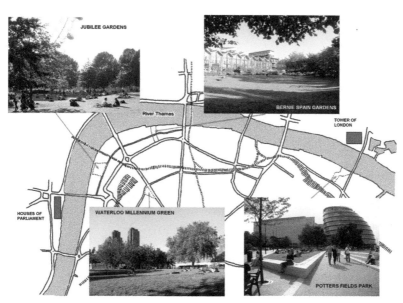

Figure 5.1 The four cases (author)

owned public spaces, where the rights associated with publicness were defined and allocated through the mechanism of planning obligations, and focuses attention on those that still belong to local governments but whose governance has been fully and successfully transferred to other social actors. They are particularly important as the former tend to represent new, additional public space (although not always), whereas the latter refer to existing and often long-standing public spaces.

The first case is Potters Fields Park, a one hectare park across the river from the Tower of London. It was leased to the Potters Fields Management Trust by Southwark Council in 2005 for a period of 30 years, renewable for another similar period. The Trust is a not-for-profit company constituted to redevelop the park and subsequently manage it. It is run by a Board of Directors made up of two representatives from the local authority, one from the Greater London Authority, one representative from each of the two neighbouring residents' associations, one from the adjoining More London business estate and one representative from the local BID. The lease gives the Trust full autonomy to manage the park, including the right to raise income through hiring parts of it for private events. As with other leases of this kind, it includes a Service Level Agreement with detailed specifications on cleaning, health and safety, maintenance, gardening and hiring the park for events.

Waterloo Millennium Green is a relatively small but centrally located park just south of Waterloo railway station. It was leased in 2014 by Lambeth Council to Bankside Open Spaces Trust (BOST), in an exceptionally long lease (999 years). The Trust, set up in 2000, is a charity specialist in horticulture, gardening and the management of urban open spaces in the South Bank area of London. It is governed by a board of 12 trustees and has connections with several residents' groups from public and private housing estates. The lease gives the Trust full responsibility for management and maintenance, which includes securing funding and empowering the local community to take on greater responsibility for the park.

The other cases involve land that belonged to the Greater London Council (GLC), the former London-wide government disbanded in 1986, and subsequently transferred to other public organisations before being leased out to the managing bodies described here. Jubilee Gardens is a highly visible park by the Thames, across the river from the government buildings in Whitehall and next to the famous London Eye. It was originally a patch of grass transferred to the Arts Council England and leased out to the Southbank Centre (a complex of theatres, concert halls and exhibition space), which gave a 135-year sublease to the Jubilee Garden Trust in 2012. The Trust is a charity set up in 2008 to take over the management of the park after its redevelopment. Its board has up to 16 trustees representing neighbouring landowners, local businesses, residents and up to four co-opted members (the local authority being one of them). It is chaired by the Chief Executive Officer of the South Bank Employers Group, a partnership of 17 of the major organisations in the South Bank area, created to promote it as a destination for leisure and business, and which now works as the executive arm of the South Bank Business Improvement District. The lease gives the Trust full responsibility for managing the park, including enforcement of rules and regulations, but significantly not the power to generate income from the park.

Nearby Bernie Spain Gardens is also located on land that previously belonged to the GLC. It is a small central park facing the busy Thames riverside walkway and bordering the Coin Street housing cooperative buildings. It was leased to the Coin Street Community Builders (CSCB) for 99 years, renewable for a similar period. CSCB is a social enterprise that owns the lease on the land and the cooperative housing around the park, controlled by a board elected by its members, all local residents. Its main activities are the development of cooperative housing and accompanying facilities in sites around the park. The lease gives CSCB full autonomy in the management of the park and adjacent Thames riverside walkway, including its initial redevelopment, its maintenance and revenue-raising rights.

All four sites are open to the wider public without significant barriers. All allow for a great variety of activities to happen in them, akin to a local authority-managed public space. There are differences, though. The extent of the governance rights residing with the management bodies, notably in the Jubilee and Bernie Spain gardens, makes them almost solely responsible for setting out regulations for access and use of the spaces, with codes of behaviour and restrictions on some activities (Figure 5.2). These restrictions might include activities such as cycling, using skateboards, ball games, large and/or political gatherings and rough sleeping, and they have their origin in concerns with legal liability, but they also express the needs and aspirations of the stakeholders those bodies represent. In Potters Fields and Waterloo Millennium Green, such regulations are the result of complex negotiations between

Figure 5.2   Jubilee Gardens use regulations (author)

the local authority freeholder and the trust and, although not dissimilar to the two previous cases, they tend to be closer to the by-laws applying to other surrounding public spaces. Nevertheless, in all four spaces the 'local community' (surrounding residents, landlords and businesses) have a greater impact on the way openness and accessibility are defined and regulated than any other stakeholder, and in that they differ, even if subtly, from local authority-managed public spaces.

Accountability rights refers to the right of stakeholders to have a voice in the governance of a public space. The four cases in this category have a trust board as their main locus of accountability, providing a direct and transparent forum for all those stakeholders represented in the management body, to voice and negotiate their aspirations. However, this does not apply to all socially relevant stakes. By their own constitution, all these cases privilege the interests of particular groups of stakeholders, who have formally received the right to oversee the management of 'their' public space on behalf of themselves and the public interest.

A first group of stakeholders, clearly recognised in almost all the arrangements, is that of local residents – that is, those living in the immediate vicinity of the public space, whose interests in it as users or property owners are recognised as those of the 'local community'. They are directly represented on the boards of three of the four charitable trusts (Potters Fields, Jubilee Gardens and Bernie Spain Gardens), albeit with different strengths. They also have seats on the steering group overseeing BOST, the managers for Waterloo Millennium Green. Locally based businesses and commercial property owners small and large are also part of the 'local community' where they are relevant: they have seats on the boards of the trusts in all cases except Bernie Spain Gardens, where surrounding business are tenants of the housing cooperative CSCB – and therefore indirectly represented by it.

Other legitimate stakeholders and the wider public have no direct access to those forums. Any accountability to them is less direct and largely depends on the mediating role of the local authority. Local authorities do have a seat on two trust boards (by rights in Potters Fields, and as a co-opted member in Jubilee Gardens). As freeholders, they have also set the scope and the limits for the trusts' power through the drafting of lease terms, as in Potters Fields and Waterloo Millennium Green, or through policy 'lock-in' with the involvement of the trusts in partnership agreements and policy initiatives, as in Jubilee Gardens and Bernie Spain Gardens. However, this indirect form of representation of interests contrasts with the direct accountability benefitting key stakeholders. Its effectiveness depends on the local authority's interpretation of the 'public interest' at any moment in time, on a match between that interpretation and the interests of any particular section of the public, on the local authority's negotiating ability, on the effectiveness of the lease terms and accompanying Service Level Agreements, and on the strength of sanctions for non-compliance with them.

To the vast majority of their users, those four spaces look and feel public and generally well managed. To a large degree, that is what they are, but the key attributes of publicness are determined and shaped largely by the particular interests and aspirations of those represented in the management trusts rather than a more inclusive 'public interest', however defined. As freeholders and lessors, local authorities or other public agencies still retain the basic rights to determine how open access shall be, which results in the general public retaining most access and use rights. However, full management rights, together with some exclusion and alienation rights (e.g. the right to lease out space for fee-charging events), now belong to surrounding residents, businesses, property owners, civic groups and other selected parts of the local community. They also own an important element of governance rights, namely the right to be heard in decisions about the space and have their aspirations and interests counted in a direct manner: it is to them that the trusts are directly accountable.

This suggests a public space governance model with a break-up of the bundle of governance rights between the local authority and what are effectively 'clubs' of local stakeholders. This particular form of governance arrangement explicitly privileges some stakeholders (i.e. surrounding residents, businesses and property owners, and civic groups with local focus) over others, and separates their needs and aspirations from other more diffuse, dispersed and less articulated but equally legitimate interests on the basis of their geography, strength of stake and mobilisation capacity. This allows for the empowerment of those with their stakes recognised in the governance arrangement; a better match between the aspirations of that 'club' of recognised stakeholders and the management of 'their' public space; and more direct and transparent accountability lines between management bodies and that community of stakeholders. However, it does so at the cost of formalising differences in rights and at the risk of disempowering other stakeholders who are not included in the governance arrangements. Whether or not that risk materialises depends on how well the governance arrangement balances the directly voiced aspirations of the 'club' and those of others, how conflicting they might be and how capable local authorities are of detecting and expressing the latter.

So far, those and similar forms of public space governance and management have worked well. All four parks are well managed and adequately meet the needs of their users while freeing their corresponding local authority from the burden of maintaining them. Conflicts between the interests of the trusts, their constituent members and other sections of the population have so far been minimal, or at any rate no more frequent than those occurring in local authority-managed public spaces. However, as the governance of more and more public spaces is transferred to groups of stakeholders with their own sets of interests, the chances of conflict increase, as does the prospect of a fragmentation of the public realm.

Conclusions

This chapter has looked at a few cases of emerging arrangements for the governance and management of public spaces in London to explore their potential implications for publicness. The first observation is that most of the debate so far about changes in public space governance in London and elsewhere has insisted on linking the off-loading of governance to third parties to an increase in corporate power and privatisation. This might hold true in some new public spaces resulting from large urban regeneration projects, especially in the so-called POPS. However, the exclusive focus on potential corporate control has ignored the subtler and finer-grained process of negotiation over the rights that make up publicness in existing public spaces and therefore fails to incorporate a more nuanced understanding of the relationship between different communities of stakeholders, elected government and society. As the four cases suggest, the disengagement of local government from public space management in London seems to be leading to a complex and varied process of reallocation of different rights over publicness attributes, creating a landscape of multiple 'publicnesses' catering to diverse groups of interests, rather than a narrow contraposition between public and private, or between individual and corporate.

The second observation is that the four spaces have remained essentially 'public' in the sense that most rights of access and use are enjoyed as they would be in a 'normal' public space and are experienced as such by most people. Municipal by-laws still regulate access and use in some of those spaces, and when they do not, the rules that apply are not very different from them. However, there is a fundamental difference, which might not be perceived and felt in the daily use of those spaces: this concerns who has the right to have a say in the governance and management of the space, that is, the right to make public space management bodies accountable. In all the cases these rights were transferred to something akin to a club of self-selected stakeholders, whose membership was defined by where they reside or work or the strength of the stake they or their business might have in the public space. This is particularly important as it is through that right that stakeholders can realise their aspirations for public spaces, including the way they look and feel, and ultimately what might or might not happen in them.

What would then be the implications if we consider the aggregate impact of these arrangements for London as a whole, or for any other large city following the same path? The disengagement of local government with public space governance and the transfer away of responsibilities to others provides answers to real demands upon public spaces, and therefore this trend is likely to continue. Local authorities can divert their shrinking budgets to other public services, financial and social capital from people with a stake in a particular space can be mobilised and invested, and business and residents can ultimately exert more control over their operating and living environment. The four cases examined in this paper suggest a city increasingly made up of constellations of public spaces with different governance systems, with fine-grained differences in publicness, playing different functions and catering for different sets of interests. This is a much more complex characterisation of the physical public realm than the dichotomy public/private often portrayed in the academic and professional debate.

The London cases so far have not presented the dilemmas associated with restrictions in public access reported in the American literature. However, as public space governance arrangements that secured inclusion in most of the 20th century evolve to become something different, new challenges emerge. Foremost among these is how to benefit from the resources and commitment of groups and individuals prepared to invest in a public space, and at the same time ensure the protection of all other legitimate interests in that space, including those of wider society. This applies to the arrangements discussed in this chapter, but also to POPS and other forms of private management. Key here is the ability and the political will to create judiciously designed ways to decide whose aspirations and interests should count when devolving the governance of public spaces. In a foreseeable future of continued economic uncertainty and further public expenditure cuts in which stakeholder involvement in urban governance is a necessity, local authorities should pay close attention to ensure that, in the ensuing reallocation of rights and power, the 'public interest' and various legitimate aspirations for public spaces are protected and do not become collateral damage.

Notes

1. It should be noted that POPS in places such as Toronto, Hong Kong or New York are more clearly defined in their location, characteristics, opening hours and so forth through a regulated exchange between developers and local government of public goods or development rights above normal zoning parameters. Their equivalents in London, where there are no zoning mechanisms, are the result of case-by-case negotiations, with variable requirements for provision and long-term management, depending on the objectives sought by developers and local authorities.
2. BIDs are legally defined associations of occupiers and/or owners of commercial property in a locality, with powers to decide on a compulsory surtax, ring-fenced to pay for additional services and improvements to that locality. In the US, Canada and indeed most countries, BIDs are mostly composed of and run by local commercial property owners, whereas in the UK they are predominantly made up of commercial property occupiers.

References

Audit Commission. 2002. *Street Scene*. London: Audit Commission.

Benn, Stanley I. and Gauss, Gerald F. (eds). 1983. *Public and Private in Social Life*. London: Croom Helm.

Blomley, Nicholas. 2014. 'Property, Law, and Space'. *Property Law Review* 3:229–35.

Boydell, Spike and Searle, Glen. 2014. 'Understanding Property Rights in the Contemporary Urban Commons'. *Urban Policy and Research* 32(3):323–40. https://doi.org/10.1080/08111146.2014.901909.

Carmona, Matthew. 2015. 'Re-theorising Contemporary Public Space: A New Narrative and a New Normative'. *Journal of Urbanism* 8(4):373–405. https://doi.org/10.1080/17549175.2014.909518.

Carmona, Matthew and Wunderlich, Fiona. 2012. *Capital Spaces: The Multiple Complex Public Spaces of a Global City*. London: Routledge.

Colding, Johan, Barthel, Stephan, Bendt, Pim, Snep, Robbert, van der Knaap, Wim and Ernstson, Henrik. 2013. 'Urban Green Commons: Insights on Urban Common Property Systems'. *Global Environmental Change* 23(5):1039–51. https://doi.org/10.1016/j.gloenvcha.2013.05.006.

De Magalhães, Claudio and Freire Trigo, Sonia. 2017a. 'Contracting Out Publicness: The Private Management of the Urban Public Realm and its Implications'. *Progress in Planning* 115:1–28. https://doi.org/10.1016/j.progress.2016.01.001.

De Magalhães, Claudio and Freire Trigo, Sonia. 2017b. '"Clubification" of Urban Public Spaces? The Withdrawal or the Redefinition of the Role of Local Government in the Management of Public Spaces'. *Journal of Urban Design* 22(6):738–56. https://doi.org/10.1080/13574809.2017.1336059.

Eizenberg, Efrat. 2012. 'Actually Existing Commons: Three Moments of Space of Community Gardens in New York City'. *Antipode* 44(3):764–82. https://doi.org/10.1111/j.1467-8330.2011.00892.x.

Ellin, Nan. 1996. *Postmodern Urbanism*. Oxford: Blackwell.

Foster, Sheila R. 2011. 'Collective Action and the Urban Commons'. *Notre Dame Law Review* 87(1):57–133.

Garnett, Nicole S. 2012. 'Managing the Urban Commons'. *University of Pennsylvania Law Review* 160(7):1995–2027.

Gursozlu, Fuat. 2015. 'Democracy and the Square: Recognizing the Democratic Value of the Recent Public Sphere Movements'. *Essays in Philosophy* 16(1):26–42. https://doi.org/10.7710/1526-0569.1519.

Hastings, Annette, Bailey, Nick, Gannon, Maria, Besemer, Kirsten and Bramley, Glen. 2015. 'Coping with the Cuts? The Management of the Worst Financial Settlement in Living Memory'. *Local Government Studies* 41(4):601–21. https://doi.org/10.1080/03003930.2015.1036987.

Hayden, Dolores. 2006. 'Building the American Way: Public Subsidy, Private Space'. In *The Politics of Public Space*, edited by Setha Low and Neil Smith, 35–48. New York: Routledge.

Kohn, Margaret. 2004. *Brave New Neighbourhoods: The Privatisation of Public Spaces*. London: Routledge.

Kohn, Margaret. 2013. 'Privatization and Protest: Occupy Wall Street, Occupy Toronto, and the Occupation of Public Space in a Democracy'. *Perspectives on Politics* 11(1):99–110. https://doi.org/10.1017/s1537592712003623.

Langstraat, Florian and van Melik, Rianne. 2013. 'Challenging the "End of Public Space": A Comparative Analysis of Publicness in British and Dutch Urban Spaces'. *Journal of Urban Design* 18(3):429–48. https://doi.org/10.1080/13574809.2013.800451.

Law, Lisa. 2002. 'Defying Disappearance: Cosmopolitan Public Spaces in Hong Kong'. *Urban Studies* 39(9):1625–45. https://doi.org/10.1080/00420980220151691.

Lee, Shin and Webster, Chris. 2006. 'Enclosure of the Urban Commons'. *GeoJournal* 66(1):27–42. https://doi.org/10.1007/s10708-006-9014-3.

London Assembly. 2011. *Public Life in Private Hands: Managing London's Public Space*. London: Greater London Authority.

Low, Setha and Smith, Neil (eds). 2006. *The Politics of Public Space*. London: Routledge.

Lowndes, Vivien and Pratchett, Lawrence. 2012. 'Local Governance under the Coalition Government: Austerity, Localism and the "Big Society"'. *Local Government Studies* 38(1):21–40. https://doi.org/10.1080/03003930.2011.642949.

Lubin, Judy. 2012. 'The Occupy Movement: Emerging Protest Forms and Contested Urban Spaces'. *Berkeley Planning Journal* 25(1):184–97. https://doi.org/10.5070/bp325111760.

Minton, Anna. 2006. *What Kind of World Are We Building? The Privatisation of Public Space*. London: Royal Institution of Chartered Surveyors.

Minton, Anna. 2009. *Ground Control: Fear and Happiness in the Twenty-first-century City*. London: Penguin.

Mitchell, Don and Staeheli, Lynn A. 2006. 'Clean and Safe? Property Redevelopment, Public Space and Homelessness in Downtown San Diego'. In *The Politics of Public Space*, edited by Setha Low and Neil Smith, 143–75. London: Routledge.

Németh, Jeremy. 2012. 'Controlling the Commons: How Public Is Public Space?' *Urban Affairs Review* 46(6):811–35. https://doi.org/10.1177/1078087412446445.

Németh, Jeremy and Schmidt, Stephan. 2011. 'The Privatization of Public Space: Modelling and Measuring Publicness'. *Environment and Planning B: Planning and Design* 38(1):5–23. https://doi.org/10.1068/b36057.

Ostrom, Elinor. 2003. 'How Types of Goods and Property Rights Jointly Affect Collective Action'. *Journal of Theoretical Politics* 15(3):239–70. https://doi.org/10.1177/0951692803015003002.

Peck, Jamie. 2012. 'Austerity Urbanism'. *City* 16(6):626–55.

Peel, Deborah, Lloyd, Greg and Lord, Alex. 2009. 'Business Improvement Districts and the Discourse of Contractualism'. *European Planning Studies* 17(3):401–22. https://doi.org/10.1080/09654310802618044.

Pestoff, Victor and Brandsen, Taco. 2010. 'Public Governance and the Third Sector: Opportunities for Co-production and Innovation?' In *The New Public Governance? Emerging Perspectives on the Theory and Practice of Public Governance*, edited by Stephen P. Osborne, 223–36. London: Routledge.

Raco, Mike. 2013. *State-led Privatisation and the Demise of the Democratic State*. Farnham: Ashgate.

Sorkin, Michael. 1992. *Variations on a Theme Park: The New American City and the End of Public Space*. New York: Macmillan.

Varna, Georgiana. 2014. *Measuring Public Space: The Star Model*. Farnham: Ashgate.

Vincent-Jones, Peter. 2000. 'Contractual Governance: Institutional and Organisational Analysis'. *Oxford Journal of Legal Studies* 20(3):317–35. https://doi.org/10.1093/ojls/20.3.317.

Ward, Kevin. 2006. '"Policies in Motion": Urban Management and State Restructuring: The Trans-local Expansion of Business Improvement Districts'. *International Journal of Urban and Regional Research* 30(1):54–75. https://doi.org/10.1111/j.1468-2427.2006.00643.x.

Webster, Chris. 2002. 'Property Rights and the Public Realm: Gates, Green Belts and Gemeinschaft'. *Environment and Planning B* 29(3):397–412. https://doi.org/10.1068/b2755r.

Whitfield, Dexter. 2012. *In Place of Austerity: Reconstructing the Economy, State and Public Services*. Nottingham: Spokesman.

6
London, its infrastructure and the logics of growth
Daniel Durrant

In fast-growing, global cities such as London and Toronto the social and physical infrastructural systems they depend upon are often stretched. As a combination of global and local drivers increase demand through rising population and inflows of capital, it is these systems that need to catch up and, in some cases, will constrain the abilities of cities to grow. As discussed by Theresa Enright, some of these systems, in particular those geared towards mobility, face outwards, connecting cities to patterns of global circulation of people and capital. Yet not all systems facilitate this sort of global engagement so directly. They also function at a more local and regional level, enabling cities, for example, to process the waste they produce, to relieve pressure on their housing markets through accessing land beyond their boundaries and to connect in other ways to regional and national economies.

In the same way, the politics of infrastructure is both global and local at the same time. Both London and Toronto share the experience of populist former mayors for whom infrastructure is part of their appeal to voters, be that cycle infrastructure (and its removal) for Rob Ford or the Garden Bridge for Boris Johnson. There are similarities in the political geographies that pit suburban against urban voters (Walks 2014). Yet there are also differences, with Johnson's use of the bicycle as his choice of urban transport functioning as a symbol of his approach to the city and Ford's preference for the SUV communicating a very different position. While the challenges of globalisation and accommodating growth are something infrastructural systems share, the geographies they serve and the regimes by which they are planned, delivered and governed can also be highly context specific. Mega-infrastructure projects in particular seem to generate their own politics yet they also spring from local political cultures. They are costly and disruptive, and voters have good reason to be sceptical of the claims made by the civic boosters that promote them (Flyvbjerg 2014). Nevertheless, the politics still often remain local, and the groups that are affected by and oppose megaprojects differ, as do the justifications that are made.

This chapter looks at one element of the justification used for two of London's recent megaprojects: the Thames Tideway Tunnel and High Speed Two (HS2).

This is unique to the UK, London and its history as an imperial capital, harking back to an era of Victorian prowess. The following sections establish the context in which this discourse sits. Firstly there is the city itself, its recent growth and the way London has promoted itself as a place where a distinctive 'megaproject ecology' has apparently resolved the difficulties global cities around the world face in meeting their infrastructural needs. In the case of London these needs and the infrastructural systems that seek to accommodate them are rarely fully contained within the city's boundaries, constantly spilling over both physically and politically. This is reflected in a description of the two projects themselves, their history and the opposition to them. While they are different in terms of their scale, form and function, the following section discusses their political framing as responses to 'our Victorian forebears'. The concluding discussion reflects upon the extent to which such responses can be seen as responding to common global challenges as opposed to being the products of very local context- and time-specific discourses.

London: Its infrastructure and 'megaproject ecology'

London's position in the first and second decades of the twenty-first century as a contender for the role of premier global city comes after a recent history of post-war, post-industrial decline. The political response to this, the way it has shaped the city with the globally connected Docklands development and the infrastructure that has enabled one form of global trade to replace another, is reflected in the narrative and politics of infrastructure. As a national capital, London, its economy and its infrastructure serve a symbolic and economic function which is often hard to disentangle from the country as a whole, despite significant regional disparities. Thus, the perception of a country seen as economically moribund and paralysed by political strife (between labour and capital) was reflected in the belief that the country struggled to deliver major infrastructure, a story also played out in the capital. There was a narrative of interminable public inquiries, such as those over the expansion of London's airports in the 1960s, and a series of 'planning disasters', which again often centred on London, its motorways and civic infrastructure (Hall 1980). As with the wider economy, the Thatcher government was seen as the turning point in the ability of the country to deliver projects, seen in both the infrastructure required to support what became a global hub in London's Docklands and a growing appetite for megaprojects. The anecdote of the then Prime Minister's fury at the unfavourable comparison between French and British rail infrastructure and the British inability to complete their high-speed rail connection on time made by French President François Mitterrand is often treated as a pivotal moment in which a political commitment to infrastructure delivery was forged (Faith 2007).

Following this, a team from the consultancy Arup appeared successful in breaking the deadlock of the Channel Tunnel Rail Link (CTRL, later rebadged as

HS1) where the former nationalised rail provider British Rail had failed. In connecting London to Paris via high-speed rail, Arup was able to design a route that minimised the demolition and threat to property values that had united urban and rural opposition to the initial British Rail proposals. The local politics that saw successful lobbying for stations in Kent to placate rural opposition and at Stratford in east London was fortunate, as it would be the same link to the optimistically named 'Stratford International' that was to become a key component of London's bid to host the 2012 Olympics. This enabled the then Mayor Ken Livingstone to connect the mega-event to the ongoing planned regeneration of the east of London, turbo charging the development of brownfield land with the Olympic Park at Stratford.

The significance of this for the way infrastructure was planned and delivered was that from a perceived inability of UK governance systems and constructors to manage large infrastructure, an alternative narrative of success emerged. Buoyed by the successes of CTRL and the 2012 Olympics, it was in many ways the zenith of what its advocates had begun to describe as 'London's megaproject ecology' (Davis 2017). London is a centre for not only global finance but also construction, engineering and architecture, with a dense network of consultancies. This network was boosted by the quasi-public Olympic delivery and legacy organisations, the growing role for Transport for London and recently bodies such as HS2Ltd and Bazalgette Engineering that are delivering the projects discussed in this chapter. This nexus of skills, knowledge and personnel aligned neatly with a city and wider political culture in which both parties were eager for infrastructure development.

In tandem with this turnaround, the system for planning major infrastructure has seen an overhaul in the form of the 2008 Planning Act. Driven by the perception that the previous public inquiry process was prohibitively slow, and by the use of key projects such as Terminal 5 at Heathrow (London's main airport) to create narratives of delay, the new system was heavily skewed towards rapid delivery of consent (Marshall and Cowell 2016). Furthermore, the wider institutional framework around infrastructure has also been reconfigured, most prominently in the establishment of a National Infrastructure Commission in 2015 by the former Conservative Chancellor of the Exchequer under the Coalition and Cameron governments, George Osborne. The Non-Departmental Public Body is charged with producing a National Infrastructure Assessment once in each parliament, setting out the needs of the UK and monitoring the government's performance. While tasked with offering impartial advice to government, the Commission is made up of key figures from industry, construction and finance. The Commission promotes what it defines as 'economic infrastructure', with the recent history of infrastructure provision described as an 'endless cycle of delays, prevarication and uncertainty' that has 'limited growth' (Armitt 2018, 3).

HS2 and the Thames Tunnel are not the only significant infrastructure projects underway. In recent years London's megaproject ecology has fostered a return to several, once rejected, transport projects. Crossrail, a new regional rail link, is currently under construction and will connect the West of London and Heathrow

Airport to both Canary Wharf in the Docklands and the north-east, beyond London's boundaries into Essex (Hebbert, 2014). The project was due in 2018 but at the time of writing (mid-2019), the final completion date is becoming increasingly uncertain. Plans to expand Heathrow Airport, scrapped by the incoming Coalition government of 2010, are currently back on the agenda, with a new National Policy Statement on airports (DfT 2018) setting out government support for expansion under the 2008 Act. There are other major investments in transport infrastructure, such as the extension of the Underground's Northern line opening up the Vauxhall Nine Elms Battersea Opportunity Area, home of the iconic Battersea Power Station (Ward et al. 2016) – yet another in a series of projects that appear to have come to fruition after what had been years of deliberation and false starts.

The politics of London's infrastructure is played out at different scales, and at the local level there are opponents of the specific impacts of projects. These, nevertheless, will often connect to wider national and global issues such as the costs to taxpayers or the environmental damage caused. The narrative of projects such as the expansion of Heathrow or HS1 in the past often reflected the desire for global connectivity discussed by Enright (see Chapter 4), yet there is always a distinct character to this. The former, for example, has been framed as an important signifier that via London's main airport the post-EU referendum UK is still 'open for business'. Yet there is also an important internal dimension to the national politics of London's infrastructure. The way in which the city constantly rubs up against its institutional boundaries has recently proved contentious in its transport connections to the wider South East of England where a significant proportion of its workforce actually live. The national (Conservative) government has been unwilling to allow Transport for London (controlled by Labour Mayor Sadiq Kahn) to govern the wider rail networks that connect to the city in what is seen as an unpalatable overreaching of mayoral authority into areas that are not represented (see O'Brien et al. 2018 for a detailed discussion). More generally the advocates of London are keen to stress that investment in the city's infrastructure is of benefit to the UK as a whole (London First 2015). Yet this view has never been without contestation, Cobbett's (1821) dismissal of the 'metropolis of empire' (as proclaimed by the civic boosters of the day) as the 'Great Wen'[1] being a notable example. More recently and specifically this can be seen in the annual, unfavourable, comparisons between per capita infrastructure spending in London and the less affluent regions of the UK (Raikes et al. 2018), a comparison that is particularly acute given that infrastructure spending in the capital held up well in contrast to the recent austerity inflicted disproportionately upon local governments.

HS2

HS2 is intended to provide a high-speed rail link connecting London, the Midlands and ultimately the North of England. It is currently planned to run from Euston Station in central London via an interchange on what has become a major brownfield redevelopment at Old Oak Common in the north-west of the city. From here the initial phase runs directly to Birmingham, passing through the Chiltern Hills Area of Outstanding Natural Beauty (AONB) in Buckinghamshire with a second phase planned to split, forming the 'Y', to connect to Leeds and Manchester. The overall costs of the project are hard to discern at the time of writing, as they have risen from an initial estimate of £32 billion to around £65 billion (Haylen 2019), with a review of the project ongoing, as discussed below. Phase 1 and part of phase 2 have been granted consent via a hybrid Bill, a parliamentary process distinct from the 2008 Planning Act, the same consenting regime used for Crossrail. It is being delivered by HS2Ltd, a company wholly owned by the Department for Transport (DfT), with the costs shouldered directly by central government. In contrast to previous UK megaprojects of this scale – the Channel Tunnel (Gourvish 2006) and CTRL (Faith 2007) – HS2 has had a relatively short gestation given its origins in the lobbying of a number of influential rail industry executives, Jim Steer of Steer Consulting in particular. Steer's initial suggestion that the UK should consider additional high-speed rail lines, indeed a whole network, came in the form of a report from the consultancy Atkins, commissioned in 2003. The report itself is a technical analysis framing the issue as one of increasing rail capacity on the overburdened lines into London and sets out a broadly similar network to the one proposed by the government in 2010 (Atkins 2003).

Initially conceived under the Labour government, the project was adopted largely unchanged by the incoming Coalition (2010–15). A significant figure within this transition was Lord (Andrew) Adonis, a vocal advocate of the project who as a Labour peer embodies the cross-party consensus on infrastructure, having recently served as Chair of the National Infrastructure Commission. Since 2010 the key political figures championing the project have always been Conservatives, with DfT led by a Conservative minister under the Coalition and with Conservative administrations from then on. Thus, the framing of the project, and to a certain extent its form and approach, have been via the lens of Conservative Party politics. As discussed, the basic form of the project has, thus far, changed little, and some of the approach, such as an aggressive strategy to acquire land and to secure rapid parliamentary consent, can be explained in part by the small 'p' politics of infrastructure. The early stages are crucial as the infrastructure delivery industry is well aware of the political risks of cancellation, which, it could be argued, explains the overly optimistic estimates of cost and delivery time. Some of this is also fed by the narrative of delay that has shaped the streamlining of infrastructure planning, indeed planning more generally, as a project that has spanned the party political divide. The specific Conservative dimension to the project can be seen in the removal of regional development objectives attached to the project under New Labour and its framing as a component in George Osborne's 'Northern Powerhouse' agenda. While the mostly Labour leaders of Birmingham and Manchester have always been vocal in their support, the extent to which the benefits of the project will flow from London rather than to it is highly contested, clouded in rhetoric and based on limited evidence (Tomaney and Marques 2013).

There has been a party political character to the opposition, with civil society groups in the Labour-controlled London Borough of Camden mounting a challenge to the widespread demolition of housing and businesses required by the expansion of Euston Station. Yet, in contrast, the Chilterns AONB is a Conservative heartland. Until recently opponents here have felt marginalised within a Conservative Party that has seen central figures supportive of the project. Yet the febrile politics of Brexit has seen Boris Johnson promise a review of HS2 as part of his appeal to the wider party. The Chilterns has also been the centre of some of the key civil society opposition, in particular HS2 Action Alliance, led by two former rail economists who have taken what they describe as an 'evidence-based approach' to criticisms of the technical and economic arguments for the project. There has also been organised opposition from local authorities through the 51M group led by Buckinghamshire County Council. National and regional media maintain ongoing scrutiny of the project, which saw peaks during the initial consenting phase, but as of early 2019 this seemed to be ramping up, with a number of documentaries pointing to rising costs and the impact on those households and businesses in the path of HS2 from both the BBC and independent broadcasters Channel 4. This could be considered a success for those opposed to the project given that one target of the campaigning organisations has been the economic case, a tactic that has proved effective in other struggles against transport megaprojects (see Griggs and Howarth 2013, 294, for a further discussion of the way opposition groups sought to undermine the economic arguments for airport expansion).

Thames Tideway Tunnel

On the face of it the Tideway Tunnel is, in contrast to HS2, located completely within London, conceived as an addition to the city's Victorian waste water system designed and built by the engineer Joseph Bazalgette. It is intended to enhance London's capacity to deal with rainwater which, flowing into the sewers from an increasingly impermeable urban environment, results in the discharge of raw sewage into the Thames. It is framed explicitly as a 'necessary extension to the legacy of the Victorians' (Halliday 2013 cited in Loftus and March 2017), as grafting new infrastructure onto the still functioning system in order to accommodate London's growing population (Stride 2019). However, where this framing of the project and particularly its solution is apparent is in the construction of excess capacity. The initial study conducted by the Thames Tideway Strategic Study Group (TTSSG), a multi-agency group established by the Department for the Environment, Farming and Rural Affairs (DEFRA) in 2005, set out the project's objectives as ensuring compliance with the EU Directive on Urban Waste Water, which the discharge of sewage into the Thames threatened to breach. Yet a 2017 report on the project by the UK's National Audit Office identifies an additional objective. Added in 2014 (considerably later than the initial reports setting out the need for the project), it is to ensure 'that a lack of strategic sewer capacity does not constrain London's growth over at least the next hundred years' (NAO 2017, 42). This commits the project to the construction of a larger system than is necessary with a view to future expansion of the city.

Unlike HS2, the Tideway Tunnel is private sector-led, delivered by a consortium of investors that provide construction finance with the ultimate client being a privatised utility, Thames Water. Yet on closer inspection, as is the case with many large infrastructure projects, many of these boundaries and distinctions become decidedly fuzzy. The Tideway itself (the tidal reaches of the Thames that will see a reduction in sewage discharge as a result of the tunnel) stretches out through the Thames Gateway in Kent and Essex into the North Sea. The £4.2 billion cost of the project is borne by Thames Water's customers, a catchment area that spreads into the surrounding counties as far west and north as Gloucestershire and Oxfordshire. Indeed, due to the way in which investors have been incentivised (Plimmer 2017) households are currently paying on average £13 per year for the project (NAO 2017) despite a completion date of 2027. Critical analysis of the project points towards a nostalgia for Victorian achievements, combined with a form of financialisation that appears to encourage the production of mega-infrastructure. Furthermore, it is argued that Thames Water's 'Neo Victorian hubris' cloaks a relative lack of ambition (Loftus and March 2017, 7). The solution is outdated and energy intensive, excluding the 'socio-ecological' integration reflected in the smaller-scale combination of environmental measures and the maximisation of the existing infrastructure.

In contrast to the often frenzied coverage of HS2, the Tideway Tunnel has seen less media scrutiny. However, the UK broadsheet the *Financial Times* has given considerable coverage to critical voices highlighting the role of Thames Water and its 'opaque' corporate structure (Allen and Pryke 2013), which includes holding companies in the Cayman Islands and sees it paying little in the way of corporation tax (Plimmer 2017). Opposition to the project has been more localised and technical, with residents' groups and London local authorities raising concerns about the impact of construction on their residents. The latter group formed the Thames Tunnel Commission in 2011, which called for a re-evaluation (Dolowitz et al. 2018, 84) in line with the green infrastructure options and called for further critical analysis from water industry experts and engineers. Of particular significance among this group is the opposition to the project from Professor Chris Binnie. As the original Chair of the 2005 TTSSG, he had originally recommended the tunnel solution to DEFRA, the government department with oversight of the privatised water companies, at its original estimated cost of £1.7 billion. Binnie now argues that in its current form it represents a costly and unnecessary solution to which alternative solutions in the form of Sustainable Urban Drainage and the greening of London's built environment (in order to attenuate flows of stormwater) are available (Binnie et al. 2014).

Unlike HS2, the broadcast media has been kinder to the Tideway Tunnel in the form of a recent hagiographic documentary from the BBC. This gave minimal coverage to any countervailing voices, seemingly beguiled by both the scale and momentum of the construction phase of the project. Recently, though, both HS2 and the Tideway Tunnel have seen opposition as part of a new wave of direct action. This has always been a feature of UK infrastructure politics, having been successful in opposing London's urban motorways in the 1960s, the large Conservative national road building programme in the 1990s and plans for the expansion of Heathrow Airport in the first decade of this century. Most recently, both projects have been the target of direct action from the environmental campaign Extinction Rebellion, with tunnel sites blocked in protest against the impact of lorry movements on local air quality and the carbon emissions of the vast amounts of concrete used in their construction. For HS2 there has been some localised protest in Camden, particularly around the destruction of a local park and cemetery, St James Gardens, and more recently the occupation of trees due to be felled at the Colne Valley nature reserve in the west London Borough of Hillingdon.

Matching up to 'our Victorian forebears'

The allure of megaprojects such as the Tideway Tunnel or HS2 not only captivates broadcasters; such projects also work their magic on decision-makers. At times the logics by which they are justified are as projections of national virility, with infrastructure such as Heathrow Airport, the Channel Tunnel and its rail link connecting the national capital to the outside world. Mega-events such as the Olympics showcase the city, its infrastructure and in this case its capacity for regeneration. Yet decision-makers must also justify projects both to themselves and to the publics who are affected and bear the costs. This justification is particularly important in those early stages where the political risks are high and the benefits of such massive investments are far from being realised. In order to explain the hold such projects have over their promoters, both in politics and within London's megaproject ecology, it is useful to look at one feature of the discourse through which such costly additions to the capital's infrastructure and outward connections are justified. This is a logic that connects the technocratic boosters from within the city's megaproject ecology to national politicians, fitting neatly with a specific narrative within contemporary Conservatism, and may go some way to explaining one framing of the current appetite for mega-infrastructure.

First, though, in order to understand the unique hold megaprojects have over the political imagination of 'growth coalitions' (Molotch 1976), it is necessary to explore the discourse, narrative and logics that underpin the mythic quality of these hegemonic projects. In Flyvbjerg's addition to Frick's (2008) application of the concept of the 'technological sublime' to explain the impact that the sense of awe generated by megaprojects has on both the physical form of infrastructures and the politics surrounding them, Flyvbjerg adds three – political, economic and technical – to the now four 'megaproject sublimes' (Flyvbjerg 2014). The language used to describe them is in itself revealing of the psychological content. There is the *enjoyment* political leaders derive from the 'ceremonious ribbon cutting', the *delight* of business and trade union leaders at profits and jobs and the *pleasure* generated by these iconic structures (Flyvbjerg 2014, 9, italics added).

In focusing upon the discourses through which such coalitions operate it is important to acknowledge that, as Glynos and Howarth (2007) point out, there is never a single logic that justifies political projects such as investment in the capital's infrastructure. Logics are plural and multidimensional. The technical dimension, however, cannot be simply ignored. There are perfectly valid reasons to increase the capacity of both the capital's waste water systems and the rail system that serves it, yet these have to be appraised against alternative solutions for attenuating and managing demand. The materiality of both systems means they generate their own timescales through the lifespans of the physical elements from which they are constructed (Anand 2015) – the 318 million bricks of Bazalgette's sewer system, the mortar that binds them together, the stations and tunnels of the rail network were all built in a different era and are ageing (albeit remarkably well). It is also true that both these infrastructural systems were either constructed, or saw major inflows of investment, at a time when London was the capital not merely of the United Kingdom but of a dominant, expansionist global empire, with all the resources that entailed. From that early investment these systems have been subject to the ravages of time, although in the case of the transport system, relatively recent analysis concluded that it is still fit for the needs of modern Britain, or at least the way its economy was envisaged as of 2006, cautioning against the 'pursuit of icons' (Eddington 2006).

Cycles of investment in the built environment, the way problems are conceived and options are explored (or rejected) have been shown to be intrinsically shaped by discursive constructions (Weber 2016; Griggs and Howarth 2013). Such constructions do not only shape or frame the reality of the way the problems of London, its growth and infrastructure are defined, they also establish hegemony and permitted solutions. Within these discourses, multiple elements (words, things, humans and non-humans) are assembled and crucially reconfigured, given their contingency. Thus, one key element of the discourse in this case, Victorian infrastructure and prowess, and the Victorian era more generally, can be seen to be deployed in different ways by different discourse coalitions. The contingency of the way a concept such as the Victorian era operates within the structure of the discourse that frames each project is revealed in the different ways it appears and is used in both cases. With the Tideway Tunnel, though it can be seen to be used in a rhetorical sense by Boris Johnson (cited in Loftus and March 2017, 7), generally it is very much front and centre embodied by one person. Joseph Bazalgette was the renowned Victorian who, as Chief Engineer of the Metropolitan Board of Works from 1856 to 1889, oversaw the construction of London's original system of interceptor sewers. The present-day organisation delivering the 25 kilometre sewer has named various entities within the structure of holding and financing companies after Bazalgette. Bazalgette's original system of sewers was commissioned by the government of the day following the 'Great Stink' of 1858, when Parliament was unable to sit due to the stench of raw sewage discharged into the Thames by London's chaotic waste water system. As an episode in London's infrastructural history it is often depicted as a tale of political leaders finally compelled to finance new infrastructure after being forced to confront the consequences of their own inaction (Stride 2019).

In the case of HS2, the Victorian era is deployed in what are portrayed as technical arguments, as in the case of the Tideway Tunnel; however, there is also a more overtly political use. The establishment of the Victorian era as both a problem and a benchmark against which modern Britain ought to be measured has been heavily, but not exclusively, associated with politicians of the liberal right and the Conservatives. Early policy documents, in which the DfT began to release the proposals for the project, problematise the 'acute connectivity limitations of the Victorian rail network'. The same documents apply a strong temporal framing to the 'once in a generation opportunity' to meet this 'twenty-first century transport challenge' (DfT 2010). This is a framing of the project that survives the change of government, with the language becoming more strident under the Coalition. In the first public consultation on the route, then (Conservative) Secretary of State for Transport Philip Hammond describes the current network as a 'tribute to our Victorian forebears' but also states: 'Our current railway system dates back to the Victorian era and will not be sufficient to keep Britain competitive in the twenty-first century' (DfT 2011, 7), here further problematising the Victorian network, not only in terms of its capacity but also in terms of national competitiveness. HS2 is presented as a national project rather than one centred on London. It is an essential feature of the UK's 'Twenty First Century economy', with Hammond evoking the 'horrific fantasy' (Griggs and Howarth 2013, 415) of the country being 'left behind'. The fantasy in this case serves a similar function to the way competitiveness and fear of the consequences of a reluctance to invest in infrastructure have been deployed in the discourse around aviation and the expansion of the capital's airport capacity, albeit by the 1997–2010 Labour administration (Griggs and Howarth 2013).

Where this combination of global competitiveness, infrastructure investment and the way the Victorian legacy is deployed in the case of HS2 has a unique character is in the intersection with the notion of a 'global race' that was a broader feature of the political milieu during the Coalition administration. While adopted by figures such as David Cameron in reference to HS2, its clearest exposition came in a polemic authored by a group of young MPs from the wing of the Conservative party that under Boris Johnson triumphed in the internecine struggles over Brexit. *Britannia Unchained* sets a narrative of national economic decline in the context of a retreat from Britain's 'Victorian Liberal principles' (Kwarteng et al. 2012, 8). The solution is given as an investment in skills development, but crucially this is cou-pled with a combination of massive deregulation and infrastructure investment. This group and the ideas they expound form one of the overlapping and com-peting views of the direction the country ought to take on leaving the European Union. The significance of this vision for London can be seen in the current popular description of this option as *Singapore on Thames* (Wolf 2019), placing the capital and its further deregulated financial sector at its centre.

Conclusion: The logics of growth

In the attempts to construct hegemonic narratives in support of both the Tideway Tunnel and HS2 it is possible to see the 'radical contingency' of the Victorian era, Victorian engineering and Victorian engineers. As objects within the discourse, they are deployed by different actors and in different ways yet always to buttress a narrative in which investment in costly mega-infrastructure is the only possible response to the pressures facing London. They cut across the city's megaproject ecology, dovetailing neatly with the narratives political leaders construct for them-selves. These are narratives that are startlingly devoid of reflection on the iniqui-ties of an imperial project that had established London as the premier global city of a previous era. Were these narratives simply confined to the realm of politics, then perhaps they would be little more than background noise to the functioning of London and the infrastructure that connects the city to both its immediate sur-roundings and the wider world. Yet as hegemonic projects the risk is that they do more than this. At a time when the claims of the boosters of London's megaproject ecology are looking hollow, with uncertainty over the time taken and the cost of Crossrail and the delivery of HS2, coupled with growing concerns about the envi-ronmental costs, they actively exclude and silence the countervailing voices. These are voices advancing solutions to contemporary challenges that are not dependent upon damage to the ecology of London, its hinterlands and urban environment, and that are not predicated upon global circulation or financialised infrastructures directing revenues offshore.

Such tensions between global drivers of growth and the pressure they place upon infrastructural systems are not unique to London or Toronto, nor are trends in politics, such as the rise of right-wing populism which has touched both cities. Yet crucially they have touched both cities in different ways and at different times and via different individuals. Thus, while the logics that appear to determine the growth of such global cities must have a global dimension, the narratives through which they are articulated, that frame urban problems and justify certain (mega) infra-structural solutions over others, are also highly contextual. They are constructed and maintained by key figures within urban growth coalitions and so reflect their psychology, their view of themselves, the world and the extent to which they do, or do not, match up to their mythic forebears.

Note

1. Wen meaning boil or pustule.

References

Allen, John and Pryke, Michael. 2013. 'Financialising Household Water: Thames Water, MEIF, and "Ring-fenced" Politics'. *Cambridge Journal of Regions, Economy and Society* 6(3):419–39. http://doi.org/10.1093/cjres/rst010.

Anand, Nikhil. 2015. 'Accretion'. *Fieldsights, Theorizing the Contemporary*. Accessed 22 July 2020. https://culanth.org/fieldsights/accretion.

Armitt, John. 2019. 'Sir John Armitt's Foreword to the 2019 National Infrastructure Assessment'. Accessed 13 August 2020. https://www.nic.org.uk/wp-content/uploads/CCS001_CCS0618917350-001_NIC-NIA_Accessible.pdf#page=8.

Atkins. 2003. *High Speed Line Study: Summary Report*. Accessed 22 July 2020. https://webarchive.national-archives.gov.uk/+/http:/www.dft.gov.uk/pgr/rail/researchtech/research/hspeedlinestudysummaryreport.pdf.

Binnie, Chris, Byatt, Ian, Lord Berkeley and Blaiklock, Martin. 2014. *Thames Tideway Tunnel Alternatives to the Tunnel: A Strategic Plan*. Accessed 12 September 2019. http://bluegreenuk.com/references/industry/xt140402 TTT Strategic Plan v9 april 2%5B1%5D.pdf.

Cobbett, William. 1821. *Rural Rides*. T. Nelson & Sons. Accessed 10 September 2019. http://www.gutenberg.org/files/34238/34238-h/34238-h.htm.

Davis, Andrew. 2017. *Projects: A Very Short Introduction*. Oxford: Oxford University Press.

DfT (Department for Transport). 2010. *High Speed Rail*. Accessed 13 September 2019. https://assets.publishing.service.gov.uk/government/uploads/system/uploads/attachment_data/file/228887/7827.pdf.

DfT (Department for Transport). 2011. *Rail: Investing in Britain's Future Consultation*. Accessed 13 September 2019. https://www.gov.uk/government/consultations/high-speed-rail-investing-in-britains-future-consultation.

DfT (Department for Transport). 2018. *Airports National Policy Statement: New Runway Capacity and Infrastructure at Airports in the South East of England, National Policy Statement*. Accessed 10 September 2019. https://assets.publishing.service.gov.uk/government/uploads/system/uploads/attachment_data/file/714106/airports-nps-new-runway-capacity-and-infrastructure-at-airports-in-the-south-east-of-england-web-version.pdf.

Dolowitz, David Peter, Bell, Sarah and Keeley, Melissa. 2018. 'Retrofitting Urban Drainage Infrastructure: Green or Grey?' *Urban Water Journal* 15(1):83–91. http://doi.org/10.1080/1573062X.2017.1396352.

Eddington, Rod. 2006. *The Eddington Transport Study, the Case for Action: Sir Rod Eddington's Advice to Government*. London: HM Treasury. Accessed 13 August 2020. https://webarchive.nationalarchives.gov.uk/20081230093524/http://www.dft.gov.uk/about/strategy/transportstrategy/eddingtonstudy.

Faith, Nicholas. 2007. *The Right Line: The Politics, Planning and Against-the-odds Gamble Behind Britain's First High-speed Railway*. London: Segrave Foulkes.

Flyvbjerg, Bent. 2014. 'What You Should Know about Megaprojects and Why: An Overview'. *Project Management Journal* 45(2):6–19. http://doi.org/10.1002/pmj.21409.

Frick, Karen. 2008. 'The Cost of the Technological Sublime: Daring Ingenuity and the New San Francisco–Oakland Bay Bridge'. In *Decision-Making on Mega-Projects: Cost-Benefit Analysis, Planning and Innovation*, edited by Hugo Priemus, Bent Flyvbjerg and Bert van Wee, 239–63. Cheltenham: Edward Elgar.

Glynos, Jason and Howarth, David. 2007. *Logics of Critical Explanation in Social and Political Theory* (1st edition). Abingdon and New York: Routledge.

Gourvish, Terry. 2006. *The Official History of Britain and the Channel Tunnel*. Abingdon and New York: Routledge.

Griggs, Steven and Howarth, David. 2013. *The Politics of Airport Expansion in the United Kingdom*. Manchester: Manchester University Press.

Hall, Peter. 1980. *Great Planning Disasters*. Berkeley: University of California Press. Accessed 22 July 2020. http://www.jstor.org/stable/10.1525/j.ctt1ppx64.

Haylen, Andrew. 2019. *High Speed 2: The Business Case, Costs and Spending Briefing Paper CBP-8601*. Accessed 22 July 2020. https://researchbriefings.parliament.uk/ResearchBriefing/Summary/CBP-8601#fullreport.

Hebbert, Michael. 2014. 'Crossrail: The Slow Route to London's Regional Express Railway'. *Town Planning Review* 85(2):171–90. https://doi.org/10.3828/tpr.2014.11.

Kwarteng, Kwasi, Patel, Priti, Raab, Dominic, Skidmore, Chris and Truss, Liz. 2012. *Britannia Unchained: Global Lessons for Growth and Prosperity*. Basingstoke: Palgrave Macmillan.

Loftus, Alex and March, Hug. 2017. 'Integrating What and for Whom? Financialisation and the Thames Tideway Tunnel'. *Urban Studies* 56(11):2280–96. https://doi.org/10.1177/0042098017736713.

London First. 2015. *London's Infrastructure: Investing For Growth.* Accessed 10 September 2019. https://www.londonfirst.co.uk/sites/default/files/documents/2018-05/Londons_Infrastructure_Investing_for_Growth.pdf.

Marshall, Tim and Cowell, Richard. 2016. 'Infrastructure, Planning and the Command of Time'. *Environment and Planning C: Government and Policy* 34(8):1843–66. https://doi.org/10.1177/0263774X16642768.

Molotch, Harvey. 1976. 'The City as a Growth Machine: Toward a Political Economy of Place'. *American Journal of Sociology* 82(2):309–32. https://doi.org/10.1086/226311.

NAO (National Audit Office). 2017. *Review of the Thames Tideway Tunnel.* London. Accessed 11 September 2019. https://www.nao.org.uk/wp-content/uploads/2017/03/Review-of-the-Thames-Tideway-Tunnel.pdf.

O'Brien, Peter, Pike, Andy and Tomaney, John. 2018. 'Governing the "Ungovernable"? Financialisation and the Governance of Transport Infrastructure in the London "Global City-region"'. *Progress in Planning* 132: article 100422. https://doi.org/10.1016/j.progress.2018.02.001.

Plimmer, Gill. 2017. 'London Super Sewer Causes Stink over Opaque Funding Structure'. *Financial Times,* 7 August. Accessed 11 September 2019. https://www.ft.com/content/bb99abb4-7203-11e7-aca6-c6bd07df1a3c.

Raikes, Luke, Millward, Leah and Longlands, Sarah. 2018. *State of the North 2018: Reprioritising the Northern Powerhouse.* Institute for Public Policy Research. Accessed 10 September 2019. https://www.ippr.org/files/2018-12/sotn-2018-web.pdf.

Stride, Phil. 2019. *The Thames Tideway Tunnel: Preventing Another Great Stink.* Stroud: History Press.

Tomaney, John and Marques, Pedro. 2013. 'Evidence, Policy, and the Politics of Regional Development: The Case of High-speed Rail in the United Kingdom'. *Environment and Planning C: Government and Policy* 31:414–27. https://doi.org/10.1068/c11249r.

Walks, Alan. 2014. 'Stopping the "War on the Car": Neoliberalism, Fordism, and the Politics of Automobility in Toronto'. *Mobilities* 10(3):402–22. https://doi.org/10.1080/17450101.2014.880563.

Ward, Eric John, Dimitrou, Harry, Wright, Phil and Dean, Marco. 2016. 'Application of Policy-led Multi-criteria Analysis to the Appraisal of the Northern Line Extension, London'. *Research in Transportation Economics* 58:46–80. https://doi.org/10.1016/j.retrec.2016.08.004.

Weber, Rachel. 2016. 'Performing Property Cycles'. *Journal of Cultural Economy* 9(6):587–603. https://doi.org/10.1080/17530350.2016.1212085.

Wolf, Martin. 2019. 'The Brexit Delusion of Creating "Singapore upon Thames"'. *Financial Times,* 7 February. Accessed 13 September 2019. https://www.ft.com/content/a70274ea-2ab9-11e9-88a4-c32129756dd8.

7
Governing urbanisation in the global city: A commentary

Alan Walks and Mike Raco

Even before the COVID-19 pandemic erupted, global cities such as London and Toronto – and their extended metropolitan regions – were (as Brail and Vinodrai in Chapter 2 highlight) at a crossroads. Dealing simultaneously with changes occurring in the global economy in which they are keenly and uniquely embedded, as well as the ever deepening national and regional politics of neoliberalism and austerity, these urban regions find themselves faced with a set of options for identifying and navigating pathways forward, one that the potential for pandemics has made even more urgent.

However, not only are these metropolitan areas at the cutting edges of changes occurring with the larger global political economy, but because of their privileged position and influence the policies and modes of governance they adopt to deal with emergent issues become models for how other cities located elsewhere respond. It thus becomes imperative to understand how governance in these cities has been evolving in response to the local and global pressures tied to their status. Their experiences can also be used to challenge broader narratives of 'urban ungovernability' that are resurfacing internationally on the (neoliberal) political right. As Le Gales and Vitale (2013) argue, the 2000s have seen the re-emergence of Douglas Yates's (1977) ideas on the supposed inability of state actors to manage cities and populations or to 'buck' markets through the regulation of capital. Such narratives have been used to legitimate broader pro-market deregulation and privatisation programmes. The chapters here, conversely, show that policy-making and political decisions still matter enormously and have a direct impact on urban built environments and communities.

There are some clear similarities, but also differences, in the challenges faced by London and Toronto. Both are the largest and most dynamic metropolitan regions in their respective nations, the pre-eminent global cities for the UK and Canada. Both London and Toronto concentrate substantial financial sectors of global reach and importance, and their embeddedness within global financial networks is one of the key things that makes their economies unique. In many ways, the economies of both metropolitan regions live off the hard work done in other places. This is not least because so much of their financial profits derive from lending to people and firms located elsewhere, but also because the terms of trade are stacked in favour of the most developed nations, and because of the 'wall' of money being invested in financial products since the bursting of the dot-com bubble in the early 1990s (Aalbers 2016).

The timing and evolution of their respective financial industries differs, though. Previously the centre of a global ('British') empire with some of the world's largest and most global banks, London's economy has, since the end of the Bretton Woods fixed-rate monetary exchange system, become the global centre for foreign currency exchange. Upon this, it has built sizeable expertise in over-the-counter derivatives, especially foreign exchange swaps. In part, London's rise is a result of its status as a location for global arbitrage – one can make trades in the UK using US dollars that one cannot do (because of US federal regulations) in New York or other US cities (Gowan 2009). Toronto's more recent rise, meanwhile, has been built on its foundation as a national financial centre with a highly regulated oligopolistic banking structure, with its strong banks increasingly expanding into the US economy and selected other nations in the face of their crisis-derived weaknesses. Whereas London has been a top-tier global financial centre for much of the post-war period, Toronto has been moving up the hierarchy in rapid fashion since the 1990s (see also Chapter 2 by Brail and Vinodrai).

London and Toronto are also the largest recipients of immigrants, and because of this the most diverse metropolitan areas, in their respective nations. While Toronto scores a lot higher than London on this (with roughly half of Toronto's population foreign born, and since 2016 more than half of the metropolitan population identifying as a visible minority, making Toronto a 'minority-majority' urban region), both metropolitan areas rank far above their national urban counterparts on these variables. This sets both Toronto and London apart from their respective nations socially, culturally and politically. The contrast between how voters in London and other places in England voted in the Brexit referendum is but one example – and outcome – of this discrepancy. In both cities, local populations are far more used to living and working alongside people who are different from themselves, and in turn have become far more tolerant and cosmopolitan than residents in other cities. Residents of both the London and Toronto regions see themselves differently from the rest of the country and are often visibly different. Residents of other places often resent those who live in Toronto and London, and their politicians, not least because they tend to be wealthier because of the booming financial sector. This creates similar political dynamics, albeit situated within national political contexts that differ due to very different national historical trajectories.

And of course, many of the local social and infrastructural dynamics are also similar. By concentrating workers in one of the most remunerative economic sectors (finance), and with the largest flows of immigrants and refugees, global cities exhibit greater income inequality and racialised inequality than most other cities. It is mainly in the global cities that the wealthiest people are found, often in gentrifying neighbourhoods close to downtown, displacing poorer households. Rising rents, land values, deconversion of tenanted homes into owner-occupation leading to a lack of rental housing, and homelessness are, unsurprisingly, outcomes of this, especially in the context of deregulation of housing, finance and labour markets (let alone the lack of sufficient new rental housing). London and Toronto are among the poster-children of urban social polarisation, despite the fact that their labour markets remain stronger than those of many other cities and wages are generally higher.

These factors present notable challenges for urban governance in both places. As the chapters in Part I make plain, national (and sub-national, i.e. Province of Ontario in the Canadian context) governments look to both cities as key to their sustained global economic competitiveness and advantage. Both London and Toronto are expected to disproportionately produce jobs, economic growth and tax revenues for their respective national populations and to incubate the technology-based firms said to be the key to future prosperity. At the same time, however, governance at the national, sub-national and local (urban) scale all have to navigate the resentments and jealousies of those living in different places, especially given that sustained competitiveness requires significant public spending on urban infrastructure in these global cities, but from an equity perspective it doesn't appear to many other people fair to spend more money in the wealthier cities. It is in this context that a politics of automobility and transit (in whose interests are state infrastructure investments?), of immigration (e.g. Brexit in the UK), connectivity (transport infrastructure to other nations, airports, etc.) and planning (should foreign investors and residents be welcomed or controlled, especially given the vulnerabilities of globally connected cities to pandemics? How to get more rental housing built in the absence of funding from upper levels of the state?) have evolved.

National and sub-national levels of the state, for decades, have been adopting various neoliberal reforms and have pushed city municipal governments to do the same (for Toronto, see Boudreau et al. 2009). State-owned firms and infrastructure (British Rail in 1993, Ontario's Highway 407 in 1999, etc.) were privatised, and public–private partnerships were promoted for building everything from roads and rail infrastructure to hospitals. Meanwhile, a host of public services including education, public health, libraries and job training were either cut or reformed with an eye to using private agencies (see also Joe Penny's chapter in Part III of this book). Yet it is also important to note that both cities also have a long history of public–private sector interactions that continue to shape current practices and urban politics. In the London case, even during the perceived high-water mark of strong, modernist planning during the 1960s, developers and private actors were notorious for exploiting loopholes in regulations and were able to bypass the city's core planning restrictions and social policy regulations. Indeed, Jenkins (2019) argues that the city's planning system has always played catch-up with the private sector and historically has been unable to meaningfully regulate the city's development. Similar arguments have been made about London's core transport infrastructure, much of which was originally built by private entrepreneurs in the Victorian period and sought out routes of greatest profitability, rather than those that might address public needs and strategic concerns (Wolmar 2008). The importance of such legacies are exemplified in the chapters on both cities, including those by Durrant and Enright, that shed light on the culturally mediated assumptions of what qualifies as legitimate and illegitimate forms of state intervention.

Housing systems have been particularly affected by neoliberalism. Not only were most social/public housing plans shelved and responsibilities downloaded to local municipalities, but state policies promoted private innovations in mortgage finance that encouraged lenders to push new kinds of mortgage loans for homeownership (see Walks 2014 for the Canadian story). Social/public housing units were sold to private owners under Thatcher's right-to-buy scheme through the 1980s and 1990s, and in Toronto under the Ford administration's sales of 'scattered-site housing' (Walks 2012). As a number of chapters in Part II of this book note, this has led to a significant loss of rental housing units which has been particularly acute in London and Toronto. Both London and Toronto are also political capitals and major seats of power (London is the national capital; Toronto is the capital of Canada's largest province, Ontario). Because of this, they are highly visible to their respective states, and these cities are often first to bow to the force of the state governments who host them – and often make them into an example. For instance, the Greater London Council was disbanded by the Thatcher government in 1986 to thwart the local power of then Mayor Ken Livingstone; Toronto was the first city to be amalgamated by the Conservative Ontario provincial government in 1998, in part to force new market-based taxation systems on the city and to thwart the power of local left-leaning councillors (see Boudreau 2000; Keil 2000; Sancton 2000).

All these challenges are felt keenly in the realm of city building. How the processes of urbanisation are governed in each metropolitan region develops in response to both imperatives emanating from the global scale, as well as national, sub-national and local politics around who will and should benefit. This is most obvious in the case of infrastructure. As the chapters by Durrant and Enright demonstrate, transport infrastructure is highly fraught, especially that which connects the world to the city via links to key international airports. Global cities require global connections, but to negotiate local politics, and to sustain local working-class labour, they also involve a highly localised politics around where the lines and stops will be. The case studies suggest it is well-heeled elite areas that typically fight against proposals to locate this infrastructure nearby on the grounds of negative externalities (see Durrant's chapter for discussion of Camden's local opposition to the HS2 line to Heathrow Airport in London), whereas working-class neighbourhoods, where locals need access to jobs, ask to have stops built nearby in the light of their positive externalities (see Enright's chapter for Weston's local insistence on having a stop on Toronto's Union Pearson Express airport line). Given that many residents, even within the cores of these regions but especially in the various suburbs, do not have access to adequate transit nor could hope to afford to live in the transit-rich neighbourhoods of the inner city, it is not surprising that such infrastructure is contested on equity grounds and highly politicised. To connect to the world, some will be granted privileged access to transit, while others will be compelled to drive in a hopelessly congested and frustrating city. Who should get that access? For whom is this infrastructure built? These questions lie at the intersection of the global and local pressures compelling the focus on local infrastructure. It also helps explain why transport would be more politicised than, say, sewage treatment (see Durrant's chapter). The latter is expanded to deal with what might be called 'residuals' of past urbanisation, while the former strongly shapes the way future urbanisation will impact local residents.

The tensions between the need to foster global connections and competitiveness on the one hand, and to address the very real social and political problems that are disproportionately felt in global cities on the other hand, have been significantly heightened by the push towards neoliberalism on behalf of national and sub-national governments. City planning processes in each metropolitan region have had to negotiate these tensions, and in doing so have attempted to walk a fine line between a state-led promotion of the public interest and a deregulated pro-market neoliberal promotion of private sector investment. As the chapters by Raco and Livingstone, Moreira de Souza, Brail and Vinodrai, and De Magalhães demonstrate, there have arisen what Raco and Livingstone call 'radical ambiguities' affecting how planning is practised. Both the London Plan and the London Housing Strategy privileged the roles of private sector investors and developers, and explicitly sought to enrol them as key agents in meeting urban growth targets, thus fulfilling the demands of the neoliberal state to promote markets. However, in doing so, these processes encouraged investors to buy up much-needed housing for their own use and to prioritise developments that had less benefit for local residents, forcing planning and public policy to innovate in new ways to regulate and compel development in the public interest when it becomes clear that local populations are not benefitting. A specific arena of such regulation involves the licensing of private rental housing providers and rent controls which, as Moreira de Souza notes, has evolved into a fragmented multi-jurisdictional scheme, which not only limits the application of knowledge and universal rights, but facilitates arbitrage on behalf of investors. In Toronto, meanwhile, as Brail and Vinodrai note, the amalgamation of the six central municipalities into one large City of Toronto in 1998, undertaken by the neoliberal Mike Harris provincial government, left a similarly fragmented 'ghost' regime of licensing and regulation for specific sectors, including the licensing of rooming houses, which are still illegal in several areas of Toronto (see also Campsie 2018).

Such radical ambiguities are also borne out in De Magalhães' study of quasi-privatisation of public parks in London, where private trusts are given extended contracts to manage parks (thus freeing municipal budgets from some of the expense), but in the joint interests of both the trust and the public (partly regulated by the municipality). This puts formerly public space in the hands of self-interested 'club realms', and although the parks still *feel* public, they create a fragmented regulatory and governance structure that creates differential rights and limits how much say the actual public might have in how they are maintained and used. In the Toronto region, such differential rights are rooted in the different approaches among municipal councils, some of whom – like the City of Toronto – have tended to prioritise public accountability while others – especially some of the 905 suburban municipalities – prefer a form of urban managerialism that puts decision-making in the hands of hired managers, trusts or other quasi-public forms of governance (Cowen 2005). De Magalhães argues that, extended to the logic of urban governance more broadly, such neoliberal forms of public space management 'suggest a city increasingly made up of constellations of public spaces with different governance systems, with fine-grained differences in publicness, playing different functions and catering for different sets of interests' (see Chapter 5). Such is one of the legacies of neoliberal governance in the global city that has been asked to perform multiple functions for multiple publics.

The development of differential forms of rights for different users, citizens, residents, firms and other kinds of 'stakeholders' in global cities such as London and Toronto means that rights are not held in consistent and universal fashion. Indeed, the critique of planning inherent in Raco and Livingstone's chapter questions whether planning itself can be expected to remain a process by which universal and consistent rules are applied in the public interest. Instead, there arises an incentive for actors to engage in jurisdictional arbitrage and to seek approval to skirt existing regulations in the name of local distinctiveness, process efficiency and/or the promotion of entrepreneurialism. Because growth pressures have been felt most acutely in global cities such as London and Toronto in the post-industrial era – what Allen Scott (2011) calls the process of 'third wave urbanization' – it is in urban regions such as London and Toronto that both the innovations in governance, and the outcomes of the multiple pressures and tensions bearing on policy-making, have been first articulated. The fragmented and ambiguous ways that urban development has been governed in the recent period, however, call into question whether they could be conceived as a model for how other cities might respond to the slightly different mix of factors impacting on planning and governance there.

The chapters in Part I also highlight a growing mismatch between the scale of challenges being faced by urban agencies and their resources and capabilities to introduce effective forms of regulation. The 2010s have witnessed the growth, for instance, of new digital technologies and big data forms of private sector-led accumulation and organisation (Zuboff 2019). Attempts to regulate firms such as Uber and Airbnb have created new challenges for authorities in both cities, with policy-makers once again caught in an ambiguous position of seeking to promote cutting-edge technologies and private sector dynamism, while also ensuring that existing residents and firms are protected from the worst effects of (relatively) unregulated activities. As noted by Hawes and Grisdale in Chapter 11 of this book, Fields's (2019) recent work on the growing power of 'automated landlords' in shaping urban rental markets, and Wachsmuth and Weisler's (2018) powerful critique of Airbnb, underscore some of the direct challenges that new forms of data-led capitalism are having on the ability to govern urban environments and manage tensions among urban social groups, even before the COVID-19 pandemic layered new logics and tensions over this landscape. As authors such as Yeung (2017) have argued, the capacity of territorially organised urban administrations to manage and shape these new forms of enterprise has thus far been lacking. State capacities in cities such as London and Toronto are hollowed out by neoliberal reforms and these cities are increasingly governed by complex constellations of public, private and civil society actors, creating political vulnerabilities but also opportunities. The chapters here highlight some of the emerging tensions that authorities are facing in global cities and their responses to new challenges.

References

Aalbers, Manuel. 2016. *The Financialization of Housing: A Political Economy Approach*. London: Routledge.
Boudreau, Julie-Anne. 2000. *The Mega-City Saga: Democracy and Citizenship in this Global Age*. Montreal: Black Rose Books.
Boudreau, Julie-Anne, Young, Douglas and Keil, Roger. 2009. *Changing Toronto: Governing Urban Neoliberalism*. Toronto: University of Toronto Press.
Campsie, Phillippa. 2018. *Rooming Houses in Toronto 1997–2018*. Toronto: University of Toronto Cities Centre Research Paper No. 242. Accessed 22 July 2020. http://neighbourhoodchange.ca/documents/2018/04/campsie-toronto-rooming-houses.pdf.
Cowen, Deb. 2005. 'Suburban Citizenship? The Rise of Targeting and the Eclipse of Social Rights in Toronto'. *Social and Cultural Geography* 6:335–56. https://doi.org/10.1080/14649360500111212.
Fields, Desiree. 2019. 'Automated Landlord: Digital Technologies and Post-crisis Financial Accumulation'. *Environment and Planning A*. https://doi.org/10.1177/0308518X19846514.
Gowan, Peter. 2009. 'Crisis in the Heartland'. *New Left Review* 55 (Jan–Feb):5–29.
Jenkins, Simon. 2019. *A Short History of London*. London: Penguin.
Keil, Roger. 2000. 'Governance Restructuring in Los Angeles and Toronto: Amalgamation or Secession?'. *International Journal of Urban and Regional Research* 24(4):758–781. https://doi.org/10.1111/1468-2427.00277.
Le Gales, Patrick and Vitale, Tommaso. 2013. *Governing the Large Metropolis*. Sciences-Po Working Papers. Accessed 22 July 2020. https://hal-sciencespo.archives-ouvertes.fr/hal-01070523.
Sancton, Andrew. 2000. 'Amalgamations, Service Realignment, and Property Taxes: Did the Harris Government Have a Plan for Ontario's Municipalities?'. *Canadian Journal of Regional Science* 23(1):135–56.
Scott, Allen J. 2011. 'A World in Emergence: Notes toward a Resynthesis of Urban-economic Geography for the 21st Century'. *Urban Geography* 32:845–70. https://doi.org/10.2747/0272-3638.32.6.845.
Wachsmuth, David and Weisler, Alexander. 2018. 'Airbnb and the Rent Gap: Gentrification through the Sharing Economy'. *Environment and Planning A* 50:1147–70. https://doi.org/10.1177/0308518x18778038.
Walks, Alan. 2012. *Anything but Scattered: The Proposed Sale of Toronto Community Housing's Standalone Scattered-Site Housing and Implications for Building an Inclusive Toronto*. Toronto: University of Toronto City Centre Policy Brief No. 2. Accessed 22 July 2020. http://neighbourhoodchange.ca/wp-content/uploads/2012/08/Walks-TCHC-Anything-But-Scattered-NCPG-Policy-Brief-2-Aug-2012.pdf.
Walks, Alan. 2014. 'Canada's Housing Bubble Story: Mortgage Securitization, the State, and the Global Financial Crisis'. *International Journal of Urban and Regional Research* 38(1):256–84. https://doi.org/10.1111/j.1468-2427.2012.01184.x.
Wolmar, Christian. 2008. *Fire and Steam*. London: Atlantic Books.
Yates, Douglas. 1977. *The Ungovernable City*. Cambridge, MA: MIT Press.
Yeung, Karen. 2017. 'Algorithmic Regulation: A Critical Interrogation'. *Regulation & Governance* 12:505–23. https://doi.org/10.1111/rego.12158.
Zuboff, Shoshana. 2019. *Surveillance Capitalism*. London: Profile Books.

Part II
Real estate and housing

8

Governing urban development on industrial land in global cities: Lessons from London

Jessica Ferm

Deindustrialisation, global cities and the fate of industrial land: London and Toronto in context

The impact of deindustrialisation in European and North American cities has been hugely varied. Transformations in the global economy since the 1970s saw the mass relocation of routine manufacturing jobs from the hitherto industrialised world to locations with cheaper land and labour. A new international division of labour emerged, with a spatial separation of production and services across global locations. Key cities such as London and Toronto emerged as locations for multinational headquarters (Friedmann 1986) and centres of global financial control with agglomerations of finance, law, accounting, advertising and consulting (Sassen 2012). According to the Global Financial Centres Index 2019, London ranks as the second most important financial centre, after New York. Toronto now occupies seventh place, following the Asian cities of Hong Kong, Singapore, Shanghai and Tokyo (Miaschi 2019). London, described in the 1960s by Peter Hall (1961, 23) as the 'single most important seat of manufacturing' in the UK, started this process of deindustrialisation and restructuring in the 1970s (GLA Economics 2016). The city established itself as a leading financial centre in the late 1980s and featured in Sassen's (1991) book, *The Global City*, alongside New York and Tokyo. Deindustrialisation in Toronto happened a little later. In the early 1980s, the City of Toronto's financial district was relatively small and was still eclipsed by Montreal, but within a decade it had emerged as the clear leader, and by the 1990s it was home to the majority of Canada's banks, foreign banks and trust companies (Sassen 2012).

Yet, as Massey (2007) argues in the context of London, the global city thesis places too much emphasis on the importance of the financial and business services sector, and on the command and control functions of global cities. It underplays the importance of economic and social diversity, and the relationship between global cities and their national economies. Moreover, she claims there 'is a politics … in this continual characterisation of London as overwhelmingly global and in the high-lighting of this particular element (global finance and business services) of its complex, diverse economy'. In doing so, it 'relegates to comparative invisibility the host of activities that keep the economy going' (41). Many of these economic activities have no obvious location in space – courier workers, plumbers, carpenters, mobile carers and others. Many economic activities take place on industrial land or in buildings that are physically separated in space from the high-income jobs of the financial district, the centres of tourism and entertainment, or residential neighbourhoods. It is the fate of this industrial land, or what is referred to as employment lands in the Toronto context, and the activities therein which is the subject of this chapter.

For despite the shift of production to developing nations, some industry remains in global cities – either because it needs to be close to its market or to other related businesses in the production or value chain, or because it directly serves and supports other businesses or residents (see Ferm and Jones 2017 for further elaboration). As Edwards and Taylor (2017) point out, the significant role still played by industry in cities such as London and the city's dependence on the production of goods (no matter where that production takes place) renders the use of the term *post-industrial* rather meaningless. In both cities, demand for industrial space is growing, vacancy rates are considered to be low and there has been a stabilisation of employment in manufacturing (CAG 2017; Toronto City Planning 2019). Importantly, industrial land also performs a broader function: it accommodates a diversity of enterprises and activities, not only industrial ones, who are occupying premises there because of their relative affordability and flexibility (Ferm and Jones 2015). As Lehrer and Wieditz (2009) show in Toronto, employment lands have been the site of multiple rounds of industrial gentrification; for example, a declining manufacturing district became the site for Toronto's studio district – a cluster of film, television and related firms – which in turn was threatened with redevelopment into a big box retail complex. Such industrial displacement as a result of real estate speculation for higher-value uses has been documented in a range of other North American cities such as New York (Curran 2007, 2010), San Francisco (BSB Advisory Board 2007), Chicago (Rast 2001) and Vancouver (Powell 2018), as well as in global Asian cities such as Seoul (Michael 2019).

In this context, the question of how to strategically handle remaining parcels of industrial land emerges as a critical issue. London is an interesting case study because it is at a crucial juncture in its approach to industrial land policy. Between 2001 and 2015, the Greater London region lost 16 per cent of its industrial land capacity, the majority to residential development, accelerating in the last five years of this period when the annual loss of industrial land was three times the target in the London Plan, and almost eight times the target in central parts of London (AECOM 2016). This is a loss comparable to Toronto, where land zoned for employment shrank by almost 10 per cent between 2006 and 2018 (Dingman

2018). In line with actual and projected downward trends of industrial employment, the Mayor of London had been actively planning for the redevelopment of some industrial land since 2004. However, this prompted the mayor and his London Plan team to revisit its approach in the new London Plan (GLA 2019), introducing policies that simultaneously aim to halt the further loss of industrial capacity and to accommodate new housing within mixed-use environments on industrial land (see illustration in Figure 8.1). Following a review of the drivers for change, this chapter tells the story of how London got to this point and provides some critical reflections on emerging policy, whether it will work and what the lessons for other global cities might be.

Drivers of change

Theoretical perspectives on the separation of industry and housing

Although industry was an inherent and accepted part of the urban mix in nineteenth-century industrial cities, in the early twentieth century conflicts between industry and housing led to the increasing use of planning tools to manage these tensions – through statutory zoning in the North American context and protected industrial areas in local plans in the UK. In addition to the traditional arguments for

Figure 8.1 Architects' illustration of a mixed-use industrial and residential development, included in the *Industrial Intensification and Co-Location Study* (We Made That 2018), commissioned by the Greater London Authority (© We Made That)

the separation of industry and housing on the basis of noise and pollution, there are also arguments that support planning intervention in order to correct market failures. For example, allowing land use allocations to be determined by the price signal alone might not result in the most economically efficient land use allocation in the long term: it will not support the location of small businesses in central areas during the incubation phase or the provision of flexible space suitable for move-on businesses, and it will not promote social equity, including the provision of jobs near to residents who need those jobs (see Chapple 2014; Heikkila and Hutton 1986). In removing competition from higher-value uses, particularly housing, the separation of land uses has the effect of suppressing land values and allowing price-sensitive businesses to locate close to their customers and markets, and other complementary businesses, in the city.

On the other hand, arguments against the separation of land uses through statutory or policy means are based on both economic factors (see Heikkila and Hutton 1986 for a summary) and increasingly adopted norms about what makes good urbanism. Mainstream, neoclassical economic theory holds that markets – left to their own devices – will determine the most efficient allocation of scarce land resources, and that businesses will choose an optimum location based on a balance between their need to co-locate with other businesses and access markets, customers and employees. On this basis, if it is not economically or practically efficient for businesses to be near housing, they will not be; hence, heavy industry still needs to be separated from residents.

In addition, separating land uses is increasingly seen as outmoded. Accepted good practice in urbanism is to promote mixed-use, compact urban environments, which can accommodate a range of uses in dense development, promoting walkable urban environments and discouraging sprawl. In Europe, this has been underpinned by an environmental sustainability agenda of compact cities, promoted by the European Commission in the 1990s and the UK government in the early 2000s as part of its drive for an 'urban renaissance' to address inner city decline. The trend towards mixed-use, compact cities and urban renaissance has its parallels in the 'new urbanism' and 'smart growth' movements in the North American context.

Housing as a competing driver for change

The move by the middle classes back to the inner city – sites of former industrial activity – is well documented in the gentrification literature. In the early 2000s, the term 'super-gentrification' was used to describe the next wave in parts of inner London, where this time middle-class residents were being displaced by super-wealthy professionals working in the financial services of London (Butler and Lees 2006). London's current housing market and evidence of its extreme unaffordability is described elsewhere in this book (see chapters by Gabrieli, Raco and Livingstone). Prior to the recent fall in residential values – assumed to be a Brexit effect – in 2015, research for the Greater London Authority (GLA) showed that they were on average more than three times industrial land values across London, and almost eight times the value in the centre (AECOM 2016, table 4.1). In this context, there are grounds for some grave concerns about a laissez-faire approach when it comes to accommodating industry in the city. Scholars in other post-industrial cities have argued that industrial decline is only a limited part of the story of the loss of industry, and that real estate speculation is often supported by political motivations (Rast 2001) and alliances between the real estate and financial sectors and the mass media (Indergaard 2009; Zukin 1988). In her detailed study of the loss of industry in Williamsburg (Brooklyn, New York), Curran (2007, 2010) argues that the loss of industry was not only the result of global competition or increasing labour costs, but also of real estate speculation for residential conversion, actively promoted and reinforced by developers, city planners, policy-makers, landlords and individual gentrifiers, in the absence of public and political support for industrial uses in the city. In London, there is also increasing evidence that deindustrialisation is no longer the main cause of the loss of industry. For example, a review of employment land studies in inner boroughs consistently showed a shortfall of supply relative to demand, and there is evidence even in outer London boroughs of speculation for redevelopment of industrial sites and landlords offering short and insecure leases to facilitate redevelopment (see Ferm and Jones 2015).

In London, population growth – projected to rise more than 20 per cent to reach 10.8 million by 2041 (GLA 2017a) – is accompanied by a crisis of housing affordability. The primary policy tool to address this currently is to boost housing supply overall, and the mayor has set local authorities ambitious housing targets; some outer London boroughs have seen their annual targets double since the last London Plan in 2016, and one inner London borough now has targets more than seven times those previously set.[1] The pressure this places on planning officers, in making day-to-day decisions on planning applications, is evident and has been one of the key drivers behind the accelerated loss of industrial sites in London (Ferm and Jones 2016). The changing relationship between planners and real estate actors is also key here: as the funding for direct provision of public services and infrastructure has decreased, planners have been left with little alternative but to support the principle of the 'highest and best use' on any given site in order to secure maximum public benefit from the development through planning gain mechanisms (see also Wolf-Powers 2005; Rydin 2013). Housing becomes the preferred use, not only because of its high value and pressure to meet housing targets, but also because it provides accommodation for workers in the higher-value economic sectors that are seen as the drivers of the economy (Jonas et al. 2010). Furthermore, real estate actors have become more powerful in the production of both knowledge and planning frameworks that guide decision-making, which allows 'their values and objectives to predominate in the decision making process' with decisions being made 'based on quantitative metrics and financial projections' (Robin 2018, 10). Understanding the complex way in which urban environments are transformed and produced, and the role and power of different actors, is critical to establishing the likely effectiveness of policy.

Pressure for change

The changes to London's policy on industrial land, which will be detailed in the next section, were influenced by the work of grassroots activists and industry lobbyists, as well as mounting evidence that further loss of industrial capacity would be detrimental to London. In 2013, Just Space – a London-wide network of community groups and activists set up to influence the London Plan – formed a subgroup, Just Space Economy and Planning (JSEP). Whereas the wider network campaigns on planning and development matters more broadly (see e.g. Sendra and Fitzpatrick's chapter on Just Space's activism work to protect social housing), JSEP came together with a shared interest in alternative economic models and a desire to influence the direction of the London Plan with respect to the economy. The group was initially supported by Myfanwy Taylor, as part of her action-based doctoral research on contested urban economies, and includes a range of activists, community groups, small business owners, interested academics, architects and economists.[2] One strong area of interest, established early on, was in response to what the group perceived as a crisis of affordable workspace and more particularly industrial accommodation. In 2015, it published a handbook for community groups fighting a loss of workspace (JSEP 2015), held two themed seminars on affordable workspace and industrial land, as well as a bigger ideas workshop, 'Making the City' – which GLA officers attended – and accompanying pamphlet, 'London's Future Has Industry' (Just Space 2016a). In addition, London Metropolitan University's Cass Cities unit, led by Professor Mark Brearley and Jane Clossick, started a campaign, *London Is Eating Itself*, informed by their students' ongoing work researching industrial businesses in London.[3] The campaign attracted media attention, including articles in *The Observer* and *Guardian* newspapers, 'London: The City That Ate Itself' (Moore 2015) and 'Made in London No More: Will Property Speculation Kill Industry in the Capital?' (Wainwright 2017).

In 2016, the election of a new Mayor of London, Sadiq Khan, prompted the announcement of a new London Plan. At this point, Just Space started work on a 'Community-led Plan for London' (Just Space 2016b). This proactive approach also involved setting up meetings with the teams responsible for the London Plan and the various mayoral strategies. Members of JSEP met three times with the team preparing the Economics Evidence Base for London and facilitated a roundtable meeting (held on 15 May 2017) on the issue of workspace with officers across the various teams. When the new London Plan was published for consultation (GLA 2017a), the Just Space written response included a detailed critique of the 'Economy' chapter.[4] Members of JSEP also gave evidence to a panel of inspectors at the Examination in Public (EiP) on the London Plan, at sessions focusing on industrial land policies and affordable workspace.

The other influential group has been the London Industrial and Logistics Sounding Board, set up in July 2017 and initiated by officers at the GLA and London First, a London-wide business lobbying organisation. This group includes industrial and logistics developers (Segro), industrial owners and asset managers (Capital and Industrial), occupiers (DHL, Safestore, Ocado), local authorities, Transport for London, the Federation of Small Businesses, Society of London Manufacturers, Port of London Authority, London Chamber of Commerce, Industrial Business Improvement Districts network, Turley (planning consultants), CBRE (planning and property consultants), Dentons (planning lawyers) and myself as an academic. The role of the Sounding Board was 'to ensure that London's industrial sector has a voice in shaping London's emerging planning policy and contributes to good growth'.[5] Although convened by the GLA, and limited to invited members, the group has played an important role in enabling representatives from the industrial and logistics sector to influence the London Plan.

Another source of pressure was mounting evidence that the demand for industrial sites was no longer declining. Signs of this were evident in the property market, in declining vacancy rates and high rental levels due to a mismatch between supply and demand. Evidence given to the London Assembly Planning Committee in September 2017 suggested that vacancy rates had fallen from around 16 per cent in 2001 to 11 per cent in 2015 across London.[6] In many inner London boroughs, vacancy rates were less than 5 per cent and on one of the largest industrial estates in London (Park Royal), vacancy rates were described as 'dangerously low' at 2 per cent, with long occupier waiting lists. These figures are supported by evidence of a projected positive net demand for industrial land in London (CAG 2017). This was confirmed by the industrial developers and asset managers at the panel of the planning committee, who reported increased demand for warehousing and logistics facilities due to growth in online retailing, as well as higher demand for sites closer to central London from time-sensitive and so-called last-mile businesses. In addition to these changes in the distribution economy, Mark Brearley (proprietor of a manufacturing business and professor at Cass Cities, London Metropolitan University) explained that the growth in the population of London is, in turn, linked to a growth in businesses that serve this population: 'more people need more pints of milk, more buildings, more school dinners, more hospital bedsheets'. As prosperity in London increases, this also fuels growth in 'everything niche and differentiated'. As a result, a range of industrial businesses are growing, including builders' merchants, self-storage, public transport and courier depots, catering, higher-end and just-in-time food and drink production, art and artisan production, garment and accessory making, printing, culture-related production and logistics (such as set and prop makers), bespoke furniture and joinery, steel fabrication and building fit-out, waste handling and recycling – all at the small and medium scale. The more skilled and entrepreneurial people are attracted to London, the more people create and grow industrial businesses there. In response, the deputy mayor for planning, regeneration and skills claimed in the committee that 'we are on the cusp of a real problem' and acknowledged that this 'has come about through the release of industrial land in recent years, over the last decade or so, that has way outstripped the benchmark'.

Alongside more optimistic projections on the future industrial economy, there was evidence that the structure of London's economy was changing. In 2013, London documented a slowing of growth in its financial and insurance services sector, with a projected decline by 2030 (Wickham 2015, Figure 3a), undermining London's prior model of economic growth heavily reliant on its success as a global financial centre. In response, the GLA's own economics team placed greater emphasis on economic diversity as a resilience strategy, particularly amid concerns about the impact of Brexit (GLA Economics 2016). The GLA's regeneration team led on important work auditing businesses on industrial land. The highest profile of these was the *Park Royal Atlas* (GLA 2014), but smaller internal pieces of work were completed in a range of other industrial locations. This work helped to build an important evidence base and raise the profile of industrial land within the GLA, also providing impetus and a methodology for further auditing work undertaken by students at London universities (London School of Economics, London Metropolitan and UCL).

A critique of the new London Plan's approach to managing industry

When the mayor's new London Plan was published for consultation in 2018, a seemingly bold approach to industrial land policy was set out. Firstly, in order to halt the loss of industrial capacity, Policy E4 states that there will be 'no net loss' of industrial

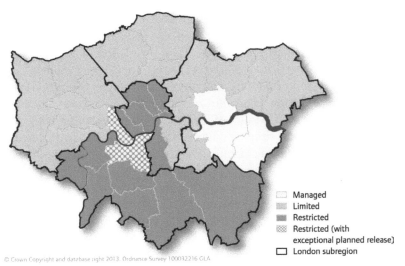

Figure 8.2 Map of London boroughs showing the management of the transfer of industrial land to other uses under the policies in the London Plan 2016 (GLA 2016)

floor space across London. Under previous London plans, the 32 London boroughs (local or municipal authorities with planning powers) were each given targets for the transfer of industrial land to other uses, with some boroughs identified as suitable for 'restricted' release, some for 'limited' release and a few for 'managed' release (the latter facilitating the highest quantum of transfer). Figure 8.2 illustrates this approach of 'managed decline' and contrasts it with the new approach in the London Plan (Figure 8.3), in which only three east London boroughs – Newham, Barking and Dagenham, and Havering – are still identified for some limited release of industrial land, with the remaining boroughs required to either retain or provide new industrial capacity, such that – overall – there is no net loss.

This has been complemented with a second new policy (E7), which promotes industrial intensification and co-location of industrial and residential uses. This is intended to stimulate denser development, both in the form of multi-storey

Management of Industrial Floorspace Capacity
Borough Level Categorisations

● Provide Capacity

● Retain Capacity

● Limited Release

Source: GLA Planning

Contains OS data ©
Crown copyright and
database right (2017)

Figure 8.3 Map of London boroughs showing the management of industrial land capacity under the policies proposed in the Draft London Plan 2017 (GLA 2017a)

industrial, and mixed-use industrial and residential development. The policy was supported by work undertaken on the viability of intensification and the urban design solutions required (GLA 2017b; We Made That 2018).

There is much to commend in the new London Plan's approach to managing industrial land. Importantly, it moves away from the previous policy of managed decline and sends a clear signal, through introducing an approach of 'nil net loss' of industrial land across London, that it is seeking to halt any further loss and support London's industry moving forward. The ambition to integrate industry and housing also has many merits in principle, at least for much contemporary industry, working towards 'industrious cities', where industry is given more prominence in the city, allowing it to be celebrated and avoiding the parcelling off of industry in anonymous sheds. It has stimulated lively discussions and innovative architectural design solutions to the challenge of co-locating industry and housing, some of which we are starting to see come forward as (private sector-led) demonstration projects.

However, the change in approach we see in the new London Plan appears to be an attempt to develop a win–win solution: deliver more housing and, at the same time, accommodate existing industrial businesses and future projected demand for industry. The mantra of growth underpinning the London Plan since its beginnings (Taylor 2013) shows no sign of waning, despite the current mayor framing it in the new London Plan as 'good growth'. The latest plan has 48 Opportunity Areas – areas of growth where thousands of new jobs and homes are planned – which is double the number identified in the original 2004 Plan. New and planned major transport infrastructure serves as the basis for this growth, but much of it (the planned Bakerloo line extension, Crossrail 1 and Crossrail 2) runs through London's largest reservoirs of industrial land. With little political appetite for building on London's Green Belt, industrial areas became an easy target for accommodating large-scale housing development. The ambition to preserve existing industrial capacity and accommodate new accommodation in this context is challenging to say the least and requires a political ambition at both the London regional and local authority scales. Such leadership is currently lacking. In fact, the wider growth ambitions of the city, and a commitment to solving the housing crisis, are clear political priorities that are eclipsing the few voices that are speaking up for the importance of retaining and providing industrial accommodation. These struggles are already being played out in many of the Opportunity Areas, where development is progressing – in the Old Kent Road, in Tottenham, in Charlton Riverside – as well as on industrial sites close to existing Opportunity Areas that are feeling the impact of development pressure beyond the boundary, such as Camley Street north of King's Cross.

If the London Plan is to succeed in its ambitions to increase capacity for both industry and housing, it will depend crucially on the deliverability of the nil net loss policy in practice and on the viability of intensification and co-location across London. If owners and developers of industrial assets do not bring forward sites for redevelopment in line with policy, or if the nil net loss policy is difficult to enforce, then the signal that co-location is acceptable in policy terms is likely to facilitate the further loss of industrial land to residential or mixed use with no guarantee of industrial accommodation. The fear is that the London Plan is overly optimistic in assuming its policies will be easy to implement at the local level, and that the unintended consequence of this suite of policies will further fuel real estate speculation and rising hope values. Lessons can already be learned from experience at the local borough level, where there has been a softening of policy on industrial land for a number of years, with Strategic Industrial Sites being variously renamed as Mixed Use Employment Areas, Regeneration Areas and so forth, but little employment delivered on these sites (see Ferm and Jones 2016).

At the London Plan EiP session on this matter,[7] there was a consensus among participants that there was an over-reliance on industrial intensification to achieve housing targets and deliver additional industrial capacity in the London Plan. London boroughs giving evidence at the session insisted that the viability of intensifying industrial and co-locating residential land use had not been adequately demonstrated. Developers and asset managers emphasised the lack of commercial incentives to redevelop sites in line with policy, if this would mean losing yard space or developing space that was less attractive to occupiers and harder to rent. These discussions suggest that the challenges in making this policy succeed lie not so much in finding the right design solutions – there are many good examples coming forward already – but in incentivising developers and investors to build and invest in schemes for which there is little demonstrable occupier appetite.

One glaring weakness of the nil net loss policy as it stands is that it only applies to industrial sites that are considered in policy terms as 'strategic' or 'locally significant'. Thirty-six per cent of the total industrial land in London falls outside these policy designations (AECOM 2016, 1) and is therefore not considered in the targets allocated to the 32 boroughs. Leaving out non-designated sites is possibly strategically deliberate. In the 'Housing' chapter of the new London Plan, a new 'small sites' policy has been introduced which seeks to encourage smaller residential developers to deliver more housing. The small sites policy is critical to achieving the housing targets in the London Plan, and non-designated industrial sites are likely to be an important source for bringing forward small sites for housing.

For planning officers in individual boroughs seeking to work with, implement and enforce a nil net loss policy, there are mixed messages in the Plan and a lack of guidance for policy- and decision-making to be effective. For example, in parallel to the nil net loss policy, the Plan actively encourages (more than before) residential and mixed-use development on all industrial sites, even those labelled 'strategic' (as long as there is a coordinated plan-led approach to consolidation and redevelopment). Given this permissive approach on all types of industrial land, there now appears to be less distinction between the three categories of *strategic*, *locally significant* and *non-designated* sites. Applying this policy at a London-wide scale is very broad and it is difficult to see how it would govern local decisions, especially given the lack of detailed, up-to-date audits of many of the industrial areas in question against which monitoring can take place. At the EiP, Just Space criticised the GLA for leading on, or being involved as strategic partners in, planning frameworks that involve development on industrial land, as this undermines their role in defending policies in the Plan. There was concern that the new London Plan allows for strategic industrial sites to be lost through rather vague master-planning exercises that are not required to follow statutory planning processes and proper consultation.

Just Space requested stronger wording on the need to involve industrial businesses in the preparation of plans that change the character of an industrial area or involve any relocation of those businesses. Whether or not there is any real commitment to retaining existing industrial businesses is unclear. In many of the demonstration projects that are cited as good practice examples (see We Made That 2018), the industrial space seems to be targeted more at maker firms of the new economy. The research evaluating these emerging schemes has yet to be undertaken, but based on my previous work evaluating redevelopment of industrial sites for residential and 'affordable workspace', developers' preferences for occupiers that help to market the more profitable residential component of the schemes is the main driver of outcomes, which leads to displacement of the original occupiers – a form of industrial gentrification (Ferm 2014).

Conclusion

London's changing approach to managing the relationship between industry and housing has been documented in this chapter. It is an experience that has relevance for Toronto and other post-industrial cities that are grappling with problems of the displacement of industry by higher-value uses, in a context where deindustrialisation is no longer the main driver of the loss of industry, and there are signs of growth in the sector. Many of these same cities are also grappling with a housing crisis, which is politically a higher priority.

In the past, industrial land was arguably a legitimate source of land for housing, given the projected ongoing decline of industrial employment. In London at least, the trend is reversing and for the first time there are projections of net future demand for industrial accommodation. This has required some innovation and creative thinking by policy-makers, and the solution has been to promote integration of housing and industry and intensification of existing low-density sites, in the hope that both housing and industrial capacity can be accommodated – a win–win solution. However, this chapter argues that there is an element of 'wishful thinking' in this approach, with a reliance on many (as yet) untested assumptions. Integration between industry and housing may well be a laudable long-term aspiration. But given the speed of change, departing from a clear protectionist stance on industrial land is, in the short term, likely to favour housing and lead to its continued loss.

The lobbying work that has been undertaken in the last decade, described in this chapter, has certainly raised awareness of the importance of protecting the industry that remains and accommodating any future projected growth – for the functioning of London's broader economy if nothing else – but there is little evidence of any serious challenge to London's growth model, to its reliance on highly specialised financial and business services sectors, or – referring back to Massey (2007) – a real appreciation of the economic (and social) diversity that underpins London's global city status. Other issues are seen as having higher priority politically. Activists questioning the granting of planning permission for residential towers on strategic industrial land are criticised openly on social media for standing in the way of delivering much-needed 'affordable housing'. This points to a deeper problem of the financial development models we have come to rely on to secure the delivery of affordable housing and broader social infrastructure. As long as these remain unchallenged, there is unlikely ever to be any strong political leadership supporting the retention of industry in our cities.

Acknowledgements

I would like to extend my thanks to fellow members of Just Space (particularly the Economy and Planning sub-group) and the London Industrial and Logistics Sounding Board, who have indirectly provided much content and inspiration for this chapter. Thank you also to Michael Edwards (UCL and Just Space) and Ben Posford (CBRE) who provided useful written summaries of the EiP session featured here.

Notes

1. Author's own calculations based on a comparison of table 4.2 of the new London Plan (GLA 2019) and table 3.1 in the 2016 London Plan (GLA 2016). Boroughs with the highest hike were chosen for reflection (Barking and Dagenham, Barnet and Tower Hamlets).
2. See Taylor and Edwards (2016) for an account of JSEP's work and impact in the first two to three years.
3. A selection can be viewed at: https://casscities.co.uk/research.
4. Accessed here: https://justspace.org.uk/2018/02/24/london-plan-write-now.
5. Drawn from the group's Terms of Reference (not available publicly online).
6. The London Assembly is made up of elected members, whose function is to hold the mayor to account by publicly examining policies and programmes. A transcript of the meeting of 7 September is available under 'Committee Meetings' at: http://www.london.gov.uk/about-us/london-assembly/london-assembly-committees/planning-committee.
7. This was considered as Matter 62 (Land for Industry, Logistics and Services to Support London's Economic Function) held on 19 March 2019 at 9.30 am.

References

AECOM. 2016. *London Industrial Land Supply and Economy Study 2015*. London: Greater London Authority.
BSB (Back Street Businesses) Advisory Board. 2007. *Made in San Francisco*. Accessed 22 July 2020. https://sfgov.org/ccsfgsa/back-streets-business-advisory-board.

Butler, Tim and Lees, Loretta. 2006. 'Super-gentrification in Barnsbury, London: Globalization and Gentrifying Global Elites at the Neighbourhood Level'. *Transactions of the Institute of British Geographers* 31(4):467–87. https://doi.org/10.1111/j.1475-5661.2006.00220.x.

CAG Consultants. 2017. *London Industrial Land Demand*. Accessed 18 September 2019. https://www.london.gov.uk/sites/default/files/ilds_revised_final_report_october_2017.pdf.

Chapple, Karen. 2014. 'The Highest and Best Use, Urban Industrial Land and Job Creation'. *Economic Development Quarterly* 28(4):300–13. http://doi.org/10.1177/0891242413517134.

Curran, Winifred. 2007. '"From the Frying Pan to the Oven": Gentrification and the Experience of Industrial Displacement in Williamsburg, Brooklyn'. *Urban Studies* 44(8):1427–40. https://doi.org/10.1080/00420980701373438.

Curran, Winifred. 2010. 'In Defense of Old Industrial Spaces: Manufacturing, Creativity and Innovation in Williamsburg, Brooklyn'. *International Journal of Urban and Regional Research* 34(4):871–85. https://doi.org/10.1111/j.1468-2427.2010.00915.x.

Dingman, Shane. 2018. 'Toronto Land Zoned for Employment Use Is Shrinking'. *The Globe and Mail*, 25 September. Accessed 18 September 2019. https://www.theglobeandmail.com/real-estate/article-toronto-land-zoned-for-employment-use-is-shrinking.

Edwards, Michael and Taylor, Myfanwy. 2017. 'Re-industrialisation as Progressive Urbanism: Why and How?'. In *Urban Re-industrialization*, edited by Krzysztof Nawratek, 21–8. Santa Barbara, CA: Punctum Books.

Ferm, Jessica. 2014. 'Delivering Affordable Workspace: Perspectives of Developers and Workspace Providers in London'. *Progress in Planning* 93:1–49. https://doi.org/10.1016/j.progress.2013.05.002.

Ferm, Jessica and Jones, Edward. 2015. *London's Industrial Land: Cause for Concern?* UCL Working Paper. Accessed 18 September 2019. http://discovery.ucl.ac.uk/1461419.

Ferm, Jessica and Jones, Edward. 2016. 'Mixed Use "Regeneration" of Employment Land in the Post-industrial City: Challenges and Realities in London'. *European Planning Studies* 10(4):1913–36. https://doi.org/10.1080/09654313.2016.1209465.

Ferm, Jessica and Jones, Edward. 2017. 'Beyond the Post-industrial City: Valuing and Planning for Industry in London'. *Urban Studies* 54(14):3380–98. https://doi.org/10.1177/0042098016668778.

Friedmann, John. 1986. 'The World City Hypothesis'. *Development and Change* 17:69–83.

GLA (Greater London Authority). 2014. *Park Royal Atlas*. Accessed 19 September 2019. https://www.london.gov.uk/what-we-do/regeneration/regeneration-publications/park-royal-atlas.

GLA (Greater London Authority). 2016. 'The current London Plan'. Accessed 2 August 2020. https://www.london.gov.uk/what-we-do/planning/london-plan/current-london-plan.

GLA (Greater London Authority). 2017a. 'New London Plan'. Accessed 22 July 2020. https://www.london.gov.uk/what-we-do/planning/london-plan/new-london-plan.

GLA (Greater London Authority). 2017b. *Industrial Intensification Primer*. Accessed 19 September 2019. https://www.london.gov.uk/sites/default/files/industrialintensificationprimer.pdf.

GLA (Greater London Authority). 2019. 'Intend to Publish London Plan 2019'. Accessed 2 August 2020. https://www.london.gov.uk/what-we-do/planning/london-plan/new-london-plan/intend-publish-london-plan-2019.

GLA (Greater London Authority) Economics. 2016. *Economics Evidence Base for London 2016*. Accessed 19 September 2019. https://www.london.gov.uk/what-we-do/research-and-analysis/economic-analysis/economic-evidence-base-london-2016.

Hall, Peter. 1961. *The Industries of London since 1861*. London: Hutchinson & Co.

Heikkila, Eric and Hutton, Thomas. 1986. 'Toward an Evaluative Framework for Land Use Policy in Industrial Districts of the Urban Core: A Qualitative Analysis of the Exclusionary Zoning Approach'. *Urban Studies* 23(1):47–60. https://doi.org/10.1080/00420988620080051.

Indergaard, Michael. 2009 'What to Make of New York's New Economy? The Politics of the Creative Field'. *Urban Studies* 46(5–6):1063–93. https://doi.org/10.1177/0042098009103855.

Jonas, Andrew, While, Aiden and Gibbs, David. 2010. 'Managing Infrastructural and Service Demands in New Economic Spaces: The New Territorial Politics of Collective Provision'. *Regional Studies* 44(2):183–200. https://doi.org/10.1080/00343400802662666.

Just Space. 2016a. 'London's Future Has Industry'. Accessed 19 September 2019. https://justspace.org.uk/2016/05/17/londons-future-has-industry.

Just Space. 2016b. 'Towards a Community-led Plan for London'. Accessed 19 September 2019. https://just-spacelondon.files.wordpress.com/2013/09/just-space-a4-community-led-london-plan.pdf.

JSEP (Just Space Economy and Planning). 2015. 'London for All! A Handbook for Community and Small Business Groups Fighting to Retain Workspace for London's Diverse Economies'. Accessed 19 September 2019. https://justspacelondon.files.wordpress.com/2015/09/workspacehandbook_highres.pdf.

Lehrer, Ute and Wieditz, Thorben. 2009. 'Gentrification and the Loss of Employment Lands: Toronto's Studio District'. *Critical Planning* 16:139–60.

Massey, Doreen. 2007. *World City*. Cambridge, UK: Polity Press.

Miaschi, John. 2019. 'Which Cities Are the World's Financial Centers?'. 25 July. Accessed 19 September 2019. https://www.worldatlas.com/articles/the-world-s-top-financial-cities.html.

Michael, Chris. 2019. 'I'm Panicking: Seoul Rips out its Manufacturing Heart'. *The Guardian*, 20 February.

Moore, Rowan. 2015. 'London: The City that Ate Itself'. *The Observer*, 28 June.

Powell, Naomi. 2018. 'Shortage of Industrial Real Estate Is Pushing Companies out of Vancouver'. *Financial Post*, 26 February. Accessed 19 September 2019. http://business.financialpost.com/real-estate/property-post/shortage-of-industrial-real-estate-is-pushing-companies-out-of-vancouver.

Rast, Joel. 2001. 'Manufacturing Industrial Decline: The Politics of Economic Change in Chicago, 1955–1998'. *Journal of Urban Affairs* 23(2):175–90. https://doi.org/10.1111/0735-2166.00082.

Robin, Enora. 2018. 'Performing Real Estate Value(s): Real Estate Developers, Systems of Expertise and the Production of Space'. *Geoforum*, 1 June. https://doi.org/10.1016/j.geoforum.2018.05.006.

Rydin, Yvonne. 2013. *The Future of Planning: Beyond Growth Dependence*. Bristol: Policy Press.

Sassen, Saskia. 1991 (2001). *The Global City: New York, London, Tokyo*. Princeton, NJ: Princeton University Press.

Sassen, Saskia. 2012. *Cities in a World Economy*. London: SAGE.

Taylor, Myfanwy. 2013. 'Rethinking London's Economy and Economic Future'. In *Imagining the Future City: London 2062*, edited by Sarah Bell and James Paskins, 131–5. London: Ubiquity Press.

Taylor, Myfanwy and Edwards, Michael. 2016. 'Just Space Economy and Planning: Opening Up Debates on London's Economy through Participating in Strategic Planning'. In *The Participatory City*, edited by Yasminah Beebeejaun, 76–86. Berlin: Jovis.

Toronto City Planning. 2019. *Toronto Employment Survey 2018*. City of Toronto. Accessed 19 September 2019. https://www.toronto.ca/wp-content/uploads/2019/03/8fd3-Toronto-Employment-Survey-2018-Bulletin.pdf.

Wainwright, Oliver. 2017. 'Made in London No More: Will Property Speculation Kill Industry in the City?' *The Guardian*, 6 February.

We Made That. 2018. *Industrial Intensification and Co-location Study: Design and Delivery Testing*. Accessed 19 September 2019. https://www.london.gov.uk/sites/default/files/136_industrial_intensification_and_co-location_study_-_design_and_delivery_testing_reduced_size.pdf.

Wickham, Melisa. 2015. *Updated Employment Projections for London by Sector and Trend-based Projections by Borough*. GLA Economics Working Paper 67. London: Greater London Authority. Accessed 20 August 2020. https://www.london.gov.uk/sites/default/files/gla_migrate_files_destination/Working%20Paper%2067.pdf.

Wolf-Powers, Laura. 2005. 'Up-Zoning New York City's Mixed-Use Neighborhoods Property-Led Economic Development and the Anatomy of a Planning Dilemma'. *Journal of Planning Education and Research* 24(4):379–93. https://doi.org/10.1177/0739456x04270125.

Zukin, Sharon. 1988. *Loft Living: Culture and Capital in Urban Change*. London: Radius.

9

Global city, global housing bubble? Toronto's housing bubble and its discontents

Alan Walks

Introduction

The key 'global' command-and-control cities are at the cutting edge of many of the changes occurring as a result of the extension of a finance-led global capitalism. For decades before the emergence of COVID-19, the spread of a global market for financial securities linked to housing has provided credit for the purchase of land and housing in a number of cities, which pushes up not only house and land prices but also rents, as landlords seek to cover their mortgage costs. Yet many of the factors that have been driving up urban housing costs are not well understood. Lack of understanding of these factors not only has the potential to fuel problematic forms of 'populist' politics but has also led to policies that arguably have made the situation worse. This chapter provides an examination of the Toronto case, with an eye to understanding the effects of housing market processes and housing policies with relevance not only for Toronto but for many key global cities around the world, including London. The chapter begins by explaining the cause of Toronto's 'bubble'. It then examines some of its implications, and it concludes by drawing on this history to outline basic solutions to the affordable housing situation in the city.

Toronto and its housing bubble

As noted by Vinodrai and Brail in Chapter 2, greater Toronto is Canada's largest metropolitan area (containing between 5.9 and 8.1 million people, depending on how the metropolitan area is defined/bounded), with Canada's largest city at its heart (the City of Toronto, with 2.73 million people in 2016). It is also Canada's predominant immigrant reception urban region, attracting over 36 per cent of all immigrants to Canada, approximately double its share of the country's population. In turn,

Toronto is Canada's most diverse metropolitan area, and people from all 255 types of ethnicity tracked in the 2016 census of Canada are present in Toronto, far more than in most other Canadian cities. Toronto is Canada's pre-eminent 'global city'.

As Canada's premier financial centre, Toronto has done better than many other cities in the transition from a Fordism dominated by manufacturing to a globalised post-Fordism characterised by finance-led capitalism, and Toronto has remained among the wealthiest regions in the country. Yet economic restructuring has had spatial and political implications in Toronto, with most of the dwindling industrial sector located in the suburbs and exurbs, while the booming financial sector is concentrated in the central business district (CBD) (Walks 2015; see also Chapter 2 by Brail and Vinodrai). This has led to rapid gentrification of the inner city, de-conversion of many older housing units from rental tenure to owner-occupation and a slow shift of the immigrant reception neighbourhoods into the suburbs (Walks and Maaranen 2008a, 2000b; Walks 2011).

High housing costs and declining levels of housing affordability are perennial issues affecting 'global' cities such as Toronto and London. Of course, it is difficult to define exactly what 'affordability' means. In the Canadian tradition, housing is unaffordable if payments take up more than 25 per cent of before-tax income, but this was raised to 30 per cent in the late 1980s. As Chapter 11 by Hawes and Grisdale shows, this is also when affordability generally became worse, and by the 2000s roughly half of Toronto's renter households, and a third of owners, had payments that exceeded this threshold. Another common definition of affordable housing is housing that rents at 80 per cent (or less) of the average market rent – this has been the definition used by the Province of Ontario to assess rental affordability (see MMAH Ontario 2011). Since the 1980s, Toronto in particular has suffered from an inadequate production of rental housing within either of these affordability criteria, driving up average costs (Suttor 2016; Walks 2006). With the advent of the 2008–9 Global Financial Crisis (GFC), which saw house prices in the United States decline, housing costs in Toronto counter-intuitively escalated to record levels. Rents followed suit after a lag. By February 2017, one of the largest Canadian banks (Bank of Montreal: BMO) declared the Toronto region housing market 'in a bubble' even as housing markets in most other Canadian cities were 'well-behaved' (Gray 2017). In September 2019, the Swiss bank UBS declared Toronto's housing market the second most overvalued of any city on the planet, and the worst in North America (McClelland 2019). In a 2019 survey, Toronto ranked dead last among Canadian cities in renter satisfaction (Lewis 2019).

That an already expensive housing market had crossed a line into bubble territory had already become a common sentiment in Toronto (Febbraro 2019). Of course, 'housing bubble' is a fraught and contested term meaning different things to different audiences. Joe Stiglitz was among the first to solidify a scholarly definition. In his view, a bubble occurs when real estate valuations significantly deviate from the underlying fundamental values supporting those prices, such as the rents the units can garner in the open market and the incomes of those who make the payments, with the result that bubble prices may be vulnerable to decline (Stiglitz

1990). This is typically how a bubble has been defined within the economics discipline ever since (see Abildgren et al. 2018). However, Stiglitz (1990) also noted that one can only determine whether a particular housing market has been in a 'bubble' by looking in the rear-view mirror based on the evolution of underlying values. Konings (2018) and Bichler and Nitzan (2009), meanwhile, argue that there are no fundamental values upon which to base prices, whether for housing or otherwise. Instead, valuations result merely from willingness and ability to pay, and thus from the confidence that buyers (including those buying for use value as well as investors buying for exchange value) have that values will not fall. Thus, housing bubbles – even those seemingly (far) out of line with incomes and rents – may not always be prone to decline, but instead could be held aloft as a result of ongoing investment demand and institutional factors. It depends on confidence, the sources of demand and how the market is structured.

Regardless of how one might define a bubble and identify its presence, it is clear that average house prices in the Toronto census metropolitan area (CMA) rose much faster following the GFC than house prices in most other metropolitan areas in Canada (Figure 9.1). Although Toronto house prices have always been

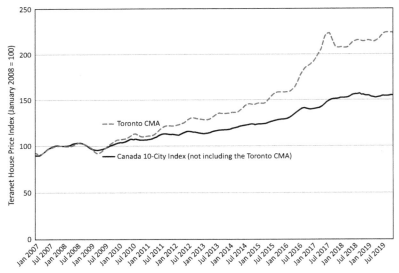

Figure 9.1 House prices in the Toronto census metropolitan area compared with house prices in other large metropolitan areas in Canada. Created by the author, using data from the Teranet House Price Index dataset (Teranet 2020). The Canada 10-City Index was calculated using the Teranet indices and weights for the Montreal, Vancouver, Calgary, Edmonton, Ottawa, Winnipeg, Quebec City, Hamilton, Victoria and Halifax metropolitan areas (CMAs), that is, 10 of the 11 metros in the Teranet 11-City Index (i.e. without the Toronto CMA). Teranet only collects information on 11 CMAs. January 2008 = 100

higher than the Canadian average, they have typically moved up or down in a similar pattern to the rest of urban Canada. Things changed after 2008, with Toronto (and Vancouver) witnessing significantly stronger house price inflation than most of the rest of urban Canada, leading to unexplainably elevated prices – the situation I refer to here as the 'bubble'.

Not only did the affordability gap widen between the Toronto region and other CMAs, but the difference in the rate of price increases widened as well. Between 2009 and 2016, Toronto prices grew *almost twice* as fast as the average of the other 10 metros in Teranet's 11-City Index (which includes Vancouver): 63.2 per cent in Toronto (for an annualised rate of 9 per cent) vs 32.3 per cent in the other 10 metros (annualised rate of 4.6 per cent). During the hottest 18 months between January 2016 and July 2017, Toronto CMA house prices rose *almost three* times faster (41 per cent in Toronto vs 14.7 per cent in the other 10 metros, for an annualised 27.5 per cent vs 9.8 per cent increase). Although concerted efforts by the federal and provincial governments from mid-2017 onward were successful in reducing the pace of inflation, prices after a short mini-correction in early 2017 continued rising, and even during the more muted rises in 2018 and 2019, Toronto's annualised rate of price increases (7.6 per cent) was *over four times faster* than that for the other 10 metros (1.8 per cent). By summer 2019, the average-priced home had become out of range of the entire bottom 90 per cent of the CMA population, despite Toronto having some of the wealthiest households in the country (Febbraro 2019), and then continued rising through most of 2020 despite the ongoing pandemic. And as private landlords need to cover their costs (including mortgage costs), rents rose along with values all the way up to the pandemic onset.[1]

Toronto is not the only city facing unaffordable and rapidly rising housing costs. Fairly similar patterns, but established even earlier than those in Toronto, are found in Vancouver (Canada), London (UK), Sydney (Australia), New York City (US) and a host of other 'global cities' (Ley and Murphy 2001; Ley 2017; Moos and Skaburskis 2010; Skaburskis and Moos 2008; Wetzstein 2017). High and rising housing costs that price out regular households appear to be a form of global city 'disease', and this has raised many questions among scholars, policy-makers and housing activists. What explains such high costs and the rapid house price inflation of the most recent decade? What are the implications of such high housing costs? Given these causes and implications, what might be done to make housing more affordable? The rest of the chapter deals with these questions, using Toronto as its case study.

Explaining Toronto's housing bubble

While a number of factors have contributed to sky-high housing costs, there have also arisen a number of erroneous claims and misconceptions about certain causes driving the housing bubble. It is important to critically examine such claims and to ascertain their relative importance. One of these misconceptions relates to the impact of rising inequality and the investment patterns of transnational elites in driving up local housing costs. It is clear that inequality in income and wealth (as revealed by the shares of each belonging to the top 10 per cent and top 1 per cent of earners) has been increasing since the 1980s in many developed nations, albeit to different degrees depending on national policies (Piketty and Saez 2014; Alvaredo et al. 2017). There were, by the mid-2010s, many more high net-worth individuals (HNWIs) searching for the best places to invest their wealth, especially from the US due to the rapid rise of inequality there since Ronald Reagan's presidency (Piketty et al. 2018) and from Russia since the collapse of the Soviet Union (Novokment et al. 2018). Coupled with the development of global information technology networks that have made it easier to move money around the world, this understandably has allowed many transnational elites to purchase housing in different cities. There is no doubt that global cities such as London, New York City, Vancouver and Sydney have come to act 'as a safe deposit box for the transnational wealth elite' (Fernandez et al. 2016; see also Rogers and Koh 2017).

But are high and rising housing costs in global cities mainly a result of this phenomenon? In Canada, many people are convinced that an influx of money from foreign buyers, especially from China, has created those bubbles and priced out Canadian home buyers (Todd 2017; Kalinowski 2018). Even some Canadian scholars (Ley 2010, 2017) have promoted the idea that rising house prices are largely due to demand from foreign buyers. Responding to public anger over the prospects of foreign buyers outbidding for housing in Vancouver, the British Columbia (BC) provincial government in 2016 imposed a 15 per cent (raised to 20 per cent in 2018) 'foreign home-buyers tax' on house purchases in Vancouver and Victoria (Todd 2017). With rising prices starting to produce a similar politics of resentment in Ontario, in 2017 the Ontario government imposed a similar 15 per cent 'non-resident speculation tax' on house sales within Greater Golden Horseshoe – the larger area that contains not only the Toronto CMA, but Hamilton, Oshawa, Barrie, Guelph and St Catharines – as part of their 'Fair Housing Plan' (Kalinowski 2018). Furthermore, reports by the BC government (Maloney et al. 2019) as well as non-governmental organisations such as Transparency International Canada (see Lee-Shanok 2019) have suggested that the Toronto and Vancouver housing markets were being used by international crime syndicates to launder money. The BC report suggested that C$6.3 billion had been laundered through Vancouver and Victoria housing markets in 2015, representing roughly 5 per cent of real estate transactions and causing a roughly 5 per cent (only)[2] increase in housing prices (Maloney et al. 2019).

But how much blame might foreign buyers actually deserve for rising housing costs? The evidence suggests that their impact in Toronto (and even Vancouver) is less important than many local residents, and the BC and Ontario governments, have thought. First of all, the alarming BC report was not based on actual flows of investment into BC, but instead on estimates of total global flows of money laundering activity, with rough projections (without actual evidence) of how much of this might flow into Vancouver; thus, it is not a reliable source of data. Actual data, however, were estimated by the Canada Mortgage and Housing Corporation (CMHC), suggesting that before the BC foreign home-buyer tax was implemented in 2016, roughly 13 per cent of buyers in Vancouver were foreign nationals (CMHC 2016). This is the exact same percentage (13 per cent) identified in a 2017 study of transactions in the London (UK) housing market (Fraser 2017). This is enough to increase house prices at the margin, but it also means that 87 per cent of home buyers were Canadian (or in London, from the UK). The effect of foreign buyer demand is even smaller in Toronto, where a subsequent analysis found that only 4.7 per cent of homes were purchased by foreign buyers in the year before the imposition of Ontario's non-resident speculation tax (Kalinowski 2018); thus, 95.3 per cent of all such purchases in Toronto were made by Canadian residents, and this went to almost 100 per cent after the imposition of the tax (Kalinowski 2018). Another study found that only 2.5 per cent of Toronto's overall condo stock was owned by foreign nationals (CMHC 2017). Although foreign buying is real, it is thus not the main, nor potentially even the secondary, cause of rapid house price inflation in global cities. The vast majority of demand is local, even in London, and even more in Toronto.

The role of public policy in Toronto's housing bubble

If house price inflation is mainly the result of local demand, why have prices risen more quickly since the GFC, which began with a recession (not a boom) and was followed by slow (not fast) economic growth and wage growth, than in the decades before the GFC? The riddle of a housing bubble during and after a recession is among the many puzzling phenomena that lead to suspicions about foreign buyers. The missing puzzle piece is not foreign buyers but the influx of cheap available credit to local buyers that has flooded mortgage markets in the aftermath of the GFC, coupled with the ways that 'financialisation' has evolved to incentivise riskier lending. When the GFC erupted, governments all over the world (including Canada, the UK and others, following the US lead) forced down central bank interest rates to as close to zero as they could (producing negative real interest rates; quantitative easing in the US, UK and EU did this as well), in order to stimulate lending and protect borrowers from insolvency. But this spurred many banks to lend, and to make riskier loans than they would have, including across national borders. Because of the ways that mortgage securitisation has evolved, much of the cheap credit that was made available went into mortgages for residential real estate, and banks no longer bore much of the risk of default (see Aalbers 2016; Walks 2019 for a longer discussion). One could suddenly acquire a larger mortgage, at a lower interest rate, on looser terms, than in the past, and this incentivised investors to put their money into housing, including second homes that they would rent out for profit (benefitting professional landlords, and turning many households into amateur landlords).

In effect, governments facing recession purposefully stimulated credit creation and real estate investment as a way of spurring economic growth and jobs in the face of crisis. Scholars have referred to such a policy approach as 'privatized Keynesianism' (Crouch 2009), in that instead of governments doing the borrowing and spending in order to stimulate the economy and put people to work (as in traditional 'Keynesianism'), it is now private individuals and households that are incentivised to borrow and spend in order to stimulate the economy. However, one result is rapidly rising debt levels among individuals and households, a negative outcome of this policy approach which in the long run makes those households, and their local economies, more vulnerable and susceptible to economic crisis (Walks 2013).

If transnational elites buying up property in global cities is not a primary factor driving up their house prices, does this mean that rising inequality cannot be blamed for the housing bubble? No, in fact rising inequality has played an important role in driving up house prices through wealthy individuals' investments into mortgage markets. Increasing income inequality provided the wealthy with greater ability save more of their income than in the past. With declining returns in manufacturing and other industries, they have invested much of their savings in financial securities of various kinds. As Lysandrou (2011) notes, the various funds that absorb these savings (including hedge funds, mutual funds, money market funds, pension funds, etc.) find it easier to invest in financial markets than to move funds around the world directly into hard assets. This has created what Aalbers (2016) calls a 'wall of money' searching for yield in global financial markets. Because national and international public policies (including the various Basel accords; see Major 2012) have provided incentives to invest in financial securities that flow funds into mortgage markets, and because of innovations in mortgage securitisation that make lending for mortgages almost riskless for banks, a large proportion of these savings flow into channels that provide credit for mortgage lending. Neoliberal policies that reduce taxes for the rich, and that reduce welfare-state spending for universal programmes, are thus in part responsible for creating this wall of money flooding into mortgage markets and, in turn, more available and cheaper mortgage credit available to borrowers. The US and UK have an interest in promoting neoliberal policies that create inequality around the world. With the world's largest financial sectors, the US and the UK have a competitive advantage in providing financial securities and services to HNWIs, and their economies end up absorbing a portion of this investment, making both countries richer than they would otherwise have been (see Walks 2019 for more discussion). Financialisation allows the US and UK to extract ('expropriate' according to Lapavitsas 2009; as a form of 'tribute' in Gowan's 2009 analysis) a portion of global profits from housing investment, helping to explain why these countries have been so slow to reform their financial sectors.

The Canadian federal government implemented a number of policies that took the risk 'off the books' of Canadian banks and encouraged them to lend for mortgages. These policies included creating new mortgage-backed securities programmes in which the federal government either directly purchased or insured mortgages and related securities (see Walks 2014 for details). This made private mortgage lending virtually risk free for banks and other mortgage lenders and helped flood mortgage markets in Canada with cheap and abundant credit. Canadian buyers, able to access so much credit, competed to outbid each other for existing housing, rapidly bidding up prices, especially in those cities where (due to a lack of rental housing) investors were incentivised to buy up second properties to rent out (the 'buy-to-let' market) – creating the 'bubble' evident in Figure 9.1.

It must be noted that – as discussed by Hawes and Grisdale in Chapter 11 – the housing bubble in cities such as Toronto would not have occurred without policies and processes that reduced access to affordable rental housing and encouraged investment in owner-occupied housing at the expense of rental housing. If there had been sufficient affordable rental housing, average rents would not have risen at a rate exceeding income increases, households facing rising house prices would not feel compelled to buy (instead of rent) and investors would not have been incentivised to buy up housing units at inflated prices to rent out. Three factors have conspired to reduce the amount of affordable rental housing available in Toronto.

First of all, gentrification – specifically the conversion of formerly rental housing into owner-occupation – has eaten away at the stock of formerly affordable rental housing. In just 20 years, across the Toronto CMA the total stock of rental units with rents below 80 per cent of the average CMA rent (the Province of Ontario's official definition of 'affordable rental housing'; see MMAH Ontario 2011) declined from 237,816 units in 1991 (41.3 per cent of the rental stock, and 17.4 per cent of all Toronto CMA housing units) to 173,783 units in 2011 (27.5 per cent of the rental stock, and only 8.7 per cent of all housing units).[3] Because social rental units have not disappeared, the brunt of these declines have been felt in the privately rented affordable stock. In the 1991–2011 period, privately rented housing units affordable under the provincial definition (80 per cent of average rent or less) declined by over 70 per cent within Toronto's inner city (Walks et al., forthcoming). This was *on top of* the major waves of gentrification that occurred from the late 1960s through the late 1980s which had already resulted in many former inner city rental units being de-converted to owner-occupation (Walks and Maaranen 2008b). This has implications not only for housing costs, but also for the ability to maintain an innovative and authentic arts scene (see Chapter 15 by March).

Second, as Hawes and Grisdale discuss in Chapter 11, upper levels of government halted funding for new social affordable housing, preferring instead to allow private sector actors to produce condo units for the owner-occupier market, under sway of an 'asset-based welfare' approach to housing, and with the idea that some of these would end up as (higher-priced) rentals (Walks 2006; Walks and Clifford 2015; Suttor 2016). However, the Ontario government (the provincial governments are the level that regulates rental housing) chose not to apply rent controls to condo units built after 1991, the majority of which were located in Toronto, a policy that clearly led to rising average rents (Rosen and Walks 2015; Hale 2018). Although a short-lived New Democratic Party (Canada's party of the left) government invested in new social units in the early 1990s (roughly 14,000 within the City of Toronto), subsequent Ontario provincial governments have built very few new units and downloaded responsibility for existing units to municipalities. The roughly 15,000 new social rental units built since 1990 have done little to make up for the loss of roughly 123,000 affordable rental units that occurred within Toronto's inner city alone over this period (see Walks et al. forthcoming). The result has been a rapid decline of affordable rental units over time and the development of a rental housing crisis.

Third, as Hawes and Grisdale discuss, a significant proportion of rental stock was shifted out of the long-term market and into the short-term rental market geared to tourists and visitors (and marketed through online sites such as Airbnb). While the COVID-19 pandemic disrupted this shift, by 2020 the number of long-term rental units in Toronto was already diminished.

With all these factors at play, it is no surprise that international investors have eyed Toronto's rents as likely to continue rising, spurring real estate investment trusts (REITs) and other large financialised corporations to buy up older rental buildings to capitalise on such rent increases (see August and Walks 2018; Chapter 11 by Hawes and Grisdale, for more information).

The final piece of the puzzle is the employment effect of policies put in place in the face of the GFC. Governments around the world – including Canada and the UK – implemented policies that bailed out the financial sector and those sectors that depended on it, such as housing and automobile sales. While this prevented a global depression, it also meant that apart from housing construction it was mainly in the financial sector that jobs and wages continued to grow. Global cities such as Toronto and London are 'global' largely *because* they are the main financial centres of their respective nations. Policies bailing out the financial sector supported job growth in Toronto at the expense of many other places in Canada. Fifty-five per cent of the 50,775 jobs created within the FIRE sector (finance, insurance and real estate) in urban Canada between 2011 and 2016 were located in the Toronto CMA, which captured 25.2 per cent of the total job growth (of all new urban jobs) over this five-year period (representing 197,305 new jobs).[4] This disproportionately attracted young adults aged 20–29 to Toronto (many via migration from other places in Canada), and this age cohort increased in Toronto by the most (66,685 people) of any CMA, representing 34.3 per cent of their total growth across urban Canada, helping to spur local demand for rental housing in Toronto at exactly the same time it was becoming extremely scarce due to the factors discussed above.

Faced with a lack of rental housing and rising house prices in the owner-occupied sector, new households in Toronto were incentivised to buy housing as soon as they could, further bringing demand forward from the future and help-ing bid up the price of remaining properties. One might expect that the construc-tion industry would have responded by ramping up housing starts and in doing so help rebalance demand and supply. In fact, they did this, but mainly in the owner-occupied condo sector where demand kept rising from both sides (households looking for a place to live, and investors in the buy-to-let market, both of whom increasingly relied on mortgage financing) in the face of rising prices (Rosen and Walks 2015; Chapter 11 by Hawes and Grisdale). But as is usual during a credit-fuelled bubble, production has not been able to keep up with rising demand, so even in the condo sector sale prices rose faster than incomes and rents. But even with rapidly rising rents, many investors in the buy-to-let sector were not earning a very high profit, if any (Kalinowski 2020a), due to the already high land and housing costs.

Implications, discontents and policy responses

The housing bubble in Toronto (and other cities such as Vancouver) has had a num-ber of important repercussions. One of these is high and rising levels of indebted-ness, as households take on ever greater mortgages in order to purchase housing, and as tenants use debt to smooth consumption in the face of rising rents. One stand-ard measure of indebtedness is the ratio of total debt to annual disposable income, a measure that controls for inflation. Across all households in Canada this ratio stood at 107.8 per cent in the first quarter of 1999, but then rose by 56.3 per cent to a ratio of 167.46 per cent in the first quarter of 2016.[5] Tellingly, households in Toronto saw their debt levels rise at almost *twice* this pace, from 105 per cent in 1999 to 210 per cent in 2016 (Gellatly and Richards 2019, 4). Furthermore, debt is highly skewed, with the poorest one-fifth of households experiencing levels of indebted-ness 2.6 times greater than richer households (420 per cent of disposable income, vs 162 per cent). This has contributed to widening the distribution of wealth: in 1999 the average net worth of the richest quintile in the Toronto CMA was 78 times that of the poorest quintile, but by 2016 this had increased to 131 times, largely because wealthier households now own much of the real estate that is increasing in price, while poorer households either remain tenants or take on larger debts in order to get owner-occupied housing (Gellatly and Richards 2019, 6–7). High levels of house-hold debt are not only a key economic vulnerability facing the country but are also linked to rapidly widening levels of wealth inequality.

When local prices and availability of housing are clearly out of alignment with other local conditions such as incomes and the availability of jobs, and the population is feeling the combined stress of rising inequality and indebtedness, the inclination is for local residents to suspect something is amiss and to look for someone or something to blame. This is at the heart of policies that point the finger at foreign buyers, including the foreign/non-resident buyers/speculation taxes, which largely aim to address suspicions that wealthy Chinese investors were pricing locals out of housing in Toronto and Vancouver (Kalinowski 2018; Todd 2017). Misunderstandings about the underlying causes of the bubble also fuel so-called populist political movements attempting to capitalise on confusion and resentment. Although his new political party – the People's Party – did not win many votes in the 2019 election, leader Maxime Bernier campaigned on a promise to reduce Canada's intake of immigrants, which he argued would reduce house prices via lower demand (Pinkerton 2019).[6]

Two other scapegoats in the rush to assign blame are the planning system that has been in place to manage and direct urban growth, and rent controls that prevent landlords from raising rents faster than the rate of inflation. The Doug Ford-led Conservative Ontario government eliminated rent controls on new units in late 2018, arguing it would spur developers to build more rental housing, but the main immediate outcome was a 6.8 per cent rise in rents – three times the rate of inflation (Kalinowski 2020b), while the COVID-19 pandemic spurred many developers to abandon their plans (including the Google-affiliated Sidewalk Labs plan for Toronto's waterfront). Although the capitalist free market has never built affordable housing for poor people (especially purpose-built rental housing) without strong government dirigisme (see Suttor 2016), a so-called YIMBY (Yes In My Back Yard) movement has arisen across North America that seeks to attack government regulation, relax density and zoning requirements, and speed up or remove altogether the development permitting system so that new high-density housing can be built quickly by private market actors (McCormick 2017). In Toronto, John Lorinc has been leading the fight for cutting development charges and allowing developers to build at higher-density zoning, in what he calls the 'yellow belt' of single-family homes – with the idea that this will solve Toronto's housing affordability crisis (Lorinc 2019). What such groups miss is the fact that governments at all levels have been allowing developers more and more flexibility for years, but this has often led to *higher* land prices due to land speculation, gentrification and forms of redevelopment that price out the poor. Furthermore, high housing costs have resulted from a lack of affordable rental housing alternatives coupled with a credit-driven rush into owner-occupied housing. Loosening regulations on developers will only mean more (expensive) owner-occupied condos.

Misconceptions about the causes of housing unaffordability have led to proposed policy solutions that would only make it worse. The ending of rent controls under the Ford government is one example. In another, scholars and politicians on the right of the Canadian political spectrum, including the leader of the Conservative Party from 2017 through 2020, Andrew Scheer, and Premier of Alberta Jason Kenney, have advocated reducing or eliminating regulations that limit how much of a mortgage loan prospective homebuyers can borrow from federally regulated lenders (Scoffield 2019).[7] This would only further drive up both wealth inequalities and housing prices, as buyers able to borrow larger amounts would seek to outbid each other for the same housing, while higher-income house-holds would benefit most from the additional credit. It is not the solution to a bub-ble. Nor is the elimination of rent controls or planning regulations a solution – these approaches only lead to higher rents, higher land values, more speculation, more gentrification and a housing system that is increasingly rigged against renters, even in the face of a pandemic.

Conclusion: Toward a more contented housing system?

The rise of house prices in global cities such as Toronto and London is explainable by the fact that, in a post-GFC world where the financial system was bailed out and encouraged to increase its lending, it is mostly in the financial centres where jobs, wages and demand for housing have grown, while mortgages have become easier to acquire. And because the financial sector is one of the most spatially centralised within cities (typically located in the downtown core), this has spurred rapid gen-trification – including the de-conversion of rental units to owner-occupation – in such cities. While housing in global cities such as Toronto and London is certainly used as a place to park wealth on behalf of a transnational elite, this has not been the main cause of the bubble. The vast majority of demand for real estate is from local residents: it is because more people were able to access larger mortgages than in the past (and at negative real interest rates) that house prices inflated so quickly. Coupled with cheap credit, a lack of affordable rental alternatives encouraged new (and often amateur) landlords to enter the buy-to-let market, along with large financialised corporations (e.g. REITS) that buy up older rental buildings, to take advantage of growing demand for rental housing. This added to overall demand for units and hence increased prices. Those needing to find housing in global cit-ies end up as the 'unwilling subjects' of housing financialisation (Fields 2017), not only due to the lack of affordable choices, but also due to the fact that financialisa-tion has resulted in a concentration of work (and often the *only* new jobs, as manu-facturing and retail jobs disappear) in global cities.

Misunderstanding about the reasons for the bubble has given rise to both a populist politics searching for scapegoats and a host of proposed solutions that would make the situation worse. Removing regulations on lending will only lead to more predatory forms of debt and more indebted households. The COVID-19 pan-demic has made this situation potentially more dangerous. The Canadian federal government and the Bank of Canada have responded to the pandemic by slashing interest rates and implementing a new, larger Insured Mortgage Purchase Program meant to encourage banks to lend for mortgages in order to stimulate the economy. Not only has this led to a renewed bubble and the resumption of predatory forms of credit, but it could saddle more households with unsustainable debts. Instead, mortgage finance needs greater regulation specifically to avoid speculation and to shape lending in the public interest. Those who would relax rent controls and zoning, reduce development charges and otherwise incentivise capitalist development will only end up benefitting developers at the expense of rising rents, higher land costs, more speculation and heightened gentrification. Capitalism has never found it profitable to build quality affordable housing. It will be necessary for the state to require, if not also fund, a greater range of affordable housing choices. Inclusionary zoning, in which higher-income owners and renters in condo buildings cross-subsidise lower-income households (with the units allocated by housing agencies rather than the condo boards or developers), would have helped – and will still help – to increase the availability of moderately priced rental units. Community land trusts have the ability to keep land costs down and empower local communities to collectively manage housing units to meet real needs, rather than private greed (see Bunce, Chapter 19). State provisions that prevent de-conversion of older rental housing would help limit gentrification and maintain affordable housing in the older accessible stock. Lastly, new state-funded social housing would help provide affordable units, keep rents down and dis-incentivise speculators and predatory finance from turning rental buildings into cash cows for global elites. Global cities, including Toronto, require a mix of these solutions as well as, eventually, the socialisation and democratisation of finance itself.

Notes

1. All data in this paragraph calculated by the author using the Teranet House Price Index dataset. Note that Figure 9.1 anchors the values for both sets of data to 100 in January 2008.
2. According to the Teranet House Price Index, house prices in Vancouver rose 12.5 per cent in 2015, so even the flawed and biased estimate produced by the authors of this BC report effectively suggests that more than a majority (60 per cent) of the increase in house prices resulted from local factors.
3. Calculated by the author using data from the 1991 Census of Canada, the 2011 Census of Canada and the 2011 National Household Survey (for details, see Walks et al. under review).
4. This is well in excess of its share of the total CMA population (22.4 per cent) and urban labour force (22.7 per cent), meaning that the Toronto CMA brought in labour from the rest of Canada during this time, creating a roughly 5 per cent jobs deficit between the rest of Canada and the Toronto CMA. All the data in this paragraph calculated by the author using data from the 1991 Census of Canada, the 2011 Census of Canada and the 2011 National Household Survey.
5. Calculated by the author using data from Statistics Canada, CANSIM II Table 3780123.
6. In an interview with the *Toronto Star* newspaper, Bernier said 'immigration will be a solution. Fewer immigrants, you'll have less pressure on the housing market so pressure will be lower' (Pinkerton 2019).
7. This includes removing the so-called stress test that requires non-insured borrowers to qualify for a mortgage at the higher of the official posted rate or the rate that the lender offers them plus two percentage points. This is in place to protect the lenders (or the investors buying financial securities backed by mortgages) by making sure borrowers will still be able to pay their mortgages if and when interest rates rise. The Conservatives advocated eliminating the stress test and relaxing other regulations.

References

Aalbers, Manuel. 2016. *The Financialization of Housing: A Political Economy Approach*. London: Routledge.
Abildgren, Kim, Hansen, Niels L. and Kuchler, Andreas. 2018. 'Overoptimism and House Price Bubbles'. *Journal of Macroeconomics* 56:1–14. https://doi.org/10.1016/j.jmacro.2017.12.006.
Alvaredo, Facundo, Chancel, Lucas, Piketty, Thomas, Saez, Emmanuel and Zucman, Gabriel. 2017. 'Global Inequality Dynamics: New Findings from WID.world'. *American Economic Review* 107(5):404–9. https://doi.org/10.1257/aer.p20171095.

August, Martine and Walks, Alan. 2018. 'Gentrification, Suburban Decline, and the Financialization of Multi-Family Rental Housing'. *Geoforum* 89:124–36. https://doi.org/10.1016/j.geoforum.2017.04.011.

Bichler, Shimshon and Nitzan, Jonathan. 2009. 'Contours of Crisis II: Fiction and Reality'. *Dollars and Sense*, 28 April. Accessed 22 July 2020. http://dollarsandsense.org/archives/2009/0409bichlernitzan.html.

CMHC (Canadian Mortgage and Housing Corporation). 2016. *Housing Market Insight: Vancouver CMA – Preliminary Impacts of the Foreign Buyers Tax on the Vancouver Housing Market*. Ottawa: CMHC. Accessed 22 July 2020. ftp://ftp.cmhc-schl.gc.ca/chic-ccdh/MAC/HousingMarketInsightVancouver/68556_2016_M10.pdf.

CMHC (Canadian Mortgage and Housing Corporation). 2017. *Housing Market Insight: Canada: Non-Resident Ownership of Condominium Apartments*. Ottawa: CMHC.

Crouch, Colin. 2009. 'Privatised Keynesianism: An Unacknowledged Policy Regime'. *British Journal of Politics and International Relations* 11(3):382–99. https://doi.org/10.1111/j.1467-856x.2009.00377.x.

Febbraro, Jenny. 2019. 'Toronto's Housing Bubble Predicted to Pop: Report'. *Toronto Storeys*, 31 July. Accessed 22 July 2020. https://torontostoreys.com/toronto-housing-bubble-pop.

Fernandez, Rodrigo, Hofman, Annelore, and Aalbers, Manuel B. 2016. 'London and New York as a Safe Deposit Box for the Transnational Wealth Elite'. *Environment and Planning* A 48(12):2443–61.

Fields, Desiree. 2017. 'Unwilling Subjects of Financialization'. *International Journal of Urban and Regional Research* 41(4):588–603. https://doi.org/10.1111/1468-2427.12519.

Fraser, Isabelle. 2017. '"Almost No Evidence" of London Homes Owned by Foreign Buyers Being Left Empty'. *The Telegraph*, 14 June. Accessed 22 July 2020. https://www.telegraph.co.uk/property/house-prices/almost-no-evidence-london-homes-owned-foreign-buyers-left-empty.

Gellatly, Guy and Richards, Elizabeth. 2019. *Indebtedness and Wealth among Canadian Households*. Ottawa: Statistics Canada. Accessed 22 July 2020. https://www150.statcan.gc.ca/n1/en/pub/11-626-x/11-626-x2019003-eng.pdf?st=mrHp1M3H.

Gowan, Peter. 2009. 'Crisis in the Heartland'. *New Left Review* 55(1):5–29.

Gray, John. 2017. 'BMO Declares Toronto Housing Bubble amid "Dangerously" Hot Prices'. *BNN Bloomberg*. Accessed 22 July 2020. https://www.bnnbloomberg.ca/bmo-declares-toronto-housing-bubble-1.672542.

Hale, Kenn. 2018. 'Ontario Government Goes Back to Failed Rent Control Policy'. Toronto: Advocacy Centre for Tenants Ontario (ACTO), 27 November. Accessed 22 July 2020. https://www.acto.ca/ontario-government-goes-back-to-failed-rent-control-policy.

Kalinowski, Tess. 2018. 'Did Ontario's Real Estate Tax Close the Deal?' *Toronto Star*, 25 April. Accessed 22 July 2020. https://www.thestar.com/business/real_estate/2018/04/25/foreign-buyers-dwindle-after-ontario-launches-real-estate-tax.html.

Kalinowski, Tess. 2020a. 'Condo Prices Are Set to Put Many Investors in the Red as Rents Fail to Meet Carrying Costs, Experts Warn'. *Toronto Star*, 12 January.

Kalinowski, Tess. 2020b. 'Toronto Rents Shoot Up on High Demand'. *Toronto Star*, 16 January.

Konings, Martijn. 2018. *Capital and Time: For a New Critique of Neoliberal Reason*. Stanford, CA: Stanford University Press.

Lapavitsas, Costas. 2009. 'Financialized Capitalism: Crisis and Financial Expropriation'. *Historical Materialism* 17:114–48. https://doi.org/10.1163/156920609x436153.

Lee-Shanok, Philip. 2019. 'Criminals Hiding Billions of Dollars in GTA Real Estate, Watchdog Claims'. *CBC News Online*, 21 March. Accessed 22 July 2020. https://www.cbc.ca/news/canada/toronto/anti-corruption-group-claims-criminals-laundering-money-through-toronto-real-estate-1.5065777.

Lewis, Michael. 2019. 'Toronto Ranks Last in Renter Satisfaction'. *Toronto Star*, 3 December.

Ley, David. 2010. *Millionaire Migrants: Trans-Pacific Pipelines*. Malden, MA: Blackwell.

Ley, David. 2017. 'Global China and the Making of Vancouver's Residential Property Market'. *International Journal of Housing Policy* 17(1SI):15–34. https://doi.org/10.1080/14616718.2015.1119776.

Ley, David and Murphy, Peter. 2001. 'Immigration in Gateway Cities: Sydney and Vancouver in Comparative Perspective'. *Progress in Planning* 35(3):119–94. https://doi.org/10.1016/s0305-9006(00)00025-8.

Lorinc, John. 2019. 'How Reducing Development Charges Will Spur the "Missing Middle"'. *SpacingToronto*, 14 January. Accessed 22 July 2020. https://spacing.ca/toronto/2019/01/14/lorinc-how-reducing-development-charges-will-spur-the-missing-middle.

Lysandrou, Photis. 2011. 'Global Inequality as One of the Root Causes of the Financial Crisis: A Suggested Explanation'. *Economy and Society* 40(3):323–44. https://doi.org/10.1080/03085147.2011.576848.

McClelland, Colin. 2019. 'Toronto Is Now the World's Second Most Overvalued Property Market: UBS'. *Financial Post*, 30 September. Accessed 22 July 2020. https://business.financialpost.com/real-estate/toronto-is-now-the-worlds-second-most-overvalued-property-market.

McCormick, Erin. 2017. 'Rise of the Yimbys: The Angry Millennials with a Radical Housing Solution'. *The Guardian*, 2 October. Accessed 22 July 2020. https://www.theguardian.com/cities/2017/oct/02/rise-of-the-yimbys-angry-millennials-radical-housing-solution.

Major, Aaron. 2012. 'Neoliberalism and the New International Financial Architecture'. *Review of International Political Economy* 19(4):536–61. https://doi.org/10.1080/09692290.2011.603663.

Maloney, Maureen, Somerville, Tsur and Unger, Brigitte. 2019. *Combatting Money Laundering in BC Real Estate*. Victoria: Government of British Columbia. Accessed 22 July 2020. https://news.gov.bc.ca/files/Combatting_Money_Laundering_Report.pdf.

MMAH (Ministry of Municipal Affairs and Housing) Ontario. 2011. *Investment in Affordable Housing for Ontario: Program Guidelines*. Accessed 9 October 2020. https://www.msdsb.net/images/ADMIN/correspondence/2011/IAH-Guidelines.pdf.

Moos, Markus and Skaburskis, Andrejs. 2010. 'The Globalization of Urban Housing Markets: Immigration and Changing Housing Demand in Vancouver'. *Urban Geography* 31(6):724–49. https://doi.org/10.2747/0272-3638.31.6.724.

Novokmet, Filip, Piketty, Thomas and Zucman, Gabriel. 2018. 'From Soviets to Oligarchs: Inequality and Property in Russia 1905–2016'. *Journal of Economic Inequality* 16(2SI):189–223. https://doi.org/10.1007/s10888-018-9383-0.

Piketty, Thomas and Saez, Emmanuel. 2014. 'Inequality in the Long Run'. *Science* 344(6186):838–43. https://doi.org/10.1126/science.1251936.

Piketty, Thomas, Saez, Emmanuel and Zucman, Gabriel. 2018. 'Distributional National Accounts: Methods and Estimates for the United States'. *Quarterly Journal of Economics* 133(2):533–609.

Pinkerton, Charlie. 2019. 'People's Party Housing Affordability Plan Features no Housing-specific Policies'. *iPolitics*, 24 September. Accessed 22 July 2020. https://ipolitics.ca/2019/09/24/peoples-party-housing-affordability-plan-features-no-housing-specific-policies.

Rogers, Dallas and Koh, Sin Yee. 2017. 'The Globalisation of Real Estate: The Politics and Practice of Foreign Real Estate Investment'. *International Journal of Housing Policy* 17(1):1–14. https://doi.org/10.1080/19491247.2016.1270618.

Rosen, Gillad and Walks, Alan. 2015. 'Castles in Toronto's Sky: Condoism as Urban Transformation'. *Journal of Urban Affairs* 85(1):39–66. https://doi.org/10.1111/juaf.12140.

Scoffield, Heather. 2019. 'Conservatives Take Swing at Fragile Housing Market'. *Toronto Star*, 25 September.

Skaburskis, Andrejs and Moos, Markus. 2008. 'The Redistribution of Residential Property Values in Montreal, Toronto, and Vancouver: Examining Neoclassical and Marxist Views on Changing Investment Patterns'. *Environment and Planning A* 40(4):905–27. https://doi.org/10.1068/a39153.

Stiglitz, Joseph E. 1990. 'Symposium on Bubbles'. *Journal of Economic Perspectives* 4(2):13–18.

Suttor, Greg. 2016. *Still Renovating: A History of Canadian Social Housing Policy*. Montreal-Kingston: McGill-Queen's University Press.

Teranet. 2020. Teranet 10-City House Price Index. Accessed January 2020. https://housepriceindex.ca.

Todd, Douglas. 2017. 'How Would Vancouver's Housing Bubble Burst? Look to China'. *Vancouver Sun*, 18 February. Accessed 22 July 2020. https://vancouversun.com/opinion/columnists/douglas-todd-how-would-vancouvers-housing-bubble-burst-look-to-china.

Walks, Alan. 2006. 'Homelessness, the New Poverty, and Housing Affordability'. In *Canadian Cities in Transition* (3rd edition), edited by Trudi E. Bunting and Pierre Filion, 419–37. Oxford: Oxford University Press.

Walks, Alan. 2011. 'Economic Restructuring and Trajectories of Socio-spatial Polarization in the Twenty-first-century Canadian City'. In *Canadian Urban Regions: Trajectories of Growth and Change*, edited by Larry S. Bourne, Tom Hutton, Richard Shearmur and Jim Simmons, 125–59. Toronto: Oxford University Press.

Walks, Alan. 2013. 'Mapping the Urban Debtscape: The Geography of Household Debt in Canadian Cities'. *Urban Geography* 34(2):153–87. https://doi.org/10.1080/02723638.2013.778647.

Walks, Alan. 2014. 'Canada's Housing Bubble Story: Mortgage Securitization, the State, and the Global Financial Crisis'. *International Journal of Urban and Regional Research* 38(1):256–84. https://doi.org/10.1111/j.1468-2427.2012.01184.x.

Walks, Alan. 2015. 'Stopping the "War on the Car": Neoliberalism, Fordism, and the Politics of Automobility in Toronto'. *Mobilities* 10(3):402–22. https://doi.org/10.1080/17450101.2014.880563.

Walks, Alan. 2019. 'Affordability and Housing Policy in the World's Cities: Excavating the Global Housing Bubble'. In *A Research Agenda for Housing*, edited by Markus Moos, 47–65. Cheltenham: Edward Elgar.

Walks, Alan and Clifford, Brian. 2015. 'The Political Economy of Securitization and the Neoliberalization of Housing Policy in Canada'. *Environment and Planning A* 47(8):1624–42. https://doi.org/10.1068/a130226p.

Walks, Alan, Hawes, Emily and Simone, Dylan. Forthcoming. 'Gentrification in Large Canadian Cities: Tenure, Age and Exclusionary Displacement 1991–2011'.

Walks, Alan and Maaranen, Richard. 2008a. 'Gentrification, Social Mix, and Social Polarization: Testing the Linkages in Large Canadian Cities'. *Urban Geography* 29(4):293–326. https://doi.org/10.2747/0272-3638.29.4.293.

Walks, Alan and Maaranen, Richard. 2008b. *The Timing, Patterning and Forms of Gentrification and Neighbourhood Upgrading in Montreal, Toronto, and Vancouver 1961 to 2001*. Toronto: University of Toronto Cities Centre Research Paper 211.

Wetzstein, Steffen. 2017. 'The Global Urban Housing Affordability Crisis'. *Urban Studies* 54(14):3159–77. https://doi.org/10.1177/0042098017711649.

10
Trends and issues in the (unaffordable) London housing market

Tommaso Gabrieli

Introduction

This chapter aims to describe and analyse some of the fundamental trends and policy issues in the London housing market. Focusing on the unaffordability problem for first-time buyers, the chapter will show how this emerges as a market outcome where price dynamics, foreign investments, speed and type of development activity interrelate and play a major role. The chapter employs a descriptive economic analysis to explain detailed empirical evidence on demand, supply and prices across the London housing system; the economic analysis will describe the institutional and market links between planning, development and housing demand and will exemplify how those links impact on market prices and affordability. Under an institutional economic approach, I will describe how the fundamental activities/functions of development, investing and planning are linked by prices and financial variables, and how those activities shape market outcomes, henceforth describing and making sense of recent market trends. In view of this institutional analysis, I will then critically present the most recent policy proposals and discussions.

The problem

The empirical evidence is stark: London is not affordable for the average earner, as first-time buyers are in the top 20 per cent of city household income distribution. Research from Halifax (2019)[1] shows that the average first-time buyer pays a deposit of £110,656 (26 per cent of the purchase price); this is about three times more than in 2008, when it stood at £38,335. Unsurprisingly this implies that first-time buyers are now older than they were in 2008 – aged 31 nationwide and aged 33 in London – up by two years. The primary reason for this dramatic lack of affordability is that housing has become increasingly expensive in the last 15 years.

According to Office for National Statistics (ONS) data, house prices have increased in every region of England since 2004. Prices per square metre in London increased far more than in any other region, leading to a widening gulf between it and other regions. In 2004, the average price per square metre in London varied from £2,310 in Barking and Dagenham to £8,190 in Kensington and Chelsea, but by 2016 these figures had risen to £5,970 and £19,440 respectively. The top 19 most expensive local authorities by price per square metre are all in London, with Elmbridge (Surrey) the twentieth most expensive non-London area. Barking and Dagenham, the cheapest borough in London, is still more expensive than the priciest local authorities in the South West, Midlands or North.

If we associate those figures to data on first-time buyers we unequivocally notice that London remains too expensive for many young first-time buyers, with research from Hometrack (2018) showing that £84,250 was the average income required to buy an average property. Average first-time buyer property prices in the capital have increased by 50 per cent in 10 years and now stand at £426,857. Within the context of a national affordability crisis, there is a particular disparity between the previous figures for London and the rest of the UK, where property prices went up by one-fifth (21 per cent) since 2008, with the average price up from £172,659 in 2008 to £212,473 today, while the average deposit is now £32,841, up by 70 per cent from £19,364 in 2008.[2] Moreover, research from Trust for London (2017) shows that the high cost of housing in the capital largely explains the higher rate of poverty in London (27 per cent of Londoners, compared with 21 per cent across England, after housing costs).

There are various measures of affordability.[3] The most commonly used indicator in the UK is the ratio of house prices to incomes or earnings – and indeed this is also used in many other countries. Based on the 2018 release of ONS data, Figure 10.1 illustrates the median affordability ratio, which is the ratio of median price paid for residential property to the median workplace-based gross annual earnings for full-time workers. We notice that in London the ratio is at 20, twice the UK average. There are broad differences; the figure shows the least affordable and the most affordable boroughs.

More generally, ONS (2018) shows that over the past five years, more local authorities in London and surrounding regions have fallen into the least affordable category. In 2018, eight of the 10 least affordable local authorities in England and Wales were in London, with two being in the surrounding South East region. The most affordable local authorities in 2018 were in the North West, Wales and the East Midlands. It is also interesting to look at some international comparisons. A survey by Demographia (2019) shows that the median ratio for London is in the severely unaffordable category,[4] alongside cities such as Hong Kong, Sydney, Los Angeles and Vancouver.

Extremely high prices and unaffordability, especially for first-time buyers, can also explain why London's overall homeownership rate has fallen in recent decades, but there are stark differences in the trends for different age groups. Research

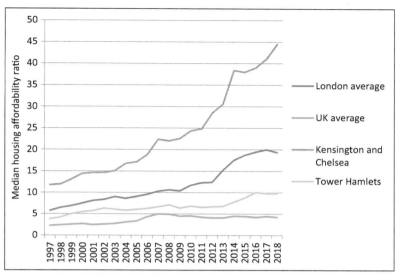

Figure 10.1 Median housing affordability ratio (author, data from ONS 2018)

from the Greater London Authority (GLA 2018) shows that in 1990, 25 per cent of households in London headed by someone aged 16–24 and 57 per cent of households headed by someone aged 25–34 owned their home. However, by 2017 these figures had fallen to 8 per cent and 28 per cent respectively. Homeownership rates also fell for households headed by someone aged 35–44 (from 69 per cent to 49 per cent) and 45–54 (71 per cent to 52 per cent) over the same period. During this period, the ownership rate for households headed by someone aged 55–64 initially rose, but over the last decade it has fallen back to its original level at 63 per cent. Finally, the proportion of households headed by someone older than 65 who owned their own home rose relatively steadily from 49 per cent in 1990 to 72 per cent in 2017.

An economic analysis

This section presents various descriptive statistics and trends, with data about tenure, ownership, foreign investments, speed and volumes of development activity, lending market and price trends. It will then present a narrative of how those various activities interact and contribute to unaffordability.

The outcome described in the previous section can be understood in terms of dynamics of demand and supply, where demand for housing in London has constantly grown in the past two decades. Looking to demand, evidence from the GLA (2018) shows that since 1997 both London's population and its economy have grown rapidly, although the job market trends are considerably more cyclical. Between 1997 and 2017, the number of jobs in London grew by 1.73 million, or 42 per cent, while the population grew by 1.81 million (26 per cent). However, this rapid economic and demographic growth was not matched by an increase in the housing stock, which grew by only 500,000 homes (16 per cent) over the same period. The last five years have also seen a wide disparity, with the number of jobs growing by 14 per cent between 2012 and 2017, the number of people by 6 per cent and the number of homes by 4 per cent. This increase in demand has not been matched by an equal increase in supply.

Why is demand so strong? London is an international financial centre. Lizieri (2009) notes that among world cities, a small subset of cities known as international financial centres (IFCs) play a major role in the global system of finance. Those cities act as centres for asset management and product innovation. Economies of scale and agglomeration, which are the benefits that firms obtain by respectively increasing in size and locating near each other, have resulted in an ongoing concentration of high-order financial services – such as equity trading, bond trading, foreign exchange activity, derivatives trading and wealth management – in a few key global cities.

In a global economy dominated by the free and fast movement of international funds, IFCs compete with each other in order to attract capital, with London usually being considered one of the most global cities (Sassen 2001). The attractiveness of London as a destination for both commercial and residential real estate capital has led to the city being described as a 'safe deposit box' (Fernandez et al. 2016). Looking at foreign investments, Wallace et al. (2017) found that 13 per cent of new build properties sold in London between 2014 and 2016 went to overseas buyers.[5] Research by Sá (2016) shows that with no foreign investment in the housing market in England and Wales between the years 2000 and 2014, house prices would be 19 per cent lower than they are now.

House prices can be theorised as an outcome of the dynamics of demand and supply: when housing demand grows more than supply, prices increase. At the same time, demand and supply are not fixed and do respond to prices; the standard economic tool to analyse those mutual links between demand, supply and prices is the general equilibrium model. However, since demand is constantly growing and developers' incentives to supply housing are often changing because of changes in planning policies, a concept of long-run equilibrium is not very useful to analyse London house price dynamics. The well-known Four Quadrant Model of DiPasquale and Wheaton (1992) is a more immediate and useful general equilibrium tool to understand how the complex interaction between development and investment inevitably creates market dynamics, volatility and cycles.[6] Essentially, the model considers the specific and joint dynamics of property, investment and development markets, where shocks in one market will have an effect, albeit with lags, on other markets through changes in prices and rents. For example, a demand shock in the property market affects property valuations, which in turn will have an effect on investments for new constructions, which will ultimately feed back as new supply to the property market, with the possibility of overshooting demand and therefore reversing the cycle. Just as in many other developed cities, this has not happened in London, where supply has not increased rapidly following periods of rapid price increase. In order to understand the reasons behind a slow supply process, we need to refer to intrinsic features of planning, development and the housebuilding industry that jointly determine the supply dynamics.

The UK planning system is local, as planning applications have to be decided in line with the relevant local planning authority's development plan. The approval process usually involves a negotiation around planning obligations, also known as Section 106 agreements (based on that section of the 1990 Town & Country Planning Act); those are private agreements made between local authorities and developers and can be attached to a planning permission to make acceptable development that would otherwise be unacceptable in planning terms. In particular, planning obligations are used for three purposes: (i) to prescribe the nature of development (e.g. requiring that a given portion of housing is affordable); (ii) to compensate for loss or damage created by a development (e.g. loss of open space); and (iii) to mitigate a development's impact (e.g. through increased public transport provision). This process is intrinsically discretionary, with decisions on permitted development on a particular site made on a case-by-case basis, following a negotiation process about developer contributions to affordable housing and other community infrastructure through Section 106. Extensive research documents that the approval process can take months or even years and that delay and lack of certainty are factored into developers' financial models,[7] increasing required returns and stopping marginal developments from going forward.

Potential lack of competition in the housebuilding industry has been long debated in the UK (see e.g. Ball 2010). Given extensive evidence that developers purchase large quantities of land without developing it, the existence of barriers to entry, increased market shares of the largest builders and weak supply responsiveness might suggest that developers do so with the intent of pushing up prices, a practice known as land hoarding – a stronger version of land banking.[8]

Despite those known issues, housing supply in London increased substantially in recent years. The GLA (2018) shows that since the turn of the millennium the net increase in London's housing stock has been relatively rapid. The GLA (2018) reports that an average of 20,000 homes a year were built in London between 2011 and 2016 according to the new build statistics, but the net increase in the dwelling stock was greater at around 25,400 a year, due to a combination of relatively few demolitions and substantial new housing supply coming from conversions and changes of use,[9] as well as the undercount in the new build statistics. Increase in the planned capacity was key for actual supply to increase: data from the GLA (2018, 22) document that the 2004 London Plan identified capacity for 23,000 new homes, which then rose to 30,500 in the 2008 Plan, 32,200 in the 2011 Plan, 42,400 in the 2015 Plan and 60,000 in the 2018 Draft Plan; however, the same data show the systematic underachievement of actual supply in terms of planned capacity, given the discussed slow process to translate capacity into completions.

Mortgage availability is the main financial channel impacting on affordability, with cheap liquidity being one of the factors that accelerated demand before the Global Financial Crisis. GLA (2018) data show that the level of new homebuyer mortgage lending continues to be subdued, with new home mover mortgages close to levels last seen during the crash. In 2017 there were 42,800 new loans to first-time buyers in London, up 1 per cent from 2016, and 30,500 to home movers, down 2 per cent. While lending to first-time buyers has recovered partially after 2009, the level of lending to home movers is very subdued. Two thousand fewer home mover loans were made in 2017 than in 2009. The number of home mover loans has fallen by one-fifth (19 per cent) since the second quarter of 2016. The typical first-time buyer in London borrowed 4.04 times their income in 2017, up from just 1.88 in 1980. Home movers, who usually bring some equity from the sale of their previous home, have typically borrowed at a somewhat lower income ratio than first-time buyers. However, the two have now converged. Home movers in London borrowed an average of 4.02 times their incomes in 2017, up from 3.93 in 2016 and 1.71 in 1980. The Bank of England recommended in June 2014 that mortgage lenders do not extend more than 15 per cent of new residential mortgages at loan to income ratios at or greater than 4.5. This is expected to progressively constrain further increases in median loan-to-income ratios for buyers in London.

Most first-time buyers typically need high loan-to-value ratios (LTVs); however, the availability of mortgage loans with high LTVs fell dramatically in the wake of the 2007/8 financial crisis. Loans with LTVs of more than 90 per cent comprised one-third of all lending to first-time buyers in London in 2005/6, but this share fell to just 1 per cent in 2010/11 and 2011/12. In the last two years the proportion of loans at LTVs of between 90 and 95 per cent has risen again, reaching 14 per cent in the year to September 2017. Loans at LTVs of more than 95 per cent are still virtually non-existent. Loans with LTVs of 50 per cent or less have risen significantly in both absolute and percentage terms since 2014/15, and in the last year comprised 23 per cent of total first-time buyer mortgage loans. This is primarily driven by the Help to Buy policy, an equity loan scheme which provides government-backed equity loans of up to 40 per cent of the property value, thereby reducing the amount to be covered by a mortgage. In 2016/17, there were 2,990 homes bought in London with assistance from this scheme, with an average loan value of £152,300. The typical income of households buying with assistance from Help to Buy London was around £66,500. The number of Help to Buy equity loan purchases in 2016/17 is equivalent to 13 per cent of the number of new build private completions in London in that year (up from 9 per cent in 2015/16). The Help to Buy London share of the homeowner market may actually be larger, as some of these new homes would have been bought by investors and rented out. By this measure, Help to Buy London plays a particularly significant role in outer London, accounting for over one-quarter of sales in several boroughs.

Policies

This section will describe proposed policies through the lenses of the previous analysis. In broad terms, policies in the following categories will be discussed and reviewed: (i) policies to increase supply; (ii) policy towards the affordable sector: shared equity, shared ownership, social rent; (iii) policies towards the Green Belt; and (iv) demand-based policies.

Recent policy documents demonstrate a strong commitment to increasing housing supply and in particular the supply of affordable homes. The Draft London Plan (2018) reports that the mayor's Strategic Housing Market Assessment has identified a need for 66,000 additional homes per year and a strategic target that 50 per cent of new homes should be affordable, given the declared key objective of Mayor of London Sadiq Khan in the 2016 mayoral election to increase the provision of homes that are genuinely affordable for Londoners. According to the Plan, these homes are to be delivered through a range of sources, including partnerships with registered providers, the allocation of affordable housing grants as part of the mayor's Affordable Housing Programme 2016–21 and within private developments. Given the many challenges around increasing housing supply that we have covered in the previous section, and that only around 20,000 homes are built every year, the current plan presents a very ambitious target.

When we look specifically at affordable housing, data from the GLA (2018) show that the percentage of affordable housing secured through the planning process fell each year between 2007/8 and 2014/15 (from 30 per cent to less than 15 per cent). Yet the number of GLA-funded affordable homes started in London was 8,940 in 2016/17, a figure which increased to 12,530 in 2017/18, the highest since 2010/11. Of the affordable homes started in 2017/18, 6,730 (54 per cent) were intermediate (shared ownership or intermediate rent), while 2,830 (23 per cent) were at social rents or London affordable rent levels, also the highest figure since 2010/11. The remainder (24 per cent) were other homes for affordable rent.

According to the government definition, affordable housing is social rented, affordable rented and intermediate housing, provided to eligible households whose needs are not met by the market. Eligibility is determined with regard to local incomes and local house prices. In particular, the London Plan states that affordable rented housing is let by local authorities or private registered providers of social housing to households who are eligible for social rented housing. Affordable rent is subject to rent controls that require a rent of no more than 80 per cent of the local market rent, including service expenses. Intermediate housing includes homes available for sale or rent at a cost above social rent but below market levels. These can include shared equity (shared ownership and equity loans), other low-cost homes for sale and intermediate rent, but not affordable rent. Households whose annual income is in the range £18,100–£66,000 should be eligible for new intermediate homes. For homes with more than two bedrooms, which are particularly suitable for families, the upper end of this eligibility range will be extended to £80,000; these figures are updated annually.

Intermediate housing in the form of shared ownership (SO) and shared equity (SE) products constitutes the only types of affordable ownership schemes backed by government policies. Whitehead (2010) notes that those schemes have been part of UK housing policy since the 1970s, as they were originally developed to address affordability issues at times of high inflation, when people who could easily afford to buy over their working lifetime were excluded by high payments in the early years. Later they became one of a range of low-cost homeownership initiatives aimed at extending homeownership, based on expectations that house-holds' incomes would increase so that they could move to 100 per cent purchase within a reasonable time (see e.g. Booth and Crook 1986). More recently, SO/SE products have been used to provide subsidies to increase homeownership rates by enabling marginal purchasers to buy as house prices rose faster than incomes and more households were excluded. While there have been many different versions over the years, government policy has concentrated on two core models: shared ownership, where the purchaser buys a proportion of the property with a tradi-tional mortgage while the other portion is owned by a social landlord who receives rent on this element; and shared equity, where the purchaser buys 100 per cent of the property but obtains an equity loan to cover part of the value.[10] Research by Whitehead (2010) shows that those instruments may be too expensive and too risky in the case of depreciations; research by Meen (2018b) shows that those poli-cies are primarily of benefit to those already on the fringes of homeownership.

Together with the recommendation of resourcing authorities' planning capacity, delivering a variety of sites for development, speeding up and monitoring build-out rates, supporting small and medium developers, research from Scanlon et al. (2018) recommends that one way of expanding construction output – includ-ing the affordable type – for boroughs and other public landowners would be to commission housing in partnership with developers. This so-called direct commis-sioning could be seen as a descendant of the council housebuilding programmes of the 1960s and 1970s, which provided hundreds of thousands of homes per year at the height of production. According to this view, the benefits of this approach are that it would effectively introduce a source of cheap land but also a long-term source of revenue. Most importantly, by having a guaranteed customer, build-out rates could be faster than those achieved by speculative for-sale developers. There are few examples of existing partnerships between local authorities and developers with different legal structures; research on the pros, cons and controversies around those schemes is limited.[11]

A number of high-profile reports mentioned by Wacher (2018) discuss the negative impact that viability assessments have played in reducing the level of affordable housing negotiated by local planning authorities through Section 106. While the statutory planning framework has remained one that is plan-led, the prevalence and influence of viability assessments on affordable housing and other planning outcomes has resulted in what could be termed a viability-led planning system. A range of factors have led to this scenario. As a proposed remedy, policy H6 of the Draft London Plan sets out details of the threshold approach to affordable housing. This enables schemes delivering 35 per cent affordable housing, and 50 per cent on public and industrial land, to be assessed under a fast-track route without needing to provide detailed viability information. A key benefit of the threshold approach is that it provides greater certainty to the market, particularly when developers purchase land. Similarly, at the national scale, the government issued a set of proposals for consultation (DCLG 2017) including an approach to viability based on area-wide assessment at local plan stage; according to this policy proposal, where a proposed development is in line with all the relevant policies in an up-to-date development plan, the development should be assumed to be viable and no further assessment of viability is needed. Scanlon et al. (2018) mention that many commentators have argued that site-specific issues are so important that this is not feasible, especially on larger sites and indeed in London, and that, contrary to what is intended, uncertainty would be exacerbated.

London's metropolitan Green Belt has been singled out as a brake on land supply and therefore a driver of rising house prices by various economic analyses.[12] According to this view, constraints on land supply, often justified for reasons of 'urban containment' and densification, are credited with turning housing into an especially attractive asset class. The issue is controversial, and it has been heavily debated both in academia and in evidence sessions at the UK Parliament.[13] Given an economic rationale that there should be a cost–benefit analysis between land in any use and its alternative proposed use, and a recognition that the Green Belt land serves an important purpose, building on it is a complex issue. However, an opinion that is gaining momentum is that wherever major infrastructure changes accessibility and provides benefits to communities, there should be a review of the costs and benefits of modifying the designation of affected land – with the full understanding that any Green Belt acreage lost should be replaced by more environmentally valuable land (see Mace et al. 2016). Edwards (2016), however, comments that in the more general context of people's interest in maintaining house values and the strong tradition of amenity protection that generate 'not in my back yard' (NIMBY) resistance to new development in many rural and urban areas, the strong commitment of central government and the mayor to protecting the Green Belt from residential development may be politically inevitable.

A recent and growing body of research is expanding the policy discussion towards demand-side policies. The introduction of a stamp duty supplement on most buy-to-let investments and changes in the rate of tax relief on privately let properties and second homes are the only examples, albeit with small potential impact on prices, of this type of policies. Meen (2018b) comments that although increases in housing supply continue to play an important part in improving affordability, it has been known since the review of housing supply by Barker (2004) that increases in supply have to be large and long-lasting to have a major effect on affordability, and therefore suggests that the benefits to those on low incomes from market provision alone are unlikely to be adequate, and that an important role for expansion of social rented housing remains. An alternative view is that housing shortages could be reduced if owner-occupiers could be persuaded with a tax to reduce 'over consumption' of housing and downsize. Meen (2018b) demonstrates the consequences of changing the tax system so that property taxes are proportional to income and the housing costs of older households would rise considerably; he suggests that were this to be considered, any changes would need to be introduced over a long period of time and/or offset in other ways. Referring to a broader perspective on financialisation of housing, Gallent et al. (2017) also suggest that the solution to the unaffordability crisis could lie in demand management policies, despite this often being considered unworkable.

Conclusions

It is difficult and complex to anticipate what the future holds for London house prices as the general political and economic uncertainty related to the Brexit process continues; the future outlook might be characterised by a general depreciation trend, which would imply a different market context from the one described in this chapter. ONS data from June 2019 show that average house prices in London fell modestly over the year each month from March 2018; from their recent peak and trough of £489,000 in July 2017 and £467,000 in June 2019, average London house prices have fallen 5.1 per cent. In principle, a decrease in average house prices may enable some wealthier potential first-time buyers to buy; however, it is fair to say that a strong depreciation could only happen in a scenario of financial turmoil and economic recession and therefore with many negative implications for the affordability of both first-time buyers and renters, especially the less wealthy. Moreover, depreciations would be particularly harmful for current holders and providers of SE and SO products.

Questions over future price trends are only one part of the methodological challenges in monitoring future trends; another fundamental issue for effective policy-making is that while there is no strict definition of housing need, this is usually understood as the amount of housing required for all households to live in accommodation that meets a certain normative standard. The number of households is often used as a proxy for housing need, but this measure cannot give the whole picture. For this reason policy-makers need information to track the changes in key indicators in a timely way, as well as to set specific goals or targets while making clear what a given measure is meant to achieve and by when; lessons and good practices over such issues may be learned across countries.

Research and policy publications cited in this chapter tend to agree that while increasing supply is of critical importance – and there is no 'silver bullet' that can remove all obstacles that still limit housing supply – the issue of affordability in both the private and social housing sectors needs to be tackled directly with more financing of affordable housing. Filling the huge existing funding gap for affordable housing is challenging, and many experts are debating a more direct role for the public sector in the delivery of what is missing, as well as suggesting looking to land value capture and tax increment finance mechanisms used by other countries. The chapter by Biggar and Siemiatycki (in this volume) analyses land value capture mechanisms such as the density bonus used in Toronto in a similar context of low affordability; notwithstanding some of the fundamental challenges that relate to the negotiation process between planning authorities and private developers that have been highlighted for both London and Toronto, such mechanisms might in principle be used to divert more resources from private development directly into affordable housing.

If policy-makers really want to ensure that more affordable homes are built where people want to live, as is often declared across the political spectrum, radical changes may be inevitable. The debate around the Green Belt described in this chapter shows the benefits of providing a careful economic analysis on the impact of a policy proposal on house prices; if pros and cons are clearer, more informed decisions ultimately can be left to the political realm. Likewise, a clear understanding of the complex interaction between demand and supply – and in particular of the effects of possible depreciation cycles, new transport connections and increasing density – is of paramount importance when evaluating innovative ideas on demand-side policies, land value capture mechanisms or a greater role for the public sector in the delivery of affordable housing.

Notes

1. Based on data from Council for Mortgage and Lenders, Halifax house price database and Office for National Statistics data.
2. Those figures imply a widening of the disparity between London and the rest of the UK after the Global Financial Crisis of 2008–9. Moreover, data from Costar show a relatively slower growing divide for commercial properties: between 2008 and 2018 sold commercial property prices per square foot grew 139 per cent in London and 92 per cent in the rest of the UK.
3. See Meen (2018a) for a comprehensive review.
4. See Figure 10.1; the denominator of the ratio is median household income.
5. There are some measurement issues based on the Land Registry's data. A British expat buying property in the UK is an 'overseas buyer' by their correspondence address, as is a UK resident buying via an overseas company; some overseas residents might buy property via a UK-based address if they have one. It is argued that a rough measure of the scale of overseas investment in London's residential market is perhaps a third of upmarket properties, but significantly less across London as a whole.
6. See Miller (2015) for a simple video lecture on the model.
7. See for example Whitehead (2017).
8. Research by OFT (2008) found no evidence that homebuilders have the ability to individually affect market prices by buying land, but Hall and Ward (2014, 228) found this conclusion at odds with the experience of many experts; recent research by Gabrieli (2018) offers an explanation for this puzzle by arguing that even if developers cannot affect land prices, weak pre-emptive competition implies that the best strategy for developers is to be slow at starting developments.
9. Clifford et al. (2018) show that between 2009 and 2012 a total of 39,000 residential units were delivered in London through conversions of B1 floor space through full planning permission, which represents an average of 13,000 units per year. Subsequent to the extension of Permitted Development in 2013, 4,757

residential units were delivered through office-to-residential conversions between 2013 and 2015, representing an average of 2,378 units per year − 18 per cent of the average prior to 2013.

10. As explained in the previous section, the current SE scheme is the Help to Buy, where the government lends a first-time buyer (or other buyer for a first home) up to 40 per cent of the cost of a newly built home (20 per cent outside London), which implies that a 5 per cent cash deposit and a 55 per cent mortgage are needed for a house purchase up to £600,000.

11. Without mentioning the many historical controversies and research about the direct involvement of the public sector in housebuilding, we can refer to Edwards (2017) for a commentary where various recent cases are mentioned, including Olympic Park, Old Oak Common, Croydon, Hounslow and Haringey.

12. This is in the context of a more general critique of the role of planning in constraining housing supply and reducing affordability; see Cheshire (2014) for a commentary and Hilber and Vermeulen (2010) for a comprehensive analysis.

13. Select Committee on Economic Affairs, 1st Report of Session 2016–17, Building More Homes, HL Paper 20, 15 July 2016.

References

Ball, Michael. 2010. *The Housebuilding Industry: Promoting Recovery in Housing Supply*. London: Department for Communities and Local Government.

Barker, Kate. 2004. *Review of Housing Supply. Delivering Stability: Securing Our Future Housing Needs. Final Report – Recommendations*. London: HMSO.

Booth, P. and Crook, A. D. H. 1986. *Low Cost Home Ownership: An Evaluation of Housing Policy under the Conservatives*. Aldershot: Gower.

Cheshire, Paul. 2014. *Turning Houses into Gold: The Failure of British Planning*. Accessed 22 July 2020. http://blogs.lse.ac.uk/politicsandpolicy/turning-houses-into-gold-the-failure-of-british-planning.

Clifford, Ben, Ferm, Jessica, Livingstone, Nicola and Canelas, Patricia. 2018. *Assessing the Impacts of Extending Permitted Development Rights to Office-to-residential Change of Use in England*. London: Royal Institute of Chartered Surveyors.

DCLG (Department for Communities and Local Government). 2017. *Planning for the Right Homes in the Right Places: Consultation Proposals*. London: DCLG.

Demographia. 2019. 15th *Annual Demographia International Housing Affordability Survey: 2019*. St Louis, MO: Demographia.

DiPasquale, Denise and Wheaton, William C. 1992. 'The Markets for Real Estate Assets and Space: A Conceptual Framework'. *Journal of the American Real Estate and Urban Economics Association* 20(2):181–97. https://doi.org/10.1111/1540-6229.00579.

Edwards, Michael. 2016. 'The Housing Crisis and London'. *City* 20(2):222–37. https://doi.org/10.1080/13604813.2016.1145947.

Edwards, Michael. 2017. *Haringey Development Vehicle*. Accessed 22 July 2020. https://michaeledwards.org.uk/2017/02/14/haringey-development-vehicle.

Fernandez, Rodrigo, Hofman, Annelore and Aalbers, Manuel B. 2016. 'London and New York as a Safe Deposit Box for the Transnational Wealth Elite'. *Environment and Planning A* 48(12):2443–61.

Gabrieli, Tommaso. 2018. *Strategic Entry in Real Estate Development: Implications for Housing Supply*. Paper presented at the Real Estate & Land Planning International Conference, 2018.

Gallent, Nick, Durrant, Dan and May, Neil. 2017. 'Housing Supply, Investment Demand and Money Creation: A Comment on the Drivers of London's Housing Crisis'. *Urban Studies* 54(10):2204–16.

GLA (Greater London Authority). 2018. *Housing in London 2018*. London: GLA.

Halifax. 2019. *First Time Buyer Review*, February. Halifax Bank.

Hall, Peter and Ward, Colin. 2014. *Sociable Cities: The 21st-century Reinvention of the Garden City*. London: Routledge.

Hilber, Christian A. L. and Vermeulen, Wouter. 2010. *The Impacts of Restricting Housing Supply on House Prices and Affordability – Final Report*. London: DCLG.

Hometrack. 2018. *UK Cities House Price Index – August 2018*. London: Hometrack Data Systems.

Lizieri, Colin. 2009. *Towers of Capital: Office Markets & International Financial Services*. Cambridge: Wiley-Blackwell.

Mace, Alan, Blanc, Fanny, Gordon, Ian R. and Scanlon, Kath. 2016. *A 21st Century Metropolitan Greenbelt*. London: London School of Economics.

Meen, Geoffrey. 2018a. *How Should Housing Affordability Be Measured?* CaCHE Report 2018_02_01. Glasgow: UK Collaborative Centre for Housing Evidence.

Meen, Geoffrey. 2018b. *Policy Approaches for Improving Affordability*. CaCHE Report 2018_02_02. Glasgow: UK Collaborative Centre for Housing Evidence.

Miller, Norm. 2015. 'Explaining the Four Quadrant Model'. Educational video on YouTube, standard licence. Accessed 22 July 2020. https://www.youtube.com/watch?time_continue=586&v=kVwHvliV1pA.

OFT (Office of Fair Trading). 2008. *Homebuilding in the UK: A Market Study*. London: OFT.

ONS (Office for National Statistics). 2018. *Housing Affordability in England and Wales: 2018*. Newport: ONS.

Sá, Filipa. 2016. *The Effect of Foreign Investors on Local Housing Markets: Evidence from the UK*. DP11658. Centre for Economic Policy Research Working Paper. London: CEPR.

Sassen, Saskia. 2001. *The Global City: New York, London, Tokyo* (2nd edition). Princeton, NJ: Princeton University Press.

Scanlon Kath, Whitehead, Christine and Blanc, Fanny. 2018. *A Sustainable Increase in London's Housing Supply?* LSE London Housing Report, January.

Trust for London. 2017. *London's Poverty Profile 2017*. Accessed 22 July 2020. https://www.trustforlondon.org.uk/publications/londons-poverty-profile-2017.

Wacher, John. 2018. 'Affordable Housing and Viability in London'. *Town & Country Planning* 87(11):448–54.

Wallace, Alison, Rhodes, David and Webber, Richard. 2017. *Overseas Investors in London's New Build Housing Market*. Working Paper, Centre for Housing Policy, University of York.

Whitehead, Christine. 2010. *Shared Ownership and Shared Equity: Reducing the Risks of Home-ownership?* Report, Joseph Rowntree Foundation, September.

Whitehead, Christine. 2017. 'Breaking Down the Barriers to Housing Delivery?'. *Journal of Planning and Environment Law* 13:26–39.

11

Housing crisis in a Canadian global city: Financialisation, buy-to-let investors and short-term rentals in Toronto's rental market

Emily Hawes and Sean Grisdale

Introduction and theoretical framework

The City of Toronto is, in 2020, arguably in the midst of a residential construction boom beyond the scope of any other city in North America. With city staff reporting almost 400,000 residential units in Toronto's development pipeline between 2014 and 2018 (City of Toronto 2019a), the unprecedented number of cranes that now dot the skyline have become emblematic of a city undergoing rapid and monumental transformation. According to a recent report from Ryerson University's Centre for Urban Research and Land Development (Clayton and Shi 2019), the City of Toronto was the fastest-growing central city in either the US or Canada for the year ending July 2018, with its 77,435 newcomers representing more than those of the next three cities combined. Even at a regional level, the 125,298 newcomers to the Toronto metropolitan region were only surpassed by migrants to metro Dallas, Texas. However, despite this scale of development, it is increasingly clear that not enough is being done to house the city's rapidly growing population, not to mention those existing populations being displaced by accelerating housing costs. In a city where almost half (47 per cent) of all households are renters (City of Toronto 2019c), the Canadian Rental Housing Index (2019) estimates that 23 per cent of those households spend more than 50 per cent of their income on rent, while high demand for rentals has kept vacancy rates persistently down, around the 1 per cent mark, and no-fault evictions have almost doubled since 2015 (CMHC 2018; ACTO 2019).

Of course, Toronto is not alone in grappling with such a housing crisis. While critical housing scholars are right to point out that housing crises have been a persistent companion to capitalist urbanisation since Engels's early studies of the first industrial towns (Aalbers and Christophers 2014; Saegert 2016), the Global

Financial Crisis (GFC) has reignited both public and scholarly attention around what has long been an unstable contradiction between housing as a place for people to live and housing as a financial asset.

However, while the increasing entanglement between housing markets and international finance – a process scholars are calling 'financialisation' – has come to the fore in critical scholarship since the GFC, this process has unfolded over decades, as neoliberal governments have worked to roll back social infrastructures such as public housing and social housing subsidies that were implemented in varying degrees by the welfare states of the post-war era. A key factor in this process was the gradual loosening of cross-border capital flows, which enabled surplus capital – what Aalbers (2016) calls the 'wall of money' – to capitalise on the highest returns available across a globalised field of potential investments. Especially in a post-GFC environment characterised by quantitative easing and low interest rates, scholars observe a preference among investors handling this 'wall of money' for the acquisition of housing assets, one of the few remaining forms of 'high-quality' collateral in a stagnating global economy (see also Walks's chapter in this volume). Meanwhile, investors have themselves become more international-facing and institutionalised into often monolithic private equity and pension funds and other institutional investment entities (Clark 2000; Aalbers 2016; Fields 2018). Finally, securitisation has been a central technology of financialisation as it has enabled otherwise 'opaque, illiquid, and unique assets – like housing and real estate' (August and Walks 2018, 125) to be turned into standardised, interest-bearing financial securities readily available for (rapid, value-seeking) exchange on financial markets (Gotham 2009; Walks 2014).

Critical scholarship has done much to document the processes through which owner-occupied residential housing markets in North America and Europe have become financialised through mechanisms such as asset-backed mortgage securitisation, in both the lead-up to and the aftermath of the GFC (see Walks's chapter in this volume). A similar literature on the financialisation of rental housing is still emerging (Beswick et al. 2016; Fields and Uffer 2016; August and Walks 2018; Fields 2018; Revington and August 2019). While disinvestment and 'roll-back' neoliberalisation tended to characterise dynamics in the social and private rental sectors of most wealthy economies in and through the post-Fordist era, scholars note how the post-GFC era has seen a striking increase in interest among private equity, pension funds and institutional investors seeking reliable yield in 'alternative assets' such as rental housing (Beswick et al. 2016).

Critical scholars have also documented the ways in which financial logics have penetrated the spaces and occupations of everyday life in a variety of contexts, noting an increasing normalisation of individualised notions of responsibility and security as manifest in concerns with balancing household budgets, the cultivation of investment portfolios to ensure retirement savings, and a heightened cultural and societal importance attached to credit scoring (Martin 2002; Langley 2008). This element of financialisation and the processes that have encouraged it have in recent decades contributed to the near-ubiquity of the notion that everyone should be an investor; investment in rental properties by small-scale, individual investors is a key example of such activity. Similarly, in what scholars have also tied to financialising processes, the rapid popularisation of short-term vacation renting, made efficient by digital platforms such as Airbnb, has also opened up significant possibilities for the commodification of housing by making myriad local rental markets accessible to international tourist demand (Wachsmuth and Weisler 2018; Grisdale 2019).

Financialising processes, then, have multiple inflections in the housing sector. Responding to Fernandez and Aalbers's (2016) call for the development of case studies that can inform an analysis of housing financialisation as a locally variegated but global totality, this chapter offers a preliminary analysis and overview of some of these processes underway in Toronto's uniquely structured rental market. Following a brief history of Toronto's private rental sector, set in the broader Canadian context, we analyse the profiles and assess the prevalence of different types of private landlords and the extent to which their roles in the sector have been changing as a consequence of broader political economic and policy decisions. We consider the present state of small-scale private letting and draw attention to emerging forms of 'buy-to-let' rental providers, including both the incursion of corporate landlords into the multi-family rental sector and the recent expansion of short-term rental letting on platforms such as Airbnb, especially among the city's rapidly increasing stock of condominiums.

A brief history of rental housing in Toronto

The prime period of Canadian private rental housing construction, which remains the source of most purpose-built rental supply today, took place from the mid-1950s to 1974 (Hulchanski 2004a; Suttor 2016). By the mid-1960s over half of new housing units built in Canada were intended for rental (Suttor 2009). In Toronto much of the apartment stock built from the late 1950s to the mid-1970s was developed in the suburbs by a handful of large firms as towers of 200+ units (August and Walks 2018). However, from the 1970s onwards renter households became increasingly low-income, as policies encouraging and subsidising homeownership that increased access to mortgage financing, as well as the increased presence of condominiums after the 1980s, led middle-income households to move from the rental sector and into homeownership (Hulchanski 2004a; Suttor 2009; Rosen and Walks 2013; Suttor 2016).

As elsewhere, the late 1970s and 1980s saw a dramatic decline in rental housing production (Hulchanski 2004a; Suttor 2009). Renters' incomes were no longer high enough for private rental production to remain profitable in light of the increased costs to production that also appeared at that time, including large increases to the costs of construction labour and land, and rising (and volatile) interest rates (Hulchanski 2004a; Suttor 2009). State support and subsidies helped to maintain private rental construction into the mid- to late 1980s, but subsequently social housing and secondary (often basement) suites became the primary sources of new rental units (Suttor 2016). In the 1980s high interest rates continued to diminish the profit motive for private rental construction and made subsidising social housing much more costly (Suttor 2009). By 1978 Canada had eschewed any responsibilities with respect to financing housing, opting instead for market approaches more susceptible to rising interest rates. Suttor (2009) estimates that private rental sector completions dropped from a national level of 88,200 completions between 1970 and 1974, to 43,000 between 1980 and 1984, to 6,200 between 1995 and 1999. While in the 1980s social rental housing accounted for 39 per cent of rental production, the period between 1984 and 1993 was characterised by rollbacks in social housing for lower-income Canadians. By 1993 the federal government had fully withdrawn all funding for new social housing (Hulchanski 2004a).

The rise of the condominium as a pillar of post-industrial re-urbanisation in Toronto has had dramatic impacts on the city's built form and has been a key factor reshaping social relations and demographics in the inner city (Kern 2007; Rosen and Walks 2015). This stock has grown especially rapidly since the early 2000s. From 2007 to 2017, condos represented 81.5 per cent of all newly completed housing, 99.1 per cent of which were in apartment-style buildings, and much of the newest construction has taken place in the downtown and waterfront area of the City of Toronto (Rosen and Walks 2015; City of Toronto 2019b). The scale of new buildings has also increased, with a dramatic rise to dominance of buildings with more than 250 units (Rosen and Walks 2015, 293). As of 2016, 26 per cent of the City of Toronto's approximately 1,113,000 housing units were condos (City of Toronto 2019c).

Meanwhile, between the turn of the millennium and 2020, very little purpose-built rental housing was constructed. Therefore, condo units – now an attractive form of speculative and cash-flow (rental) investment in a heated market – rented in the secondary market have become a crucial source of housing stock expected to meet new rental demand (along with rooming houses and non-condo secondary suites, such as basement apartments) (CMHC 2018). Between 2006 and 2016, approximately 75 per cent of all new rental housing stock was added in the form of condominiums, 23 per cent in non-condo private units and only 2 per cent in purpose-built rental housing (Grisdale 2019, 10). While purpose-built rental housing and social housing built in the 1970s and 1980s was generally intended to serve moderately low- and very low-income renters, the new secondary market stock tends to be high-end, commanding rental prices that often exclude lower-income tenants or serve as attractive spaces for the short-term rental market (see Figure 11.1) (Rosen and Walks 2015; City of Toronto 2019b).

Changing dynamics of ownership and tenure in the City of Toronto

Who owns Toronto's private sector rental stock and benefits from the enormous increases to land, property and rent prices that appeared in the 2010s? In the 1960s

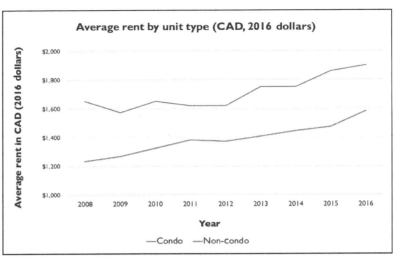

Figure 11.1 Average rents (CAD) in Toronto, 2008–16 (Canada Mortgage and Housing Corporation 2018)

and 1970s Toronto's private rental sector was dominated by large- or medium-scale corporate/commercial landlords/owners (and typically also developers), primarily of professionally managed apartment towers (August and Walks 2018; Chisolm and Hulchanski 2018). Following the decline in purpose-built rental construction things shifted and approximately half of these older multi-unit rental properties are now owned by individuals (Gibb et al. 2018; August and Walks 2018). Data from the Canada Mortgage and Housing Corporation (CMHC) indicate that at the national level in 2017, 49.3 per cent of purpose-built rental housing units were owned by individual investors, 39.7 per cent by private corporations, and the remainder were held by a combination of real estate investment trusts (REITs) (7.9 per cent), public corporations (2.5 per cent), pension funds (0.3 per cent) and real estate investment funds (CMHC 2017). However, these numbers neither reveal the scale of investors' operations within these categories nor provide any insight on the secondary rental market. Nor do they disaggregate private corporations in terms of size and corporate structure (e.g. between smaller family-owned corporations and monolithic private equity firms). Is the private rental market dominated by a small number of individual investors that own large quantities of rental units, or many small-scale investors owning only one to three rental units, as is the case in Australia and the UK (Arundel 2017; MacLennan et al. 2018)? Is it dominated instead by non-individual (corporate) landlords that have very large portfolios of rental properties? Indeed, such information is difficult to find.

In England, approximately 89 per cent of landlords (2015) are private individuals, and the vast majority hold only one rental property (Ronald et al. 2015). This situation was intensified by a period of accessible mortgage credit and property price crashes around the time of the financial crisis (Ronald et al. 2015; Arundel

2017; Chisolm and Hulchanski 2018; MacLennan et al. 2018). While in similar nations, such as Australia, the rental sector has also long been dominated by individual investors, with relatively few corporate or institutional landlords (Pawson 2018; Adkins et al. 2019), the Canadian housing landscape has long differed from these countries in important ways (Suttor 2009), and with no major housing correction (despite the financial crisis) it has experienced sustained house price inflation. New units in cities such as Toronto have been particularly concentrated in high-rise condos (Walks 2014; Chisolm and Hulchanski 2018; Gibb et al. 2018; Rosen and Walks 2015).

The rise of asset-based welfare and its implications for inequality

Understanding the proportions and profiles of individual private landlords, particularly in the secondary market, is important both because of the effects of property-based wealth on wealth (and income) inequality and because of the rental market dynamics (and dynamics of control) particular to this form of stock. Since the 1990s, Canada's federal government has absolved itself of any direct role in the rental housing sector in favour of policies promoting the premise of an 'asset-based' form of welfare (Sherraden 1991; Walks 2014). Emblematic of what critical scholars call the 'financialization of daily life' (Martin 2002), 'asset-based welfare' describes a policy orientation that aims to replace the traditional welfare state with incentives for people to accrue assets that will increase in value over time and thus be drawn on as a form of social security in old age. While the federal government devolved responsibility for social housing to the provinces in the 1990s, it continued to maintain involvement in the mortgage insurance market through the CMHC, promoting policies amenable to the interests of Canadian (and subsequently foreign) financial institutions that, in need of new revenue streams, were increasing their operations in household mortgages (Walks 2014; Kalman-Lamb 2017). In the early years of the new millennium, and intensifying with the 2008 crisis, the CMHC introduced financial products such as government-insured mortgage-backed securities. These effectively allow mortgage originators to sell mortgages to investors in secondary markets (see Walks 2014, and Walks's chapter in this volume, for details). In combination with reductions in government mortgage insurance eligibility requirements for homebuyers, these programmes enabled banks to lend en masse to aspiring and upsizing homeowners and individual investors.

Among the results were an increase in levels of household indebtedness and a shift of middle-income renters into the ownership sector, variously through (a) relatively more affordable condo purchases, (b) expanded condo development and (c) sustained, rapid house price escalation, particularly in Vancouver and Toronto (Walks 2014; Rosen and Walks 2015). However, after 2006 the national homeownership rate increased only slightly despite sustained house price inflation

(Kalman-Lamb 2017). Wage stagnation has had much to do with this, but more recent increases in government-imposed mortgage market regulations to impede households' access to homeownership have also played a role. As a result, the supposed wealth-building aims of asset-based welfare have been undermined, while financial institutions have benefitted enormously (Walks 2014).

A housing and social security system that promotes the individual (or household) ownership of assets (such as housing) as the key mode of wealth building and retirement savings has contributed to a skewed distribution of wealth; not only are those retirees that rely on their housing equity for retirement security vulnerable to market downturns, but lower-income and younger households have in many cases been locked out of the owner-occupied housing market due to a combination of high student debt levels, low wage growth, lack of supply and highly inflated urban house prices. As such, early entrants have been the main beneficiaries of these considerable wealth gains. These policies also enhance wealth inequalities between renters and owners if owners use the equity in their principal residence and – more importantly – the access to additional credit (at the lowest rates) that these assets open up to purchase rental properties as further investments for their portfolios. This has become a key reason to evaluate the extent of small-scale, individual private investor-landlords' ownership of Toronto's (and Canada's) private sector rental housing stock within both the purpose-built and secondary markets.

As Arundel (2017) has shown in the UK context, where the dominance of individual landlords in the private rental market has had important consequences for the distribution of wealth in British society, over 50 per cent of landlords in the UK are among the wealthiest 10 per cent of households in terms of housing wealth. They are also heavily concentrated among the highest-income-earning households, and the highest-income earners see the greatest returns on their rental property investments (Arundel 2017). Beyond merely providing pensioners with a retirement income boost, rental property investment has served to entrench existing wealth and income imbalances in the UK. The increased demand from investors can also serve to increase house prices and further erode the ability of aspiring owner-occupiers to access the homeownership ladder (Ronald et al. 2015).

Data constraints make replication of this analysis difficult in the Canadian context. However, young adults are living with parents longer, are facing high and escalating rental costs in major cities and are having difficulty in accessing the homeownership market; it is thus possible that a similar compounding of wealth inequalities, both within and between age groups, is already underway. In this case the housing system, rather than providing affordable shelter to all, would not even be fulfilling the promises of asset-based welfare, as the wealth gains of the already wealthiest and highest-income households occur at the expense of those who may never even hope to leave the rental sector.

It is still more difficult to find detailed ownership data for the secondary rental market in Canada. Despite it being widely understood that when condominium units are developed a significant proportion are expected to be rented out by purchasers, direct data on rental condos and their owners are somewhat scarce. Gibb et al. (2018) claim that the Canadian private rental stock is split roughly evenly between small investors on the one hand and medium and large investors on the other. A recent analysis by Statistics Canada suggests that nationally, 76 per cent of individual, resident owners of multiple residential properties (concentrated in Toronto and Vancouver) own only two properties (Bekkering et al. 2019). It is unclear whether additional properties are used as rentals. However, in Toronto 21 per cent of two-property owners owned a condo apartment and almost half (46.6 per cent) of multiple-property owners held all their properties in the vicinity of their residence, suggesting that these are primarily rentals. A 2018 consultancy report (Hildebrand and Tal 2018, 4) suggests that a significant group of Toronto's condo rental investors tend to be 'local immigrants' who are investing for their retirement portfolio or as a means to help their children access the housing market. These observations could point to a significant group of relatively wealthy, middle-aged, individual private landlords in Toronto renting condos, many of whom are new residents. What is clear in the Canadian context is that there has been a persistent income gap between owners and renters in Canada since at least the 1970s (Hulchanski 2004b). Today, nationally, owners' median income is approximately twice that of renters (Chisolm and Hulchanski 2018). In Toronto this can be seen in disproportionate housing affordability stress among renters relative to homeowners (Figure 11.2).

In 2016, only 29.6 per cent of Canadian households did not hold any debt (Statistics Canada 2017). The average price for a detached home in the Greater Toronto Area (GTA) reached $1.05 million in December 2019 (Canadian Press 2020). Facing high prices, Canadian borrowers, particularly in Toronto and Vancouver, have turned increasingly to private alternative lenders, among whom

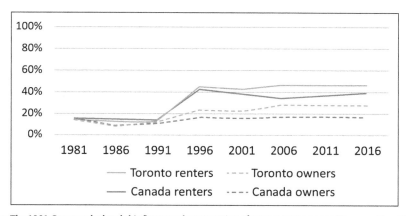

Notes: The 1981 Census calculated this figure as the proportion of owners/renters spending more than 25% of income rather than 30%. Data not available for 2011 so extrapolated between 2006 and 2016.

Figure 11.2 Proportion of owners and renters spending more than 30 per cent of income on shelter costs in Canada and the City of Toronto, 1981–2016 (custom tabulated by Sean Grisdale based on data from Canada Statistics n.d.)

mortgage delinquency rates tend to be considerably higher than average (Better Dwelling 2018; Tal 2019). In September 2019 personal insolvencies (driven by defaults in unsecured and home equity lines of credit) saw their biggest annual increase (19 per cent) nationally since 2009 (Tal and Shenfeld 2019; Heaven 2019).

If small-scale individual landlords tend to hold rental condos as their investment properties, this also has implications for rental sector stability. Condo rentals are believed to be a more volatile form of stock; their investor-landlords may not have much interest, experience or knowledge in being a landlord, and may choose to sell at any time to realise capital gains. When sold to new buyers, condo units may be returned to owner-occupied tenure, and tenants may be asked to vacate on relatively short notice if existing owners decide to use the unit for personal purposes (TOLTB 2018). A 2019 report suggests that annual increases to rental condo supply have been declining in Ontario, as fewer investors keep their units on the long-term rental market (FRPO 2019). The property industry has also recently suggested that new condo-rental investors may be unable to carry costs in the coming years if the rents needed to cover monthly costs begin to outpace renters' ability or desire to pay (Kalinowski 2020). Further, secondary condo rentals lack oversight and control by local planning authorities, in that they are market-produced stock rather than intentional components of land use planning, and the quality of rental and experience of renting may be more precarious in this housing (Rosen and Walks 2015; Gibb et al. 2018; City of Toronto 2019b).

Institutional investors: Pension funds, private equity and REITs

Recent work on the financialisation of rental housing has demonstrated the scale at which large private equity firms such as Blackstone have made inroads into those markets most heavily affected by the GFC, with Beswick et al. (2016) suggesting we may be witnessing the rise of what they call 'global corporate landlords'. Indeed, in the wake of the GFC, it was reported that Blackstone had acquired $10 billion of repossessed residential properties at foreclosure auctions – many of them single-family homes – making it the largest private landlord in the United States, and probably the world (UNHRC 2017). Beswick et al. (2016) also show how Blackstone has acquired a formidable portfolio of distressed housing, office, retail and commercial property in Ireland, Spain and Greece. However, while research does indicate an increasing interest among private equity, REITs and pension funds in acquiring ageing multi-family residential apartments in Toronto (August and Walks 2018), it is clear that the Canadian context, much like the UK rental market (Beswick et al. 2016), is experiencing dynamics divergent from economies that experienced a significant foreclosure crisis.

For the most part, Canada managed to avoid what could have been a mass foreclosure event by socialising many of the country's insolvent mortgages onto the balance sheet of the CMHC (see Walks's chapter in this volume). As a consequence, it prevented the formation of those rent gaps now exploited by firms such as Blackstone in the US, Ireland, Spain and Greece. Conversely, inflated housing prices in major Canadian cities such as Toronto and Vancouver now precipitate different problems for local communities, with processes of gentrification primarily benefitting domestic property owners, who are holding existing assets either for the purposes of long-term speculation, to milk existing rents or on the bet that they can reposition their assets to entice higher-income tenants. Indeed, according to Raj Mehta, Global Head of Private Capital and Partnerships with the property asset management company Starlight Investments, 90 per cent of this sector remains in the hands of domestic family companies and small individual investors, citing good returns amid the confluence of (a) rising rental demand as the middle class is increasingly unable or unwilling to access homeownership, (b) limited rental supply that is unlikely to be significantly offset by near-term rental completions and (c) an unwillingness to pay the capital gains taxes that come with selling (Wilcox 2018).

However, while Mehta notes the Canadian rental market continues to constitute a 'noticeable gap' in the overall portfolios of companies such as Blackstone, there are signs that this might be changing. For instance, in partnership with Starlight Investments, Blackstone recently marked their first incursion into the Canadian rental sector in 2018 with their joint acquisition of five apartment buildings between Toronto and Montreal (Wilcox 2018), while more recently the same partnership announced a second round of acquisitions, buying 1,067 units across eight mid-rise buildings in the GTA (Starlight Investments 2019). However, while the corporatisation of rental housing across the world has emerged from the ashes of many countries' distressed housing markets, it is important to note that disinvestment in Canada's multi-family apartment sector was also an important precursor to the emergence of Canadian REITs in the mid- to late 1990s. As August and Walks (2018) note, a number of overlapping historical events (see above) precipitated the legislation that would enable REITs to become the rising stars they are today.

Coincidentally, legislation enabling the first REITs was passed in 1993, the same year the federal government took its protracted leave from the rental housing market. However, as August and Walks (2018) note, the first REITs to invest in apartments would not come into existence until 1997–8 with the formation of Canadian Apartment Properties REIT (CAPREIT) in 1997 and Residential Equities REIT (ResREIT)in 1998. Today, CAPREIT is likely Canada's largest landlord, controlling approximately 64,000 rental apartment and townhouse units across Canada, the Netherlands and Ireland in 2019 (CAPREIT 2019). Canada's *Real Estate News Exchange* notes (euphemistically) how its strategy of shifting 'toward quality in its asset mix, tenant base and market selection' has paid off, with its net rental income increasing by 11 per cent between 2017 and 2018 alone (Duggan 2019b). Significantly, these REITs were formed at the exact moment that the Province of Ontario decontrolled rents, stripped back tenant protections and downloaded social housing responsibilities to municipalities, setting the stage for investors to capitalise on the deep rent gaps suddenly appearing in Toronto's ageing and disinvested apartments. There are many REITs operating in Canada's property markets, allowing both small retail investors and institutional investors such as pension funds to receive steady returns on property, without succumbing to the particular commitments and responsibilities associated with owning actual property. And as with private equity firms such as Blackstone, they have pooled their investments in the gamut of alternative property asset classes, including student housing (Revington and August 2019), office space, industrial space and even mobile homes (Duggan 2019a).

However, a number of factors make the emergence of financialised landlords a cause for concern with respect to gentrification. As globalised monoliths, they are harder to hold accountable legally or politically, while also harder to negotiate with or persuade at an affective level – opportune conditions for them to coordinate their specialised technical expertise, patient capital and market power towards maximising revenue streams and exploiting legal loopholes (Fields and Uffer 2016; August and Walks 2018). Furthermore, as ownership is shared among any variation of diverse investors in whatever vehicle ultimately owns a given pool of units, the impetus to maximise shareholder value in combination with the unique scale at which they enjoy access to credit and technical expertise entails a drive to close rent gaps that might not be as strong, or in many cases possible, for smaller landlords or firms (August and Walks 2018). Thus residents and housing activists organising in multi-family housing are stuck between a rock and a hard place: both fighting for repairs to the severely disinvested infrastructure of buildings where smaller owners are content to milk their properties into the ground, while also struggling against aggressive evictions in buildings acquired by ambitious new corporate owners interested in maximising shareholder value by attracting wealthier tenants (August and Walks 2018). While local tenant organising has produced some important successes in the form of concessions, they are up against an increasingly sophisticated, resourced and patient form of landlord.

Digital short-term rental platforms: An emergent form of financialised housing?

While dynamics underway in Toronto's multi-family apartment buildings are characterised by long-standing (though evolving) processes of disinvestment and gentrification, one unforeseen consequence of policy-makers' turn to asset-based welfare and buy-to-let rental housing provision has been the rapid expansion of digital short-term rental platforms such as Airbnb; these now serve to distort the rental market by providing a more flexible and profitable alternative to the traditional rental market (Wachsmuth and Weisler 2018; Cocola-Gant and Gago 2019; Grisdale 2019). While companies such as Airbnb represent themselves as platforms for everyday people to make extra money renting out an extra room (Airbnb 2016; 2017), scholars studying their expansion in cities around the world are increasingly demonstrating how short-term rental platforms are dominated by commercial operators capitalising on the willingness of tourists and business travellers to pay higher rates of rent than locals (Wachsmuth et al. 2017; Crommelin et al. 2018; Ferreri and Sanyal, 2018; Wachsmuth and Weisler 2018; Cocola-Gant and Gago 2019). Thus, as Wachsmuth and Weisler (2018) have theorised, the platform can be understood as enabling the exploitation of new rent gaps that have less to do with the capacity of property owners to invest in their property. These platforms are now playing an important role in the commodification and financialisation of housing; the international surplus capital invested in disruptive platforms such as Airbnb represents hedges on the platform's ability to capitalise on rent gaps emerging in parts of the city that are attractive to tourists (Wachsmuth et al. 2017, 2019; Wachsmuth and Weisler 2018; Grisdale 2019).

Drawing on a methodology and dataset developed by Wachsmuth and Weisler (2018) to assess the impact of short-term rentals on the local rental market, Grisdale (2019) finds that between June 2016 and May 2017 there were 4,479 full-time, entire-home Airbnb rentals operating in the city. Thus, at the same time that the rental vacancy rate hovered around 1 per cent, full-time short-term rental operations were shown to be removing approximately 0.85 per cent of the city's potential rental stock from the traditional long-term market. The implication is that insofar as these units could be incentivised to return to the traditional rental market, the vacancy rate could be almost doubled. Furthermore, Grisdale (2019) observes that these 4,479 full-time rentals also took home approximately 58.5 per cent of total Airbnb revenue in the city, while the average full-time Airbnb host in many downtown neighbourhoods was found to be making significantly larger profits than the average landlord. A recent report by Wachsmuth et al. (2019) suggests the industry did indeed continue to expand between 2017 and 2019. While commercial short-term rentals were supposed to be officially banned in Toronto as of summer 2020, the sector has continued to operate without oversight. And as a global city that continues to attract tourists for various reasons, the platform could only be expected to continue enticing buy-to-let property owners to take up short-term rentals insofar as it continued to offer a more profitable model for investor owners.

As Wachsmuth et al. (2019) demonstrate, short-term rental hosts running multiple listings have assumed an increasing share of both total listings and total revenue, suggesting a continuing intensification of short-term rental commercialisation in the city. In 2015, hosts running multiple listings constituted approximately 23 per cent of total listings, taking home almost 37 per cent of total revenue. By 2019 they controlled almost 38 per cent of listings while taking home just over 53 per cent of total revenue. Both the absolute number of listings and the absolute amount of revenue flowing through the sector have also increased significantly. Between 2015 and 2019, active daily short-term rental listings in Toronto increased more than five-fold, from less than 5,000 in 2015 to more than 21,000 as of 30 April 2019 (Wachsmuth et al. 2019). In terms of revenue, while between June 2016 and May 2017 hosts in the City of Toronto generated approximately $151.3 million in revenue (Grisdale 2019), they more recently took in approximately $218.9 million in the period between May 2018 and April 2019 (Wachsmuth et al. 2019), constituting a 45 per cent increase in yearly revenue in only two years.

While digital short-term rentals have come under scrutiny for a number of reasons, from over-tourism and neighbourhood disruption, to issues of safety and tax evasion, Toronto activists emphasise their impact on an already stressed local rental market, where vacancy rates are at their limit and evictions are on the rise in popular Airbnb neighbourhoods such as Kensington Market (Dingman 2019; Mathieu 2017). Just as scholars are demonstrating in the London housing market (Ferreri and Sanyal 2018; Shabrina et al. 2019), this can be understood as an unforeseen consequence of decades of neoliberal approaches to housing policy precipitating housing systems wherein the total given supply of rental stock is primarily a function of the willingness of many self-interested investors to supply their property to the traditional, regulated rental market as opposed to leaving it vacant, living in it part time or hosting tourists. Thus, the expansion of Airbnb in Toronto is particularly bound up in the city's condominium-oriented approach to urban development. As Grisdale (2019) shows, the most central neighbourhoods of Toronto, where condominium units are the dominant (in some parts only) form of residential housing (specifically the Waterfront Communities, South Parkdale–King West and the Church–Yonge and Bay Street corridors), together accounted for almost half of the city's full-time, entire-home listings (2,112 listings or 47 per cent). Together, these 2,112 listings accounted for approximately 32 per cent of the total Airbnb revenue generated in the city that year.

This appears to be in line with trends observed in London, where Shabrina et al. (2019) show that Airbnbs are most prevalent in the city's core where there is a high predominance of dense, privately rented flats (whether purpose built, converted or in commercial buildings). However, while London and Toronto are seeing buy-to-let rental stock assuming a greater proportion of the total, a trend which also contributes to potential short-term rental stock, the factors driving these processes are not entirely the same. In Toronto, new buy-to-let construction of condos has been significant and sustained in neighbourhoods popular for tourists, meaning new condo construction likely accounts for a significant proportion of the total potential short-term rental stock (City of Toronto 2019a). In comparison, the rate of new construction has been declining in London since the 1970s, suggesting that relative to Toronto, flat conversions are likely to be a more significant source of any new potential short-term rental stock (Shabrina et al. 2019). Of course, short-term rentals cannot simply be explained by the city's mix of housing tenure. Policy is also key, and though regulations banning short-term rentals in non-primary residences were set to come into enforcement in summer 2020, the platform has already done much to reshape the city. Evictions cannot be taken back, the city has lost much-needed rental stock, while many properties are likely to have undergone conversion into luxury suites that will only continue to attract higher-income tenants for the foreseeable future, whether they live there temporarily or long-term.

Conclusion

Toronto is facing a crisis of affordable housing for its lowest-income residents and for renters and prospective owners across an increasingly wider income spectrum (Chisolm and Hulchanski 2018). As the rental vacancy rate hovers at 1 per cent and rents continue to rise, 'no-fault' evictions, including those requested for renovations and the landlord's own use, almost doubled between 2015 and 2019 (ACTO 2019). In this chapter we have responded to Fernandez and Aalbers's (2016) call for analyses of the financialisation of housing in its variegated, locally inflected forms. We argue that the financialisation of rental housing in Toronto is mediated by the city's unique mix of tenure and infrastructure: the city's large stock of ageing multi-family rental housing is targeted by large institutional investors exploiting rent gaps that emerged suddenly in the wake of rent decontrol legislation (August and Walks 2018), while the more recent strategy of relying on condominiums to fulfil rental demand in the private market driven by job growth is now complicated by the rise of short-term rental platforms that can offer increasingly leveraged homebuyers higher returns in the tourism market, which particularly affects global cities such as Toronto and London. At the same time, rapid in-migration to the Toronto region and an expansion of mortgage debt driving a housing boom uninterrupted by the 2008 financial crisis are factors driving households into a rental market that is experiencing severe supply shortages. While purpose-built rental development is seeing something of a resurgence after decades of stagnation, the increase is not enough to meet rapidly growing demand in the short term, and developers are primarily positioning units to cater to the luxury and high end of the market (Lawrence 2019). Meanwhile, the prospect of returning rental units from the commercialised short-term rental market remains uncertain. While stringent regulations involving taxation, licensing of all listings and bans on listings in all secondary suites and properties that are not a host's primary residence have been legislated, the question of enforcement capacity will continue to haunt cities' attempts to govern this phenomenon.

References

Aalbers, Manuel B. 2016. *The Financialization of Housing: A Political Economy Approach*. New York: Routledge.

Aalbers, Manuel B. and Christophers, Brett. 2014. 'Centring Housing in Political Economy'. *Housing, Theory and Society* 31(4):373–94. https://doi.org/10.1080/14036096.2014.947082.

Adkins, Lisa, Cooper, Melinda and Konings, Martijn. 2019. 'Class in the 21st Century: Asset Inflation and the New Logic of Inequality'. *Environment and Planning A* (online first) 1–25. https://doi.org/10.1177/0308518x19873673.

ACTO (Advocacy Centre for Tenants Ontario). 2019. 'We Can't Wait. Preserving Our Affordable Rental Housing in Ontario'. November. https://www.acto.ca/production/wp-content/uploads/2019/11/FINAL_Report_WeCantWait_Nov2019.pdf.

Airbnb. 2016. 'The Airbnb Community in Ontario'. 7 September. Accessed 13 August 2020. http://files.newswire.ca/1503/airbnbONrep.PDF.

Airbnb. 2017. 'Airbnb Policy Tool Chest 2.0'. Accessed 13 August 2020. https://press.airbnb.com/wp-content/uploads/sites/4/2019/08/Airbnb-Policy-Tool-Chest-2.0.pdf.

Arundel, Rowan. 2017. 'Equity Inequity: Housing Wealth Inequality, Inter and Intra-generational Divergences, and the Rise of Private Landlordism'. *Housing, Theory and Society* 34(2):176–200. https://doi.org/10.1080/14036096.2017.1284154.

August, Martine and Walks, Alan. 2018. 'Gentrification, Suburban Decline, and the Financialization of Multi-family Rental Housing: The Case of Toronto'. *Geoforum* 89:124–36. https://doi.org/10.1016/j.geoforum.2017.04.011.

Bekkering, Ellen, Deschamps-Laporte, Jean-Philippe and Smailes, Marina. 2019. 'Housing Statistics in Canada, Residential Property Ownership: Real Estate Holdings by Multiple-property Owners'. Statistics Canada. Accessed 9 October 2020. https://www150.statcan.gc.ca/n1/pub/46-28-0001/2019001/article/00001-eng.htm.

Beswick, Joe, Alexandri, Georgia, Byrne, Michael, Vives-Miró, Sònia, Fields, Desiree, Hodkinson, Stuart and Janoschka, Michael. 2016. 'Speculating on London's Housing Future'. *City* 20(2):321–41. https://doi.org/10.1080/13604813.2016.1145946.

Better Dwelling. 2018. 'BoC: Private Lenders See Their Share of Canada's Mortgage Market Double Since 2015'. *Better Dwelling*, 11 June. Accessed 13 January 2020. https://betterdwelling.com/boc-private-lenders-see-their-share-of-canadas-mortgage-market-double-since-2015.

Canada Mortgage and Housing Corporation. 2018. *Housing Market Report – Greater Toronto Area, 2017 Edition*. Accessed 2 August 2020. https://assets.cmhc-schl.gc.ca/sf/project/cmhc/pubsandreports/esub/_all_esub_pdfs/64459_2017_a01.pdf?rev=7eac987e-d4b4-4d9c-87f6-3b0bfcca1201.

Canadian Press. 2020. 'Toronto Homes Sales and Average Price Both Surge in December'. *Toronto Star*, 7 January. Accessed 13 January 2020. https://www.thestar.com/business/2020/01/07/toronto-home-sales-up-174-per-cent-in-december-average-price-up-12-per.html.

Canadian Rental Housing Index. 2019. 'Overspending'. Accessed 15 January 2020. http://www.rentalhousingindex.ca/en/#overspending_cd.

CAPREIT (Canadian Apartment Properties REIT). 2019. 'About CAPREIT'. Accessed 10 January 2020. https://www.caprent.com/about-capreit.

Chisholm, Sharon and Hulchanski, David. 2018. 'Chapter Four: Canada's Housing Story'. In *Shaping Futures 21: Changing the Housing Story Final Report*, edited by Duncan MacLennan, Hal Pawson, Kenneth Gibb, Sharon Chisholm and David Hulchanski, 21–8. City Futures Research Centre. Accessed 4 January 2020. https://cityfutures.be.unsw.edu.au/research/projects/shaping-futures-changing-housing-story.

City of Toronto. 2019a. 'Profile Toronto: How Does the City Grow?' [PH7.12 Attachment 1, Part 1]. Accessed 12 January 2020. https://www.toronto.ca/legdocs/mmis/2019/ph/bgrd/backgroundfile-135021.pdf.

City of Toronto. 2019b. 'Toronto Housing Market Analysis: From Insight to Action' [PH2.5 Appendix 1]. Accessed 10 January 2020. https://www.toronto.ca/legdocs/mmis/2019/ph/bgrd/backgroundfile-124480.pdf.

City of Toronto. 2019c. *Inclusionary Zoning Assessment Report: Housing Need and Demand Analysis*. Accessed 13 August 2020. https://www.toronto.ca/wp-content/uploads/2019/05/981d-IZ-Assessment-Report-Need-and-Demand-formatted-170519-accessiblePAC.pdf.

Clark, Gordon L. 2000. *Pension Fund Capitalism*. Oxford: Oxford University Press.

Clayton, Frank and Shi, Hong Yun. 2019. 'WOW! Toronto Was the Second Fastest Growing Metropolitan Area and the Top Growing City in All of the United States and Canada'. Centre for Urban Research and Land Development, Ryerson University, 31 May. Accessed 10 January 2020. https://www.ryerson.ca/cur/Blog/blogentry35.

CMHC (Canada Mortgage and Housing Corporation). 2017. 'Housing Market Insight – Canada'. Accessed 2 August 2020. https://www.cmhc-schl.gc.ca/en/data-and-research/publications-and-reports/housing-market-insight-canada.

CMHC (Canada Mortgage and Housing Corporation). 2018. 'Rental Market Report: Greater Toronto Area'. *Rental Market Reports*, 28 November. Accessed 13 January 2020. https://www.cmhc-schl.gc.ca/en/data-and-research/publications-and-reports/rental-market-reports-major-centres.

Cocola-Gant, Augustin and Gago, Ana. 2019. 'Airbnb, Buy-to-Let Investment and Tourism-Driven Displacement: A Case Study in Lisbon'. *Environment and Planning A: Economy and Space*, Online First. https://doi.org/10.1177/0308518x19869012.

Crommelin, Laura, Troy, Laurence, Martin, Chris and Parkinson, Sharon. 2018. *Technological Disruption in Private Housing Markets: The Case of Airbnb*. Australian Housing and Urban Research Institute Limited, 8 November. Accessed 24 August 2020. https://www.ahuri.edu.au/__data/assets/pdf_file/0022/28615/AHURI-Final-Report-305-Technological-disruption-in-private-housing-the-case-of-airbnb.pdf.

Dingman, Shane. 2019. 'Evicted: The Loophole Ontario Landlords Use to Force Tenants Out'. *The Globe and Mail*, 1 May. Accessed 22 July 2020. https://www.theglobeandmail.com/canada/article-evicted-how-landlords-are-forcing-tenants-out.

Duggan, Evan. 2019a. 'Kenney Takes Over at CAPREIT, Expands Mobile Home Portfolio'. *Real Estate News Exchange*, 28 March. Accessed 22 July 2020. https://renx.ca/kenney-capreit-ceo-buy-manufactured-homes-communities.

Duggan, Evan. 2019b. 'CAPREIT Buys 23 More Canadian MHCs, CEO Talks Strategy'. *Real Estate News Exchange*, 2 April. Accessed 13 August 2020. https://renx.ca/capreit-buy-23-manufactured-homes-communities-ceo-strategy.

Fernandez, Rodrigo and Aalbers, Manuel B. 2016. 'Financialization and Housing: Between Globalization and Varieties of Capitalism'. *Competition and Change* 2(2):71–88. https://doi.org/10.1177/1024529415623916.

Ferreri, Mara and Sanyal, Romola. 2018. 'Platform Economies and Urban Planning: Airbnb and Regulated Deregulation in London'. *Urban Studies* 55(15):3353–68. https://doi.org/10.1177/0042098017751982.

Fields, Desiree. 2018. 'Constructing a New Asset Class: Property-led Financial Accumulation After the Crisis'. *Economic Geography* 94(2):118–40. https://doi.org/10.1080/00130095.2017.1397492.

Fields, Desiree and Uffer, Sabina. 2016. 'The Financialisation of Rental Housing: A Comparative Analysis of New York City and Berlin'. *Urban Geography* 53(7):1486–1502. https://doi.org/10.1177/0042098014543704.

FRPO (Federation of Rental-housing Providers of Ontario). 2019. '2018 Ontario Rental Market Update: The Supply Gap Grows Larger'. Urbanation, for Federation of Rental-housing Providers of Ontario. January. Accessed 10 December 2019. https://www.frpo.org/wp-content/uploads/2019/02/Urbanation-FRPO-Ontario-Rental-Market-Report-Winter-2019.pdf.

Gibb, Kenneth, Pawson, Hal and David Hulchanski. 2018. 'Chapter Seven: Private Renting'. In *Shaping Futures 21: Changing the Housing Story Final Report*, City Futures Research Centre, edited by Duncan MacLennan, Hal Pawson, Kenneth Gibb, Sharon Chisholm and David Hulchanski, 55–68. Accessed 22 July 2020. https://cityfutures.be.unsw.edu.au/research/projects/shaping-futures-changing-housing-story.

Gotham, Kevin F. 2009. 'Creating Liquidity Out of Spatial Fixity: The Secondary Circuit of Capital and the Subprime Mortgage Crisis'. *International Journal of Urban and Regional Research* 33(2):355–71. https://doi.org/10.1111/j.1468-2427.2009.00874.x.

Grisdale, Sean. 2019. 'Displacement by Disruption: Short-term Rentals and the Political Economy of "Belonging Anywhere" in Toronto'. *Urban Geography* 1(27) (Online First).

Heaven, Pamela. 2019. 'Posthaste: What Canada's Mysterious Rise in Insolvencies Says About the Economy'. *Financial Post*, 19 December. Accessed 13 January 2020. https://business.financialpost.com/executive/posthaste-lessons-learned-from-canadas- mysterious -rise-in-insolvencies.

Hildebrand, Shaun and Tal, Benjamin. 2018. 'A Window into the World of Condo Investors'. *Urbanation*, 6 April. Accessed 22 July 2020. https://www.urbanation.ca/sites/default/files/Urbanation-CIBC%20Condo%20Investor%20Report.pdf.

Hulchanski, David. 2004a. 'How Did We Get Here? The Evolution of Canada's "Exclusionary" Housing System'. In *Finding Room: Policy Options for a Canadian Rental Housing Strategy*, edited by David Hulchanski and Michael Shapcott, 179–94. Toronto: University of Toronto Press.

Hulchanski, David. 2004b. 'A Tale of Two Canadas: Homeowners Getting Richer, Renters Getting Poorer'. In *Finding Room: Policy Options for a Canadian Rental Housing Strategy*, edited by David Hulchanski and Michael Shapcott, 81–8. Toronto: University of Toronto Press.

Kalinowski, Tess. 2020. 'Condo Prices Are Set to Put Many Investors in the Red as Rents Fail to Meet Carrying Costs, Experts Warn'. *Toronto Star*, 12 January. Accessed 13 August 2020. https://www.thestar.com/news/gta/2020/01/12/condo-prices-are-set-to-put-many-investors-in-the-red-as-rents-fail-to-meet-carrying-costs-experts-warn.html.

Kalman-Lamb, Gideon. 2017. 'The Financialization of Housing in Canada: Intensifying Contradictions of Neoliberal Accumulation'. *Studies in Political Economy* 98(3):298–323. https://doi.org/10.1080/07078552.2017.1393911.

Kern, Leslie. 2007. 'Reshaping the Boundaries of Public and Private Life: Gender, Condominium Development, and the Neoliberalization of Urban Living'. *Urban Geography* 28(7):657–81. https://doi.org/10.2747/0272-3638.28.7.657.

Langley, Paul. 2008. *The Everyday Life of Global Finance: Saving and Borrowing in Anglo-America*. Oxford: Oxford University Press.

Lawrence, Sean. 2019. 'Purpose-built Rental Units: Answer to Toronto's Housing Crisis?' *Urban Toronto*, 3 May. Accessed 12 January 2020. https://urbantoronto.ca/news/2019/05/purpose-built-rental-units-answer-toronto%E2%80%99s-housing-crisis.

MacLennan, Duncan, Pawson, Hal, Gibb, Kenneth, Chisholm, Sharon and David Hulchanski. 2018. *Shaping Futures 21: Changing the Housing Story Final Report*. Accessed 4 January 2020. https://cityfutures.be.unsw.edu.au/research/projects/shaping-futures-changing-housing-story.

Martin, Randy. 2002. *The Financialization of Daily Life*. Philadelphia, PA: Temple University Press.

Mathieu, Emily. 2017. 'Emptied Kensington Apartments Appear on Airbnb'. *Toronto Star*, 19 June. Accessed 22 July 2020. https://www.thestar.com/news/gta/2017/06/19/emptied-kensington-apartments-appear-on-airbnb.html.

Pawson, Hal. 2018. 'Chapter Two: The "Housing Story": An Australian Perspective'. In *Shaping Futures 21: Changing the Housing Story Final Report*, City Futures Research Centre, edited by Duncan MacLennan,

Hal Pawson, Kenneth Gibb, Sharon Chisholm and David Hulchanski, 10–14. https://cityfutures.be.unsw. edu.au/research/projects/shaping-futures-changing-housing-story.

Revington, Nick and August, Martine. 2019. 'Making a Market for Itself: The Emergent Financialization of Student Housing in Canada'. *Environment and Planning A* 52(5):856–77.

Ronald, Richard, Kadi, Justin and Lennartz, Christian. 2015. 'Homeownership-based Welfare in Transition'. *Critical Housing Analysis* 2(1):52. https://doi.org/10.13060/23362839.2015.2.1.176.

Rosen, Gillad and Walks, Alan. 2013. 'Rising Cities: Condominium Development and the Private Transformation of the Metropolis'. *Geoforum* 49:160–72. https://doi.org/10.1016/j.geoforum.2013.06.010.

Rosen, Gillad and Walks, Alan. 2015. 'Castles in Toronto's Sky: Condo-ism as Urban Transformation'. *Journal of Urban Affairs* 37(3):289–310. https://doi.org/10.1111/juaf.12140.

Saegert, Susan. 2016. 'Rereading "The Housing Question" in Light of the Foreclosure Crisis'. *ACME: An International E-Journal for Critical Geographies* 15(3).

Shabrina, Zahratu, Arcaute, Elsa and Batty, Michael. 2019. 'Airbnb's Disruption of the Housing Structure in London'. March [Pre-Print]. Accessed 22 July 2020. https://www.researchgate.net/publication/332033983_Airbnb%27s_disruption_of_the_housing_structure_in_London.

Sherraden, Michael. 1991. *Assets and the Poor: A New American Welfare Policy*. London: M.E. Sharpe.

Starlight Investments. 2019. 'Starlight Investments and Blackstone Announce Second Multi-Family Acquisition with a Portfolio of Eight GTA Concrete Buildings Totaling 1,067 Units'. *Cision*, 26 February. Accessed 22 July 2020. https://www.newswire.ca/news-releases/starlight-investments-and-blackstone-announce-second-multi-family-acquisition-with-a-portfolio-of-eight-gta-concrete-buildings-totaling-1-067-units-856954637.html.

Statistics Canada. 2017. 'Survey of Financial Security, 2016'. *The Daily*, 7 December. Accessed 5 January 2020. https://www150.statcan.gc.ca/n1/daily-quotidien/171207/dq171207b-eng.htm.

Statistics Canada. n.d. 'Census of Population, years 1981–2016'.

Suttor, Greg. 2009. *Rental Paths From Postwar to Present: Canada Compared*. Cities Centre, University of Toronto, Research Paper 218.

Suttor, Greg. 2016. *Still Renovating: A History of Canadian Social Housing Policy*. Montreal: McGill-Queen's University Press.

Tal, Benjamin. 2019. 'Mortgage Stress Test: The Operation Was a Success, But …'. CIBC Economics 'In Focus', 16 April. Accessed 22 July 2020. https://economics.cibccm.com/economicsweb/cds?ID=7069&TYPE=EC_PDF.

Tal, Benjamin and Shenfeld, Avery. 2019. 'Lessons Learned from Rising Canadian Household Insolvencies'. CIBC Economics 'In Focus', 18 December. Accessed 22 July 2020. https://economics.cibccm.com/economicsweb/cds? TYPE=EC_PDF&ID=9052.

TOLTB (Tribunals Ontario Landlord and Tenant Board). 2018. 'Eviction for Personal Use, Demolition, Repairs and Conversion. Interpretation Guide 12, 15 December. Accessed 13 January 2020. http://www.sjto.gov.on.ca/documents/ltb/Interpretation%20Guidelines/12%20-%20Eviction%20for%20Personal%20Use.html.

UNHRC (United Nations Human Rights Council). 2017. *Report of the Special Rapporteur on Adequate Housing as a Component of the Right to an Adequate Standard of Living, and on the Right to Non-discrimination in This Context*. Accessed 10 January 2020. http://www.unhousingrapp.org/user/pages/04.resources/Thematic-Report-3-The-Financialization-of-Housing.pdf.

Wachsmuth, David, Belot, Charlotte, Bolt, Amy and Kerrigan, Danielle. 2019. 'Short-term Rentals in Toronto'. *UPGo City Spotlight*, August. Accessed 22 July 2020. https://upgo.lab.mcgill.ca/publication/short-term-rentals-in-toronto/short-term-rentals-in-toronto.pdf.

Wachsmuth, David, Kerrigan, Danielle, Chaney, David and Shillolo, Andrea. 2017. 'Short-term Cities: Airbnb's Impact on Canadian Rental Markets'. Urban Politics and Governance Research Group, McGill School of Urban Planning, 10 August. Accessed 22 July 2020. https://upgo.lab.mcgill.ca/publication/short-term-cities.

Wachsmuth, David and Weisler, Alexander. 2018. 'Airbnb and the Rent Gap: Gentrification through the Sharing Economy'. *Environment and Planning A: Economy and Space* 50(6):1147–70. https://doi.org/10.1177/0308518x18778038.

Walks, Alan. 2014. 'Canada's Housing Bubble Story: Mortgage Securitization, the State, and the Global Financial Crisis'. *International Journal of Urban and Regional Research* 38(1):256–84. https://doi.org/10.1111/j.1468-2427.2012.01184.x.

Wilcox, Don. 2018. 'Blackstone Enters Canadian Multi-family, JVs with Starlight'. *Real Estate News Exchange*, 28 June. Accessed 22 July 2020. https://renx.ca/blackstone-enters-canadian-multi-family-jvs-starlight.

12
Planning for densification and housing in London: Urban design and real estate agendas in practice
Michael Short and Nicola Livingstone

Introducing ideas on urban densification

Urban densification has long been seen as an approach to counteracting urban sprawl (European Environment Agency and European Commission 2006) and delivering sustainability, via more compact cities and efficient use of resources such as land, urban transport, materials and energy, for example (Breheny 1996). However, an emerging body of literature points to the shortcomings of urban densification, including challenges relating to culturally significant heritage spaces (Skrede and Krokann Berg 2019), negative outcomes for social sustainability (Dempsey et al. 2012) and decreasing social equity in compact cities (Burton 2000). An important strand within this literature sees urban transformation as an opportunity for property-led development, which is often connected to negative social impacts, for example increasing housing unaffordability, gentrification and urban inequality (Immergluck and Balan 2018). Additionally, positive trickle-down effects from regenerative property-led development to more deprived communities are not always apparent in reality (Tallon 2013).

To rebut these perspectives, it has also been argued that urban design, combined with real estate development, governance and planning strategies, can effectively create more attractive places and place-making processes, recognising that although real estate actors may enforce constraints, they can also 'facilitate the creation of successful places' (Tiesdell and Adams 2012, 60). Of course, the idea of what a 'successful place' may be is subjective, and there are tensions at play between the diverse and variegated perspectives of those operating in markets to create 'successful' housing developments, which are sustainably designed, culturally sensitive and appropriate to the context of local communities.

This chapter investigates the inherent complexities of residential densification through an analysis of recent strategies and policies adopted in London to address the housing crisis post-2010. Challenges in providing housing, ensuring sustainable development and managing densification processes are not unique to London but are prevalent in myriad global cities (see Chapter 13 by Biggar and Siemiatycki for a discussion on densification in Toronto). The chapter also provides a summary and reflection of the proposed changes to urban density policy in the incumbent London Plan, which will be finalised in late 2020, and specific guidance issued by particular London boroughs in response to this.

This chapter examines current influences on densifying the city form grounded in urban design and real estate perspectives using three case studies of residential-led development in inner London: the Heygate Estate (Elephant and Castle, London Borough of Southwark), the Victoria Opportunity Area (City of Westminster) and Woodberry Downs (London Borough of Hackney). Furthermore, it questions whether these influences can cohesively facilitate the creation of 'successful' residential and mixed-used developments, and how these might be understood as successful. Based upon empirical work undertaken in London, we seek to explore the role that urban design plays in mediating between the sometimes conflicting requirements of sustainable, progressive property-led development. In London a range of densification options have been implemented, from building tall to the purchase of social housing estates by private developers for new private, denser residential development. The chapter will first provide a brief discussion about the ways in which density has been determined, looking at quantifiable approaches versus attempts at understanding perceived densities. This will be followed by an overview of urban design and real estate agendas in relation to density. The final main section will summarise the policy position towards density in London with a discussion of how this works 'on the ground' in relation to the three case studies (as previously introduced). The conclusions will firstly seek to summarise the ways in which density is being promoted and implemented in inner London before offering some reflections upon the emerging debate about policies for densification in the new London Plan. Finally they will suggest a way forward in terms of how London boroughs might manage the issue of density on a site-by-site basis, how they may use urban design and planning strategies to achieve that, and what the prospects for a more nuanced understanding of social sustainability might mean in practice. How the ongoing debate surrounding processes of urban densification has unfolded in London is the research focus of the chapter, and the conclusions reflect on key lessons from London which may be pertinent to other global cities.

Measuring density: Numbers versus local context?

Traditionally, density is something that has been measured in terms of the number of units in a given area (e.g. Boyko and Cooper 2011; Churchman 1999). The unit may refer to the number of dwellings, buildings, rooms or individuals in a given measurable area. Thus this attempt at quantifying density characterises places by numbers of units that may, or may not, give an accurate understanding of that place. The main issue with the quantifiable approach is that it does not respond to the particularities of context and therefore, in essence, it ignores what place really means. The numerical measurements are indicative of the density more broadly, but they offer a limited and generalised perspective which only reflects one aspect of the urban housing story. A 'more context-sensitive approach that simultaneously provides planners with new tools to develop both socially and ecologically sustainable urban environments' (Kyttä et al. 2016, 34) would provide dimensionality to ideas surrounding what densification means in our urban centres.

Our understanding of density is in line with Churchman's, in that it 'can be perceived and evaluated in very different ways, by different people, under different circumstances, in different cultures and countries' (1999, 390). Similar approaches to densification have emerged in urban planning in more recent times, and in a market-led system, where planning processes are discretionary, such as those applied in London, the contextual understandings of density, coupled with myriad understandings of how the concept is understood, can be variegated across interpretations of density in the city's 32 boroughs (local authorities created by the London Government Act, 1963). Perceived density is 'defined as an individual's perception and *estimate* of the number of people present in a given area, the space available, and the organization of that space' (Churchman 1999, 390, our italics). Therefore the 'measure' of density is subjective and relational rather than objective and fixed, even though quantifiable approaches have traditionally sought to enforce numerically predefined boundaries to the idea of density. In summary, 'the lack of consensus between theory, policy and practice arguably points to a requirement for residential densities to be examined on a case-by-case basis according to the policy in place at the time as well as the particulars of the place itself' (Dempsey et al. 2012, 96).

Due to subjective experiences and perceptions, each individual understands and responds to density in a different way. This can be understood through two main lines of thinking: perceived physical density and perceived social density (Bergdoll and Williams 1990). Perceived physical density refers to the relationship between physical attributes in the built environment, while perceived social density refers to a relationship between individuals and communities and the physical setting. Furthermore, perceived social density addresses the relative relationships not only between individuals and space, but also between individuals in the space (Cheng 2009, 12), which again reinforces the importance of accounting for diverse local contexts and characteristics. Therefore, the challenge for planners and other built environment professionals is to try to understand not only the complexities of quantifiable and perceived densities, but the ways in which these interact in particular places across London's boroughs to form the built environment and respond to housing, property and urban design ambitions.

London's urban design and real estate agendas

Questions surrounding city development, including how and where people should live, have evolved across the UK since the rapid urbanisation experienced during the industrial revolution of the nineteenth century. Potential opportunities for providing effective residential housing solutions were pursued through Ebenezer Howard's garden city new towns initiative, polycentric developments and continuing urban sprawl. However, the late 1950s brought the introduction of the metropolitan Green Belt around London, while demographic shifts saw the city's population decentralise and therefore decrease. It wasn't until the 1990s, when London was once more experiencing substantial growth and a shift in housing demand, that debates on brownfield redevelopment, the so-called urban renaissance agenda, and the advocacy of the 'compact city' were considered. Indeed, processes of densification and development reflect the temporal dynamics of how cities form and evolve. Such processes are conceived by McFarlane as an interconnected triptych of densification, re-densification and de-densification, influenced by history and place, as well as actively creating new history and places, which 'bring together different temporal trajectories and places across the city, region and world' (2020, n.p.). Presently, London still has an active Green Belt policy, coupled with a rising population and ever increasing pressures on land use, and therefore since the start of the twenty-first century it has experienced rising house prices, increasing social inequity and an inability to meet housing demand. The ongoing housing crisis in the city reflects scenarios where social (public) housing developments have stalled (or are pursued in partnership with private entities – see Chapter 16 for more on housing struggle), the private rented sector (PRS) continues to grow apace (see Chapter 3 for a discussion on issues within London's PRS market) and the viability of housing developments is often impacted by land value price escalation. Densifying the space available to developers could be perceived as a potential solution to the burgeoning affordability crisis being experienced in London (see Chapter 10 for a broader discussion of housing affordability), but wider policy debates continue over how densification can and should be understood from both spatial and temporal perspectives, and whether a densification agenda should be pursued as a response to the complexities of the housing crisis.

It has been argued that 'density is a simple yet effective measure that brings together economic, environmental and social benefits, solving the problems of a sprawling society that has become disconnected, disengaged and distant from an earlier ideal of urban propinquity' (Holman et al. 2015, 2). Indeed, Churchman (1999, 389) argues that its appeal to planners and policy-makers is that it is 'objective, quantitative, and neutral', although we actively query the idea of objectivity as well as neutrality, in how density can be interpreted and operationalised in the discretionary planning system; an objective measure may be understood in a subjective, fluid and non-neutral way, depending on the particulars of a development and the London borough's approach to densification. Density is both a relational and relative concept. However, these 'multiple win–win claims for density' (Holman et al. 2015, 2) reflect a view that density is an independent variable (Boyko and Cooper 2011) that somehow potentially delivers a set of un- or ill-defined benefits. Density can, however, be perceived and therefore be experiential. This, unlike the 'measurable' indicators of density, is a relative and subjective indicator. Perceived density is not solely about the relation between individuals and their surrounding environment, but also about the relations among the individuals in the space (Ng 2010).

Academic literature that considers the spatial and temporal impacts of densification policies in line with the real estate market in contemporary cities is limited (Adams and Tiesdell 2012; Udy 2004). The real estate market's response to densification in the UK is inherently connected to the policies addressing the continued direction of city development, but there is little reflection on the 'end value' of densifying residential real estate, in line with relevant policies, development or investment processes. The impact of densification through zoning, for example (Chakraborty et al. 2010), as well as its social consequences (Glaeser and Gottlieb 2006), is explored in a more diverse way from a North American perspective (see Chapter 13 by Biggar and Siemiatycki for a Toronto perspective on land value capture and density bonusing).

From a development perspective, densification can either be 'hard' or 'soft': both types of densification can contribute to the creation of new housing and can bring different challenges for planning authorities. 'Soft' densification processes are smaller-scale, infill developments which contribute to the creation of new housing in a more discrete manner. Dunning et al. (2020) discuss how softer densification should not be overlooked by local authorities and that 'proactive policy frameworks' are necessary, as incremental changes through smaller developments can result in significant cumulative impacts in local areas. Across the UK, London has experienced the highest levels of 'soft' housing densification processes. As discussed by Bibby et al., in 'London Boroughs, various combinations of large, formal development schemes, that substantially increase site density, and those that reduce it, less intrusive infill developments and the deconversion of larger existing houses may all be proceeding simultaneously' (2020, 114); therefore, there are potential challenges in managing data relating to hard and soft densification, and a need to balance out possibilities of oversupply with development scale.

For larger-scale 'hard' densification developments, as well as potentially increasing the financial value of denser residential provision for the developer, investor and local government, value can also be reflected on in a more socially holistic way, considering local amenities, accessibility and transport links, combined with the user market's willingness to pay for properties (renting or purchasing) in line with cyclical supply and demand issues in the real estate market. Indeed, market reports relating to London (London First and Savills 2015) clearly conclude that increasing the city's residential density can result in varied types of value creation and opportunities, while contributing strategically to addressing the burgeoning housing crisis. There is no concrete guarantee that the housing produced through such strategic developments will offer accessible or affordable housing across the income spectrum within local communities. However, analysing and assessing the potential for value creation in London is subject to viability appraisals carried out by developers, and the ensuing negotiation and decision-making processes between developers, planners and local authorities can result in diverse outcomes as they are considered on a site-by-site basis.

Through viability assessments the developer will be able to reflect on costs, land values and the perceived profits relating to the proposed development in order to ascertain how much of a contribution they will make through 'planning gain' mechanisms. Local authorities seek to benefit from developments through planning obligations such as Section 106 and the Community Infrastructure Levy (CIL), agreeing a financial or tangible contribution from the developer in relation to affordable housing, contributions towards local amenities or infrastructure. The economic factors influencing developments have become increasingly important in the 2010s and are seen by many as prioritising profit and finance over other influential and important urban development influences, such as sustainability. Methods of economic modelling applied by developers in the production of affordable housing (or the lack thereof) have also been criticised as problematic, along with the planning system, suggesting that the limited level of affordable housing output is 'predictable' due to the use of viability appraisals (Sayce et al. 2017). Colenutt et al. suggest that the dominance of financial viability assessments has led the UK to a point where the 'asymmetry in the relationship between the property industry, and local authorities and the communities they serve' (2015, 453) has been reinforced, to the benefit of the developer. Crosby and Wyatt (2016) also demonstrate that viability appraisals enable developers to maximise profits at the expense of the community. However, other emerging research by Lee (2019) suggests that although viability assessments have been utilised advantageously by the developers, such scenarios weren't meant to result in asymmetry of power relations, but that these have emerged as a result of limited governmental guidance and regulation. Such are the complexities of understanding the varied scales of development processes and densities on a site-by-site, borough-by-borough basis, across discretionary planning authorities with particular institutional approaches and local characteristics.

Urban densification debates are also intimately related to sustainability discourses. Urban densification is seen as both a response to climate change and a tool for sustainable urbanisation (Burton 2000). The most influential conceptualisation for this is perhaps the 'compact city' framing, which purports that the denser a city is (in terms of buildings, infrastructure, people, uses, etc.), the better its sustainability outlook and ecological footprint. However, this is not always agreed upon by scholars. In fact, Breheny (1996) acknowledges two schools of thought: *centrists* are those who argue for compact cities, densification and intensification, mainly highlighting environmental sustainability benefits of the compact city; and *decentrists* are those who are against compact cities and advocate the benefits of decentralisation, dispersed cities and suburban living by bringing to the forefront economic and social sustainability advantages. On the one hand, densification of cities has a positive environmental impact by lowering transport needs, making more efficient use of energy and reducing the need for greenfield land for housing; it also promotes healthier and more sustainable lifestyles via walking and cycling (Burton et al. 1996). On the other hand, densifying a city can lead to congestion, lack of affordable housing, no sense of freedom and urban alienation; it also can lead to unwanted health costs by exposing a larger proportion of the population to air pollution, and by reducing urban green space. Hence, there are sustainability claims for and against urban densification. Westerink et al. (2013) classify these claims under four categories: environmental (i.e. CO_2 emissions, energy, water and noise), social (health, wellbeing, social equity, segregation/gentrification and sense of community), economic (land prices, housing affordability, real estate development and competitiveness) and institutional (politics, policy and performance monitoring). In rapidly growing cities such as London we see a shift in academic debate away from the synergy between economic sustainability and densification and towards tensions between densification and the social aspects of sustainability such as social justice and social equity.

Furthermore, in addition to the potential for increased density to affect place identity (either positively or negatively), it might be said to also represent a challenge to the conservation of cultural built heritage, given that densification projects often take place in historic urban environments (Skrede and Krokann Berg 2019). As the protection and conservation of the historic environment in 'hybrid' cities such as London is a central concern of planning, promoting higher densities should address the core question of 'how much originality, how much change?' (Larkham 1996, 38) in that urban environment. In evolving planning and conservation practice, it is recognised that 'the retention of an appropriate ... visual and sensory setting, as well as the retention of spiritual and other cultural relationships that contribute to the cultural significance of the place' (ICOMOS 2013, 5), is key. Thus we see an intrinsic dilemma for complex cities such as London, where the demands of growth and higher densities are potentially at odds with the need to protect and conserve historic environments. This relates primarily to the idea of approaches to the management of urban change, namely, for cities with an historic environment to evolve in a managed way and to not only retain their distinctiveness, but to improve on it through proper planning and contributing to a twenty-first-century city (Hobson 2004).

Urban densification in London: Querying policies and practice

Led by the London Plan (GLA 2016), we are witnessing a 'major programme of densification of areas prompted by a lack of land for new homes' (Allies and Morrison 2016, 3). London has traditionally grown outwards, yet 'this decade is the first time we are identifying growth areas in order to recycle existing neighbourhoods and land' (Allies and Morrison 2016, 1). However, density is a concept that has been embedded into London policy since the creation of the Greater London Authority and a more proactive mayoral system in 2000, with the creation of the London Plan density matrix (LPDM). The first iteration of the LPDM was based on the sustainable residential quality (SRQ) density matrix, created by consultants Llewelyn-Davies in 1998. The matrix proposed that developing at appropriate densities across different sites citywide should adopt a 'design-led' approach to density, determined by site-specific characteristics and qualities relating to sustainable development, as well as accessibility and transport links. The current LPDM has set quantifiable lower and upper density targets for sites depending on a broad characterisation (central, urban or suburban) based upon public transport accessibility level (PTAL) rating (see Table 12.1). The most recent iteration of the London Plan, which will be finalised in late 2020, consulted on whether the LPDM should continue to be applied in its current format for a number of reasons, as outlined below. Such consultative discussions have resulted in diverse and opposing perspectives as to whether densification can be used to address the need for 66,000 new homes in London annually, and if the matrix is fit for purpose.

As a strategic policy aim of the London Plan, the LPDM assumes that proximity to public transport should encourage higher density, although the matrix has been criticised as ignoring the local context and character of neighbourhoods and places (Allies and Morrison 2016). As argued by Edwards (2019), the LPDM has led to an over-reliance on PTAL which consequently ignores impacts on social infrastructure capacity, especially in inner areas. As can be seen from Table 12.1,

Table 12.1 Sustainable residential quality (SRQ) density matrix (habitable rooms and dwellings per hectare) in the adopted London Plan 2016

Setting	Public Transport Accessibility Level (PTAL)		
	0 to 1	2 to 3	4 to 6
Surburban	150–200 hr/ha	150–250 hr/ha	200–350 hr/ha
3.8–4.6 hr/unit	35–55 u/ha	35–65 u/ha	45–90 u/ha
3.1–3.7 hr/unit	40–65 u/ha	40–80 u/ha	55–115 u/ha
2.7–3.0 hr/unit	50–75 u/ha	50–95 u/ha	70–130 u/ha
Urban	150–250 hr/ha	200–450 hr/ha	200–700 hr/ha
3.8–4.6 hr/unit	35–65 u/ha	45–120 u/ha	45–185 u/ha
3.1–3.7 hr/unit	40–80 u/ha	55–145 u/ha	55–225 u/ha
2.7–3.0 hr/unit	50–95 u/ha	70–170 u/ha	70–260 u/ha
Central	150–300 hr/ha	300–650 hr/ha	650–1100 hr/ha
3.8–4.6 hr/unit	35–80 u/ha	65–170 u/ha	140–290 u/ha
3.1–3.7 hr/unit	40–100 u/ha	80–210 u/ha	175–355 u/ha
2.7–3.0 hr/unit	50–100 u/ha	100–240 u/ha	215–405 u/ha

Source: GLA (2016)

the matrix sets numerical ranges for density in relation to PTAL. For example, in suburban areas (typically with low-density detached and semi-detached housing, or residential units of two to three storeys) and a PTAL of four to six (with six being the highest/best level of accessibility), you would expect 45–90 units per hectare of development when there are 3.8–4.6 habitable rooms per unit. In central areas (dense development, city centres, six to eight storeys), at a similar PTAL level of four to six, but with fewer habitable rooms per unit at 2.7–3.0, you would expect 215–405 units per hectare of residential development.

The new Draft London Plan (GLA 2018) sets out a revised density policy which would rid the plan of upper limits for densification (Policy D6, *Optimising Housing Density*). This proposed design-led approach would see site context, connectivity and infrastructure determinants of site capacity considered; this has broadly been welcomed, yet a number of witnesses at the Examination in Public (EiP) outlined their concern about the removal of upper density limits on sites. A major concern is that the 'enforcement of clear, upper limits on density would help discourage over-bidding by developers when they are buying sites and thus help damp land price escalation – to the benefit of social housing providers as well as private develop-ers and ultimately households' (Edwards 2019, n.p.). Additionally, the new policy regime would place the onus of deciding and implementing densities upon London boroughs through site-by-site limits, design codes and the like. Again, there is con-cern about the implications for this for London boroughs in terms of their capacity, ability and need to deliver housing targets (Just Space 2019).

Furthermore, there is additional evidence that the upper limits in particular have been ignored and that there is a 'lack of any hard evidence that the exist-ence of the matrix has significantly affected either the general level or spatial pat-tern of new development densities across London, as compared with that expected from market forces interacting with borough level signals of planning acceptabil-ity' (Gordon et al. 2016, 3). Indeed, Gordon et al. indicate that the upper limits have been 'breached in the majority of the approvals actually granted' (2016, 3). Numbers indicate that the matrix 'is not being followed, 50 per cent of develop-ment is above the matrix maximum for its location, 25 per cent is double the maxi-mum and 15 per cent is below the minimum, i.e. only 35 per cent of development is within the appropriate density matrix range' (GLA 2017, 3). Other alternative perspectives suggest that although a lower/minimum level of density should be maintained, the higher/maximum level should be discontinued (Gordon et al. 2016), especially if the new Plan is considering 'optimum' rather than 'maximum' density: this perspective feeds back into the literature on the complexities inherent in decision-making across boroughs at local level, and how sites are unique. It also demonstrates how, considering the apparent lack of influence the current matrix has, decisions are subjective, market-led and multidimensional, with the LPDM being seen as advisory rather than rigidly enforced – decisions in relation to den-sity should not only be determined by PTAL and broad locational characteristics. Respondents from Highbury, however, consider that the LPDM should be retained in its entirety, as it provides a starting point from which the developers and local planning authorities can begin negotiation processes. Just Space also commented that the upper limits of the LPDM should be strictly enforced moving forward until each borough has a design code in place, thereby reducing speculation and curtailing land value escalation.

The concerns about viability have been a theme in the discussion of policies for densification at the London level; the existing policy of having lower and upper density limits on sites has resulted, in practice, in developers speculatively over-bidding for sites, therefore needing to claw back value from their consequent development proposals. The result has been ever higher densities, building heights and developers arguing 'that the price they have paid for land should be taken into account in "viability" calculations and used to justify social housing reductions' (Edwards 2019, n.p.). Viability, then, has a negative impact on how much local planning authorities can capture through planning gain obligations and Section 106/CIL and diminishes contributions towards affordable housing.

Case studies of densification in London: 'Successful' densification?

Three case studies were chosen to exemplify the nature of the density debate in London. In each of the three cases density is being addressed at different spatial scales and in different ways: in Heygate (London Borough of Southwark) the municipality has sought to relocate the social housing residents, demolish the existing housing and sell the land to developers for higher-density, mainly private residential uses. The Victoria Opportunity Area (City of Westminster) adopted supplementary planning guidance calls for an additional 1,000 dwellings in a context of nationally important infrastructure, established residential communities and a high proportion of protected built heritage (both buildings and areas). In Woodberry Down (London Borough of Hackney) around 2,000 council (or former council) homes will have been demolished and replaced with more than 5,500 units on the estate with a very limited number of social housing units, some for 'key workers', and the majority to be sold on the open market.

In each case, urban design processes seek not only to mediate between sustainability concerns and the real estate investment cycle, but additionally to mediate between the existing character of places and the aspirations of densification strategies. We use a range of methods including policy analysis, interviews and observations on site to assess the processes of densification at play in each location.

Table 12.2 summarises the particular site and proposal characteristics for each of the three case studies. For each of the cases, documents produced as part of each densification process were collected for review purposes. These include the relevant adopted and draft plans (at London and municipal level) and any planning application documents including supporting information, reports, newspaper

Table 12.2 Summary of site and development characteristics

	Heygate, LB* of Southwark	Victoria Opportunity Area, City of Westminster	Woodberry Down, LB of Hackney
Type of site	Social housing estate (with some private ownership)	Mixed – nationally important infrastructure, residential areas, built heritage, offices	Social housing estate (with some limited private ownership)
Size in hectares	9 hectares	40 hectares	64 hectares
Existing dwellings	1,214 dwellings	Unknown (established neighbourhoods)	2,013 dwellings
Number of residents	3,000 approximately	Unknown	Unknown
London Plan 2016 target	3,000 dwellings (Heygate Character Area in the Elephant and Castle OA)	1,000 new dwellings + 4,000 new jobs	5,500 dwellings over 20 years (41% social rented or shared ownership)
Density target	Between 266 and 285 dwellings per hectare, conforming with policy 3.4 requiring a density range of 140–405 dph in *Central* character area.	Not articulated in the Victoria Area Planning Brief SPD, or Westminster City Plan 2019–2040.	Not articulated in any adopted plan (Hackney Local Plan 2015)
Land ownership	LB of Southwark. Sold to Lend Lease Group (for £50 million)	Multiple	LB of Hackney. Sold to a variety of housing developers including Berkeley Homes
Proposal	Demolition of estate to provide 2,704 homes (82 socially rented)	Achieve 1,000 new dwellings through infill of vacant sites and intensification of existing sites.	Demolition of estate over 20 years, in 8 phases.

Table 12.2   Continued

	Heygate, LB* of Southwark	Victoria Opportunity Area, City of Westminster	Woodberry Down, LB of Hackney
Status of proposals/ development	Substantially completed	A number of proposals have come forward for infill/ intensification.	Phase 3 commencing on site.
Any other plans/ planning guidance	Elephant and Castle Supplementary Planning Guidance	Victoria Planning Brief SPD 2011 / Westminster City Plan 2019	Hackney Local Plan 2015 / Woodberry Area Action Plan 2004 / Woodberry Down – A Framework for Regeneration 2009 / Woodberry Down Masterplan 2014
Notes	Demolition substantially completed in 2014. New Elephant Park under construction.	It is unclear how the monitoring of intensification in relation to the plan is taking place.	Approximately 1,500 dwellings have so far been built.

Source: Author
*LB: London Borough.

articles, letters and consultation responses. The review of the documentation established the facts of each of the cases. Site observation was also undertaken for each of the case studies as it allowed for the contextualisation of the facts uncovered in the document review stage. Site observation was crucial to understanding the context of densification proposals, as well as the impact of those proposals (where redevelopment has taken/is taking place).

The three case studies reflect processes of both 'soft' and 'hard' densification: the Victoria Opportunity Area reflects the former, and Heygate and Woodberry Down reflect the latter. Interestingly, with softer processes of intensification through infill and discrete developments, as the land has multiple owners and the sites are variegated across the opportunity area, issues to do with monitoring development processes and outcomes may arise in line with the relevant literature (Bibby et al. 2020; Dunning et al. 2020). With multiple, concomitant developments actively shaping the local urban area in discrete ways, it will be curious to see what the outcomes of these developments are in the longer term in line with the LPDM, considering the lack of density-related perspectives in the City Plan or supplementary planning documents (SPD). In this respect, in the Victoria Opportunity Area, due to the 'soft' nature of active densification processes spread across a substantial geographical area (40 hectares) with myriad 'unknown' locations, it is unlikely that there will be pertinent questions emerging regarding viability, affordable housing provision and sustainable 'good growth'. Therefore, the success of the densification process will be contingent upon the capacity for the smaller-scale developments to contribute positively to and enhance the character and context of the locality and its residential community. One measurable outcome of success is likely to be whether, through effective densification, the Opportunity Area meets the target of creating an anticipated 4,000 new jobs. The spatial and temporal evolution of densification processes in Victoria is likely to have a more disjointed and less concentrated impact over a longer period when compared with the more controversial, 'harder' densification projects considered.

The other two case studies both reflect 'hard' densification processes, with residential development concentrated within defined boundaries and reflecting redevelopment of post-Second World War social housing estates, with Heygate south of the River Thames in the London Borough of Southwark, and Woodberry Down to the north of the city in the London Borough of Hackney. Woodberry Down covers a substantially larger area than the Heygate redevelopment (64 hectares compared with nine hectares) and will provide a larger number of residential units upon completion. However, although a variety of different plans and guidelines have been produced in relation to the Hackney development, they offer no specific guidance on density. This may be due to the temporal and spatial pattern of the development in Hackney, as financial viability and development plans may alter over the anticipated 20-year period, rolling out across eight phases. However, with this lack of definition over a longer period comes opportunity: moving forward, the development could adjust in line with more design-led perspectives if the LPDM were to be adjusted, incorporating additional sustainability features, and revisiting the developer's proposals for integrative urban realm. Although the development will have been fundamentally based on financial viability assessments, with negotiated planning obligations agreed with the local authority, another opportunity would be for developers to actually extract more value from the development in the longer term, depending on the responses to London's housing crisis and movements in land value costs over the lifetime of the development processes, combined with the dynamics of the real estate cycle. There may be further opportunity to actively develop additional housing units if such a shift is valuable for the developer, there is consistent demand in the local community, it is approached in a sustainable way and the adjusted proposals can be seen as representative of 'optimum' density for the area.

The redevelopment of the Heygate Estate, in comparison with the Woodberry Down case study, attracted a significant amount of controversy and media attention because the new development is seen to actively contradict Southwark Council's approach to affordable housing provision. The SPD provides details on how housing can be provided across a range of incomes to maintain the mixed communities within the borough. However, the language adopted is imprecise and open to interpretation, and indeed the new redevelopment fails to deliver on affordable housing targets (which is something that Woodberry Down does succeed at doing, providing 41 per cent of the development as social rented housing or for shared ownership). From its completion in 1972 the original Heygate Estate was home to over 3,000 residents, with over 1,200 social housing units, some of which were sold off through the right-to-buy campaign which emerged in the 1980s. The redevelopment has been criticised in the wider media, as although the number of dwellings will increase through the redevelopment from 1,214 to 2,704, only 82 of these – 3 per cent of the whole development – will be provided for social housing. In this respect, the processes of densification at play in the Heygate Estate have resulted in an area being regenerated but in a community being displaced and alienated, as tenants were relocated elsewhere within London. The Southwark case study is almost complete and is an example of 'hard' densification that, although it clearly sits within the recommended guidelines of the LPDM and provides a contemporary, design-led redevelopment, also embodies many of the negative characteristics associated with densification: profit maximisation through viability assessments by the developer, negative implications for social equity and lack of consideration for the local context or community.

Conclusions

The conclusions will firstly seek to summarise the ways in which density is being promoted and implemented in inner London before offering some reflections upon the emerging debate about policies for densification in the Draft London Plan. They will finally suggest a way forward in terms of how London boroughs might manage the issue of density on a site-by-site basis, how they may use urban design and planning strategies to achieve that and what the prospects for a more nuanced understanding of social sustainability might mean in practice.

It is clear that density is an issue that is challenging planners and planning in inner London – the density matrix, in essence, might appear to be conceived of in a way that maximises the potential of particular sites in delivering 'sustainable development', but in reality the negotiation of specific density in inner London boroughs is fraught with complexity. The three case studies presented show a range of densification challenges from 'soft' to 'hard' approaches. Each suggests a different set of issues that planners face at both the Greater London and individual London borough levels. What ties them together, however, is a vision of what increasing density might achieve, and the skills required in outlining and negotiating that vision in relation to each site. The 'hard' densification promoted in both

Heygate and Woodberry Down has seen the removal of significant numbers of social housing units and their replacement with private accommodation of various types. Should this be the aim of densification? Could a more 'soft' approach, as in Victoria, deliver more units while maintaining the social housing on which so many Londoners depend?

While there is concern about the replacement of the LPDM with targets and approaches that are designed and implemented only at the London borough level, surely a system that appears to prescribe the optimum development on a site to encourage sustainability but which, in reality, allows developers to have the maximum amount of development for the minimum amount of infrastructure provision is flawed. The LPDM promotes a quantifiable approach which does not recognise the qualitative ways in which people live and work – people's perception of the density that is being delivered is entirely absent from discussions in planning in London, and this needs to be remedied. Perceived density should be at the heart of discussions about the overhaul of planning policy to deliver density targets for the benefit of Londoners rather than developers.

References

Adams, David and Tiesdell, Steve. 2012. *Shaping Places: Urban Planning, Design and Development*. London: Routledge.

Allies and Morrison. 2016. *Historic England: London's Local Character and Density*. London: Historic England.

Bergdoll, James R. and Williams, Rick W. 1990. 'Density Perception on Residential Streets'. *Berkeley Planning Journal* 5(1):15–38.

Bibby, Peter, Henneberry, John and Halleux, Jean-Marie. 2020. 'Under the Radar? "Soft" Residential Densification in England 2001–2011'. *EPB: Urban Analytics and City Science* 47(1):102–18. https://doi.org/10.1177/2399808318772842.

Boyko, Christopher and Cooper, Rachel. 2011. *Clarifying and Re-conceptualising Density*. Amsterdam and London: Elsevier.

Breheny, Michael. 1996. 'Centrists, Decentrists and Compromisers: Views on the Future of Urban Form'. In *The Compact City: A Sustainable Urban Form?* (1st edition), edited by M. Jenks, Elizabeth Burton and Katie Williams, 13–35. London and Melbourne: E & FN Spon.

Burton, Elizabeth. 2000. 'The Compact City: Just or Just Compact? A Preliminary Analysis'. *Urban Studies* 37:1969–2006. https://doi.org/10.1080/00420980050162184.

Burton, Elizabeth, Jenks, Mike and Williams, Katie (eds). 1996. *The Compact City: A Sustainable Urban Form?* London: E & FN Spon.

Chakraborty, Arnab, Knapp, Gerrit-Jan, Nguyen, Doan and Jung Ho, Shin. 2010. 'The Effects of High-density Zoning on Multifamily Housing Construction in the Suburbs of Six US Metropolitan Areas'. *Urban Studies* 47:437–51. https://doi.org/10.1177/0042098009348325.

Cheng, Vicky. 2009. 'Understanding Density and High Density'. In *Designing High Density Cities for Social and Environmental Sustainability*, edited by Edward Ng, 3–16. London: Routledge.

Churchman, Arza. 1999. 'Disentangling the Concept of Density'. *Journal of Planning Literature* 13:389–411. https://doi.org/10.1177/08854129922092478.

Colenutt, Robert, Cochrane, Allan and Field, Martin. 2015. 'The Rise and Rise of Viability Assessment'. *Town and Country Planning* 84(10):453–8.

Crosby, Neil and Wyatt, Peter. 2016. 'Financial Viability Appraisals for Site-specific Planning Decisions in England'. *Environment and Planning C: Politics and Space* 34(8):1716–33. https://doi.org/10.1177/0263774x16636118.

Dempsey, N., Brown, C. and Bramley, G. 2012. 'The Key to Sustainable Urban Development in UK Cities? The Influence of Density on Social Sustainability'. *Progress in Planning* 77:89–141. https://doi.org/10.1016/j.progress.2012.01.001.

Dunning, Richard, Hickman, Hannah and While, Aidan. 2020. 'Planning Control and the Politics of Soft Densification'. *Town Planning Review,* forthcoming. https://doi.org/10.3828/tpr.2020.17.

Edwards, Michael. 2019. 'Density: A Walkover for Developers?' Accessed 30 July 2020. https://michaeledwards.org.uk/2019/03/05/density-a-walkover-for-developers.

European Environment Agency and European Commission (Joint Research). 2006. *Urban Sprawl in Europe: The Ignored Challenge.* Copenhagen: European Environment Agency.

GLA (Greater London Authority). 2016. *London Plan.* London: GLA.

GLA (Greater London Authority). 2017. *The Draft London Plan 2017: Topic Paper, Housing Density.* London: GLA.

GLA (Greater London Authority). 2018. *Draft London Plan.* London: GLA.

Glaeser, Edward L. and Gottlieb, Joshua D. 2006. 'Urban Resurgence and the Consumer City'. *Urban Studies* 43:1275–99. https://doi.org/10.1080/00420980600775683.

Gordon, Ian, Mace, Alan and Whitehead, Christine. 2016. *Defining, Measuring and Implementing Density Standards in London.* London Plan Density Research Project 1. London: LSE.

Hobson, E. 2004. *Conservation and Planning: Changing Values in Policy and Practice.* London: Routledge.

Holman, Nancy, Mace, Alan, Paccoud, Antoine and Sundaresan, Jayaraj. 2015. 'Coordinating Density Working through Conviction, Suspicion and Pragmatism'. *Progress in Planning* 101:1–38. https://doi.org/10.1016/j.progress.2014.05.001.

ICOMOS (International Council on Monuments and Sites). 2013. *The Burra Charter for Places of Cultural Significance.* Canberra: ICOMOS Australia.

Immergluck, Dan and Balan, Tharunya. 2018. 'Sustainable for Whom? Green Urban Development, Environmental Gentrification and the Atlanta Beltline'. *Urban Geography* 34(4):546–62. https://doi.org/10.1080/02723638.2017.1360041.

Just Space. 2019. *Just Space Response on Matter M39 Density 2718.* Accessed 22 May 2019. https://justspacelondon.files.wordpress.com/2019/01/m39-density-just-space-2718.pdf.

Kyttä, Marketta, Broberg, Anna, Haybatollahi, Sayyed M. and Schmidt-Thomé, Kaisa. 2016. 'Urban Happiness: Context-Sensitive Study of the Social Sustainability of Urban Settings'. *Environment and Planning B Planning and Design* 47:1–24. 10.1177/0265813515600121.

Larkham, Peter J. 1996. *Conservation and the City.* London: Routledge.

Lee, Gerald. 2019. *Has the Rise of Financial Viability Assessment in the British Planning System Reinforced the Asymmetry in Relationship between the Property Industry, Local Authorities, and the Communities that They Serve?* 19 December 2018. Accessed 13 August 2020. https://papers.ssrn.com/sol3/papers.cfm?abstract_id=3345921.

London First and Savills. 2015. *Redefining Density: Making the Best Use of London's Land to Build More and Better Homes.* London: London First.

McFarlane, Colin. 2020. 'De/Re-densification: A Relational Geography of Urban Density'. *City* 24(1–2):314–24. Accessed 22 July 2020. http://dro.dur.ac.uk/30115/1/30115.pdf?DDD14+dgg0cm1+kswl88.

Ng, Edward (ed.). 2010. *Designing High-density Cities for Social and Environmental Sustainability.* London: Earthscan.

Sayce, Sarah, Crosby, Neil, Garside, Peter, Harris, Rob and Parsa, Ali. 2017. *Viability and the Planning System: The Relationship between Economic Viability Testing, Land Values and Affordable Housing in London.* Cirencester: Royal Agricultural University.

Skrede, Joar and Krokann Berg, Sveinung. 2019. 'Cultural Heritage and Sustainable Development: The Case of Urban Densification'. *The Historic Environment: Policy & Practice* 10:83–102. https://doi.org/10.1080/17567505.2019.1558027.

Tallon, Andrew. 2013. *Urban Regeneration in the UK.* London: Routledge.

Tiesdell, Steve and Adams, David. 2012. *Urban Design in the Real Estate Development Process.* Hoboken, NJ: Wiley-Blackwell.

Udy, John. 2004. *Man Makes the City: Urban Development and Planning.* Victoria, BC: Trafford Publishing.

Westerink, Judith, Haase, Dagmar, Bauer, Annette, Ravetz, Joe, Jarrige, Françoise and Aalbers, Carmen B. E. M. 2013. 'Dealing with Sustainability Trade-Offs of the Compact City in Peri-Urban Planning Across European City Regions'. *European Planning Studies* 21:473–97. https://doi.org/10.1080/09654313.2012.722927.

13

Addressing equity concerns in land value capture: The spatial distribution of community benefits in Toronto's urban redevelopment

Jeff Biggar and Matti Siemiatycki

Introduction

In high-growth cities such as Toronto and London, creating public good from private land development to provide social and physical infrastructure is a key driving force of city planning. Booming economies and soaring land values in local property markets raise the stakes for cities to capture gains arising from the approval of new development and for planners to ensure this development contributes positively to communities. In this context, land value capture (LVC) mechanisms such as density bonusing (used in Toronto) and planning obligations (used in London) apply the idea that some of the profits gained from private development should be reinvested in public amenities and infrastructure. Toronto and London share a similar legislative foundation for planning based on a discretionary process. Each planning case is decided on its own merits, accounting for local plans but not legally bound to them (Booth 1996; Tewdwr-Jones 1999; Smit and Valiante 2015). Discretion enables flexibility in the planning system to adapt to rapid change in an urban environment, which may move at a faster speed than planners can respond to and predict. Out of these systems emerge development-led planning practices that, on the one hand, allow for creativity to adapt to changing trends such as infill and brownfield development, but, on the other, reduce the role of plan-led, comprehensive planning to provide the stability and guidance cities and their planners benefit from to achieve specific goals for the built environment.

This chapter investigates the LVC practice of density bonusing in Toronto's planning system. The chapter begins with an overview of the principles of land value capture and related planning instruments. The details of the research project are then presented, followed by a discussion of the research findings and their relevance for local governments to plan for growth with equity as a model for future cities.

LVC: Political-economic context and conceptual framework

Land value capture refers to any policy or legal instrument whose purpose is to capture value arising from an increase in the price of property and to use that increase for specific purposes (Alterman 2012; Walters 2013). LVC is conceptually rooted in the notion of unearned increment, which emerged among nineteenth-century political economists such as John Stuart Mill and Henry George, who saw the rise in land values derived from public decisions and market conditions, not individual landowners (Hendricks et al. 2017). Smolka and Amborski (2000) define LVC as the process of securing all or part of the value increase caused by public intervention through regulatory or policy means. Other scholars, such as Alterman (2012), suggest LVC may contribute to the public good in the form of windfall capture, an understanding shared by Ingram and Hong (2012), who state that the unearned increment of individually owned private property is created from public action and should therefore be reallocated to society. Examining urban development from a social equity perspective means that gains in value resulting from government action (subsidies to developers, the building of a park, improvement of schools, provision of transit, rezoning of land, etc.) are derived collectively and therefore the benefits likewise should be enjoyed by many, not few (Kohn 2016; Fainstein 2012, 25). The idea of density bonusing resonates with debates on LVC and equity as a process of public action (e.g. rezoning sites for more density) and value creation (e.g. securing community infrastructure).

The rise of LVC comes amid important changes to the political economy of cities. The financialisation of urban development in market-intensive, neoliberal environments sees governments rely more on user fees and voluntary taxes to fund local public facilities, amenities and services rather than general taxation (Fainstein 2016; Gielen and Tasan-Kok 2010; Sagalyn 1997). Incentivising development to receive public benefits is considered politically favourable for local governments looking to keep taxes low and residents satisfied. Canadian cities such as Toronto are no exception to this trend. A political climate promoting fiscal austerity in municipal budgets has kept taxes low and successive provincial governments have downloaded responsibility for affordable housing, transit and social services, resulting in chronic underfunding and no choice but to look beyond property taxes to make up revenue shortfalls to fund major infrastructure and services (Fanelli 2009; Joy and Vogel 2015). Since 2012, property tax increases have been kept at or below inflation and population growth, with the city relying on reserve funds, fluctuating land-transfer taxes and user fees towards already underfunded services and infrastructures (Block and Macdonald 2019).

In these conditions, LVC is one avenue to capture some of the gains of market speculation from private development. Beginning in the mid-1980s, many North American cities extended these provisions to include institutional infrastructure requirements to address affordable housing shortages and other social needs, such as schools, libraries, day care centres, and low-income and affordable housing

(Altshuler and Gomez-Ibanez 2000). Government intervention in land markets informs the LVC paradigm, whereby governments attempt to recoup part of the value derived from offloading infrastructure requirements to the private sector. While gains made through LVC pale in comparison with broad-based taxation (e.g. a tax on the value of land, progressive income taxes), if governments lack resources to fund local infrastructure, LVC tools bring capacity to fill in infrastructure gaps and thus must not be overlooked (Alterman 2012; Muñoz Gielen and Lenferink 2018). Alterman and Kayden (1988) use an umbrella term, 'developer provisions', to describe how value capture techniques work in practice (see Table 13.1).

Incentive-based (negotiated) developer provisions providing public benefits are common in cities such as Toronto and London through density bonusing and planning obligation instruments (Campbell et al. 2000; Moore 2013). In England and Wales, Section 106 planning obligations and the Community Infrastructure Levy (CIL) make up the system of developer provisions to mitigate the social and environmental effects of development. Affordable housing is the primary contribution funded through planning obligations; however, similar to Toronto, there are local variations in the value of these obligations (Lord et al. 2018). The CIL is a standard planning charge with a set formula that is voluntary and applies on most new buildings. In combination they provide for the provision of affordable housing and community infrastructure (Burgess et al. 2013).

Density bonusing in Toronto

Toronto's rapid growth trajectory is a key driving force of the use of LVC practices. Toronto is experiencing a high-rise development boom with an unprecedented volume of construction globally and leads North American cities in total active construction cranes at 120 in 2019 (O'Neil 2019). Strong market forces (consistently

Table 13.1   Conceptual typology of developer provisions, showing differences between LVC instruments

How are they obtained	What is provided	How are they provided
Exaction-based provisions	Infrastructure (roads, sewers, schools, libraries) that directly serves the physical and social needs of a development	Conditional obligations through in-kind/cash contribution
Incentive-based provisions	Benefits such as cultural facilities, parks and recreation centres serving a larger community area beyond the needs of a given development	Negotiations between government actors providing cash in lieu/ in-kind contribution

Source: Alterman and Kayden (1988)

low interest rates, foreign direct investment and speculation on small land supply) are a prevailing narrative for the residential condo boom in Toronto (Filion et al. 2015; Rosen and Walks 2015). The application of density bonusing depends on a booming economy and a perceived value for density by builders and developers, making Toronto a rich urban context to study LVC practices.

Most Canadian cities, including Toronto, use development fees or charges to finance the costs of infrastructure to ensure growth pays for growth (Skaburskis and Tomalty 2000). The provision of public infrastructure and facilities are secured through more fixed public revenue streams, such as development charges, property taxes, commercial business levies, provincial tax transfer payments and federal excise taxes such as the gas tax (Côté 2009). Additional infrastructure money is secured through indirect sources such as density bonusing. It has been the City of Toronto's view that density bonusing was not intended to be a direct revenue tool nor a substitute for other revenue streams such as development charges, but used 'above and beyond' these mechanisms following policy objectives (City of Toronto 2007).

In Toronto, density bonusing is referred to as Section 37 of the Planning Act. When a development is proposed beyond what is otherwise permitted in the zoning by-law, the developer must provide capital 'facilities, services or matters' (affordable housing, parks, public art, libraries) in return for the incentive of additional height or density. These facilities must 'bear a reasonable planning relationship' to a proposed development and have 'an appropriate geographical relationship to the development' that addresses associated planning issues (City of Toronto 2007, 5). Once a development application is approved, the process is facilitated through a community benefit agreement: a voluntary, discretionary agreement between a developer and a municipality outlining the density incentive provided and the agreed upon public benefit,[1] which may be in the form of cash or cash in lieu, and put towards a specific capital project. In practice, the ward councillor – not city planners – negotiates density bonus agreements with developers, and the city council (an elected body) has the final say on all zoning by-law amendments (City of Toronto 2007, 7). The developer, city planner and councillor then agree on what they consider an appropriate value. Density bonusing is triggered by two key public and private actions: (1) the rezoning of land for more height and/or density and change in use, and (2) a transaction where the city extracts public value (cash or cash in lieu) in return for permitting a developer to build a larger or denser building(s).

Section 37 agreements are intended to promote city building objectives of the official plan, a means by which the city can achieve 'responsible, balanced growth' (City of Toronto 2007), and provincial means to provide 'desirable visual amenities to enhance the development site or surrounding neighbourhoods' (MMAH 2009). Like all local planning decisions, Section 37 decisions must consider higher-level provincial legislation and policies to which they are subordinate (Sorensen and Hess 2015). The province of Ontario specifies that municipalities must demonstrate a 'reasonable planning relationship' between the proposed public benefit and the development site (MMAH 2009). If it can be proven that the relationship is untenable, then planning decisions may be appealed by the developer to the Ontario Municipal Board (OMB) and more recently the OMB's successor, the Local Planning Appeals Tribunal – a third-party appeal board appointed by the province to settle land use disputes, as well as interpret and enforce municipal planning decisions.[2] OMB rulings regarding what constitutes a reasonable planning relationship or nexus have produced conflicting rulings over the past decade. Accordingly, the OMB's approach sends mixed signals to planners as to what is considered an appropriate geographical relationship and, more broadly, whether a level of equitable distribution is permitted by legislative frameworks.

Methodology

A mixed-method approach was employed to explore circumstances holistically through various data collection and analysis techniques (Creswell and Creswell 2017). We first collected and assembled density bonusing data (Section 37 community benefit agreements) provided by the City of Toronto planning department to create a unique dataset that includes council approval date, ward location, location of development project, type or value of bonus secured (i.e. cash or non-cash), community benefit description and project notes. The data enabled an assessment of the types of projects that received funding through the density bonus programme, as well as their spatial distribution. Additionally, 20 semi-structured interviews were conducted between June 2015 and April 2016 with key stakeholders (planners, politicians, councillors and developers) involved in negotiating or determining community benefit agreements. Lastly, the analysis included a content analysis of relevant provincial and local level policies, plans, acts, guidelines and protocol and related materials, as well as a review of media articles, industry reports and development industry blog entries. Taken together the data provide insights on the application and outcomes of LVC arrangements in Toronto.

Analysis of community benefit agreements

Between the years 1998 and 2014, the City of Toronto generated 630 community benefit agreements. Each agreement contains one or multiple benefits. Across all agreements, there were approximately 2,000 individual community benefits. Seventy-nine per cent of benefits were paid in cash and 21 per cent were described as non-cash benefits. Each community benefit agreement is tied to a specific development project and secured in a zoning by-law.

The aim of density bonusing policy in Toronto is to provide a range of social, environmental and physical benefits such as public space, provision of affordable housing and day care centres. Moore (2013) found that the city primarily secures benefits that provide a cosmetic treatment to the built form. As shown in Figure 13.1, the findings both confirm and extend this observation as the majority of benefits are still secured under roads and streetscapes. However, social benefits referred to as 'community, culture and recreation' are the second-most secured category of benefits, with investment going towards community and recreation facilities: day care centres, early learning centres, theatre space and artist live/work units. The benefits realised under roads and streetscapes tend to be for beautification over measures such as traffic calming, as density bonusing is not intended to address hard infrastructure requirements such as sewer upgrades, road widening and traffic signalling – capital costs supported through development charges (City of Toronto 2015b; Tomalty and Skaburskis 2003).

Lehrer and Wieditz (2009) argue that Section 37 mostly provides public art and park space over affordable housing and community facilities because the former favours the developer by driving up property values. Politicians also aim to use Section 37 agreements to fund highly visible 'wish list' projects such as park improvements and community arts and culture amenities that appeal to constituents and enhance their chance of re-election. The findings confirm this proposition: after roads, community and cultural facilities, parks and public art make up the largest recipients of Section 37 funds; by contrast, affordable housing makes up 20 per cent of the funds collected.

Overall the analysis demonstrates that Section 37 LVC agreements favour the physical environment through investments in roads and streetscapes over social infrastructure through investments in affordable housing. This imbalance shows that the city struggles to use density bonusing as the strategic implementation tool it was intended to be, minimising the equity gains possible and falling short

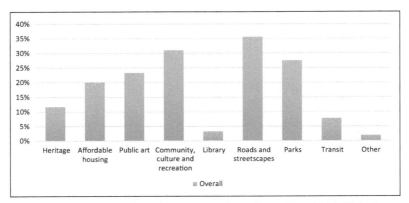

Figure 13.1 Percentage of total Section 37 benefits, 1997–2014. This figure shows the total breakdown of Section 37 benefits by type and percentage of total benefits secured (Biggar 2015; City of Toronto 2015)

in supporting the bigger challenge of new development outpacing existing and planned social infrastructure.

Public perception of density bonusing has prompted many commentators to refer to the process as 'let's make a deal planning', which some claim reduces the legitimacy of the planning process in the public eye. The optics of councillors negotiating directly with developers to determine the amount of funds captured through a Section 37 agreement does not abate suspicions of corruption and cronyism (Jeffords and Warmington 2012; Devine 2008). Moreover, the high volume of cash transactions put aside and pooled for future community benefits makes it unclear whether a rational 'nexus' between a proposed development and the location of public benefit will transpire (Healey et al. 1993). Toronto's ability to secure cash permits councillors to invest community benefits anywhere within ward boundaries and pushes the majority of benefits off the site where the development is taking place. Toronto has seen a general increase in total cash contributions from projects in the last decade. Figure 13.2 shows total cash payments for community benefits scale upward over a 17-year period, the exception being a brief dip in the median cash payment in 2011. The median cash payment was $450,000 across the data sample, with the highest median cash payment of $987,000 in 2014. Based on historical projections, it is not surprising that many councillors and practitioners consider density bonusing an important and reliable source for funding municipal projects.

Spatial analysis of community benefit agreements

Public benefits secured through density bonusing occur at the ward scale – there were 44 wards in Toronto at the time the study was completed. The amount of funds is closely tied to development and thus unequally generated between the city centre and key nodes in the city that are growing most rapidly, and those areas primarily in the inner suburbs where less development is taking place. The largest

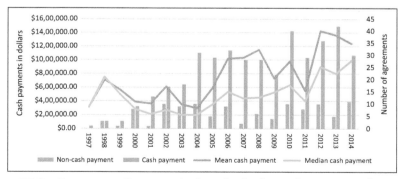

Figure 13.2 Frequency of community benefits by form of payment and year (Biggar 2015; City of Toronto 2015)

amount of public benefit investment provided through this policy tool is spatially concentrated within the downtown and midtown areas, key growth centres in the city. The four wards that comprise the downtown core, in particular, have received the lion's share of bonusing funds – approximately 53 per cent of total public benefits across the city to a combined total of $200 million in cash value. The second-highest concentration of benefit agreement funding is along major avenues in the inner suburbs, where city plans aim to concentrate growth and there has been an uptick in development. By contrast, the inner suburbs in Toronto have received the least amount of development and therefore smaller amounts of funds generated through LVC.

The links between benefits through LVC and wealth show that most benefits are located in affluent yet uneven and gentrifying downtown neighbourhoods. Across Toronto, 64 per cent of benefits are in wards with a median household income below $63,000. In the downtown, this number is lower at $55,000. For example, one ward that received a large share of public benefits is also the most socially and economically divided, with higher-income households in single-family dwellings existing alongside lower-income public housing complexes (Delacourt 2016). Yet the majority of the density bonus funding came from developing new high-rise housing in the lower-income part of the ward, as compared with the single-family neighbourhood where little intensification has occurred (see Figure 13.3 for distribution of density bonusing funds). Thus, it is important to take into account socio-spatial inequities within wards. Even if social benefits such

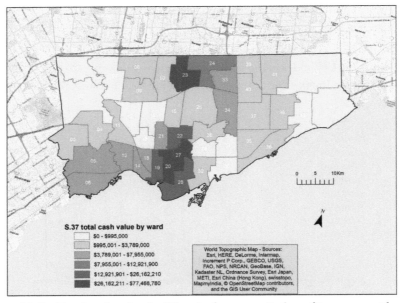

Figure 13.3 Total cash value (millions) of community benefit agreement by ward (Biggar 2015; City of Toronto 2015)

as affordable housing units (the city's minimum target is 10 per cent of total units) are included in new owner-occupied units in lower-income sections of the ward, they are likely not substantial enough to stabilise the rising market value of the rezoned land on which they were built.

Discussion

Toronto has secured a wide variety of community benefits from density bonusing, which are spatially concentrated in areas experiencing rapid growth rather than dispersed geographically and more equally across all parts of the city. The policy formulation of density bonusing can be considered a combination of indirect and direct value capture; however, the practice of density bonusing does not conform to existing conceptualisations of value capture as described by Alterman (2012). In general terms, the rationale for density bonusing is partly about anticipating the negative impacts of a proposed development (indirect value capture) and offsetting them, and partly about the uplift in economic value gained from a planning permission for rezoning (direct betterment capture). After viewing the material distribution of community benefits, little evidence of the 'betterment capture' or 'sharing the wealth' idea of value capture applies to the findings (Alterman 2012; Booth and Albrechts 2012). This is not surprising considering that public benefits are concentrated in high-density areas where regional policy directs growth. In addition, legal requirements and related case precedents at the OMB direct planners and councillors to provide off-site community benefit contributions close to the development site, limiting the distribution of funds to low-income neighbourhoods. But interpreting proximity is not straightforward as views of what counts as a reasonable distance from a given site vary. In Ontario, the OMB does not always provide a rationale when ruling on the lack of nexus between development and benefit, sending mixed signals to planners and politicians.

Interviews with government and private sector actors provide insight into the process behind community benefits. Table 13.2 summarises interview results. A further explanation as to why political influence over local planning matters occurs is the discretionary nature of Toronto's planning system. Local councillors may weigh in and direct decisions about where community benefits go and how much value should be captured. Interviews with councillor staff suggest that in some instances a small yet vocal contingent of residents are successful in lobbying their councillor to direct community benefits according to their wishes over the higher-order needs of a neighbourhood. This is not surprising, because the ward electoral system in Toronto influences who benefits from density bonusing since outcomes are tied equally to political boundaries and to geographical ones. Individual councillors are primarily beholden to constituents within a certain catchment area, so there is little incentive for one councillor to share the wealth of his or her negotiated community benefit with another (Moore 2013).

Table 13.2 Interview themes. This table shows the three main themes derived from the interview analysis

Interview Themes	Characteristics
Uneven distribution of benefits	The scale of public benefit is uneven. Site-specific planning addresses local needs at the expense of citywide needs. Density bonusing is indicative of development-rich areas in the downtown and development-poor areas on the periphery and parts of the suburbs. Rationale for benefits to stay on-site, or close to site, poorly understood by development actors and public alike.
Artificial valuation of density	The development industry was a proponent of formulas to base valuation on actual numbers, not artificial ones lacking methodological rigour and reliability. Respondents felt current approach creates unfairness towards development industry and overall lower contribution amounts from additional density for the city. Some planners opposed to discussing financial details of community benefits transaction because they don't want them to compromise good planning. This leads to conflict with the development industry.
Broad political discretion	Legislative discretion granted to city councillors has politicised the negotiation process where councillors ultimately are the strongest voice in determining community benefits. Going by general guidelines and no set standards, councillors have wide latitude in choosing what type of benefit will be selected and how much value it will be worth. This dynamic has created an uneven playing field across the city's political boundaries.

Source: author

The open-ended nature of LVC practices, such as density bonusing, that have few standards presents an arena for councillors to exercise discretionary power to great effect, which in Toronto's environment leads to variation in process and outcomes. The findings show the effects of a municipal structure that grants broad-based political discretion to councillors. Factors such as knowledge sharing, understanding of the development process and policy competence among local councillors and planners play into how much value will be captured, if any. The skill and negotiating acumen of councillors varies by geography, as does their ideological conviction over what benefits should be selected. Some councillors may be more talented negotiators than others based on their experience and knowledge of planning. In the right circumstances, councillors may leverage their position to negotiate a higher or lower amount of the uplift from new development projects.

For example, one downtown councillor had a previous career in the real estate industry and used this experience when negotiating with developers (personal communication, councillor's assistant). The councillor negotiated a deal ($5.5 million) with a developer for the same amount as a deal by her predecessor in the same ward, except the councillor's project was half the density. Similarly, a former councillor possessed the 'architectural and economic language' to reason with developers and acknowledged the value they place on speed and efficiency (personal communication, member, downtown community association). Some councillors have overlooked opportunities to achieve any public benefits because they were unfamiliar with how the process works, whereas others have taken creative steps to 'bend the rules in the name of social equity ... by doling out money to neighbourhoods who were not getting the attention they deserved for affordable housing' (former city councillor, City of Toronto, personal communication).

The data reveal that some individual community benefit project agreements deviate from legal requirements to use density bonuses for permanent capital projects and use them on operational projects of a social nature. For example, a community activist advocated for a developer's community benefit contribution of $200,000 to fund a breakfast programme for neighbourhood children. Another example saw the organisers of AIDS2006 – an international AIDS conference – receive $150,000 for conference expenses, and a business improvement area receive $20,000 for 'economic development programs' (Jeffords 2012). Other community benefits demonstrate the use of land leases to provide eight below-market-rate rental units for artists and visiting professors for a downtown university, OCAD, and a non-profit arts and cultural organisation (Biggar and City of Toronto 2015; City of Toronto 2015b).

In the context of considerable discretion residing with the individual city councillors, the amount negotiated or value of benefit is also influenced by the openness and transparency of financial considerations. Some developer respondents bemoaned the lack of rigour and consistency surrounding the valuation of Section 37, because they believe planners have a general lack of interest in the economic components of a development application. When it comes to economics in the development process, planners and developers are at different ends of the spectrum and appear to talk past each other. Planners withdraw from discussions about financial details despite their integral role in building construction and city building more broadly. Developers are often willing to engage in discussions of economics because they consider Section 37 a cost, not a benefit or gain to the public. When planners do consider the economic dimension of bonusing, the extent to which development controls accurately reflect the true costs of benefits and negative externalities inflicted on the built environment is unknown. One aim of LVC is to capture full or partial amounts of 'unearned increment' (Smolka and Amborski 2000). Most planning jurisdictions in Toronto do not explicitly define the value of the 'uplift' (gains from added density) they hope to capture from intensification in a set formula, instead following a negotiated approach that determines the value of density on a case-by-case basis. Citing confidentiality reasons, the City of Toronto and developers do not disclose the details of negotiations that outline the total costs of the bonus contained within the developer's pro forma.

Interviews with planners revealed that value capture increment was as low as 4 per cent in some instances, and some councillors establish their own measures based on unofficial standards, such as the value secured in other development projects in their ward. Interviews with city councillors revealed inconsistency in the understanding of how uplift works. For example, one downtown councillor stated in an interview that they secured 15 per cent of the uplift on each project, regardless of the scope and specific financial details (personal communication, city councillor, City of Toronto). The arbitrary assigning of value also occurs among some developers. The respondent's perspective below shows that the value of density is not necessarily proportional to a specific project and may be arbitrarily applied: 'Most Section S.37s are in that swing of 10 per cent. That just evolved, I don't know who invented it. People like round numbers, but you rarely find exact amounts' (personal communication, Developer 3). These perspectives suggest that planners and councillors have no definitive way of knowing whether the gains extracted from development meet or exceed the development's proportionate share of the costs associated with community infrastructure needs. Moreover, land values may be derived artificially as all numbers are not fully disclosed.

Achieving equity from LVCs

A social equity lens to value capture conceptualises the object of development as not just efficiency (highest and best use), but also how development addresses (or does not address) social disadvantage and contributes to the quality of life for the broader public (Fainstein 2012). An assessment of the scale and scope of public benefits in Toronto, and the accompanying factors that help explain variation in both type and value, reflect broader interpretations of value capture as being 'messy' and associated policies as confusing (Alterman 2012; Campbell et al. 2000; Fox-Rogers and Murphy 2015). The inequitable geographic and material outcomes of density bonusing point to larger consequences of relying on private development to fund public infrastructure. While the intention of policy tools such as density bonusing is not to redistribute wealth beyond the vicinity where it is derived, the lack of distributive policy function raises more complicated questions about a growing equity gap in Toronto: areas that have development get additional public investment and areas that don't remain stagnant. The findings call into question the related problem of neighbourhoods outside up-zoned areas that do not directly benefit from increased density but may still be negatively impacted by new development. A growth model that hinges on developing with density does not work towards an equitable spatial order of the city. In this regard, density bonusing can be considered a potential but not fully developed approach to capturing the value of development to allocate to social purposes. In the absence of an explicit redistributive policy objective, areas in need of community infrastructure improvements will not receive bonusing finds. These issues matter, especially given the budget pressures being faced by Toronto, which relies more and more on one-off funds through Section 37 instead of predictable general taxation revenue streams for community infrastructure. Nevertheless, if local governments such as Toronto lack predictable resources to supply the ever changing infrastructure needs for localities, discretionary and indirect mechanisms such as density bonusing will continue to be applied. These results leave questions of how to maintain the flexibility inherent in density bonusing to accommodate shifting public needs while bringing coherence in the form of structure or standards that predetermine the actual costs of public facilities and amenities based on need.

These perspectives call for a bigger conversation about basic principles that have gone unaddressed: who should stand to benefit, and how can community needs match the benefits that are prioritised? A 'sharing the wealth' rationale for value capture means that land value captured from development may extend beyond the vicinity of the development where value is derived. The site-specific nature of density bonusing in Toronto demonstrates that benefits derived from a single development tend to stay close to a given site and produce one-off investments, as is the policy intent. In its current form, this policy area occurs in a vacuum, but the notion of community benefit extends beyond the regulatory apparatus of land use planning and zoning to other public sector policies, such as workforce development and local economic development as seen in the US and UK through community benefit agreements (Wolf-Powers 2010).[3] On its own, Section 37, like other forms of incentive-based indirect forms of value capture, generates a small amount of revenue and was intended by planners to supplement, not replace, funding to address the infrastructure gaps faced by the city (City of Toronto 2007). However, current conditions of budgetary austerity leave councillors with few options but to rely entirely on Section 37 to fund local projects. Between 2016 and 2019, the city has secured upwards of $90 million to fund 150 community facility projects (e.g. childcare, libraries, recreation centres), making contributions toward the City of Toronto's ten-year capital plan (City of Toronto 2019). But the site-specific composition of this planning activity in Toronto is indicative of what Margalit and Alfasi (2016) refer to as 'splintered planning', where the primacy of deal making is strongly connected to growing flexibility and fragmentation in entrepreneurial planning, resulting in one-off deals that create a fractured and disconnected vision for a city. Planning becomes oriented toward the site, not an area or the city as a whole. Cast in this light, LVC tools such as density bonusing and planning obligations are indicative of larger trends in planning; they facilitate uneven development and create spatial and financial inequities in cities, on the one hand, and provide creative 'win–win' solutions from density for narrow public interests, on the other hand. Toronto's municipal structure reinforces case-by-case planning due to the 'ward boss' system that responds to individual constituents in a 'one property at a time scale of development process' (Valverde 2012, 133). Political boundaries within the ward system of electing local representatives focus councillors' attention on parochial issues, which shapes the expectations of citizens to make one-off demands to benefit their block or neighbourhood, not the city.

Conclusion

This chapter investigated the LVC mechanism of density bonusing in Toronto. It assessed the allocation and distribution of community benefits derived from this policy area and considered the extent to which benefits create equity from development projects. The chapter found that benefits are spatially concentrated, not evenly distributed, and that public benefits are localised and pertain to the physical form of the city. The results showed that government actors' discretionary control of negotiations surrounding density bonusing was a key factor in explaining variation in the amount of value captured, which reportedly varies significantly, ranging from 4 per cent to 15 per cent of the value from additional height and/or density permitted to developers through site-specific rezoning outcomes. For areas that received a high amount of public benefits, the negotiating acumen of individual councillors and the type of developer were key factors in influencing the range of value and types of benefits secured. Political influence in planning matters also distorts how planning frameworks in Toronto fit into broader understandings of the purpose of public benefits, including whether equity is considered.

The findings were consistent with the view in the literature that LVC is messy and lacks clear rationales in its application (Alterman 2012; Walters 2013). Some outcomes suggest the purpose of density bonusing is to create localised effects for those immediately affected by development, whereas others suggest the notion of a public benefit may be shared with the wider community – also known as 'sharing the wealth' of extracted public value. Importantly, fees derived from land use tools such as density bonusing depend entirely on a strong real estate market boom and developer confidence to ask for additional planning permissions beyond 'as-of-right' zoning. And density bonusing has limited value in many land markets across the city, particularly in large parts of the inner suburbs where little development is taking place. In other words, the cost–benefit ratio must offer a favourable return to a developer making an investment – if developers do not perceive a financial benefit in the trade-off between additional density and amenity, an agreement will not be made. Even with these constraints, for cities planning in a capitalist, market-intensive economy, planners and other city officials must find creative ways to apply shared resources to reach common goals and to move further towards equitable distribution of public benefits derived from high-density development.

Notes

1. Suggested benefits include non-profit child care facilities, affordable housing, public art, parks improvement, streetscape improvements, heritage conservation and improvement to transit facilities.
2. The OMB has since been replaced by the Local Panning Appeals Tribunal (LPAT). The key difference from the OMB is that LPAT follows a standard appeals process, reviewing municipal decisions but not making a decision or overruling/substituting that of a municipal council.
3. Community benefit agreements (CBAs), most common in the US and UK, are led by community–developer legal agreements that outline the benefits a community will receive from the development in return for supporting the proposed project (e.g. construction jobs for low-income residents, apprenticeship and training, social enterprises and community amenities ranging from day cares to public art). CBAs are a relatively new practice in Toronto (Nugent 2017).

References

Alterman, Rachelle. 2012. 'Land Use Regulations and Property Values: The "Windfalls Capture" Idea Revisited'. In *The Oxford Handbook of Urban Economics and Planning*, edited by Nancy Brooks, Kieran Donaghy and Gerrit-Jan Knaap, 755–86. New York: Oxford University Press.

Alterman, Rachelle and Jerold Kayden. 1988. 'Developer Provisions of Public Benefits: Toward a Consensus Vocabulary'. In *Private Supply of Public Services: Evaluation of Real Estate Exactions, Linkage, and Alternative Land Policies*, edited by Rachelle Alterman, 22–34. New York: NYU Press.

Altshuler, Alan A. and Gomez-Ibanez, Jose, A. 2000. *Regulation for Revenue: The Political Economy of Land Use Exactions*. Washington, DC: Brookings Institution Press.

Biggar, Jeff and City of Toronto. 2015. Section 37 Database. [Dataset]

Block, Shelia and Macdonald, David. 2019. *A New Revenue Tool: The Case for a Greater Toronto and Hamilton Area Sales Tax*. Toronto: Canadian Centre for Policy Alternatives. Accessed 22 August 2019. https://www. policyalternatives.ca/publications/reports/new-revenue-tool.

Booth, Philip. 1996. *Controlling Development: Certainty and Discretion in Europe, the USA and Hong Kong* (Vol. 9). London: Psychology Press.

Booth, Philip A. and Albrechts, L. G. H. 2012. 'The Unearned Increment: Property and the Capture of Betterment Value in Britain and France'. In *Value Capture and Land Policies*, edited by Gregory K. Ingram and Yu-Hung Hong, 74–96. Cambridge, MA: Lincoln Institute of Land Policy.

Burgess, G., Crook, T. and Monk, S. 2013. *The Changing Delivery of Planning Gain through Section 106 and the Community Infrastructure Levy*. Cambridge, UK: Cambridge Centre for Housing and Planning Research.

Campbell, Heather, Ellis, Hugh, Henneberry, John and Gladwell, Caroline. 2000. 'Planning Obligations, Planning Practice, and Land-use Outcomes'. *Environment and Planning B: Planning and Design* 27(5):759–75. https://doi.org/10.1068/b2683.

City of Toronto. 2007. *Implementation Guidelines for Section 37 of the Planning Act and Protocol Negotiating Section 37 Community Benefits*. Toronto: Toronto City Planning.

City of Toronto. 2015a. *Toronto 2015 Budget*. Accessed 23 June 2020. https://www.toronto.ca/city-government/budget-finances/city-budget/previous-budgets/2015-city-budget.

City of Toronto. 2015b. *2015 Annual Report, City Planning – Your City*. Accessed 25 June 2019. https://www.toronto.ca/legdocs/mmis/2016/pg/bgrd/backgroundfile-90606.pdf.

City of Toronto. 2019. *Proposed Bill 108 (More Homes, More Choice Act, 2019) and the Housing Supply Action Plan – Preliminary City Comments*. Accessed 22 July 2020. https://www.toronto.ca/legdocs/mmis/2019/cc/bgrd/backgroundfile-133165.pdf.

Côté, Andre. 2009. *The Maturing Metropolis: Governance in Toronto a Decade on from Amalgamation*. Toronto: Institute on Municipal Finance and Governance.

Creswell, John W. and Creswell, J. David. 2017. *Research Design: Qualitative, Quantitative, and Mixed Methods Approaches*. Thousand Oaks, CA: SAGE.

Delacourt, Susan. 2013. 'Toronto Centre: Byelection Riding Has Huge Income Gap'. *Toronto Star*, 16 November. Accessed 22 July 2020. https://www.thestar.com/news/canada/2013/11/16/toronto_centre_byelection_riding_has_huge_income_gap.html.

Devine, J. P. 2008. 'Section 37: An Update on "Let's Make a Deal" Planning'. Working paper. Toronto: Fraser, Milner, Casgrain, LLP. Accessed 21 July 2015. http://www.fmclaw.com/upload/en/publications/2008/RealEstate_Mar2008_Devine_Sliwa_Section37.pdf.

Evans, Pete. 2014. 'Skyscraper Gap in N. America Narrows, but Toronto Leads with 130'. *CBC News*, 21 January. Accessed 22 July 2020. https://www.cbc.ca/news/business/130-highrise-building-projects-in-toronto-lead-north-america-1.2504776.

Fainstein, Susan. 2012. 'Land Value Capture and Justice'. In *Value Capture and Land Policies*, edited by Gregory Ingram and Yu-Hung Hong, 121–40. Washington, DC: Lincoln Institute of Land Policy.

Fainstein, Susan. 2016. 'Financialisation and Justice in the City: A Commentary'. *Urban Studies* 53(7):1503–8. https://doi.org/10.1177/0042098016630488.

Fanelli, Carlo. 2009. 'The City of Toronto Fiscal Crisis: Neoliberal Urbanism and the Reconsolidation of Class Power'. *Interdisciplinary Themes Journal* 1(1):11–18.

Filion, Pierre, Charney, Igal and Weber, Rachel. 2015. 'Downtowns that Work: Lessons from Toronto and Chicago'. *Canadian Journal of Urban Research* 24(2):20–42.

Fox-Rogers, Linda and Murphy, Enda. 2015. 'From Brown Envelopes to Community Benefits: The Co-option of Planning Gain Agreements under Deepening Neoliberalism'. *Geoforum* 67:41–50. https://doi.org/10.1016/j.geoforum.2015.09.015.

Gielen, Demetrio Muñoz and Tasan-Kok, Tuna. 2010. 'Flexibility in Planning and the Consequences for Public-value Capturing in UK, Spain and the Netherlands'. *European Planning Studies* 18(7):1097–131. https://doi.org/10.1080/09654311003744191.

Healey, Patsy, Ennis, Frank and Purdue, Michael. 1993. *Gains from Planning? Dealing with the Impacts of Development*. York: Joseph Rowntree Foundation.

Hendricks, Andreas, Kalbro, Thomas, Llorente, Marie, Vilmin, Thierry and Weitkamp, Alexandra. 2017. 'Public Value Capture of Increasing Property Values: What Are "Unearned Increments"'. In *Land Ownership and Land Use Development*, edited by Erwin Hepperle, Robert Dixon-Gough, Reinfried Mansberger, Jenny Paulsson, Józef Hernik and Thomas Kalbro, 257–81. Zürich: vdf Hochschulverlag.

Ingram, Gregory and Hong, Yu-Hung. 2012. 'Land Value Capture: Types and Outcomes'. In *Value Capture and Land Policies*, edited by G. Ingram and Yu-Hung Hong, 3–18. Cambridge, MA: Lincoln Institute of Land Policy.

Jeffords, Shawn. 2012. 'Following the Section 37 Cash Trail'. *Toronto Sun*, 27 October. Accessed 22 July 2020. https://torontosun.com/2012/10/27/following-the-section-37-cash-trail/wcm/9dea93f2-a9be-42ff-8bec-1edf6cd3e6b3.

Jeffords, Shawn and Warmington, Joe. 2012. 'City Plays "Let's Make a Deal"'. *Toronto Sun*, 8 October. Accessed 22 July 2020. https://torontosun.com/2012/10/08/city-plays-lets-make-a-deal/wcm/bab3a8e7-872d-4881-8cc5-25baa18d6bd6.

Joy, Meghan, and Vogel, Ronald K. 2015. 'Toronto's Governance Crisis: A Global City under Pressure'. *Cities* 49:35–52. https://doi.org/10.1016/j.cities.2015.06.009.

Kohn, Margaret. 2016. *The Death and Life of the Urban Commonwealth*. New York: Oxford University Press.

Lehrer, Ute and Wieditz, Thorben. 2009. 'Condominium Development and Gentrification: The Relationship between Policies, Building Activities and Socio-economic Development in Toronto'. *Canadian Journal of Urban Research* 18(1):140–61.

Lord, Alex, Dunning, Richard, Dockerill, Bertie, Burgess, Gemma, Carro, Adrian, Crook, A. D. H., Watkins, Craig and Whitehead, Christine. 2018. 'The Incidence, Value and Delivery of Planning Obligations and Community Infrastructure Levy in England in 2016–17'. Accessed 22 September 2019. https://www.lse.ac.uk/geography-and-environment/research/lse-london/documents/Reports/Section-106-and-CIL-research-report.pdf.

Margalit, Talia and Alfasi, Nurit. 2016. 'The Undercurrents of Entrepreneurial Development: Impressions from a Globalizing City'. *Environment and Planning A: Economy and Space* 48(10):1967–87. https://doi.org/10.1177/0308518x16651872.

MMAH (Ministry of Municipal Affairs and Housing), Provincial Planning Policy Branch. 2009. *Height and Density Bonusing (s. 37): Building Blocks for Sustainable Planning 5*. Toronto: Queen's Printer for Ontario.

Moore, Aaron. 2013. *Trading Density for Benefits: Toronto and Vancouver Compared*. Toronto: Institute on Municipal Finance and Governance, University of Toronto.

Muñoz Gielen, Demetrio and Lenferink, Sander. 2018. 'The Role of Negotiated Developer Obligations in Financing Large Public Infrastructure after the Economic Crisis in the Netherlands'. *European Planning Studies* 26(4):768–91. https://doi.org/10.1080/09654313.2018.1425376.

Nugent, James. 2017. 'The Right to Build the City: Can Community Benefits Agreements Bring Employment Equity to the Construction Sector?' *Labour/Le Travail* 80: 81–114.

O'Neil, Lauren. 2019. 'Toronto Has More Construction Cranes than Anywhere Else in North America'. BlogTO. Accessed 22 July 2020. https://www.blogto.com/real-estate-toronto/2019/07/toronto-construction-cranes.

Rosen, Gillad and Walks, Alan. 2015. 'Castles in Toronto's Sky: Condo-ism as Urban Transformation'. *Journal of Urban Affairs* 37(3):289–310. https://doi.org/10.1111/juaf.12140.

Sagalyn, Lynne B. 1997. 'Negotiating for Public Benefits: The Bargaining Calculus of Public–Private Development'. *Urban Studies* 34(12):1955–70. https://doi.org/10.1080/0042098975169.

Skaburskis, Andrejs and Tomalty, Ray. 2000. 'The Effects of Property Taxes and Development Cost Charges on Urban Development: Perspectives of Planners, Developers and Finance Officers in Toronto and Ottawa'. *Canadian Journal of Regional Science* 23(2):303–28.

Smit, Anneke and Valiante, Marcia. 2015. *Public Interest, Private Property: Law and Planning Policy in Canada.* Vancouver: UBC Press.

Smolka, Martim O. and David Amborski. 2000. *Value Capture for Urban Development: An Inter-American Comparison.* Cambridge, MA: Lincoln Institute of Land Policy.

Sorensen, Andre and Hess, Paul. 2015. 'Building Suburbs, Toronto-style: Land Development Regimes, Institutions, Critical Junctures and Path Dependence'. *Town Planning Review* 86(4):411–36. https://doi.org/10.3828/tpr.2015.26.

Tewdwr-Jones, Mark. 1999. 'Discretion, Flexibility, and Certainty in British Planning: Emerging Ideological Conflicts and Inherent Political Tensions'. *Journal of Planning Education and Research* 18(3):244–56. https://doi.org/10.1177/0739456x9901800306.

Tomalty, Ray and Skaburskis, Andrejs. 2003. 'Development Charges and City Planning Objectives: The Ontario Disconnect'. *Canadian Journal of Urban Research* 12(1):142–61.

Valverde, Mariana. 2012. *Everyday Law on the Street: City Governance in an Age of Diversity.* Chicago: University of Chicago Press.

Walters, Lawrence C. 2013. 'Land Value Capture in Policy and Practice'. *Journal of Property Tax Assessment & Administration* 10(2):5–21.

Wolf-Powers, Laura. 2010. 'Community Benefits Agreements and Local Government: A Review of Recent Evidence'. *Journal of the American Planning Association* 76(2):141–59. https://doi.org/10.1080/01944360903490923.

14

Real estate and housing: A commentary Dynamics of a housing crisis – the politics and planning of housing in London and Toronto

Susannah Bunce and Nicola Livingstone

London and Toronto are cities in the grip of housing crises. Buoyed by real estate markets directed by multi-scalar financialisation practices, supportive governmental policies and regulations, and large corporate and individual investment in residential property for financial gain, the resultant impacts on the commodification of housing and, conversely, the availability of affordable housing have been grave in both cities. The production of uneven real estate and housing landscapes has formed stark cleavages in social relations in London and Toronto, where the divisions between investors and/or residents who own property and those who rent, are underhoused or without housing have increasingly become visible markers of either financial 'success' or struggle.

These indicators are etched into the aesthetic and visceral experiences of everyday life in both cities: through the presence of tall construction cranes building luxury residential towers, via the real estate marketing of gentrifying neighbourhoods, in the form of costly 'bidding wars' for houses, in the prevalence of Airbnb and other short-term lets, in queues for an ever decreasing supply of affordable rental units, and in the growing number of rough sleepers and an amplified reliance on temporary shelters. In Toronto and London, the housing crisis is intimately tied with situations of income disparity and racialisation across both cities, with persons with lower incomes, racialised communities, longer-settled and more recent immigrants and refugees, and other individuals experiencing discrimination and marginalisation significantly bearing the consequences of inadequate and unaffordable housing (Hulchanski 2010; Mensah and Williams 2013; Millington 2012).

In this commentary, we identify and outline two common themes that emerge from chapters in Part II that seek to explain the housing crisis and connected issues in London and Toronto: firstly, the rise of financialisation and assetisation practices that have worked to further commodify housing and housing tenures, and secondly, the role of local governments in formulating housing policy and planning approaches that connect with the aims of private, market-led residential development. The practices that coalesce to form the contemporary real estate and housing landscape in London and Toronto are numerous and complex. Writ large, we observe complicated relational associations between private market actors and government interests in real estate and housing in both cities.

The real estate and housing sectors in both cities are continually being reconstituted and reformed through networked connections and interactions between markets, governments and individual actors, from a local to a global scale, that mediate and incentivise urban investment. These networks and associations are understood as both active responses to and products of late-stage capitalism, where financial gains are prioritised over community benefits and social justice. The financialised terrain of real estate and housing, as noted in examples of multinational corporate investment in new large-scale residential developments and existing housing, real estate investment trusts and direct foreign ownership, is increasingly connected to practices of state policy formation, deregulation and re-regulation that connect with and generally augment this investment logic. The chapters in Part II reflect on the impact of market-led real estate and housing dynamics and ever changing state systems of governance and planning (for more on London and Toronto's governance, see Part I). Through the discussions in the six chapters within Part II, we note similarities framed by these relational, and at times contradictory, practices that have emerged in both cities, where private sector and government actors seek multiple ways to address supply-side opportunities and limitations to produce amenable investment spheres. The chapters examine diverse real estate and housing issues such as the policies and implementation of residential densification (Chapter 13 in Toronto, Chapter 12 in London); the forms and functions of deregulated and re-regulated planning systems such as the role of planning gain and development levies (Chapter 13 in Toronto, Chapters 8 and 12 in London), the impacts of financialisation, the creation of housing bubbles and market precarities, and the challenges of housing affordability (Chapters 9 and 11 in Toronto, Chapter 10 in London) and the intricacies of local politics (interwoven through all the chapters).

Across all the chapters we see how policy framings and directives become concrete in the geographies of real estate and housing markets, drawing out antagonisms relating to variegated spatial and temporal experiences and embodying how the local processes at play are inherently influenced by relational processes at a regional, national and international scale. Changes in the global economy are embedded locally in both Toronto and London, as we witness tensions emerging in relation to socio-economic inequalities, the loss of key commercial real estate land use, viability assessments and inflated perceptions of land value, resulting in both cities experiencing and responding to their respective housing crises in differentiated yet similar ways. The housing crisis in both cities – bluntly encapsulated by disequilibrium in demand and supply, deep unaffordability, reductions in social housing provision and a seemingly ever increasing wealth gap – is explored throughout the chapters in Part II. In this commentary, we consider how historic and global processes have impacted the housing markets and examine local perspectives, policies and responses in both cities.

Perspectives on housing: Financialisation, assetisation and affordability

As noted in the previous section, London and Toronto are key financial centres and important seats of governance and regulation, with shifting population trends and demographics. Since the beginning of the twenty-first century both cities have continued to grow in population size (as discussed in Chapters 9 and 10). Similar historic trends have shaped both London's and Toronto's housing markets, leading to the current experience of housing crises formed by both global and local processes and transforming housing into a multidimensional investment opportunity through financialisation and assetisation processes. The introduction of contemporary financing strategies in a neoliberal and deregulated world brings the opportunity for change in the market processes of late capitalism, which sees investment and surplus capital as a 'wall of money' (Aalbers 2016) consistently branching out into new arenas in search of profit maximisation. Securitised interests in real estate, housing and mortgages become interests to be traded (with varied levels of risk and potential return) as they are repackaged into vehicles for global exchange. As a tangible asset, housing transforms into an investment vehicle with increased liquidity characteristics. Thus housing undergoes a process of assetisation, where it has local, national and international exchange value through the operationalisation of investment vehicles, in addition to maintaining exchange and utility values in the local market.

Growth in such investment vehicles has been facilitated by the expansion and movement of capital globally since the 1980s, as markets have become increasingly interconnected and open to investors anywhere in the world. In a normative sense, the integration of housing-related vehicles (e.g. asset-backed mortgage securities) into wider investment strategies offers the potential for increasingly diversified portfolios for investors and brings a multidimensionality to the function of housing. However, we argue that 'financialisation' processes are often broadly defined and are problematic due to subjective and varied interpretations of what the term means. Definitions of financialisation reflect 'a new form of competition which involves a change in orientation towards financial results' (Froud et al. 2000, 104), and one where 'the increasing dominance of financial actors, markets, practices, measurements and narratives, at various scales, [is] resulting in a structural transformation of economics, firms, states and households' (Aalbers 2017, 544).

As an umbrella term, however, financialisation successfully illustrates the dynamics across the global investment market and can help us ascertain how market-led processes are forming the real estate and housing markets in Toronto and London – with uneven spatial and temporal impacts (Bond 2013; McNally 2009). As per Fernandez et al. (2016), Hawes and Grisdale (Chapter 11) observe that the financialisation of housing can be seen as locally variegated but also as a global totality. Both Walks (Chapter 9) and Hawes and Grisdale (Chapter 11) draw our attention to the importance of the 'wall of money' and how this global totality is expressed through finance strategies developed to accommodate capital through housing markets via innovative structures such as private equity vehicles, institutional investments such as pension funds and real estate investment trusts (in Canada these are much more advanced in structure than their UK counterparts, especially in relation to housing). Impacts of financialisation are culturally, temporally and spatially specific in both urban markets, where the wider economic contexts are conducive to the development of both direct and indirect investment vehicles, which derive value from housing as an underlying asset.

In Toronto, the local real estate market responded very differently to the 2008 Global Financial Crisis, with a significant construction boom and rapid house price inflation that has formed an over-inflated housing market ('housing bubble') due to disconnects between household income and property values, and increased levels of household financial indebtedness. As detailed by Walks (Chapter 9), between 2009 and 2016 Toronto's housing prices grew nearly twice as fast as the average of the ten other major cities in Canada (with the lowest-income quintile of Toronto census metropolitan area households having a debt-to-income ratio of 420 per cent). This has been stimulated by the availability of cheap mortgage credit and riskier lending as a form of 'privatised Keynesianism' (Crouch 2009), which has led to an increase in social inequalities (Chapter 9). In London, house prices dropped off after 2008 and recovered slowly due to a longer-term market recession and a period defined by government-led austerity measures – with the housing market still being out of reach, however, for many residents. The impact and uncertainties of Brexit discussions since 2016, combined with fluctuating housing prices in London, have incited caution in many investors in the residential market, both domestic and international. While Toronto has experienced a recent, albeit small, uptick in foreign investment in the real estate market that has had an effect on housing prices, the London market has noticeably more entrenched networks and forms of investment from foreign capital, which has resulted in housing becoming a 'safe deposit box for the transnational wealth elite' (Fernandez et al. 2016). Certain boroughs, such as Kensington and Chelsea, have a substantial number of luxury homes targeted towards foreign investors and the very wealthy, and Kensington and Chelsea is one of the most unequal local authorities across the city in terms of housing. In Toronto, as Walks (Chapter 9) notes, the actual quantity of foreign-owned housing has less of an impact on real estate prices than domestic ownership (in 2017, only 4.7 per cent of Toronto's housing was owned by non-residents, compared with 13 per cent in London).

Affordability questions are at the centre of discussions across all the chapters in Part II, and like the concepts of financialisation and assetisation, ideas and definitions of affordability are dynamic, policy dependent, market-led and complex. In Toronto, the commodification and assetisation of housing has been encouraged by policy shifts, as more traditional welfare policies have evolved into approaches related to 'asset-based welfare' (see Chapter 11) that encourage people to purchase housing as an asset in order to enhance their financial security in later life. In the UK market we have also seen a consistent drive towards investment in housing as a way to build and secure assets through owner-occupied housing and as a way to derive investment returns from the purchase of rental properties. On the other side of this residential investment landscape, we see an increased struggle for renters who lease housing through growing private rental markets rather than through the social housing sector. Walks (Chapter 9), in reference to Toronto, and Gabrieli (Chapter 10), in relation to London, reflect on how the housing crises in both cities have shifted relations of owner occupation and widened the income and social gap between renters and owners. In Toronto, the financialisation and investment focus of the private rental market, coupled with regulatory changes such as the eradication of vacancy control, has led to skyrocketing rental prices over the past few years, a very low vacancy rate for low and moderately priced rental units (around 1 per cent) and a market that is increasingly geared towards luxury rentals (ACTO 2019). In Toronto, nearly half (47 per cent) of the population are renters, and 47 per cent of these renters spend more than 30 per cent of their income on rent (see Figure 11.2 in Chapter 11). In London, anecdotally, spending more than one-third of your income on rent and housing costs is generally considered to be unsustainable.

In both cities there are strong correlations between instances of poverty and lack of housing affordability that impacts renters. Gabrieli (Chapter 10), for example, notes that the high cost of housing in London largely contributes to the higher rates of poverty in the city by comparison with the poverty rate for the UK. In terms of affordability in London, Gabrieli discusses how the cost of housing in London remains substantially higher than the rest of the UK and too expensive for the majority of first-time and local-income earners: the mean affordability ratio, representing the cost of property as a ratio to earnings, sits at 20 in London, double the UK average. If you are unable to purchase a house in London and become entangled in the private rental sector, the concept of 'affordable rent' sits at 80 per cent of the local market rent. Considering the discrepancies between local boroughs, this 80 per cent can demonstrate significant differences in affordability across the capital (as per Gabrieli).

As well as affordability issues, changes in tenure, accessibility, use class and other pressures on markets, including densification practices (Chapters 12 and 13) and loss of industrial land (Chapter 8), contribute to the imbalance of both residential and commercial stock in both city markets. Additionally, the rental landscape is further complicated by the rise of short-term rentals such as Airbnb and other short-term lets (see Chapter 11). As Hawes and Grisdale (Chapter 11) note, in Toronto, nearly 5,000 homes were rented on the Airbnb platform between 2016 and 2017, taking much-needed long-term private rental units out of the market and further accentuating a low vacancy rate. In London, the short-term rental market is similarly impactful, with Airbnb especially prevalent in areas where there are high levels of private rental sector housing, with some areas currently seeing up to 20 per cent of the local market lost to platform rentals (Shabrina et al. 2019), contributing to an already overheated residential market and exacerbating underlying housing inequalities.

New configurations of local government involvement in housing policy and planning

The housing policy terrain in London and Toronto is tied together with the aforementioned processes of real estate financialisation and housing commodification. The formation of housing policies and the planning regimes in both cities have rapidly adapted to neoliberal market dynamics, in keeping with the notion of neoliberalism as being a series of 'roll-back and roll-out' processes of government deregulation in order to reduce public investment and re-regulation to ameliorate other investment conditions (Peck and Tickell 2002). State-led housing policy and legislation approaches, apart from market regulation tweaks to modulate some of the tensions between household debt and property over-inflation – such as 'mortgage stress tests' and the implementation of provincial non-resident buyer taxes in Canada, as noted by Walks (Chapter 9) – have largely emphasised 'innovative' methods by which to decrease public responsibility for housing provision and encourage more flexible forms of private–public activity. In both Canada and the UK these methods have been constituted by changing ideological strategies of governmental austerity, an agenda which has been more intensely felt in the UK context, particularly in the last decade.

New arrangements for the public–private governance and planning of housing that emphasise the private delivery of housing alongside mitigated forms of government involvement are noted in the Toronto context by Biggar and Siemiatycki (Chapter 13). They discuss the rise of private sector-developed condos in the city and the role of local government in utilising planning regulations to ensure community benefits. They describe the role of 'uplift' planning mechanisms such as Section 37 'density bonusing', which allows for increased height and density in a private development in return for the construction of public infrastructure, such as libraries, parks and day care centres in the development area, as well as the ad hoc and inconsistent local government use of Section 37. Similar issues are present in the London market, where planning gain is captured through larger 'hard' densification projects, with a payment from the developer to the local authority, typically towards amenities, infrastructure or affordable housing via Section 106 and Community Infrastructure Levy contributions. However, as discussed by Short and Livingstone (Chapter 12), recent consultations around the density matrix and the new London Plan (due for completion in 2020) have seen those consulted question whether the matrix remains fit for purpose as well as whether density should be 'optimised' rather than 'maximised'. If the former, then how can a notion of optimal be consistently defined? As with Toronto, the impact of density and the concomitant contributions extracted through the planning gain system are on a site-by-site basis and can be subjectively interpreted across local authorities and between public and private actors.

In Chapter 8, on industrial/employment land in London and Toronto, we can further observe tensions embedded at local levels of governance through the planning mechanisms in place as industrial land is lost, frequently to accommodate residential development: the Greater London region lost 16 per cent of its industrial capacity (2001–15), and land zoned for employment in Toronto has shrunk by almost 10 per cent (2006–18). As the new London Plan is reconsidering its approach to dealing with density, it is also reconsidering how best to address the issues surrounding loss of industrial land through policies E4 and E7, which aim to ensure there will be 'no net loss' of industrial space and promote the idea that housing can be accommodated through intensification, by creating mixed-use environments on industrial land. As Ferm (Chapter 8) reflects, the journey to this point was informed by local consultants and lobbying groups such as Just Space, who are acting to preserve and protect industrial land. However, concerns remain over how the policies can be implemented, especially considering the viability mechanisms used to measure and assess the potential of a scheme by developers. Ferm expresses concern for the effectiveness of these new policies and how they will be enforced, considering their application at the local level and on a site-by-site basis; benefits captured through a discretionary planning system are not necessarily always as effective as they could be, as they are negotiated between public and private actors, and could result in actual loss of industrial land and increasing real estate speculation. In Chapters 8, 12 and 13 we note increasingly complex arrangements between local governments, local consultants and private developers in both cities, where private investors and developers lead new housing and mixed-use developments and local governments pursue these interests while at the same time attempting to generate some public benefits from this housing.

Other housing policy and planning approaches of local government that are evident in Toronto and London include an emphasis on 'intensification' or 'densification' as a way to encourage more compact urban form through taller and more dense housing developments. However, in line with the points outlined in the previous paragraph, enforcing densification strategies at local level can be complex and problematic. Toronto's government has employed intensification as an official comprehensive planning strategy since 2002. Intensification has been packaged by politicians and planners as an environmentally sustainable planning strategy that encourages more compact use of land within city boundaries and decreases sprawled development on the suburban fringes of Toronto (Bunce 2004, 2018). At the same time, policies for intensification have dovetailed with the logic of new private sector-delivered, market-led housing in Toronto and, indeed, have coalesced to rationalise the planning and development landscape of Toronto's 'condo boom' over the past two decades (as described in Chapters 11 and 13), a form of densification that has been particularly visible in brownfield areas such as the central waterfront and along major arterial streets of the city.

Short and Livingstone (Chapter 12) detail the continued interest in densification planning in London, directed by the London Plan that is due for publication in late 2020. They note that densification is employed as a way to address the lack of available land in London for new residential development and that this strategy encourages the identification of 'growth areas' within borough and neighbourhood boundaries for new housing, the primary delivery of which is market-led. Their three case studies reflect on the differentiated impacts of densification and how it can be interpreted, with diverse implications. Although each case study demonstrates how densification can definitively increase housing provision in London, in the Victoria Opportunity Area, Woodberry Down, and Elephant and Castle, there are differences in relation to social housing production and contribution (or the lack thereof), as well as varied levels of density. There are also issues and differences between hard and soft processes of development across a variegated spectrum of size and scale, in planning guidance at local level, and in developer contributions and discretionary negotiations. In the chapters in Part II that address housing policy, it is clear that the complexities in the form, function and production of policy mechanisms in London and Toronto are dynamic and flexible; however, these processes also create tensions and difficulties in the interpretations of their purpose, with subjective impacts.

Conclusions

The chapters in Part II carefully point to the nuanced dynamics that constitute and shape the housing crisis in London and Toronto. In particular, two important themes that emerge from the chapters are the impacts of an increasingly complex financialised housing market and the directives of new housing policies that join together well with, and in some instances help to guide, housing market dynamics in both cities. As the chapters in Part II illustrate, the complex processes and outcomes of the housing crisis require the need for multifaceted solutions that work to address issues of social disparity and injustice. It is simply not enough to explain the financial processes and impacts of the housing crisis in London and Toronto. An articulation of its social fallout is increasingly necessary as the landscapes of both cities become more uneven and the experiences of people facing daily cost of living struggles become more visible. We end here by suggesting that a comparison of housing contexts in London and Toronto, as shaped through the chapters of Part II, offers valuable insights for other global cities facing similar issues and outcomes of financialisation, affordable housing constraints, and housing policy transformation.

References

Aalbers, Manuel. 2016. *The Financialization of Housing: A Political Economy Approach*. Abingdon: Routledge.

Aalbers, Manuel. 2017. 'The Variegated Financialization of Housing'. *International Journal of Urban and Regional Research* 41(4):542–54. https://doi.org/10.1111/1468-2427.12522.

ACTO (Advocacy Centre for Tenants Ontario). 2019. *We Can't Wait: Preserving Our Affordable Rental Housing in Ontario*. Toronto: ACTO.

Bond, Patrick. 2013. 'The Uneven and Combined Geographical Development of Financialised Capitalism'. *Transformation: Critical Perspectives on South Africa* 81/82:179–207. https://doi.org/10.1353/trn.2013.0016.

Bunce, Susannah. 2004. 'The Emergence of "Smart Growth" Intensification in Toronto: Environment and Economy in the New Official Plan'. *Local Environment* 9(2):177–91. https://doi.org/10.1080/1354983042000199525.

Bunce, Susannah. 2018. *Sustainability Policy, Planning, and Gentrification in Cities*. Abingdon: Routledge.

Crouch, Colin. 2009. 'Privatised Keynesianism: An Unacknowledged Policy Regime'. *British Journal of Politics and International Relations* 11(3):382–99. https://doi.org/10.1111/j.1467-856x.2009.00377.x.

Fernandez, Rodrigo, Hoffman, Annalore and Aalbers, Manuel. 2016. 'London and New York as a Safe Deposit Box for the Transnational Wealth Elite'. *Environment and Planning A* 48(12): 2443–61. https://doi.org/10.1177/0308518x16659479.

Froud, J. Haslam, C, Johal, S. and Williams, K. 2000. 'Shareholder value and financialisation: consultancy promises, management moves'. *Economy and Society* 29(1): 80-110.

Hulchanski, David. 2010. *The Three Cities within Toronto: Income Polarization Among Toronto's Neighbourhoods, 1970–2005*. Toronto: Cities Centre Press.

McMichael, Philip. 2013. 'Land Grabbing as Security Mercantilism in International Relations'. *Globalizations* 10(1):47–64. https://doi.org/10.1080/14747731.2013.760925.

McNally, David. 2009. 'From Financial Crisis to World-Slump: Accumulation, Financialisation, and the Global Slow Down'. *Historical Materialism* 17:35–84. https://doi.org/10.1163/156920609x436117.

Mensah, Joseph and Williams, Christopher. 2013. 'Ghanaian and Somali Immigrants in Toronto's Rental Market: A Comparative Cultural Perspective of Housing Issues and Coping Strategies'. *Canadian Ethnic Studies* 45(1–2):115–41. https://doi.org/10.1353/ces.2013.0013.

Millington, Gareth. 2012. '"Man Dem Link Up": London's Anti-riots and Urban Modernism'. *Sociological Research Online* 17(4).

Peck, Jamie and Tickell, Adam. 2002. 'Neoliberalizing Space'. *Antipode* 34(3):380–404. https://doi.org/10.1111/1467-8330.00247.

Shabrina, Zahratu, Arcaute, Elsa and Batty, Michael. 2019. 'Airbnb's Disruption of the Housing Structure in London'. Centre for Advanced Spatial Analysis (CASA), University College London.

Smith, Susan. 2005. 'Residential Segregation: A Geography of English Racism?' In *Race and Racism: Essays in Social Geography*, edited by Peter Jackson, 22–41. London: Allen & Unwin.

Part III
Community, activism and engagement

15

DIY: Making space in Toronto's 'Creative City'

Loren March

Introduction

Since the early 2000s, cities around the world have been enthusiastically restructuring their policy agendas in hopes of becoming globally competitive, and cultural policy has become an increasingly important aspect of urban planning as cities strive to become 'creative'. Culture is now strategically deployed in the interests of urban regeneration and increasingly understood to play a complex role in processes of gentrification and displacement. In cities such as Toronto and London, the perceived authenticity of arts communities has been capitalised upon in the production of landscapes of desire in post-industrial downtown spaces and disinvested neighbourhoods. Yet as grassroots arts ecologies are instrumentalised in urban redevelopment, they are also disrupted and displaced. In the case of downtown Toronto this has long been the case, as rising property values and rapid upscaling continue to pose serious challenges to the establishment of sustainable place-based scenes and sites of cultural production, necessitating a variety of survival tactics and forms of 'making do'.

This chapter discusses a specific form of bottom-up 'place-making' which has long been an important aspect of Toronto's arts scenes and now appears as a collective and individual response to intensifying gentrification, urban redevelopment and top-down arts-led regeneration in the city: 'do-it-yourself' (DIY). DIY emerges not only as a popular scene in the city, but also as an important political and spatial practice and survival tactic in the face of urban change. I discuss the history of DIY's employment in creative scenes and contexts in Toronto's downtown, and its emergence in the context of Creative City planning. This chapter is part of a larger research project I conducted on spatial production in DIY spaces in downtown Toronto in 2018. I draw upon observations from site visits, semi-structured interviews conducted with 16 DIY practitioners working in downtown Toronto, and vernacular photographs taken by these participants, as well as upon policy and media analysis. I argue that DIY can be politically generative when taken up collectively and is an increasingly important form of self-provisioning as space in Toronto becomes less accessible, but that it is also potentially isolating for individual practitioners and can be more generally interpreted as an expression of precariousness.

This chapter is divided into three sections. The first section details Toronto's particular evolution of strategic cultural policy and the deployment of Creative City discourse. The second explores DIY practices, touching upon cases in the Toronto and London arts scenes. Here I also trace the ongoing 'crisis' of creative space in Toronto, highlighting the emergence of unique models of organisational spatial provision in each city. The third section discusses Toronto's largely invisible geography of DIY spaces, as well as the often elaborate spatial practices of artists working under persistent threat from processes of gentrification that they themselves often contribute to. I conclude with a discussion of the Toronto case and the broader implications of DIY practices.

Becoming 'creative'

In the 1990s, when hype around creativity emerged, Toronto's planning and governance paradigms were strengthening neoliberal urban trajectories that were already being fostered in the 1980s (Desfor et al. 2006; Kipfer and Keil 2000). Intensified doctrines of competition and a distinctly entrepreneurial approach to planning and governance were levelled against a long-standing angst about the city's perceived 'lag' in urban investment and development (Kipfer and Keil 2002). Large-scale redevelopment and revitalisation, ambitious place-making initiatives and visionary megaprojects were pursued with gumption in hopes that they would increase the city's competitiveness. There was a concerted push for deregulation and intensification of development in Toronto's downtown. The removal of provincial rent controls in the 1990s allowed for a rapid turnover of tenants across many downtown residential areas, while the deregulation of zoning in formerly industrial or manufacturing areas permitted unbridled development to quickly move in, allowing a kind of 'instant gentrification' to take place (Teelucksingh 2009). These changes allowed for widescale demolitions, conversions into high-end studios and commercial galleries, and for rapid upscaling through the development of luxury lofts and condominiums, the marketing of which centred around lifestyle and drew upon the perceived authenticity of displaced cultural scenes (Crawford 1993; Palmer 2000).

The Creative City rhetoric, as it emerged in Toronto, fit nicely into the city's push to achieve a more globally competitive image. The doctrine put forward in the work of Richard Florida (2002; see also Landry 2000; Landry and Bianchini 1995) was enthusiastically taken up in urban policy, in the style of 'fast' (Peck and Theodore 2015) policies that are easily transportable between cities. 'Creative' policies have been differently taken up by coalitions in cities around the world, generally attempting to position culture and creativity as development opportunities and consumer amenities, but following place-specific trajectories with unique social outcomes and implications (Grodach and Silver 2012). In London, for instance, 'creative' policies emerged in the mid-1990s, promoting the development of cultural hubs and clusters and focusing on the targeted funding and provision of arts spaces in ways that are different than what we have seen in Toronto, with different results. There are, however, similarities. Take, for example, the lack of clarity around the meaning or definition of culture and creativity (Neelands and Choe 2010; Pratt 2005); the explicit instrumentalisation of creativity in urban regeneration (Moreton 2013); and the tensions that have been observed between these policies' social goals of inclusion (culture for everyone) and their neoliberal economic goals promoting competitiveness, consumption, meritocracy and the citizen-consumer (Coates 2001; Oakley 2006).

In Toronto, the Creative City planning model largely provides a 'brand identity' and a 'unifying language' to gloss over what are rather conventional economic development practices (Grodach 2013). Its strategy is geared towards urban economic growth and the instrumentalisation of creativity for economic purposes, subjecting cultural production to performance evaluation while promoting a kind of 'creative' citizenship which entangles notions of authenticity and self-actualisation with participation in consumption and entrepreneurship, and the adoption of a 'dutiful neoliberal lifestyle' (Grundy and Boudreau 2008, 351). Culture is valued insofar as it supports economic growth (Catungal et al. 2009; Finch 2015). Emphasis is placed upon the development of major institutions and the production of spectacular and exclusionary consumption-oriented landscapes of privilege (McLean 2014; McLean and Rahder 2013). Little attention is paid to already existing grassroots arts ecologies, to informal spaces, to politicised or subversive forms of art or to the actual labour involved in cultural production (Finch 2015; Hracs and Leslie 2014; McRobbie 2011; Rantisi and Leslie 2010; Reid 2006). In its attempt to become 'creative' at the beginning of the 2000s, in an initiative known as the 'Cultural Renaissance', Toronto spent over $900 million on culture-led development downtown. The Creative City discourse conveniently complemented urban redevelopment, revitalising major cultural institutions and sites of tourism and producing designated cultural districts through targeted place-making initiatives.

DIY as a place-making tactic

In the face of widespread urban change, DIY has offered a means to stay in place. While the term DIY has increasingly come to have a specific meaning and to connote particular places, we can understand both Toronto's and London's creative scenes to have histories of using DIY tactics to establish spatial stability in the city. Urban theorist Kimberley Kinder (2016) observes that DIY is a necessary form of adaptive self-provisioning in situations of urban disinvestment, filling gaps where particular needs are not being met. As a coping mechanism not necessarily directed towards effecting systemic social change, it is nevertheless meaningful. As an individual practice that connects with broader social networks, it offers real benefits to those who engage in it. In both North American and European cities, we can see an increasing turn to collective self-help and mutual aid practices to accommodate both informalised working practices and the rise in freelance labour (Merkel 2015, 2018) – an important yet severely unrepresented part of the creative industries in both London and Toronto (Bain and McLean 2013; Mould et al. 2014). As a creative practice itself, DIY is also frequently associated with amateurism, craft movements and folk traditions (Dawkins 2011; Hawkins 2017). Practitioners are not always professionalised or recognised institutionally.

In Toronto, DIY holds a considerable amount of cultural capital due to its connection with particular arts scenes. Scenes, as urban cultural theorist Will Straw (2015) points out, are 'publicly observable clusters of urban sociality' that 'perform the often invisible labour of pulling together cultural phenomena in ways which heighten their visibility' (2015, 483). They are dynamic, shifting and impermanent. Daniel Silver and Terry Nichols Clark (2015, 425) define them as 'multi-dimensional complexes of meaning embedded in material, local practices'. Conceptually, scenes connote a fluidity and 'slipperiness' (Straw 2002, 249) that is lacking in terms such as 'community', while also designating a tangible and publicly visible 'space of enlistment and convergence' (Straw 2015, 478) wherein people connect around particular tastes, practices, people and cultural happenings. In Toronto, a number of place-based arts scenes have emerged around DIY practices and politics, as well as specific venue or gallery spaces, which have been generative of a sense of unity and collective politics.

Over the years, an extensive DIY infrastructure has been established in Toronto at the grassroots level, including performance spaces, labels, collectives, online networks and studios, although a 'DIY space' is commonly presumed to imply a venue. Such spaces became highly visible after a wave of high-profile venue closures in Toronto's downtown in early 2017. In recent years, DIY community spaces have provided important safe, accessible gathering places and much-needed alternative programming for marginalised practitioners who have lacked recognition and representation, and the persistent threat of losing them has ignited concern that the city's grassroots arts ecologies are not properly appreciated by policy-makers (Finch 2015; Ross 2017). Some DIY practitioners believe that the City of Toronto is 'not really interested in the arts' (Interview, 22 February 2018). Many perceive the City of Toronto to be out of touch with their needs, expressing frustrations and disappointment with local institutions. One noted: 'I don't know much about any of the city's cultural policies … But do they impact me? Yes. Insofar as some of the venues I've performed in have been closed or shut down' (Interview, 6 February 2018). Of the city self-identifying as 'creative', another observed: 'It's very cute. It's very cute that they're down to identify as that … but being creative involves doing things that they are very bad at, which includes turning a blind eye to DIY spaces and noise complaints and just allowing these things to exist' (Interview, 22 February 2018).

DIY scenes posit competing imaginaries of what a 'creative city' might be (Finch 2015; Worth 2006). Such scenes in Toronto often differentiate themselves from dominant institutions and express a sense of alienation from the top-down Creative City framework and its orientation around consumption. Nevertheless, while they tend to take an oppositional stance, they are also faced with the difficult task of maintaining this stance as they become successful or drawn into the mainstream (Finch 2015). Much-needed attention from the public and policy-makers can be a double-edged sword and can be costly, as visibility draws attention to the ways in which many spaces operate outside existing legal frameworks, subjecting them to scrutiny and potential closure (Rancic 2016). Practitioners complain that the City of Toronto is more inclined to close DIY spaces than to assist in bringing them up to code. In recent years, many DIY spaces and studios have had to 'go underground', becoming 'hidden' and 'less accessible' to avoid inspection (Interview, 22 February 2018). The tension between visibility and invisibility will be discussed further below.

Despite the seemingly recent emergence of DIY, Toronto's creative scenes have a very long history of engaging with it. Looking to cultural historian Rosemary Donegan's (1986) accounts of the evolutions of different cultural scenes in Toronto's downtown through the twentieth century, we can see DIY as a long-standing and deeply embedded collective practice that is reliant on place-specific factors. Such practices were employed by artists forming their own scenes in the Adelaide and Yonge Street areas at the end of the nineteenth century. Donegan's work reveals how through the twentieth century there was an increasing shift away from the bourgeois club mentality of previous generations, towards a style that pushed back against the cultural forms of dominant cultural institutions. Through this period, place-based scenes established themselves in Toronto's downtown around Gerrard Village, Yorkville and along Queen Street West (see Figure 15.1), achieving spatial stickiness by relying upon localised and largely informal horizontal networks

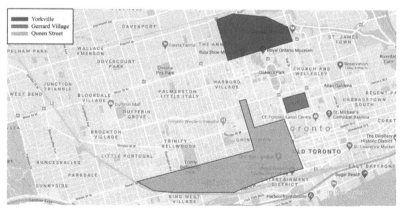

Figure 15.1 Map of different place-based creative scenes in Toronto. Individual DIY spaces are not mapped here to protect the privacy of tenants (map by L. March)

of support, as well as a large stock of unused industrial buildings and affordable live/work spaces (Bain 2006; Bain and March 2019; Donegan 1986). Scenes also made use of key informal venues or 'third-spaces' (Rantisi and Leslie 2010), which acted as gateways into various parts of the scenes and were used for networking, horizontal philanthropic practices, organising and creative experimentation (Bain and March 2019). The Queen Street scene in particular has been described at length as a complex social world in which economies of giving and co-creation, resource-sharing, anti-capitalist/anti-state/anti-art-market political imperatives and organisation around self-governance were prevalent amid the usual rivalries, divergences, tensions and internal dramas of a scene (Monk 2016; Tuer 1986). Many practitioners countered the established institutions they did not see as serving them, creating a 'parallel universe' (Bronson 2014) of organisations, some of which took up especially strong stances against the existing state-supported arts bureaucracy (Tuer 1986), and many of which are now important cultural institutions and key stakeholders in the Creative City.

Similar phenomena can be observed in the scene that established itself in various clusters throughout London's East End between the 1970s and 1990s. Like in Toronto, a large number of disused industrial buildings in the central city were able to accommodate a vast number of creative practitioners and a diverse range of creative practices (Green 1999; Harris 2012; Wedd et al. 2001). While artists were drawn to the existing infrastructure of these neighbourhoods, other factors were also at play which allowed place-based scenes to flourish. For example, in London, the 'relaxed planning regime' (Green 1999, 29) of the 1970s played a large role, allowing artists to more easily acquire real estate. Furthermore, through this period various forms of government funding were made available to artists in both cities, allowing practitioners to start artist-run centres in Toronto (Bain and March 2019) and to start studio provision organisations such as SPACE and Acme in London (Green 1999; Harris 2012). Once established, these scenes were able to collectively draw upon benefits shared within their place-based networks. However, by the 1990s the increasing visibility of London's East End scene and many of its collective antics led to rapid gentrification and extensive reinvestment in places such as Hoxton, as the social capital of artists as well as their active courting of the market generated buzz and appeal (Harris 2012). As artists and other tenants were gradually priced out, the area went from being 'the place to be' (Harris 2012, 230) to being perceived as populated by 'posers' (Pratt 2009, 1056), while its artistic identity continued to be used as a selling point by developers and real estate agents. Similar waves of gentrification in Toronto's Queen Street West have displaced artists and arts institutions alike, with members of the scene declaring 'The Queen Street is dead! Long live Queen Street!' (Monk 2007) years before it was deemed one of the world's hippest neighbourhoods by *Vogue* magazine in 2014.

Spatial stability has presented a consistent challenge to lower-income artists in Toronto. While unique convergences of land uses, cheap real estate, available infrastructure, government support and market factors have contributed to the establishment of place-based arts scenes in the downtown in the past, and DIY tactics have sustained them, the space of the downtown has been dramatically restructured over time in ways that have made this more difficult. Further complicating this is the fact that artists must seek out affordable areas with appropriate spaces to conduct their practices (Bain 2006), but tend to make these spaces attractive to higher-income groups, thus becoming implicated in gentrification and their own potential displacement in varied complex, tension-filled and context-specific ways (Bain and March 2019; Grodach et al. 2018; Ley 2003; Mathews 2010).

Already in the mid-1980s, the media were describing a 'crisis' of space for artists in Toronto's downtown, as practitioners were pitched into a kind of 'battle' (Wright 1995) against development that threatened their displacement. At the time, many artists were living precariously throughout the downtown in industrial spaces that existed in a legal grey area (Yawching 1986). The Toronto Arts Council warned that there was a scarcity of affordable spaces and recommended that the City of Toronto move to foster the development of studios and facilities for arts organisations (Hendry 1985). Whereas London's own scenes produced organisations such as SPACE and Acme, Toronto's Arts Council formed Toronto Artscape Inc. as an arms-length institution tasked with addressing the mounting spatial crisis. Artscape proceeded by renovating donated heritage properties into arts facilities and studios. A series of reports produced for the City of Toronto also encouraged the development of policy around artist housing and live/work spaces, proposing the alteration of existing zoning and building codes to allow for mixed uses (Bain and March 2019; TAC 1987). With this support, Artscape became heavily involved in so-called creative place-making initiatives, eventually becoming a major property developer, a central voice advocating for the Creative City at the international scale and a partner in many of Toronto's revitalisation projects (Lehrer and Wieditz 2009).

Meanwhile, in the London case, formalised studio providers largely came together as a sector in the early 2000s. The logics behind studio provision which emerged during this period very explicitly instrumentalise the creative workspace in urban regeneration and community development initiatives and are grounded in economic and social benefit rationales (Moreton 2013). Studio providers in this context are increasingly professionalised, repositioning themselves as property developers, providing spaces that are carefully calculated based on affordability but also on goals of revenue generation, while at the same time tending to reinforce classic romanticised ideals of the artist's studio: white walls, high ceilings, self-contained spaces. As Moreton (2013, 422) observes, these provisioned studios represent 'a spatial reconfiguration of ideas about models of creative/culture-led urban development, cultural labour and value measurement', and the ability of many artists to engage in their creative practices is now largely mediated by relationships with developers holding these ideas.

As property values in Toronto's downtown have steadily increased and the available stock of appropriate arts spaces has decreased, there has been a mounting demand for the kinds of workspaces provided by studio provision organisations

(Bain and March 2019). These kinds of studios both set the standard for creative workspaces in the city and are increasingly the only option available. Yet these spaces are also costly, difficult for more marginalised practitioners to access and inappropriate or off-limits for those with more disruptive practices (such as musicians). These kinds of formalised workspaces have also been criticised for the role they play in gentrification and the production of exclusionary space (Bain and March 2019; Catungal et al. 2009; Ilyniak 2017).

DIY workspaces: Facilitating labour under the radar

In Toronto, some practitioners have engaged in oppositional politics, mobilising against top-down cultural planning and urban regeneration which has threatened to dislodge existing pockets of artists (Silver 2012). Several DIY scenes in Toronto, such as those centred around Unit 2 or the Blank Canvas collective, have at various points mobilised around issues of gentrification and displacement, and have built strong grassroots networks in order to maintain a hold in the landscape.[1] As noted above, in 2017 a strong community reaction emerged against the mounting 'venue crisis', with artists speaking out at City Hall and organising community discussions around the issue. At the centre of much of the discourse were DIY community spaces, the places where people come together and where work is seen. The places where work is made were hardly mentioned in these conversations.

On the production side, contemporary DIY workspaces tend to be more individualised and thus to generate less political action. This fragmentation could potentially be interpreted as a reversion to the individual studio from collective spaces that emerged between the 1970s and 1990s, as the downtown's stock of disused buildings with large, shareable spaces has dwindled, options for appropriate third spaces have been reduced through gentrification and the costs of renting from formalised studio collectives have in many cases become prohibitive. In comparison with DIY community spaces, DIY workspaces tend to remain relatively invisible in the landscape, often flying 'under the radar' (Interview, 24 February 2018). Many of these workspaces bend legal parameters and policy guidelines, necessitating a degree of secrecy about their existence. Many spaces are located in practitioners' homes, an unglamorous and often underappreciated or delegitimised site of labour (Black et al. 2019) that often goes unrecognised as an essential part of the so-called Creative City. These spaces also fail to adhere to the aesthetic and functional standards now set by studio provision organisations. They adhere to no particular appearance or typology and are thus not identified as properly 'creative' spaces. Many of these spaces have been taken up as a last resort because a separate, designated studio space is too expensive. The DIY workspace exists out of necessity.

Artists working in these circumstances actively engage in practices to minimise the attention they might draw to themselves. These include altering work hours, building elaborate work setups to minimise noise and smell (see Figure 15.2),

Figure 15.2   A DIY recording studio assembled in a musician's living room in a rental apartment. The studio, in this case, has taken over most of the common area in a shared residential space. Note the practitioner's use of foam soundproofing materials and an added curtain to protect against noise and vibrations travelling into neighbouring apartments (photograph taken by research participant, 2018)

meeting with collaborators exclusively in third spaces, changing media or the scale of their work and in some cases changing their practice altogether to reduce outside impacts. Practitioners are not only aware of impacts that might get them evicted (noise, fumes, etc.), but are also aware of the role they potentially play in gentrification. While it is clear that their presence cannot be erased entirely, many sacrifices and compromises are made. As a result, in addition to being precariously employed, many practitioners work in precarious *spatial* circumstances, wrestling with conditions that are less than ideal. Practitioners often settle for live/work conditions that are below par in exchange for being able to continue their practice; they are willing to put up with more because of their lack of alternatives. As one practitioner put it (Interview, 2 February 2018), 'you find your space and you hang on and learn to love it, and you never leave it until you are evicted because it's the only option you have'. This adds further imbalances to already uneven power dynamics with landlords, which in some cases results in feelings of fear, helplessness or paranoia about eventual eviction – affective states which can ultimately make or break a creative space (see Figure 15.3).

The intentional obscurity of DIY workspaces in the landscape complicates gentrification narratives that identify artistic visibility and aestheticisation as triggers that set its processes in motion (Ley 2003; Zukin 1982). Venue and community spaces are arguably often already involved in gentrification at the neighbourhood

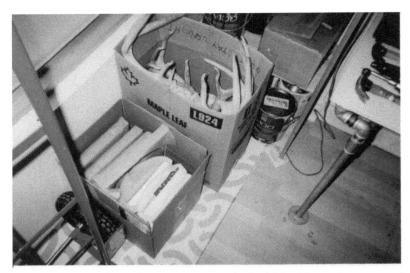

Figure 15.3 Boxes of supplies remain unpacked within this workspace, as the practitioner occupies the space with the presumption that she will soon have to move again (photograph taken by research participant, 2018)

level, due to the often consumption-oriented nature of their activities and the ways in which these attract attention and stimulate desire, contributing to the production of affluent playscapes. The necessity of visibility in public struggles over these spaces can also draw them further into complicity with the gentrification processes whether they like it or not, as 'buzz' is generated around them. Meanwhile, with DIY workspaces, practices of individual resilience to avoid displacement in many cases involve extremely elaborate attempts to draw as little attention to oneself as possible. The aim is not to develop a neighbourhood more broadly into a mutually supportive artistic milieu, but instead to maintain a small place of one's own through determined practices of secrecy. Their atomisation and obscurity make it difficult for individual DIY workspaces to generate any sense of community around them, or to catalyse political action around issues practitioners face while working within these circumstances.

Conclusion

Creative practitioners and cultural planners in so-called creative cities are often engaged in very different kinds of place-making, and there are many incongruencies between the concerns and interests of each. The impacts of 'creative' place-making strategies that focus on revitalisation threaten to drive out many of the very creatives they purport to be enticing into the city. Meanwhile, the formalisation of more collective spatial arrangements has led to the proliferation of developer-like studio provision organisations, who hold gatekeeper positions and have unique power to shape urban cultural production. In the case of Toronto, practitioners who cannot access these spaces, or can no longer afford the exorbitant cost of living in the city, migrate to the urban peripheries (Bain 2013), or beyond to nearby cities such as Hamilton, where both artist-led and municipally driven property development are already dramatically reshaping lower-income, working-class neighbourhoods (Bain 2017, 2018). Those who stay are pressured to rapidly professionalise and play the competitive game of artistic entrepreneurship or resort to alternative practices and the more horizontal support networks of DIY.

In the case of Toronto, DIY is largely taken up out of necessity, as practitioners seek more stable living conditions or success within existing Creative City frameworks which have largely served to render space less accessible to them. In this case, DIY might be perceived as an example of practitioners reacting to the 'individualisation of risk' (Bain and McLean 2013; Gill and Pratt 2008) encouraged within Creative City discourse, and adapting to rapidly changing dynamics in Toronto's downtown. These practices have tangible impacts on individual practitioners' work and lives and speak to broader precarious conditions of labour in cultural production in the city which are distorted by 'Creative' policy rhetoric.

DIY community spaces offer a more visible and public centre of convergence for political action around arts spaces, with the social benefits they offer marginalised artists backing an excellent argument for increased policy support. DIY workspaces remain in the shadows, yet these spaces represent important individual efforts to exist outside dominant frameworks in the face of precarity. While artists increasingly seem to be rendered precarious and isolated in such spaces, their plight is increasingly one that is shared. There is a collective desire for support and action around the spaces of work. Even as this research was conducted, participants expressed a strong desire to potentially meet each other to discuss challenges they face, breaking with established tendencies to shroud their work in secrecy. This speaks to a potential to generate action around them. Yet the response of arts communities to the Creative City in Toronto overall is complicated and not entirely oppositional, as many practitioners are implicated in dominant institutional and state frameworks, and many have internalised the Floridian doctrine: 'be creative or die'. Practitioners rarely respond with targeted resistance against 'Creative' policy frameworks that do not serve them.

In the meantime, DIY is an important form of self-provisioning which allows practitioners to remain downtown, offering them some freedom to engage with creativity on their own terms while the pressures of the art market and of top-down policy frameworks and conditions of precarity remain. More research into the range of emergent DIY practices in 'creative' cities is needed. DIY spaces offer means to survive current conditions in these cities while also posing alternatives, and they certainly deserve further recognition.

Acknowledgements

Many thanks to Ute Lehrer, Stefan Kipfer and Lisa Myers for their valuable input on the broader research project from which this work is derived, and to the participants who generously opened their spaces to me. The research informing this chapter was made possible with financial support from the Social Sciences and Humanities Research Council of Canada.

Note

1. Unit 2 has notably also been involved in mutual aid organising throughout the COVID-19 pandemic, directing energy and resources towards providing needed support to queer, trans and gender-diverse people, and especially those who are Black, Indigenous or people of colour.

References

Bain, Alison L. 2006. 'Resisting the Creation of Forgotten Places: Artistic Production in Toronto Neighbourhoods'. *The Canadian Geographer* 50(4):417–31. https://doi.org/10.1111/j.1541-0064.2006.00155.x.

Bain, Alison L. 2013. *Creative Margins: Cultural Production in Canadian Suburbs*. Toronto: University of Toronto Press.

Bain, Alison L. 2017. 'Neighbourhood Artistic Disaffiliation in Hamilton, Ontario, Canada'. *Urban Studies* 54(13):2935–54. https://doi.org/10.1177/0042098016658390.

Bain, Alison L. 2018. 'Artists as Property Owners and Small-scale Developers'. *Urban Geography* 39(6):844–67. https://doi.org/10.1080/02723638.2017.1405687.

Bain, Alison L. and McLean, Heather. 2013. 'The Artistic Precariat'. *Cambridge Journal of Regions, Economy and Society* 6:93–111. https://doi.org/10.1093/cjres/rss020.

Bain, Alison L. and March, Loren. 2019. 'Urban Redevelopment, Cultural Philanthropy and the Commodification of Artistic Authenticity in Toronto'. *City & Community* 18(1):173–94. https://doi.org/10.1111/cico.12359.

Black, Shannon, Fox Miller, Chloe and Leslie, Deborah. 2019. 'Gender, Precarity and Hybrid Identity in the Virtual Domestic Arts and Crafts Industry in Canada and the US'. *Gender, Place & Culture* 26(2):1–22. https://doi.org/10.1080/0966369x.2018.1552924.

Bronson, A. A. 2014. 'General Idea – Interview with AA Bronson – Centre Culturel Canadien'. *Centre Culturel Canadien* interview. Accessed 14 May 2019. https://www.youtube.com/watch?v=0istPcv8FSw.

Catungal, John Paul, Leslie, Deborah and Hii, Yvonne. 2009. 'Geographies of Displacement in the Creative City: The Case of Liberty Village, Toronto'. *Urban Studies* 46(5–6):1095–114. https://doi.org/10.1177/0042098009103856.

Coates, David. 2001. 'Capitalist Models and Social Democracy: The Case of New Labour'. *British Journal of Politics and International Relations* 3:284–307. https://doi.org/10.1111/1467-856x.00061.

Crawford, Trish. 1993. 'Downtown Living's Again Where It's At'. *Toronto Star*, 30 October.

Dawkins, Nicole. 2011. 'Do-It-Yourself: The Precarious Work and Postfeminist Politics of Handmaking (in) Detroit'. *Utopian Studies* 22(2):261–84. https://doi.org/10.5325/utopianstudies.22.2.0261.

Desfor, Gene, Keil, Roger, Kipfer, Stefan and Wekerle, Gerda. 2006. 'From Surf to Turf: No Limits to Growth in Toronto?' *Studies in Political Economy* 77:131–55. https://doi.org/10.1080/19187033.2006.11675115.

Donegan, Rosemary. 1986. 'Whatever Happened to Queen Street West?' *Fuse Magazine* 42:10–24.

Finch, Mark. 2015. '"Toronto Is the Best!" Cultural Scenes, Independent Music, and Competing Urban Visions'. *Popular Music and Society* 38(3):299–317. https://doi.org/10.1080/03007766.2014.927284.

Florida, Richard. 2002. *The Rise of the Creative Class: And How It's Transforming Work, Leisure and Everyday Life*. New York: Basic Books.

Gill, Rosalind and Pratt, Andy. 2008. 'In the Social Factory? Immaterial labour, Precariousness, and Cultural Work'. *Theory, Culture and Society* 25:1–30. https://doi.org/10.1177/0263276408097794.

Green, Nick. 1999. 'The Space of Change: Artists in the East End 1968–1980'. *Rising East* 3:20–37.

Grodach, Carl. 2013. 'Cultural Economy Planning in Creative Cities: Discourse and Practice'. *International Journal of Urban and Regional Research* 37(5):1745–65. https://doi.org/10.1111/j.1468-2427.2012.01165.x.

Grodach, Carl, Foster, Nicole and Murdoch, James. 2018. 'Gentrification, Displacement and the Arts: Untangling the Relationship between the Arts Industries and Place Change'. *Urban Studies* 55(4):807–25. https://doi.org/10.1177/0042098016680169.

Grodach, Carl and Silver, Daniel. 2012. 'Introduction: Urbanizing Cultural Policy'. In *The Politics of Urban Cultural Policy: Global Perspectives*, edited by Carl Grodach and Daniel Silver, 1–12. London: Routledge.

Grundy, John and Boudreau, Julie-Anne. 2008. '"Living with Culture": Creative Citizenship Practices in Toronto'. *Citizenship Studies* 12(4):347–63. https://doi.org/10.1080/13621020802184226.

Harris, Andrew. 2012. 'Art and Gentrification: Pursuing the Urban Pastoral in Hoxton, London'. *Transactions of the Institute of British Geographers* 37(2):226–41. https://doi.org/10.1111/j.1475-5661.2011.00465.x.

Hawkins, Harriet. 2017. *Creativity*. Oxford: Routledge.

Hendry, Tom. 1985. *Cultural Capital: The Care and Feeding of Toronto's Artistic Assets*. Toronto: Toronto Arts Council.

Hracs, Brian J. and Leslie, Deborah. 2014. 'Aesthetic Labour in Creative Industries: The Case of Independent Musicians in Toronto, Canada'. *Area* 46(1):66–73. https://doi.org/10.1111/area.12062.

Ilyniak, Sophia L. 2017. 'Non-profiting for a 'More Inclusive Creative City': Tracking the Gentrification Frontier from Toronto's Downtown to the Disinvested Inner-suburbs'. Master's thesis, Faculty of Environmental Studies. Toronto: York University.

Kinder, Kimberley. 2016. *DIY Detroit: Making Do in a City without Services*. Minneapolis and London: University of Minnesota Press.

Kipfer, Stefan and Keil, Roger. 2000. 'Still Planning to Be Different? Toronto at the Turn of the Millennium'. *Planning Review* 35(140):28–36. https://doi.org/10.1080/02513625.2000.10556731.

Kipfer, Stefan and Keil, Roger. 2002. 'Toronto Inc? Planning the Competitive City in the New Toronto'. *Antipode* 34(2):227–64. https://doi.org/10.1111/1467-8330.00237.

Landry, Charles. 2000. *The Creative City: A Toolkit for Urban Innovators*. London: Earthscan.

Landry, Charles and Bianchini, Franco. 1995. *The Creative City*. London: Demos/Comedia.

Lehrer, Ute and Wieditz, Thorben. 2009. 'Condominium Development and Gentrification'. *Canadian Journal of Urban Research* 18(1):82–103.

Ley, David. 2003. 'Artists, Aestheticization and the Field of Gentrification'. *Urban Studies* 40(12):2527–44. https://doi.org/10.1080/0042098032000136192.

McLean, Heather. 2014. 'Digging into the Creative City: A Feminist Critique'. *Antipode* 46(3):669–90. https://doi.org/10.1111/anti.12078.

McLean, Heather and Rahder, Barbara. 2013. 'The Exclusionary Politics of Creative Communities: The Case of Kensington Market Pedestrian Sundays'. *Canadian Journal of Urban Research* 22(1):90–110.

McRobbie, Angela. 2011. 'Rethinking Creative Economies as Radical Social Enterprise'. *Variant* 41:32–3.

Mathews, Vanessa. 2010. 'Aestheticizing Space: Art, Gentrification and the City'. *Geography Compass* 4(6):660–75. https://doi.org/10.1111/j.1749-8198.2010.00331.x.

Merkel, Janet. 2015. 'Co-working in the City'. *Ephemera: Theory & Politics in Organization* 15(1):121–39.

Merkel, Janet. 2018. '"Freelance Isn't Free": Co-working as a Critical Urban Practice to Cope with Informality in Creative Labour Markets'. *Urban Studies* 56(3):526–47.

Monk, Philip. 2007. 'A Proposal for a Tax in Support of Toronto Artists'. *AGYU Out There*. Toronto: Art Gallery of York University.

Monk, Philip. 2016. *Is Toronto Burning? Three Years in the Making (and Unmaking) of the Toronto Art Scene*. London: Black Dog Publishing.

Moreton, Simon. 2013. 'The Promise of the Affordable Artist's Studio: Governing Creative Spaces in London'. *Environment and Planning A* 45:421–37. https://doi.org/10.1068/a44598.

Mould, Oli, Vorley, Tim and Liu, Kai. 2014. 'Invisible Creativity? Highlighting the Hidden Impact of Freelancing in London's Creative Industries'. *European Planning Studies* 22(12):2436–55. https://doi.org/10.1080/09654313.2013.790587.

Neelands, Jonathan and Choe, Boyun. 2010. 'The English Model of Creativity: Cultural Politics of an Idea'. *International Journal of Cultural Policy* 16(3):287–304. https://doi.org/10.1080/10286630903111647.

Oakley, Kate. 2006. 'Include Us Out—Economic Development and Social Policy in the Creative Industries'. *Cultural Trends* 15(4):255–73. https://doi.org/10.1080/09548960600922335.

Palmer, Karen. 2000. 'Art and Business Live in Liberty, a Vision for Toronto: Funky Community Inspires High-tech Vision for Port Lands'. *Toronto Star*, 17 April.

Peck, Jamie and Theodore, Nik. 2015. *Fast Policy: Experimental Statecraft at the Thresholds of Neoliberalism*. Minneapolis: University of Minnesota Press.

Pratt, Andy C. 2005. 'Cultural Industries and Public Policy'. *International Journal of Cultural Policy* 11(1):31–44. https://doi.org/10.1080/10286630500067739.

Pratt, Andy C. 2009. 'Urban Regeneration: From the Arts "Feel Good" Factor to the Cultural Economy: A Case Study of Hoxton, London'. *Urban Studies* 46(5–6):1041–61. https://doi.org/10.1177/0042098009103854.

Rancic, Michael. 2016. 'DIY Can't Die: The Messy, Triumphant Story of Toronto Punk Venue S.H.I.B.G.Bs'. *Noisey*. Accessed 14 May 2019. https://noisey.vice.com/en_ca/article/rmajby/shibgbs-punk-diy-toronto.

Rantisi, Norma and Leslie, Deborah. 2010. 'Creativity by Design? The Role of Informal Spaces in Creative Production'. In *Spaces of Vernacular Creativity: Rethinking the Cultural Economy*, edited by Tim Edensor, Deborah Leslie, Steve Millington and Norma M. Rantisi, 33–45. London and New York: Routledge.

Reid, Dylan. 2006. 'The Challenges of the Creative City'. In *The State of the Arts: Living with Culture in Toronto*, edited by Christina Palassio, Alana Wilcox and Jonny Dovercourt, 50–7. Toronto: Couch House Books.

Ross, Sara Gwendolyn. 2017. 'Development versus Preservation Interests in the Making of a Music City: A Case Study of Select Iconic Music Venues and the Treatment of Their Intangible Cultural Heritage Value'. *International Journal of Cultural Property* 24(1):31–56. https://doi.org/10.1017/s0940739116000382.

Silver, Daniel. 2012. 'Local Politics in the Creative City: The Case of Toronto'. In *The Politics of Urban Cultural Policy: Global Perspectives*, edited by Carl Grodach and Daniel Silver, 249–63. London: Routledge.

Silver, Daniel and Nichols Clark, Terry. 2015. 'The Power of Scenes: Quantities of Amenities and Qualities of Places'. *Cultural Studies* 29(3):425–49. https://doi.org/10.1080/09502386.2014.937946.

Straw, Will. 2002. 'Scenes and Sensibilities'. *Public* 22(23):245–57.

Straw, Will. 2015. 'Some Things a Scene Might Be'. *Cultural Studies* 29(3):476–85. https://doi.org/10.1080/09502386.2014.937947.

Teelucksingh, Cheryl. 2009. 'Instant Gentrification: Social Inequality and Brownfields Redevelopment in Downtown Toronto'. In *Environmental Conflict and Democracy in Canada*, edited by Laurie E. Adkin, 262–78. Vancouver and Toronto: UBC Press.

TAC (Toronto Arts Council). 1987. *No Vacancy: A Cultural Facilities Policy for the City of Toronto*. Toronto: Toronto Arts Council.

Tuer, Dot. 1986. 'The CEAC Was Banned in Canada'. *C Magazine* 11:22–37.

Wedd, Kit, Peltz, Lucy and Ross, Catherine. 2001. *Artists' London: Holbein to Hirst*. London: Merrell.

Worth, Liz. 2006. 'Just Do it Yourself: The Growing DIY Movement Is Rooted in Anti-consumerist Ideals and Encourages People to Fulfill Dreams to Make Things Happen'. *Toronto Star*, 15 August.

Wright, Lisa. 1995. 'Struggling Artists Battle City for Creative Space: Bylaws for Studios Paint Tenants into a Corner'. *Toronto Star*, 23 August.

Yawching, Donna. 1986. 'The Loft Scene: Artists Find Illegal Lofts Places to Live and Work'. *Toronto Star*, 11 September.

Zukin, Sharon. 1982. *Loft Living: Culture and Capital in Urban Change*. Baltimore, MD: Johns Hopkins University Press.

16

Pragmatic fix or a farewell to welfare? Making sense of and contesting the financialisation of public land and council housing in London

Joe Penny

Introduction

Since 2010 the local state in England has been both the subject and agent of a Conservative-led project of post-crisis austerity. More than simply the unfortunate administrators of fiscal retrenchment bearing the disproportionate burden of a zealous attempt to 'pay down the national deficit', local authorities have been at the vanguard of 'the most far-reaching and precipitate attempt to achieve fundamental restructuring in an established welfare state ... in recent years' (Taylor-Gooby 2012, 61). On the one hand, they are managing unprecedented budget cuts and reducing the scale and scope of local public services. On the other hand, they continue to 'modernise' the local state, further opening up services and assets to private interests, while also catalysing and speculating on urban development to ensure their fiscal futures. In short, a distinctly English version of 'austerity urbanism' – a process pioneered across US and Canadian cities (Peck 2012) – is being constituted by and between the central *and* local state, producing new powers and liabilities; strategic dilemmas and existential exigencies; policy innovations, experiments and failures; as well as cause for contestation and politicisation (Penny 2017).

Meanwhile, the local state in London is also at the epicentre of 'an acute, pervasive and socially explosive housing crisis' (Beswick et al. 2016, 321). Here too, the role of the local state is an ambiguous one: London's boroughs are both subject, caught in the crossfire of central government policy and real estate interests, and agent, actively aligning themselves to, and so helping reproduce, a status quo predicated on ever rising land values. A key driver behind London's housing crisis today, the privatisation and de-municipalisation of council housing, was at once an attempt to develop a 'property-owning democracy' and a means to fundamentally undermine the power of the local state. Indeed, since the 1990s, with grant funding to build council housing limited and existing stock dwindling, London's boroughs have been relegated to playing an enabling planning role as part of what Samuel Stein (2019), referencing North American cities such as New York City and Toronto, has termed the 'real-estate state'. Rather than directly delivering council housing, London's boroughs enable private real estate development and then, through planning gain, try to eke out a 'commercially viable' portion of so-called affordable housing, which can be up to 80 per cent of market rents (rents inflated by those very same developments). Yet while their room for manoeuvre in this context is undoubtedly more constrained than in previous times, most London boroughs have *actively* aligned themselves with real estate interests and their inflationary and exclusionary logic of land value uplift and extraction. Even before developers were able to purchase exclusive access to planning officers, many boroughs were reluctant to use the regulatory powers at their disposal to challenge questionable viability appraisals. Others have enthusiastically entered into public–private partnerships to redevelop public land and housing estates, purposefully inflating land and property values at the expense of low-income residents in a process that will be only too familiar to those who lived in Regent Park, Toronto.

As these crises converge, London's boroughs are being transformed and are transforming themselves in profound and potentially path-changing ways. In pursuit of long-term revenues to fulfil their managerial role of meeting social housing and care needs in a zero-grant environment, they are emerging as key entrepreneurial actors in the financialisation of public land and housing. Significantly, in reconfiguring the use, management and ownership of public land and housing, turning the latter from 'machines for living' into what a resident on one London housing estate called 'machines for revenue generation', many councils are eschewing simple fire-sale privatisations of their assets. Instead, hoping to directly capture rising land values, they are drawing on the repertoires and operational models of property developers, and in some cases entangling themselves in new relationships with finance capital, to produce market, affordable and social housing themselves in distinctly novel ways. As evidence of this, council-owned local housing companies, constituted as special purpose vehicles, are being set up across London, enabling councils to build housing by circumventing fiscal and regulatory constraints, treating land and property in increasingly speculative ways as a financial asset and, in some cases, engaging financial actors through innovative financing models (Beswick and Penny 2018).

For many, these local housing companies represent a 'renaissance' (Hackett 2017) in local state housebuilding, a creative fix for the housing crisis and a vehicle for publicly directed civic improvement (Morphet and Clifford 2017; Kollewe 2017; Wainwright 2017). More broadly, they have also been posited (see Christophers 2019) as a revival of a pragmatic and progressive municipal interventionism in the face of what, to all intents and purposes, looked inevitably like the 'strange death of municipal England' (Crewe 2016). This optimism is far from groundless.

Local housing companies propose to deliver a mix of market, affordable and social housing, meeting diverse housing needs; they enable boroughs to both circumvent borrowing caps, opening up much-needed fiscal capacity, and bypass right-to-buy legislation, which has seen a relentless haemorrhaging of public housing for almost 40 years; and, of course, they promise fiscal returns which can be spent on any number of financially stretched local services – such as social care, community centres, libraries, parks and the like.

Yet for all their possibilities and promise, the emergence of local housing companies has not gone uncontested. Since 2015, facing the prospect of estate demolition, a growing number of campaigns have brought people together – in people's homes and community centres, as well as in town halls, the courts and streets – to scrutinise and fight against these companies and what, despite the assurances of local councillors and officers, some fear they portend: rising rents and living costs; a loss of democratic accountability; housing precarity, alienation and displacement; as well as new rounds of accumulation by dispossession (see Sendra and Fitzpatrick, Chapter 18).

Building on the above counter-narrative, in this chapter I critically engage with the development of local housing companies and their implications for collective urban provisioning, policy and politics. I do this in three steps. First, taking a conjunctural urban political economy approach, I situate the emergence of local housing companies in the 'causal *and* constitutive' (Pike et al. 2019, 24) context of shifting central–local relations, devolved austerity and a convergence of crises unfolding on the terrain of the local state, arguing that London's boroughs are inflating and harnessing already overheated land, property and private-rental markets in order to produce a more managed austerity urbanism. Second, I interrogate in more detail how London boroughs are setting up local housing companies, focusing on their mixed and mutating managerial, entrepreneurial and financialised rationalities, strategies and logics (Pike et al. 2019). In this section, I suggest that these companies are being designed as flexible governance spaces to circumvent a set of constraining rules and regulations. Finally, in the third and concluding section, I evaluate whether local housing companies represent a creative, pragmatic and ultimately progressive fix or rather a 'farewell to welfare approach' (Chatterjee 2014) with long-term consequences for council housing, low-income renters and local government in London and England more broadly.

The urban political economy of local state restructuring in London under austerity

In 2013, three years into his premiership, David Cameron felt confident enough to state in no uncertain terms what had been clear to many from the outset: that austerity, far from being a short-term remedy to a financial-turned-fiscal crisis, was intended as a strategically selective project of state restructuring. Speaking on the occasion of the Lord Mayor's Banquet Speech at the Guildhall in the heart of the City of London, Cameron (2013) informed an audience of political, financial and business elites that 'we are sticking to the task. But that doesn't just mean making difficult decisions on public spending. It also means something more profound. It means building a leaner, more efficient state. We need to do more with less. Not just now, but permanently.' In step with the North American experience of 'downloaded' austerity, the burden of responsibility for realising this 'permanently leaner state' has fallen decidedly on the shoulders of the local state. Local councils have been compelled to manage swingeing budget cuts at a time of rising need for social housing and care services; and they have been summoned anew as a site for 'catalysing latent potentialities for economic growth' (Ward et al. 2015, 443), encouraged to tie their fiscal prospects, and the future of local public services, to real estate interests, markets and values.

The most remarked-upon dimension of local government austerity is the deep and cumulative budget cuts that it has experienced annually since 2010, and which it will continue to be subject to until at least 2020. Set within the narrative of public sector profligacy and guided by the political decision to address the perceived public deficit crisis overwhelmingly through public expenditure reductions (Innes and Tetlow 2015), between 2010 and 2016 the Department for Communities and Local Government (DCLG) saw its budget reduced by over 50 per cent in real terms, far greater than in any other government department (Gray and Barford 2018). In a context of highly unequal central–local relations, in which the vast majority – over 80 per cent in some areas – of local state spending is funded nationally through DCLG, this reduction is significant. To put these figures into historical context, the cuts up to 2015 alone were estimated to be three times the level of those experienced during the previous notable round of austerity in English local government between 1978 and 1985 (Newman 2014).

Geographically these cuts have been distributed and experienced unevenly. Undermining long-standing commitments to territorial resource redistribution and equalisation that compensated, albeit insufficiently, for decades of a spatially selective 'finance-dominated accumulation regime' (Jessop 2014) favouring the South East and London (Massey 2007), the Coalition government's cuts purposefully severed the link between funding and social need, with predictably regressive consequences. The most deprived areas in England, where social need for housing and care is highest, have seen the deepest reductions in funding. Boroughs in inner London have been especially hard hit. Expressed in real terms, London Councils estimates that between 2010/11 and 2015/16 local government in London saw a 44 per cent reduction in core funding, the equivalent of some £2.6 billion. A further £1 billion has since been cut, representing a 60 per cent real-terms reduction from 2010/11 (London Councils 2014).

Further cuts since 2010 have come in the form of reductions in capital funds, which have fallen by 45 per cent (Hastings et al. 2017). This has had a marked effect on social housing in particular. Between 2011 and 2015, radical cuts and reforms were enacted such that central government investment in social housing was terminated in favour of a new 'Affordable Homes Programme', where rents can be set at up to 80 per cent of market rates (Adam et al. 2015). While upwards of £8 billion of public money was funnelled into Help to Buy, supporting middle-class homeownership and inflating house prices, investment in this so-called Affordable Housing Programme was reduced from £9.3 billion (the amount spent between 2008 and 2010 on social housing) to £4.7 billion (Adam et al. 2015). Unsurprisingly, the stock of social housing in England has fallen precipitously since 2010, which has contributed, along with a suite of punitive welfare 'reforms', to rising levels of housing insecurity, homelessness and rough sleeping.

Early evidence suggests that some of these austerity measures were, to a limited extent, absorbed by local councils through back-office efficiencies – or significant reductions to council work forces, affecting women and racialised minorities first and foremost – and then, with increasing severity over time, cuts to service budgets and triaging. Yet councils adopting this incremental approach are fast running out of road. Most now face the choice between going over a financial cliff-edge and fundamentally transforming how they operate (Meegan et al. 2014; Hastings et al. 2017). As early as 2013 the Public Accounts Committee (2013, 3) warned that 'if [current financial] trends continue there is a risk that the worst-affected councils will be unable to meet their statutory obligations, and that serious questions will arise about the viability of some councils'. Five years on, in February 2018, Northamptonshire County Council went as close to declaring bankruptcy as legally possible, and the National Audit Office warns others will surely follow.

In London the need for fundamental transformation has been articulated in local council policy discourse with growing urgency since 2015. Grant funding is rapidly declining as a crisis of social reproduction is developing, with demand for social housing and for social care services acute. Indeed, growth in demand for the latter alone looks set to fundamentally reorient what and who the local state is for. A social care funding gap of £285 million is expected to open up by 2020. Even as access to statutory social services is being reduced via triage, leaving thousands without adequate support, funding for universal discretionary services, such as community centres, libraries and parks, is waning, with long-term consequences for the broader legitimacy of the local state as an institution (Penny 2017).

In the absence of grant support from central government, which is set to be fully cut by 2020, the (not always clear or coherent) plan for how councils will get by and avoid the cliff-edge has entailed a selective set of risk-shifting policies that localise fundraising responsibilities and draw the local state closer to real estate developers. From the outset, any appetite that local politicians may have had for an anti-austerity municipal socialism, funded through increased local council taxes, was headed off. Taking the line that 'the public aren't going to tolerate … higher council taxes' (Pickles 2013), the Coalition government imposed new rules mandating a local referendum to approve any council tax increases above 1.99 per cent. By trusting in people's tax-averse tendencies, under the auspices of localism, the

Coalition government successfully 'locked in' a low council tax regime. Furthermore, councils already unable to borrow to pay for revenue expenditure were also blocked from borrowing money to directly build council housing through artificially low borrowing caps placed on their Housing Revenue Accounts (HRA; see below).

Instead, notwithstanding vague appeals to 'do more for less' by encouraging greater voluntary participation in public services at the expense of paid professional employees, local councils have been compelled to take responsibility for their fiscal futures by becoming more entrepreneurial, developer-friendly and speculative in orientation. Since 2010, local councils have been given a 'General Power of Competence' by central government under the 2011 Localism Act, empowering them to set up new trading companies and generate profits; incentivised to promote residential real estate developments that increase their council tax base through the New Homes Bonus scheme; and encouraged to catalyse local growth through commercial real estate development by allowing them to retain 'a proportion of the growth in their business rate revenue' (Sandford 2016, 639) from new floor space (Muldoon-Smith and Greenlaugh 2015).

As austerity deepens, the ability of the local state to fund and provide collectively consumed services is being predicated on the capacity of local actors to 'unlock' the potential of their assets. Significantly this includes exhortations to 'rationalise' the public estate through one-off asset sales (Besussi 2016), but it also entails inflating property and land values in order to extract a share of the surplus from the realisation of such values either *indirectly* through permissive pro-development strategies, planning gain mechanisms and bonuses, or *directly* through the creation of local asset-backed vehicles capable of generating new forms of long-term 'fiscal rent' (Haila 2016). While the goals of building houses, attracting inward investment and delivering economic growth are far from new in local government in England, the extent to which these activities have become central to the ability of a local authority to maintain organisational capacity, fund local services and meet its stated public policy objectives arguably is. With redistribution from the centre coming to an end, and as 'cities can no longer rely on economic growth in the nation as a source of finance' (Leitner 1990, 154), the realisation of locally derived revenue is becoming *the* primary source of income, such that an entrepreneurial outlook and orientation towards development will cease to be an important supplementary function to the managerial delivery of services (Hall and Hubbard 1996), but rather will be the principal means through which services are to be resourced and austerity urbanism managed.

Thinking outside the HRA box

In response to the shifting urban political economy of local state restructuring and increasingly acute crises of housing and social care, London boroughs have been actively devising entrepreneurial solutions to generate long-term revenues from their local asset bases. One such solution, which has generated significant buzz in recent years as a possible return to municipal intervention-ism, is the council-owned local housing company. Constituted as special purpose corporate entities, local housing companies are designed to enable boroughs to act speculatively as real estate developers, building housing on public land for market sale and rent while also cross-subsidising 'affordable' homes in line with planning requirements. In this section I will explore the rationalities, strategies and logics that animate these companies, arguing that they are being set up as flexible governance spaces, enabling councils to circumvent fiscal/regulatory constraints, treat land in speculative ways as a financial asset and engage finan-cial actors through innovative financing models. Far from representing short-lived idiosyncratic innovations, the proliferation of these vehicles (21 London boroughs now have them) portends a new mode of austerity-induced urban governance – a 'financialized municipal entrepreneurialism', as a colleague and I have termed it (Beswick and Penny 2018), with under-explored implications and risks.

Council-owned local housing companies are corporate entities limited by shares that are constituted outside a local authority's General Fund (the account from which the majority of local public services are funded) and the HRA (a ring-fenced account for the governance and maintenance of existing, and provision of new, council housing). The existence of trading companies is not new in the recent history of English local government. Section 93 of the 2003 Local Government Act, for example, allows local authorities to trade *existing* services to generate prof-its. Local housing companies, however, go beyond this by enabling a borough to acquire, build and manage real estate for market sale and rent, including outside their own territorial boundaries, and so engage in commercial activities that would until recently have been ultra vires. This was made possible in 2011 through the Localism Act's 'General Power of Competence', which allows a local authority to undertake any activity that an individual or corporation can unless specifically pro-hibited by central government legislation.

Across the different London boroughs that have set up a council-owned local housing company, a consistent set of guiding rationales is articulated. These can be summarised as follows. Firstly, councillors and officers emphasise a shared desire to build more homes, especially on council-owned land. Here the private sector is criticised for slow build-out rates and land banking practices, while the broader developer-led planning gain approach to securing affordable housing is seen as failing. Secondly, the importance of generating a financial return is stressed. The developer-led planning gain approach typically sees profits of 15–20 per cent written into, and so all but guaranteed by, developer viability appraisals. Council-owned housing companies are justified, in part, on the basis that these profits can and should be captured directly by the local state to reinvest in 'afford-able' housing or borough General Funds to reduce the impact of fiscal retrench-ment and promote financial self-sufficiency. Thirdly, and relatedly, the importance of public control, managerialism and intervention is asserted in response to market failures in housing affordability, private rental quality (which is notoriously poor in London), place-making and design and, in some outer London boroughs, disinvestment. Thus, local housing companies promise a pragmatically progressive pathway beyond the facilitative and minimal mode of neoliberal entrepreneurial housing governance that has been ascendant since the 1990s.

Yet local housing companies do 'not signal a simple return to, or revalorization of, the public-sector ethos or modus operandi' (Beswick and Penny 2018, 625). While the council-owned status of these companies is emphasised as a virtue, their operating strategies and logics ape those of the private and financial sector, suggesting a mixing and mutation of managerial with entrepreneurial and financialised modes of governance. A key feature of council-owned housing companies is that they sit outside the HRA, the account that legally governs conventional council housing. As such, these companies circumvent a number of fiscal and regulatory constraints associated with the HRA, opening up a smooth governance space in which boroughs are able to act more flexibly and 'creatively'. By developing outside the HRA, boroughs gain the ability to:

- Build homes speculatively for private sale and rent, with the possibility of cross-subsidising 'affordable' housing in line with planning requirements, which they cannot do within the HRA;
- Bypass tight borrowing restrictions placed by central government on the HRA, opening up a range of financing options, from the Public Works Loan Board to innovative forms of equity and debt financing, including with institutional investors;
- Avoid right-to-buy legislation, preventing the enforced subsidised sale of properties developed by council-owned companies;
- Set rent levels flexibly, outside those determined by the Treasury formula and the Secure Tenancy regime, making it easier to 'flex' housing units across rent/tenure or liquidate assets;
- Demolish existing council housing estates, often on high-value public land, and transfer council tenants without ballot to new developments, replacing their Secure Tenancies with less secure Assured Shorthold Tenancies (ASTs);
- Generate a long-term income stream for the General Fund to pay for local public services, which cannot be done within the ring-fenced HRA, and become more financially self-sufficient;
- Sell shares in the company to private parties, including institutional investors or hedge funds, as part of a joint venture or a takeover.

On the one hand, local housing companies are celebrated as representing an innovative – 'out of the box' – governance fix. They enable London boroughs to circumvent central government restrictions and move beyond a reliance on private developers and housing associations. Boroughs can directly build housing again and pursue broader public policy objectives in a more managerial and interventionist way. According to their proponents, local housing companies may even be a way of addressing local fiscal and housing crises. On the other hand, the way in which these public objectives are being pursued suggests an ambiguous mixing and mutating of managerial, entrepreneurial and financialising modes of governance. The development of local housing companies signals the active constitution by the local state of public land and public housing estates as financial assets first and foremost. The realisation of public objectives through these companies is predicated on the financial success of speculative real estate development, the promotion of less secure forms of housing tenure for low-income Londoners and a greater exposure to long-term financial risk. As the next section explores, this dynamic brings with it a set of tensions and trade-offs with long-term implications for council housing, low-income renters and local government more broadly.

Creative financial fix or a farewell to welfare?

If successful on their own terms, council-owned local housing companies will increase the number of good-quality homes built in London, including at social rent levels; they will prevent the erosion of council-owned homes within these companies by withholding the 'right to buy'; in stark contrast to London's current landscape of amateur landlords, they will intervene in the private rental sector and may provide better-quality institutional products; they will encourage private real estate investment in areas that have suffered from disinvestment; and they will provide flexible financial returns to cash-strapped local authorities. In the best case scenario, they would represent a creative financial fix to help address the housing crisis and manage austerity urbanism.

However, even if this best case scenario unfolds – and in the context of Brexit this is far from assured – success would come at a cost. To begin with, as noted above, local housing companies treat public land and properties as financial assets first and foremost. The generation of public value, for example in the form of social housing, is not planned for on the basis of identified social need, as it was during the Keynesian Welfare State era. Instead, mirroring the neoliberal real estate state model prevalent across North American cities including Toronto, public value is predicated on commercial and financial success. This fundamentally shifts the role of local authorities; managerialism follows speculative entrepreneurialism. The importance of this shift is becoming clear in policy literature on local housing companies. While the overwhelming housing need in London is for social housing, local housing companies are not expected to deliver significant proportions of this tenure. The Smith Institute, for example, estimates that just 10 per cent of local housing company housing will be social housing. Given the fact that local housing companies rely greatly on council-owned land to develop on, councils risk exhausting their supply of a shrinking resource with developments that benefit aspiring homeowners and middle-class renters most. Should there be a change of government policy in future years and a return to grant funding, the opportunity costs of local housing developments may become clear.

Since the commercial viability of local housing companies, and their ability to cross-subsidise more affordable homes, relies on rising land and property values, they also risk a form of state-induced gentrification as rents in general increase in nearby areas. In some disinvested boroughs of London this is an explicit policy aim, with local housing companies effectively positioned as vanguards to encourage private investment and development: 'Effectively, we are there to take development forward, to accelerate growth and development, to both build directly and also to catalyse and assist other people in building out' (Chief Executive of BeFirst, Barking and Dagenham). In other cases, more direct forms of state-led gentrification are in evidence. In the London Borough of Lambeth, for example, the council is planning to demolish up to six existing council estates to clear high-value land for mixed-tenure developments delivered by its local housing company. Lambeth council stresses that by closing the rent gaps on its estates through market sale and rent, more 'at council rent' housing can be delivered. The council also promises to rehouse all the estates' current council housing tenants. As resident campaigners note, however, the number of additional 'at council rent' houses is very small and subject to change with unexpected delays, rising construction costs and falling house prices; very little support is being offered to leaseholders whose compensation will fall far short of the costs of buying a like-for-like home on the new developments; and returning council tenants will lose their Secure Tenancies and face increased rents and living costs.

The control and flexibility that the local housing company opens up for boroughs, and indeed that is central to their commercial success, comes at the expense of the security of existing council tenants and future generations of would-be council tenants. Importantly, the affordable and social homes built by these companies are not council homes, even though they are built by a company whose sole shareholder is the council. Council housing, with secure lifetime tenancies, associated rights and centrally regulated rent regimes, can only legally exist within the HRA. The affordable homes built by local housing companies represent less secure forms of non-market homes in which rents are set by the companies, including on a project-by-project basis, and short-term tenancies (ASTs) can be used to 'flex' a development's tenure mix over time, either increasing or decreasing the proportion of affordable housing. This undoing of council tenants' security is not an unexpected outcome of providing housing outside the HRA; it is institutionally expedient as a means of circumventing central government control and it is commercially necessary as a means of ensuring financial flexibility to manage long-term risks. As the outgoing leader of the Local Government Association put it: 'I've spent all my life as a council leader trying to get out of the HRA ... If I didn't have an HRA I wouldn't go anywhere near it ... what's the advantage? Just set up a private company keep all the houses privately and you can choose what level of rent you charge on every single house, there is no way the government can interfere ...' (Inside Housing 2019).

Flexibility is an important means by which local housing companies seek to manage long-term risks. This is most clearly visible when institutional investment has been sought and where the councils in question are contractually obliged to pay fixed/indexed returns to their investors over 20-, 40- and 60-year periods. Here, flexibility becomes a means of maintaining sufficient rent envelopes to manage adverse fluctuations in interest rates as well as possible issues with voids, non-payment and other management issues. Flexibility can also be used as a means of generating more income for local authorities as and when the need arises. The disadvantages of flexibility are felt predominantly by tenants, whose security of tenure is necessarily diluted. Indeed, flexibility is predicated on providing tenants with short-term and less secure ASTs, enabling the landlord to more easily move homes across the rental spectrum from social to affordable to market rent levels. In addition to moving away from historic associations of council housing with lifetime security, this kind of flexibility is also likely to open up a variegated geography of tenant security as different councils, in negotiation with their funders, are likely to offer different kinds of AST, some with relatively long-term tenancies and others without.

Finally, local housing companies carry significant risks for local authorities and for the local state more broadly. Local housing companies, due to unfortunate timing, are being developed in a profoundly unfavourable economic context in which costs (of labour and materials) can be expected to rise and real estate values to fall. While London's land and property markets rebounded quickly after the Global Financial Crisis of 2008, there are no guarantees they will do so again should a painful and disruptive exit from the European Union take place. Yet even if such an outcome were not to occur, and local housing companies succeeded as viable and profitable ventures, the local state as an institution would still likely suffer. Local housing companies are a pragmatic response to the shifting urban political economy of local state restructuring. They reflect the turn away from Spatial Keynesianism. But they also help to reproduce it. What is good for any one local authority may not be good for local government as an institution. Over time, due to uneven geographies of investment and land values across England, geographical variegation and 'territorial injustice' (Gray and Barford 2018) are likely outcomes of the approach to local funding that local housing companies sit within. The local public services that people can access will reflect not the actually existing social need, but the ability of local actors to operate as successful real estate developers and managers.

In conclusion, while local housing companies do represent at one level a creative financial fix, they also represent a vivid example of what Ipsita Chatterjee (2014) calls a 'farewell to welfare approach'. Here, managerial welfare objectives are just about 'kept alive through a discursive life-support system in order to become the sleeping partner for municipal entrepreneurialism'. Increasingly, Chatterjee adds, 'welfarism lives in the level of discourse only and is replaced by entrepreneurial strategies in practice'. Time will tell if local housing companies are successful as companies and whether they are able to deliver some social housing through cross-subsidisation. Yet for low-income Londoners, any such success is likely to prove pyrrhic as local housing companies demolish existing council housing, take up land that could be used for future council housing and erode the security of tenure, low rents and democratic accountability that have made council housing a success – despite the decades-long ideological and material war waged upon it.

References

Adam, Stuart, Chandler, Daniel, Hood, Andrew and Joyce, Robert. 2015. *Social Housing in England: A Survey*. Institute of Fiscal Studies. Accessed 22 July 2019. https://www.ifs.org.uk/uploads/publications/bns/BN178.pdf.

Besussi, Elena. 2016. 'Extracting Value from the Public City: Urban Strategies and the State–Market Mix in the Disposal of Municipal Assets'. In *Urban Austerity: Impacts of the Global Financial Crisis on Cities in Europe*, edited by Sebastian Schipper and Barbera Schoenig, 98–102. Berlin: Theater der Zeit.

Beswick, Joe and Penny, Joe. 2018. 'Demolishing the Present to Sell Off the Future? The Emergence of "Financialized Municipal Entrepreneurialism" in London'. *International Journal of Urban and Regional Research* 42(4):612–32. https://doi.org/10.1111/1468-2427.12612.

Beswick, Joe, Alexandri, Georgia, Byrne, Michael, Vives-Miró, Sònia, Fields, Desiree, Hodkinson, Stuart and Janoschka, Michael. 2016. 'Speculating on London's Housing Future: The Rise of Global Corporate Landlords in "Post-crisis" Urban Landscapes'. *City* 20(2):321–41. https://doi.org/10.1080/13604813.2016.1145946.

Cameron, David. 2013. 'Lord Mayor's Banquet 2013: Prime Minister's Speech'. Accessed 19 August 2020. https://www.gov.uk/government/speeches/lord-mayors-banquet-2013-prime-ministers-speech.

Chatterjee, Ipsita. 2014. *Displacement, Revolution, and the New Urban Condition: Theories and Case Studies*. London: SAGE.

Christophers, Brett. 2019. 'Putting Financialisation in its Financial Context: Transformations in Local Government-led Urban Development in Post-financial Crisis England'. *Transactions of the Institute of British Geographers* (Online First).

Crewe, Tom. 2016. 'The Strange Death of Municipal England'. *London Review of Books* 38(24):6–10.

Gray, Mia and Barford, Anna. 2018. 'The Depths of the Cuts: The Uneven Geography of Local Government Austerity'. *Cambridge Journal of Regions, Economy and Society* 11(3):541–63. https://doi.org/10.1093/cjres/rsy019.

Hackett, Paul. 2017. *Delivering the Renaissance in Council-built Homes: The Rise of Local Housing Companies*. Smith Institute. Accessed 22 July 2019. http://www.smith-institute.org.uk/wp-content/uploads/2017/10/The-rise-of-local-housing-companies.pdf.

Haila, Anne. 2016. *Urban Land Rent: Singapore as a Property State*. Oxford: Wiley-Blackwell.

Hall, Tim and Hubbard, Phil. 1996. 'The Entrepreneurial City: New Urban Politics, New Urban Geographies?'. *Progress in Human Geography* 20(2):153–74.

Hastings, Annette, Bailey, Nick, Bramley, Glen and Gannon, Maria. 2017. 'Austerity Urbanism in England: The "Regressive Redistribution" of Local Government Services and the Impact on the Poor and Marginalised'. *Environment and Planning A* 49(9):2007–24. https://doi.org/10.1177/0308518x17714797.

Innes, David and Tetlow, Gemma. 2015. 'Delivering Fiscal Squeeze by Cutting Local Government Spending'. *Fiscal Studies* 36(3):303–25. https://doi.org/10.1111/j.1475-5890.2015.12056.

Inside Housing. 2019. 'Is Council Housebuilding about to Make a Comeback?' Accessed 6 August 2020. https://soundcloud.com/insidehousing/is-council-housebuilding-about-to-make-a-comeback.

Jessop, Bob. 2014. 'Financialization, Financial Crisis, and Deficit Hysteria: Neoliberalism Redux'. In *Moments of Truth: The Politics of Financial Crises in Comparative Perspective*, edited by Francisco Panizza and George Phillip, 101–19. New York: Routledge.

Kollewe, Julia. 2017. 'How One Council Is Beating Britain's Housing Crisis'. *The Guardian*, 25 March. Accessed 22 July 2019. https://www.theguardian.com/money/2017/mar/25/how-one-council-is-beating-britain-housing-crisis-sheffield.

Leitner, Helga. 1990. 'Cities in Pursuit of Economic Growth: The Local State as Entrepreneur'. *Political Geography Quarterly* 9(2):146–70. https://doi.org/10.1016/0260-9827(90)90016-4.

London Councils. 2014. *London, The Next Four Years: Long-term Financial Prospects*. Accessed 16 October 2020. https://www.londoncouncils.gov.uk/node/1771.

Massey, Doreen. 2007. *World City*. Cambridge, UK: Polity Press.

Meegan, Richard, Kennett, Patricia, Jones, Gerwyn and Croft, Jacqui. 2014. 'Global Economic Crisis, Austerity and Neoliberal Urban Governance in England'. *Cambridge Journal of Regions, Economy and Society* 7(1):137–53. https://doi.org/10.1093/cjres/rst033.

Morphet, Janice and Clifford, Ben. 2017. *Local Authority Direct Provision of Housing*. RTPI. Accessed 22 July 2019. https://i.emlfiles4.com/cmpdoc/3/8/5/5/7/files/516134_local-authority-direct-provision-of-housing.pdf.

Muldoon-Smith, Kevin and Greenhalgh, Paul. 2015. 'Passing the Buck without the Bucks: Some Reflections on Fiscal Decentralisation and the Business Rate Retention Scheme in England'. *Local Economy* 30(6):609–26. https://doi.org/10.1177/0269094215599724.

Newman, Innes. 2014. *Reclaiming Local Democracy*. Bristol: Policy Press.

Peck, Jamie. 2012. 'Austerity Urbanism: American Cities under Extreme Economy'. *City* 16(6):626–55. https://doi.org/10.1080/13604813.2012.734071.

Penny, Joe. 2017. 'Between Coercion and Consent: The Politics of "Cooperative Governance" at a Time of "Austerity Localism" in London'. *Urban Geography* 38(9):1352–73. https://doi.org/10.1080/02723638.2016.1235932.

Pickles, Eric. 2013. 'Local Luddites Must Get with the Programme'. *The Telegraph*, 3 July. Accessed 22 July 2019. https://www.telegraph.co.uk/news/politics/conservative/10156636/Eric-Pickles-local-luddites-must-get-with-the-programme.html.

Pike, Andy, O'Brien, Peter, Strickland, Tom, Thrower, Graham and Tomaney, John. 2019. *Financialising City Statecraft and Infrastructure*. Cheltenham: Edward Elgar.

Public Accounts Committee. 2013. *Department for Communities and Local Government: Financial Sustainability of Local Authorities – Public Accounts Committee*. Accessed 22 July 2019. https://publications.parliament.uk/pa/cm201314/cmselect/cmpubacc/134/13403.htm.

Sandford, Mark. 2016. 'Public Services and Local Government: The End of the Principle of "Funding Following Duties"'. *Local Government Studies* 42(4):637–56. https://doi.org/10.1080/03003930.2016.1171753.

Stein, Samuel. 2019. *Capital City: Gentrification and the Real Estate State*. London: Verso Books.

Taylor-Gooby, Peter. 2012. 'Root and Branch Restructuring to Achieve Major Cuts: The Social Policy Programme of the 2010 UK Coalition Government'. *Social Policy & Administration* 46(1):61–82. https://doi.org/10.1111/j.1467-9515.2011.00797.x.

Wainwright, Oliver. 2017. 'Out of the Box: Councils Try Innovative Projects to Provide Social Housing'. *The Guardian*, 10 February. Accessed 22 July 2019. https://www.theguardian.com/society/2017/feb/10/councils-innovative-projects-social-housing.

Ward, Kevin, Newman, Janet, John, Peter, Theodore, Nik, Macleavy, Julie and Cochrane, Alan. 2015. 'Whatever Happened to Local Government? A Review Symposium'. *Regional Studies, Regional Science* 2(1):434–56. https://doi.org/10.1080/21681376.2015.1066266.

17
Community-based responses to exclusionary processes of neighbourhood change in Parkdale, Toronto

Elena Ostanel

Introduction

Toronto's socio-spatial polarisation is proceeding at a rate much greater than elsewhere in Canada. Spatially, formerly middle-income neighbourhoods are transforming into either high or low income (Walks 2014). Toronto is becoming a strikingly segregated city, with visible minorities concentrated in low-income neighbourhoods and white residents dominating affluent areas in numbers far higher than their share of the population (Hulchanski 2009). In this context Toronto is experiencing both sustained gentrification and advanced suburban restructuring (Walks and August 2008). As Lehrer has pointed out, Toronto's urban changes are strongly impacted by the global economy exceeding the capacity of local policies to govern them (Lehrer 2006). Thus we are witnessing a policy context in Toronto where local government is retreating from public investments, giving more room to the motives of private corporations. This situation has produced problems for the social production of space in the city, as it is now heavily influenced by private property interests.

While Parkdale, a neighbourhood in the western downtown area of Toronto, was considered one of the last affordable downtown neighbourhoods for culturally diverse newcomers to Canada, the situation is rapidly changing. An analysis of 2016 census data shows a mutable situation, particularly in South Parkdale where the recent immigrant population (people arriving in the previous 10 years) is shrinking and the non-immigrant population is growing. Similarly, the population of low-income persons and recent immigrants has decreased while the population of older, Canadian-born working adults has increased. The occupations of residents are also shifting away from middle-income blue-collar jobs towards business people/professionals. A change in residential accommodation is noticeable as well. There has been an increase in apartments removed from the regular rental housing stock and made available for short-term rental through services like Airbnb[1]; advertised rents in the neighbourhood demonstrate a drastic increase over the 2015–18 period. Overall, simple unweighted average advertised rents increased by over $426 per month, or 36 per cent. The quickly changing environment of Parkdale is creating a more marked process of gentrification, where only households with higher incomes are able to afford to live in the neighbourhood.

In Parkdale, low-income people together with populations with mental health and addiction experiences, refugees and recent immigrants, and people facing homelessness are all strongly affected by these rent increases and the resulting changes in the nature and use of public spaces in the neighbourhood.[2] While the inclusivity of Parkdale is at risk, community-based activism to resist and mitigate the negative effects of neighbourhood change is getting stronger. In the last few years, a social infrastructure that is able to promote the empowerment of diverse community members in a condition where land use decision-making is particularly market-driven, compartmentalised and privatised (PCED 2016) has been built with the collaboration of diverse organisations and community allies. Through a case study of Parkdale, this chapter argues that community-based responses produce positive outcomes in response to the negative effects of neighbourhood change and disadvantage if a grounded and networked social infrastructure that can influence decision-making processes regarding neighbourhood development and planning is designed and implemented. The effectiveness of community-based action is related to the capacity of building on-the-ground and bottom-up governance mechanisms (Garcia 2010), directed at bringing equity not only to the social realm but also to governance and planning systems and practices. Viewed within this framework, Parkdale is a relevant case study due to the presence of effective neighbourhood organisations (Carrière 2016) that are connected through a multifaceted social infrastructure that supports a fundamental rethinking of local planning policy and practice (Hanna and Webber 2010).

In this chapter, I first provide a brief overview of the literature discussing the complex relationship between community-based activism and local governments. I then focus on Parkdale's path-dependent history of community-based activism, by exploring its scope and actors as well as the changing forms of organisation over the years. The chapter also examines the ability and capacity of municipal policies and planning tools and mechanisms to control the negative effects of neighbourhood change. This is based on field research that was conducted in Parkdale between November 2017 and May 2019. The research employed a mixed-method qualitative approach through a literature review of neighbourhood change and community development scholarship, analysis of background data at the City of Toronto and neighbourhood level, interviews with key stakeholders, participant observation at public meetings and in key neighbourhood spaces, and the review of City of Toronto and Parkdale neighbourhood planning documents.

Community-based practices as policy-making

Many scholars have highlighted how community-based practices in the contemporary city raise new questions around the relationship between community-based initiatives and local governments. This issue is particularly relevant within the context of global neoliberal conditions, where the state's retraction from social welfare provisions has dramatically increased in recent decades (Alford 2009; Peck et al. 2013; Savini 2016). Some scholars have argued that it is important to consider community-based organising as an arena of opportunities that emphasise bottom-up governance (Garcia 2010) and that focus on reconnecting local communities to their governments as well as scaling up processes of change in governance practices. This bottom-up approach to reconfiguring community–local government relations sits in opposition to the traditional approach to planning and activism in communities or neighbourhoods by local governments. As Uitermark (2015) explains, in the 1980s and 1990s, urban governments in Europe co-opted a great number of moderate activists through targeted neighbourhood policies that emphasised partnerships and similar participatory schemes, effectively dividing radical and moderate activists while imposing government constraints on groups operating within neighbourhood-based social movements. Uitermark points out how this approach was used to address new challenges presented by austerity and the retraction of the welfare state, but in a way that urban governments could still control neighbourhood-based activism and initiatives and ensure that they were palatable to government interests. In similar fashion, the analyses of DeFilippis and other scholars have warned about the risk of depoliticising community-based initiatives when they act as service providers and apolitical moderators between citizens and local governments. Instead, they consider community activism as a potential source for building community power and changing the root causes of social and spatial problems (DeFilippis et al. 2010). Thanks to the agency of more empowered local communities, community-based initiatives can build 'new institutions' to enhance democratic control over unfair processes of neighbourhood change. This strand of the literature considers community empowerment as essential for advocating for more responsive local government (Novy and Leubolt 2005; Swyngedouw 2005; Garcia 2010; Ostanel and Attili 2018).

Similarly, Sendra and Fitzpatrick (Chapter 18) argue that community-based activism in London has had the power to influence decisions, political agendas and the policy-making process. Even though it is not possible to present a picture of complete victory, activism creates more opportunities for further successes as it seems to have a replicating effect in terms of motivating communities to keep fighting at different scales and finding policy alternatives to a politics of austerity. These practices can be seen as part of a politics of 'counter-austerity', with each case offering a particular spatial scale of emergent forms of contestation as new policy-making (Arampatzi 2017; Sendra and Fitzpatrick, Chapter 18). According to this line of thought, conflict and collaboration can be considered as reinforcing elements in an ongoing political process, where conflict is not only unavoidable but also a necessary aspect of community participation and engagement. Real-life practices of community-based activism can foster and co-produce formal and/or informal changes in how local institutions function (González and Healey 2005; Ostanel 2020).

A path-dependent history of community-based activism in Parkdale

This section aims to reconstruct the path-dependent and context (place)-bound (Moulaert et al. 2013; Bunce 2016) history of community-based activism in Parkdale (see Figure 17.1). Community activism in Parkdale has continuously changed over time, becoming increasingly attentive to the root causes of social and spatial inequalities as well as fostering much-needed conversations across scales – moving from the micro (everyday resistance to neighbourhood change) to the macro level (policy changes and the rethinking of planning regimes). In the following sections, I explore how community activism has championed social equity and inclusivity in Parkdale in relation to planning decisions by Toronto's municipal government and neighbourhood change processes.

Competing visions for Parkdale

Contemporary local activism in Parkdale is largely rooted in community work that was started in the 1990s, when the growing divide between affluent homeowners and lower-income tenants led to a local consultation process guided by the City of Toronto government (Barna 2007). Two competing visions for the neighbourhood were raised at the time, with relatively affluent residents wanting to fight the overconcentration of social services and rooming houses/bachelorettes in the neighbourhood, considered as the cause of drug dealing, prostitution and the presence of numerous very poor residents. Gentrification processes were already at play, producing noticeable financial reinvestment in residential and commercial property and increasing social displacement, evictions and homelessness (Slater 2004). The gentrification process was actively supported by the City of Toronto from the outset (Slater 2004). Public discourse was constructed around the role of bachelorettes (very small bachelor apartments) and rooming houses, because these inexpensive rental housing options were seen by gentrifiers and local government to 'threaten the stability of family neighbourhoods', 'destroy streetscape' and 'bring a host of social problems because of the often-rowdy transients they attract as tenants' (Whitzman and Slater 2006). At the same time, some organisations active in the provision of social services conveyed a counter-vision. In their view, the main challenges of Parkdale were related to high unemployment and

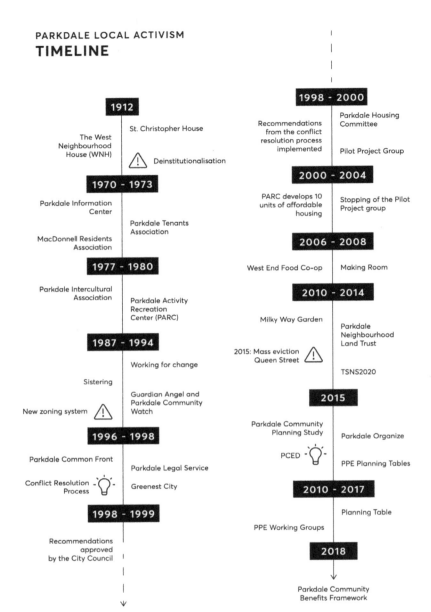

PARKDALE LOCAL ACTIVISM
TIMELINE

1912

The West Neighbourhood House (WNH)

St. Christopher House

⚠ Deinstitutionalisation

1970 - 1973

Parkdale Information Center

MacDonnell Residents Association

Parkdale Tenants Association

1977 - 1980

Parkdale Intercultural Association

Parkdale Activity Recreation Center (PARC)

1987 - 1994

Working for change

Sistering

Guardian Angel and Parkdale Community Watch

⚠ New zoning system

1996 - 1998

Parkdale Common Front

Parkdale Legal Service

💡 Conflict Resolution Process

Greenest City

1998 - 1999

Recommendations approved by the City Council

1998 - 2000

Recommendations from the conflict resolution process implemented

Parkdale Housing Committee

Pilot Project Group

2000 - 2004

PARC develops 10 units of affordable housing

Stopping of the Pilot Project group

2006 - 2008

West End Food Co-op

Making Room

2010 - 2014

Milky Way Garden

Parkdale Neighbourhood Land Trust

2015: Mass eviction Queen Street ⚠

TSNS2020

2015

Parkdale Community Planning Study

Parkdale Organize

💡 PCED

PPE Planning Tables

2010 - 2017

PPE Working Groups

Planning Table

2018

Parkdale Community Benefits Framework

Figure 17.1 The timeline of community activism in Parkdale (organisations' websites and Barna 2007)

lack of jobs. They argued there was an increased need for the provision of more social services and social housing in Parkdale. In that period, the Parkdale Activity Recreation Centre (PARC) was among the most active community-based organisations supporting a different narrative about Parkdale and working in collaboration with other dynamic social agencies in the neighbourhood, including West

Neighbourhood House, Sistering and Parkdale Intercultural Association (Barna 2007). The tension between the two competing visions for Parkdale erupted in 1996 in response to the introduction of the City of Toronto's 'interim control by-law' that prohibited any new rooming house/bachelorette development or conversion in South Parkdale designed for low-income tenants (Slater 2004).

An immediate effect of this top-down planning decision by the City of Toronto was the creation of an alliance of stakeholder groups in Parkdale. The Parkdale Common Front in Defense of Poor Neighbors group was established in 1996 to support the idea that Parkdale should remain a diverse neighbourhood and accessible to low-income people. Many non-profit organisations became part of this association, including the Bachelorette Owners Association. The City of Toronto's planning decision also resulted in the creation of more unusual alliances between groups in Parkdale and citywide organisations, such as the Ontario Coalition Against Poverty. The level of concern and conflict was so high that in 1998, the Toronto City Council decided to institute a formal conflict resolution process in Parkdale, aimed at opening up a dialogue with all stakeholder organisations in the neighbourhood. With the support of an external facilitator, different organisations and City of Toronto staff met for 12 months in order to discuss 'the approach that the City should take on the existing illegal rooming houses and bachelorettes in Parkdale' (Toronto Community Council 1999). In 1999, Toronto's City Council drafted and adopted a report with recommendations to legalize rooming houses. A Parkdale Housing Committee was created and a 'Pilot Project Group' was initiated in the neighbourhood. In 2000, the recommendations started to be implemented and 266 illegal rooming house properties were identified for potential legalisation (Barna 2007). In 2004, however, the City of Toronto abandoned the Parkdale Pilot Project. Barna highlights the lack of long-term support by the City, both from a financial and a political point of view, as one of the main reasons why the programme was stopped (Barna 2007, 37). Slater's analysis is directed at the City of Toronto's unwillingness to support single-room occupancy housing in the neighbourhood (Slater 2004).

Towards equitable planning in Parkdale: The role of PARC

Since the end of the 1990s, PARC has had a key stakeholder organising role in advocating for access to affordable housing. In 2000, PARC created and managed 10 units of supported housing on the third floor of its offices at 1499 Queen Street West. Commercial units were given to charitable or non-profit organisations in order to create a local hub for community services, thus promoting the inclusion of new community stakeholders (PARC 2007). Starting from a mission related to more traditional drop-in community services, PARC has increasingly built efforts to advocate for affordable housing and to organise against evictions caused by gentrification. PARC's first mission statement was written in 1994. It stated that 'Parkdale Activity-Recreation Centre is to be a stable and meaningful self-directed resource for the community of psychiatric consumer/survivors and socially isolated people, a focus for inspiration and a source of pride for every individual Member. We aspire to contribute to the health and well-being, comfort of person, richness of spirit, and the expression of individual truth of all PARC Members' (PARC 1994, 1). In 2007, PARC changed its mission statement to 'a community where people rebuild their lives', with a consequent decision to shift part of the mission towards supporting equitable development in the neighbourhood. PARC subsequently decided to become a landowner in Parkdale, purchasing 1499 Queen St West and 194 Dowling St to protect residents from eviction but at the same time forming closer links with both the government and the private market through this process (Epstein et al. 2017).

Starting in 2010, PARC started to seriously explore how a community land trust might work within the context of Parkdale (see Bunce, Chapter 19). In 2012, an interim board for the Parkdale Neighbourhood Land Trust (PNLT), hosted through PARC, was formed with the contribution of different organisations. In 2014, a non-profit organisation was incorporated and run by a board of directors, consisting of local non-profit organisations and groups that represent the diversity of Parkdale. These organisations included PARC, the West End Food Co-Op, Greenest City, Roncesvalles-Macdonell Residents Association, Parkdale Community Legal Services, Parkdale Village Business Improvement Association, West Neighbourhood House (formerly St Christopher House) and Sistering. PARC actively works with PNLT and other Parkdale organisations to promote community participation in guiding how neighbourhood land is used to benefit the community and exploring on-the-ground methods to keep Parkdale affordable and diverse. In 2018 the work of the PNLT pushed for the approval at the City of Toronto level of a $1.5 million fund that a non-profit could use to purchase and operate a Parkdale rooming house.

Community-based planning: Planning and organising against gentrification

The Parkdale Community Economic Development (PCED) Project (now called the Parkdale People's Economy), an initiative of PARC, has the objective of bringing diverse stakeholder efforts together to form a common strategy under the umbrella of a 'community wealth building' approach. Community wealth building is defined as 'a system approach to economic development that creates an inclusive, sustainable economy built on locally rooted and broadly held ownership' (Kelly et al. 2016, 16). The community wealth building approach explicitly emphasises the democratisation of the ownership of community assets. Starting in February 2015, different organisations met on a bi-monthly basis through a Neighbourhood Planning Table, facilitated by PARC, to develop a plan for action to support community participation in planning and organising in the face of gentrification (PCED 2018). As a product of this work, the Parkdale Community Planning Study is a plan to address displacement pressures by building decent work, shared wealth and equitable development in Parkdale. According to an analysis of meeting minutes, 63 stakeholders were present at the different planning table meetings among community-based stakeholders (both active in Parkdale and across the city), different departments of the City of Toronto (City Planning, Public Health and Social Development Finance and Administration), community services, faith groups and the University of Toronto.[3]

PCED describes it as a community planning initiative envisaging a range of tools for action: (i) community-based research and community development; (ii) direct action, demonstrations and community voting; (iii) community benefits framework; and (iv) letter writing and media campaigns. In addition to the planning table, community working groups have been set up to cover the areas of interest envisaged by the planning study, focusing on the following topics: decent work; participatory democracy; community finance; affordable housing; food security; cultural development; and community health (PCED 2016). The working groups were designed to facilitate the direct participation of residents beyond the planning table. Community groups set up their own agendas and action plans with the aim to incrementally implement the planning actions envisaged and eventually revise them.

The community planning process in Parkdale has intersected with the Toronto Strong Neighbourhoods Strategy (TSNS) 2020 (City of Toronto 2012),[4] a neighbourhood policy released by the City of Toronto in 2012 and aimed at providing 'an equitable set of social, economic and cultural opportunities for all residents, leading to equitable outcomes across all neighbourhoods' (City of Toronto 2014, 2). The Parkdale People's Economy planning table has been recognised as the institutional table of this municipal government strategy in Parkdale, a situation that seems to facilitate a smooth flow of communication between municipal departments and policies and different community groups. Nevertheless, the TSNS appears to have limited room for action regarding the more structural and systemic elements that are causing inequitable development in Parkdale, particularly in relation to constraints on affordable housing as well as democratic control over neighbourhood change.

Impacts on planning and development in Parkdale

With an increase in gentrification pressures, Parkdale community organisations have needed to reinforce their capacity to respond to how official planning and development tools and mechanisms are designed and implemented. One of the ways this is being done is through the Parkdale Community Benefits Framework, developed in 2018 by Parkdale community organisations 'to center community needs and community benefits when planning for neighbourhood growth and development rather than highest and best use, as defined by density and profit'

(PCED 2018). The vision of the Parkdale Community Benefits Framework is a 'call for equitable development that respects and benefits existing community members, that values people's lives over profits, and that promotes development without displacement' (PCED 2018). In terms of equitable development, the document calls for the use of 'transparent and fair process that ensures historically marginalized community members can share power and meaningfully participate in the development process through participatory planning and direct democracy' (PCED 2018). In order to ensure accountability, it states that 'developments can mitigate the risk of displacement through tools such as Equity Impact Studies, Inclusionary Zoning, and Community Benefits Agreements' (PCED 2018).

The Parkdale Community Benefits Framework was used in 2019 as a recommendation in the City of Toronto's consultation process on inclusionary zoning. In this consultation, Parkdale residents and organisations asked for a minimum of 30 per cent permanently affordable housing with commitments to deep affordability, accessibility and adequately sized units for families in new buildings (PCED 2018). They advocated for the approval of inclusionary zoning by the City of Toronto in order to expand housing options for low- and middle-income renters. While the City of Toronto's inclusionary zoning regulation is still being decided, what is interesting is the effort to establish a more strategic and spatial approach to social inclusion through the activism of community-based organisations in Parkdale.

Discussion and conclusion

Parkdale serves as an excellent case study for assessing the capacity of community-based initiatives to resist or mitigate the negative effects of neighbourhood change. Community activism in Parkdale shows the presence of a strong network of community organising, which is considered a condition for successful collective mobilisation for positive change (Sampson 2004; Lin Cheng-Chen and Peng 2010; Carrière 2016). This chapter showed how community activism in Parkdale has developed over time and how it is context-specific and place-bounded. Over the years, community-based activism in Parkdale has become increasingly attentive to the root causes of social and spatial inequalities, as well as fostering much-needed conversations across scales – a movement from the micro (everyday resistance to neighbourhood change) to the macro level (policy changes and rethinking of planning regimes). While community-based action is intrinsically related to different scales, it is also important that it is multi-scalar and interrelated: from everyday activism, to a broader cultural politics and agency of a neighbourhood (Rankin 2009), and to broader levels of decision-making, such as local government.

In line with this, I suggest that community-based responses such as those in Parkdale are more able to control the negative effects of neighbourhood change when they acknowledge the importance of how planning and development mechanisms are designed and implemented. This is particularly important in a context where the municipal government is weakened in the governance of land use decision-making processes because of the interests of private developers and where the benefits of improvement are not shared equitably (Walks and Maaranen 2008). As Sendra and Fitzpatrick (Chapter 18) highlight, community-based activism in London has contributed to proposing equitable community-led regeneration as well as influencing current policies, as evidenced in the cases of the West Ken and Gibbs Green communities. In a similar fashion, Parkdale's social infrastructure has pushed for and co-produced an innovative plan to preserve some of the neighbourhood's rapidly dwindling stock of affordable housing (i.e. the pilot project on rooming houses). In addition to this, community-based activism in Parkdale is advocating for mandatory inclusionary zoning regulations with high 'set asides' – defined as the percentage of a new residential building that will be made affordable and ideally provide deep affordability. The concurrent work on the Parkdale Community Benefits Framework, being inserted into a broader campaign regarding community benefits in development, is identified as an important step for envisioning what community benefits can be gleaned from future developments in Parkdale. Parkdale's social infrastructure has acknowledged that a successful inclusionary zoning policy needs to be integrated with the Toronto Official Plan, affordable housing plans and local neighbourhood plans, and geared towards the revision of municipal planning and development mechanisms. In this sense, Parkdale is particularly interesting for its capacity to merge community development practices, such as collective action and solutions to neighbourhood-based problems (Carpenter 2015), with community organising strategies directed at changes in policies and approaches at the city level and on a broader scale (Brian and Speer 2015).

Community-based activism in Parkdale confirms the idea that contestation can be considered as a valuable form of policy-making (Arampatzi 2016 in Sendra and Fitzpatrick, Chapter 18). In Parkdale, conflict and collaboration are reinforcing elements in an ongoing political process whereby disagreements (between community and local government or between competing neighbourhood visions) are not only unavoidable but also a necessary aspect of community participation and engagement (Ostanel 2020). Parkdale can be considered as a community 'trading zone' (Balducci and Mäntysalo 2013), where the ordinary structures and processes of community planning are transformed in alliance with and relation to other stakeholders and different scales of decision-making within and outside the neighbourhood sphere. The story of Parkdale's community organising and activism efforts demonstrates the creation of a strong social infrastructure in response and relation to larger institutional and structural processes and impacts. Over time, community activism in Parkdale has enabled the development of community-based interventions that combine social and economic justice approaches with building cohesive plans intended to influence the decisions of Toronto's government. In this way, community action in Parkdale exemplifies a bottom-up, networked approach to resisting impactful neighbourhood change, while at the same time challenging any detrimental 'top-down' municipal government decisions.

Acknowledgements

This chapter is the result of research conducted within the project NEIGHBOURCHANGE, which has received funding from the European Commission under the Marie Skłodowska-Curie Individual Fellowships, Horizon 2020 research and innovation programme, project NEIGHBOURCHANGE grant agreement no. 707726. This work would not be possible without the support of Parkdale People's Economy and all their partner organisations in accessing the research field. Data analysis has been provided by the Neighborhood Change Research Partnership based at the University of Toronto (Professor David Hulchanski, Principal Investigator; Richard Maaranen, Senior Data Analyst).

Notes

1. Data analysis was developed by the Neighborhood Change Research Partnership, http://neighbourhoodchange.ca.
2. Parkdale is a neighbourhood approximately 4 kilometres west of the downtown core. Queen Street, an important commercial artery for both Parkdale and Toronto, runs east–west through the neighbourhood and is used as the dividing line between North and South Parkdale. In this study, South Parkdale is the focus of the investigation. Data have been collected considering census tracts 4, 5, 7.01 and 7.02. Liberty Village neighbourhood has been analysed considering the impact of its transformation into a hub for creative and cultural industries in the late 1990s on South Parkdale.
3. During the field research I had the opportunity to participate in planning tables and working group meetings, observing interactions as well as analysing meeting schedules and minutes.
4. The TSNT was aimed at providing 'an equitable set of social, economic and cultural opportunities for all residents, leading to equitable outcomes across all neighbourhoods' (City of Toronto 2014, 2). The TSNT assessment identifies 31 out of 140 neighbourhoods 'below the benchmark' and defines place-based action plans.

References

Alford, John. 2009. *Engaging Public Sector Clients: From Service-Delivery to Co-Production*. London: Palgrave Macmillan.

Arampatzi, Althina. 2017. 'The Spatiality of Counter-austerity Politics in Athens, Greece: Emergent "Urban Solidarity Spaces"'. *Urban Studies* 54(9):2155–71. https://doi.org/10.1177/0042098016629311.

Balducci, Alessandro and Mäntysalo, Raine. 2013. *Urban Planning as a Trading Zone*. Dordrecht: Springer.

Barna, Miriam. 2007. 'Bridging Divides: An Examination of the 1998 Parkdale Conflict Resolution Process'. Toronto: University of Toronto.

Brian, Christens and Speer, Paul. 2015. 'Community Organizing: Practice, Research, and Policy Implications'. *Social Issues and Policy Review* 9(1):193–222. https://doi.org/10.1111/sipr.12014.

Bunce, Susannah. 2016. 'Pursuing Urban Commons: Politics and Alliances in Community Land Trust Activism in East London'. *Antipode* 48(1):134–50. https://doi.org/10.1111/anti.12168.

Carpenter, Mick. 2015. 'The First 50 Years of the Community Development Journal'. *Community Development Journal* 50(1):1–9.

Carrière, Jessica. 2016. *Neighbourhood Collective Efficacy: A Scoping Review of Existing Research*. Neighbourhood Change Research Partnership Research Paper. Accessed 30 April 2020. http://neighbourhoodchange.ca/documents/2016/07/neighbourhood-collective-efficacy.pdf.

City of Toronto. 2012. *Toronto Strong Neighbourhoods Strategy 2020*. Accessed 15 May 2020. https://www.toronto.ca/wp-content/uploads/2017/11/9112-TSNS2020actionplan-access-FINAL-s.pdf.

City of Toronto. 2014. *TSNS 2020 Neighbourhood equity index: Methodological Documentation*. Accessed 24 April 2020. https://www.toronto.ca/wp-content/uploads/2017/11/97eb-TSNS-2020-NEI-equity-index-methodology-research-report-backgroundfile-67350.pdf.

DeFilippis, James, Fisher, Robert and Shragge, Eric. 2010. *Contesting Community: The Limits and Potential of Local Organizing*. New Brunswick, NJ: Rutgers University Press.

Epstein, Griffin, Cambridge, Tyde Irma, Martin, Peter G., Sampson, Bernice, Hovhannisyan, John, Zareian, Omid, Timson, Bernadette and Cronyn, Hume. 2017. *Creating Change: Research Findings at the Parkdale Activity-Recreation Centre*. Toronto: PARC.

Garcia, Marisol. 2010. 'The Breakdown of Spanish Urban Growth Model: Social and Territorial Effects of the Global Crisis'. *International Journal of Urban and Regional Research* 34(4):967–80. https://doi.org/10.1111/j.1468-2427.2010.01015.x.

González, Sara and Healey, Patsy. 2005. 'A Sociological Institutionalist Approach to the Study of Innovation in Governance Capacity'. *Urban Studies* 42(11):2055–69. https://doi.org/10.1080/00420980500279778.

Hanna, Kevin and Webber, Steven. 2010. 'Incremental Planning and Land-use Conflict in the Toronto Region's Oak Ridges Moraine'. *Local Environment* 15(2):169–83. https://doi.org/10.1080/13549830903530625.

Hulchanski, J. David. 2009. *The Three Cities within Toronto: Income Polarization Among Toronto's Neighbourhoods, 1970–2005*. Neighbourhood Change Research Partnership Research Paper. Toronto: Urban Centre. Accessed 30 April 2019. http://www.urbancentre.utoronto.ca/pdfs/curp/tnrn/Three-Cities-Within-Toronto-2010-Final.pdf

Kelly, Marjorie, McKinley, Sarah and Duncan, Violeta. 2016. 'Community Wealth Building: America's Emerging Asset Based Approach to City Economic Development'. *Renewal: A Journal of Social Democracy* 24(2):51–68.

Lehrer, Ute. 2006. 'Willing the Global City: Berlin's Cultural Strategies of Interurban Competition after 1989'. In *The Global City Reader*, edited by Roger Keil and Neil Brenner, 332–8. London: Routledge.

Lin Cheng-Chen, Timothy and Peng, Tai-Kuang. 2010. 'From Organizational Citizenship Behaviour to Team Performance: The Mediation of Group Cohesion and Collective Efficacy'. *Management and Organization Review* 6(1):55–75. https://doi.org/10.1111/j.1740-8784.2009.00172.x.

Moulaert, Frank, MacCallum, Diana, Mehmood, Abid and Hamdouch, Abdelillah. 2013. *The International Handbook on Social Innovation, Collective Action, Social Learning and Transdisciplinary Research*. Cheltenham: Edward Elgar.

Novy, Andreas and Bernhard, Leubolt. 2005. 'Participatory Budgeting in Porto Alegre: Social Innovation and the Dialectical Relationship of State and Civil Society'. *Urban Studies* 42(11):2023–36. https://doi.org/10.1080/00420980500279828.

Ostanel, Elena. 2020. 'Can Social Innovation Transform Local Governments? The Experience of Naples'. In *Social Movements and Public Policies in Southern European Cities*, edited by Laura Fregolent and O. Nel·lo, 155–72. Berlin: Springer.

Ostanel, Elena and Attili, Giovanni. 2018. 'Powers and Terrains of Ambiguity in the Field of Urban Self-organization Today'. *TU – Italian Journal of Urban Studies* 4:6–17.

PARC (Parkdale Activity-Recreation Centre). 1994. *Annual Report*. Toronto: PARC.

PARC (Parkdale Activity-Recreation Centre). 2007. *History of PARC*. Accessed 15 January 2020. http://parc.on.ca/about/history-of-parc.

PCED (Parkdale Community Economic Development Planning Project). 2016. *Building a Foundation for Decent Work, Shared Wealth and Equitable Development in Parkdale*. Full Report. Accessed 20 October 2020. https://ccednet-rcdec.ca/sites/ccednet-rcdec.ca/files/parkdale_community_planning_study_2016.pdf.

PCED (Parkdale People's Economy, Parkdale Community Economy, Development Planning Project). 2018. *Parkdale Community Benefits Framework Full Report. Guide for Development without Displacement*. Accessed 9 October 2020. https://parkdalecommunityeconomies.files.wordpress.com/2018/11/parkdale-community-benefits-framework1.pdf.

Peck, Jamie, Theodore, Nik and Brenner, Neil. 2013. 'Neoliberal Urbanism Redux?'. *International Journal of Urban and Regional Research* 37(3):1091–9. http://doi.org/10.1111/1468-2427.12066.

Rankin, Katharine. 2009. 'Critical Development Studies and the Praxis of Planning'. *City* 13(2):262–374. https://doi.org/10.1080/13604810902983233.

Sampson, Robert. 2004. 'Neighborhood and Community: Collective Efficacy and Community Safety'. *New Economy* 11:106–13. https://doi.org/10.1111/j.1468-0041.2004.00346.x.

Savini, Federico. 2016. 'Self-Organization and Urban Development: Disaggregating the City-Region, Deconstructing Urbanity in Amsterdam'. *International Journal of Urban and Regional Research* 40(6):1152–69. https://doi.org/10.1111/1468-2427.12469.

Slater, Tom. 2004. 'Municipally Managed Gentrification in South Parkdale, Toronto'. *Canadian Geographer* 48(3):303–25. https://doi.org/10.1111/j.0008-3658.2004.00062.x.

Swyngedouw, Erik. 2005. 'Governance Innovation and the Citizen: The Janus Face of Governance Beyond-the-state'. *Urban Studies* 42(11):1991–2006. https://doi.org/10.1080/00420980500279869.

Toronto Community Council. 1999. *Parkdale Conflict Resolution Process (High Park)*. Accessed 9 October 2020. http://www.toronto.ca/legdocs/2000/agendas/council/cc/cc000201/to2rpt/cl027.pdf.

Uitermark, Justus. 2015. 'Longing for Wikitopia: The Study and Politics of Self-organisation'. *Urban Studies* 52(13):2301–12. https://doi.org/10.1177/0042098015577334.

Walks, Alan. 2014. 'From Financialization to Sociospatial Polarization of the City? Evidence from Canada'. *Economic Geography* 90(1):33–66. https://doi.org/10.1111/ecge.12024.

Walks, Alan and August, Martine. 2008. 'The Factors Inhibiting Gentrification in Areas with Little Non-market Housing: Policy Lessons from the Toronto Experience'. *Urban Studies* 45(12):2594–625. https://doi.org/10.1177/0042098008097102.

Walks, Alan and Maaranen, Richard. 2008. 'Gentrification, Social Mix, and Social Polarization: Testing the Linkages in Large Canadian Cities'. *Urban Geography* 29(4):293–326. https://doi.org/10.2747/0272-3638.29.4.293.

Whitzman, Carolyn and Slater, Tom. 2006. 'Village Ghetto Land: Myth, Social Conditions, and Housing Policy in Parkdale, Toronto, 1879–2000'. *Urban Affairs Review* 41(5):673–96. https://doi.org/10.1177/1078087405284673.

18

Time to be an activist: Recent successes in housing activism in London

Pablo Sendra and Daniel Fitzpatrick

Introduction

The recent period of entrenched austerity and a deepening housing crisis in London have exacerbated the poor living conditions of many people. Decreasing numbers of council homes have forced people to rely on the private rented sector, which remains under-regulated, unaffordable for a great proportion of people living in London and in poor condition. The tragedy of the Grenfell Tower fire in summer 2017, in one of the richest boroughs of the UK, has highlighted the contradictions of housing provision – with fatal results. In the aftermath, further contradictions emerged during the rehousing of the survivors and neighbours when it was revealed that there were some 1,857 vacant dwellings in the Borough of Kensington and Chelsea in July 2017 (Shrubsole 2017).

As a result of the politics of austerity imposed by central government following the crisis of 2007–8, local authorities have been exploring different ways of 'sweating' their assets in order to meet their housing targets. These strategies include the demolition and redevelopment of social housing estates, selling their housing stock or partnering with private developers in joint ventures to deliver urban renewal schemes. Cases such as the demolition of the Heygate Estate in Elephant and Castle in the London Borough of Southwark have demonstrated that such schemes do not meet the needs of the local population. Firstly, the number of social-rented homes will decrease from 1,194 to 74 when the scheme is completed, a loss justified in the developers' viability assessment (Wainwright 2015). Secondly, a report on the 'impact of overseas corruption on the London property market' by Transparency International UK (2017) found out that all flats sold in South Gardens in Elephant Park were represented by one single firm of solicitors, which 'specialises in international property investor purchases' (p.39). Thirdly, the redevelopment scheme has led to the displacement of most of its residents (London Tenants Federation et al. 2014).

The failure of the Heygate Estate was rooted in the way the redevelopment scheme neither met the needs of local people nor increased the provision of social housing; instead, it served investors, private interests and also the council's priority of attracting wealthier people into the borough. Furthermore, the typical terms used by the local authority (London Borough of Southwark) in presenting the development, such as 'consultation' and 'affordable', created frustration and distrust (see London Tenants Federation et al. 2014). This frustration was not limited to the Heygate redevelopment, but has been felt increasingly by many other groups of social housing residents across London and has been highlighted by urban scholars critical of regeneration processes across the world (Watt and Smets 2017).

Amid the tragic and fatal dynamics of under-maintenance, under-regulation, bad management, redevelopment and the accompanying displacement, expulsion and dispossession on a mass scale, there are housing movements coalescing around particular themes, including fighting redevelopment programmes and proposing alternatives, opposing joint ventures between local authorities and private developers, and influencing the policy-making process. This rise of activist movements can be linked to the struggles that many communities have suffered in relation to their housing conditions, particularly exacerbated since the introduction of austerity politics in 2010 (Watt and Minton 2016). As Ostanel (Chapter 17, this volume) explains for the case of Parkdale in Toronto, activism and community-led planning have become stronger in the context of a decrease of welfare provision by the state. In the UK, the decrease in welfare provision was a key part of the politics of austerity, which was an outcome of the Coalition government of 2010 (Conservative and Liberal Democrats) and their response to the financial crisis of 2007–8. On the surface it was a deficit-reduction fiscal programme, but it had deep social and political effects due to the reduction in public service spending and subsequent cuts to public service provision especially affecting areas such as housing and local government (Tunstall and Pleace 2018).

After nearly a decade of a rise in activism which has resulted in a range of campaigns around housing, many are succeeding in stopping regeneration schemes, in reversing the intention of selling public land to private developers, in preventing joint ventures and in influencing housing policy. The rise of such activism has emerged as part of a broader questioning of and resistance to not only the social injustices caused by austerity but also more widely neoliberal capitalism, including financialisation. In recent history, housing struggles and resistance to capitalism have generated alternative housing provision, in a similar way to that in which the squatting movement of the 1970s was linked to the emergence of housing cooperatives (Vasudevan 2017). Other examples include the regeneration protests that led to the establishment of London's Coin Street Community as community-led cooperative housing (Tuckett 1988; Baeten 2000, 2001; Brindley 2000), or the community-owned housing association of Walterton and Elgin Community Homes (WECH) in the late 1980s and early 1990s (Bunce 2016; Rosenberg 2011, 2012; Bailey 2012).

This chapter argues that the rise of activism, including denouncing situations of injustice, has gained momentum and power to shape decisions, political agendas and the policy-making process to the point where in some cases there has been a reverse of, or indeed the development of policy alternatives to, a politics of austerity. This is within a context in which local authorities in London, who have a responsibility to provide housing for their residents, employ decision-making processes that either minimise or ignore local communities' involvement. The chapter also argues that these 'victories' create more opportunities for further successes, as they have a replicating effect by motivating other activist groups to resist and fight for their rights, as well as generating knowledge transfer between campaigns.

The chapter concentrates on three particular themes that are related to local authority (council) provision of social housing and maintenance of their housing stock: firstly, social housing estate redevelopment, which has been widely contested across London (Watt and Minton 2016; Lees and Ferreri 2016; Sendra 2018); secondly, the opposition to joint ventures between local authorities and private developers, a common strategy that local authorities are adopting to deliver housing in times of austerity (Beswick and Penny 2018); and thirdly, the influence that campaigns have had on the draft planning documents published by the Mayor of London: the Estate Regeneration Good Practice Guide (December 2016), the Housing Strategy (September 2017) and the London Plan (December 2017)

Three case studies are used to address these three particular themes, reflecting the scale of campaigning intervention: social housing at a neighbourhood scale, at a borough scale and at London-wide metropolitan scale (see Figure 18.1). The

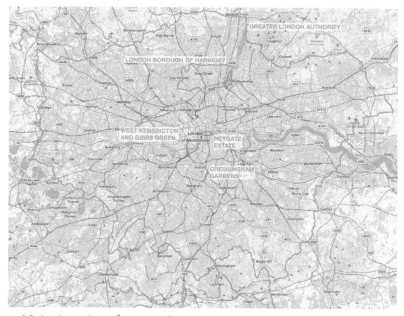

Figure 18.1 Location of case studies and examples mentioned in the chapter. Elaborated by the authors from Open Street Map cartography and boundary data (© OpenStreetMap contributors. Data are available under the Open Database Licence, and the cartography is licensed as CC BY-SA. https://www.openstreetmap.org/copyright)

first case study is that of West Kensington and Gibbs Green Community Housing, a community group that after nine years of campaigning managed to make their local authority (London Borough of Hammersmith and Fulham) reconsider the sell-off of their homes to a private developer for demolition and redevelopment. The second case study is the campaign against the Haringey Development Vehicle, a joint venture between the local authority (London Borough of Haringey) and the private developer Capco, which managed to stop the creation of a special purpose vehicle (SPV); and finally, we examine how community groups responded to the consultation on the planning documents published by the Mayor of London (Mayor's Good Practice Guide for Estate Regeneration, Housing Strategy, the proposed new funding condition to require resident ballots in estate regeneration, and the London Plan). This involves looking at the achievements and limitations of policy proposals such as no loss of social housing in redevelopment schemes or resident ballots as a Greater London Authority (GLA) funding condition for regeneration schemes that involve demolition.

This chapter is part of a research project titled 'Community-led social housing regeneration: between the formal and the informal', funded by a British Academy/Leverhulme Grant, developed by Pablo Sendra and Daniel Fitzpatrick in collaboration with Just Space, a London-wide network of community groups and activists. The research project explores, in the context of London's housing crisis and the UK's politics of austerity, what strategies community groups are using to oppose social housing demolition and redevelopment and how they have been able to propose alternative community-led plans for regeneration. For the research project, residents, community organisers, activists, campaigners, architects and a diverse range of people involved in campaigning against housing estate demolition were interviewed and, as part of the November 2017 Just Space community conference on the Draft Housing Strategy, a workshop was organised with community groups to develop a collective response to the consultation process and to reflect on how estate regeneration could be led by residents or communities themselves. The authors also contributed to Just Space's responses to the Draft Housing Strategy, the Mayor's Ballots Requirement to Estate Regeneration, and participated in the discussion on the Draft London Plan consultation (see also Ferm, Chapter 8).

Stopping the selling of social housing to private developers: An important milestone in a long struggle

Most of the campaigners we interviewed, engaged with and/or studied in this research project were facing dispossession and the demolition of their homes. In this chapter we focus on one particular case study of a group that has achieved an important milestone in their campaign: West Kensington and Gibbs Green estates in the London Borough of Hammersmith and Fulham (LBHF) in west London.

The residents started to campaign against the council's plans for redevelopment in 2009.[1] The council intended to sell the land to a private developer in order to carry out a mega-redevelopment scheme covering a large site in west London, specifically in the neighbourhood of Earls Court, which is spread over two local authorities. The two social housing estates – West Kensington Estate and Gibbs Green – are within the London Borough of Hammersmith and Fulham, while the remaining area of the Earls Court redevelopment scheme is in the Royal Borough of Kensington and Chelsea.

The residents approached Jonathan Rosenberg, who joined them as community organiser. Rosenberg had succeeded, in the late 1980s, in stopping Westminster Council from selling the Walterton and Elgin estates to developers and in completing the transfer of housing stock from Westminster Council to a community-owned housing association – WECH – in the early 1990s, using a piece of legislation that did not remain in effect for long, the 1988 Tenants Choice.

One of the first moves of West Kensington and Gibbs Green residents after Rosenberg joined them as community organiser was to set up the Community Land Trust West Ken and Gibbs Green Community Housing (WKGGCH) with the aim of applying for a Right to Transfer. Community land trusts are a practice for community-based land stewardship and affordable housing creation (Bunce 2016) or, in the case of West Ken and Gibbs Green, protection of social housing against demolition. As Bunce further reflects in Chapter 19, the emergence of community-based, resident-led and non-governmental organisation-supported actions, in cities such as London and Toronto, against gentrification pressures has led to people finding solutions at the community or neighbourhood scale. In the case of West Ken and Gibbs Green, the Right to Transfer legislation was still being passed and therefore not in place but was intended to allow residents to acquire collective ownership and control of their homes and therefore then to propose their own regeneration scheme, as the Walterton and Elgin residents had done thanks to the 1988 Tenants Choice legislation. The new legislation was not in place until November 2013, so the residents were only able to present a Right to Transfer notice in August 2015. In the meantime, they asked Architects for Social Housing to help them draft a People's Plan, which proposed building between 200 and 300 new homes without the need to demolish any existing houses. This notice was rejected by LBHF in September 2015 and both LBHF and WKGGCH asked for a determination from the Secretary of State. This came on July 2019 and determined that LBHF's rejection of the notice was valid. In March 2020, WKGGCH gave a Right to Transfer notice again, and this time it was accepted by LBHF in April 2020.[2]

Although the transfer has not happened yet, the experience does provide a good example of knowledge transfer from past experiences and also serves as an example of testing a new piece of legislation. Thus, WKGGCH's ambition to gain community ownership and control of their homes as a response to the threat of privatisation and demolition was inspired by WECH's success in the late 1980s and early 1990s. Campaigns learn from each other and also learn from past experiences.

Another campaign in London that has also served notice for the Right to Transfer is the group of residents of Cressingham Garden in the Borough of Lambeth (see Chapter 3 in Sendra and Fitzpatrick 2020). This experience was also useful to test whether the new legislation worked in granting residents ownership and control of their homes. In this sense, Rosenberg highlighted the problems of the new legislation compared with the 1988 Tenants Choice legislation that WECH used in the early 1990s.[3]

At the same time as the community was preparing to serve notice for the Right to Transfer, the council was continuing in its plans to sell the land to the developer and this was challenged through judicial review by the residents (see Chapter 11 in Sendra and Fitzpatrick 2020). While the judicial review did not manage to stop the Conditional Land Sale Agreement (CLSA), it did delay it. In 2013, the council signed a CLSA with the developer Capco, with the signing taking place a few months before the Right to Transfer legislation was finalised.

Despite it being a long campaign, the West Ken and Gibbs Green community remained strong and united for many years and gained support from politicians, professionals, scholars, urban planning students and other activists. In January 2018, as a result of years of campaigning and the use of diverse strategies, planning tools and actions (see Sendra 2018), the new council, which had changed from Conservative to Labour, demanded that the developers hand back the estate to the council. By February 2018, the council launched an investigation into the previous administration's deal which had sold off the site to Capco in 2012 (Prynn 2019).

This was an important milestone in the residents' effort to avoid displacement and gain control of their neighbourhood's future. It was also an important achievement in that it can influence other councils and residents across London, and it provides a demonstration of the positive impact that collective action and campaigning can have. While writing this chapter, the authors attended a preview screening of a film about the campaign along with a series of other historical films on tenants and residents across the UK taking control of housing. The event, held in the estate's community centre, was packed and attended by many residents as well as people who had supported or sympathised with the campaign in different ways over the years, and the atmosphere of the event was optimistic.

Haringey Development Vehicle: Has it been stopped?

In its attempts to deal with housing shortages and the poor quality of social housing stock in the borough, Haringey Council in north London decided to undertake a £2 billion deal with a private partner, Lendlease, through which the council would provide the land and the developer would undertake a regeneration programme of all housing on council-owned land. The SPV set up for this purpose, known as the Haringey Development Vehicle (HDV), was approved in July 2017 as a 50/50 partnership between Haringey Council and Lendlease. This leading property group was chosen following a supposedly lengthy process, despite their reputation for having been involved in the plans for the aforementioned demolition of the Heygate Estate, in the London Borough of Southwark. The decision to create such an SPV as a joint venture was partly so that the council could draw on the developer's real estate experience in speculative interventions while maintaining some semblance of control, albeit not openly accountable or transparent to the public. Furthermore, the logic of the HDV, as in many of the other London cases of housing SPVs, was based on developing affordable housing through the cross-subsidies of speculative market housing to sell on the private market and treating public land as a financial asset (Beswick and Penny 2018).

Local residents, political groups, housing campaigners and other local organisations representing a diverse range of local views came together very quickly to create a multi-stranded campaign to prevent the HDV from going ahead. Their two main concerns were the lack of social housing in the business plan on which the HDV was based and the lack of accountability in the governance of the SPV (Chakraborty 2017a). There was also a dimension of local political ideologies playing out within the local Labour Party which ran the council, along lines dividing the older, establishment Labour elements in the council, including councillors and the leader, and the newer, more grassroots Labour group, which included Momentum as the activist wing of the party, as made explicit in the Labour manifesto and general election of 2017 (Chakraborty 2017b). However, the struggle did not play out as a purely internal Labour Party rift, but echoed the wider concerns of residents in most boroughs across London, especially around housing, affected by forms of property-led regeneration heavily dependent on financialised and viability-dependent modes of planning (Raco and de Souza 2018).

The main concerns about the SPV's lack of accountability and its governance began with the process that led to the particular SPV being set up as well as the future plans for its governance. The proposed quantity of social housing was also unclear: the land to be used by the HDV had around 1,400 social homes, and Lendlease was originally proposing to build 6,400 new homes, presumably by demolishing large swathes of the existing social housing stock, while only promising that 40 per cent of new homes would be 'affordable', with no explicit provision for social-rent housing (Chakraborty 2017a). The council's strategy was one of growth, which the then leader of the council, Claire Kober, described in her letter of resignation as 'the only option for a council like Haringey determined to control its own destiny' (Kober 2017). The question for residents, however, was what form this growth would take.

There were also concerns about the ability of the developer to complete the job given its failure in the regeneration of the Heygate Estate, if one applies such evaluative criteria as increasing social housing provision and having meaningful resident participation and engagement in the development process, rather than the displacement of original residents. Moreover, there were wider concerns about how developers would exploit viability assessments to reduce the number of social housing units provided, as in the case of Heygate (Wainwright 2015), and eventually transform the schemes into enclaves for wealthier residents (Lees 2014; Lees and Ferreri 2016).

In October 2017, the campaign that had coalesced around the StopHDV group, a coalition of Haringey residents opposed to the HDV, took Haringey Council and Lendlease to court. They challenged the decision to set up the HDV through a judicial review. The case was refused by the judge in February 2018. A secondary outcome, however, was the resignation of the Labour leader of the council Claire Kober, who stepped down.

In the run-up to local elections and as a result of the StopHDV campaign a swathe of deselections of local Labour candidates took place and the elections in May 2018 resulted in a new administration taking over the council, which remained in overall Labour control. In July 2018, the newly formed Labour cabinet, in keeping with their election manifesto pledge, voted not to approve the formation of the HDV and therefore scrapped the agreement with Lendlease (Haringey 2018). This resulted in a claim being filed against the council by Lendlease for the expenditure incurred after being picked as partner in the SPV. In an out-of-court settlement in February 2019, Haringey agreed to pay £520,275 to Lendlease (Jessel 2018).

With greater control over the future regeneration of Haringey's estates, it is unclear what strategy is going to be used to replace the joint venture SPV. More recently, concerns have arisen regarding the proposal for a scheme on the Broadwater Farm estate which requires the demolition of two blocks – Tangmere and Northolt – being exempt from resident ballots. An application was made to the GLA to consider whether Haringey could be exempted from balloting on the grounds of safety (London Assembly 2018). Local groups have nonetheless expressed concerns over the lack of balloting, not because residents disagreed with the options to demolish but, more importantly, they believed that resident ballots on schemes involving the demolition of social housing should be carried out as it is a decision for tenants to make.[4]

More serious concerns have been raised over the other regeneration sites that were exempt from resident ballots as they had already been scheduled for demolition before the mayoral requirement for balloting for estate regeneration was approved. In many cases, it would undermine the original concerns that resident ballots sought to address, namely as an instrument to reinforce the principles of participation and greater resident involvement in the decision-making process with regard to housing management and regeneration. These are some of the main drivers of residents' involvement and their concerns with the processes of social housing regeneration. The way in which these concerns have been articulated can be further seen in the case of community groups' involvement in the consultation process at the larger spatial scale of the mayoral draft planning documents, including the mayor's Good Practice Guide for Estate Regeneration, the Resident Ballots Funding Requirement, the Housing Strategy and the London Plan.

Consultation on the Mayor of London's policy documents: An opportunity?

Community groups and housing activists have campaigned simultaneously in multiple dimensions. Although the aforementioned campaigns may seem isolated and disconnected, they are networked and form part of a new conscience for activism in London. This network has crystallised in organisations such as Just Space, a London-wide 'informal alliance of … community groups, campaigns and concerned independent organisations' (JustSpace.org.uk), as well as other groups such as Axe the Housing Act, Radical Housing Network, Generation Rent, Demolition Watch and other organisations, some locally based. Just Space as a network was born in the early 2000s, soon after the formation of the GLA and the election of the first Mayor of London in the year 2000, with the aim of uniting the voices of communities to influence planning in London (Lipietz et al. 2014). This network has played a very important role in supporting community groups, sharing knowledge between the different campaigns, developing partnerships with academia to establish collaborations between communities, researchers and students, and putting together collective responses to consultation processes on planning policy documents. They have also created their own 'Community-led London Plan' (Just Space 2016), where they have a series of well-researched policy proposals. As Ferm touches on in Chapter 8, the Just Space network has done much work on highlighting the economy and planning at a local level and changing the approach to industrial land, for example, taken in the London Plan, but here we reflect on another strand of Just Space's work focused on housing and regeneration.

In May 2016, Sadiq Khan (Labour Party) won the election for Mayor of London. In his campaign he promised to address the housing crisis. As Raco and Livingstone explore in Chapter 1, there are a series of ambiguities in the implementation of policies to address the housing crisis which have resulted in opposite effects. This is a result both of the rhetoric used around the governance of residential development in London and also the unintended consequences of policy implementation. In reference to estate regeneration, Khan stated that it would only take place where 'there is resident support, based on full and transparent consultation'. In the first couple of years of his mandate, he published three draft documents to address the issue of estate regeneration: the 'Draft Good Practice Guide for Estate Regeneration' (December 2016), the 'Draft Housing Strategy' (September 2017) and the 'Draft New London Plan' (December 2017). The Resident Ballot was also consulted on as a separate policy within the 'Good Practice Guide for Estate Regeneration' during April 2018. For each of the documents, the Mayor of London opened a consultation process in which individuals and organisations could provide responses to the documents. In February 2018, the mayor published a revised version of the 'Good Practice Guide for Estate Regeneration', where he took on board some of the comments that were provided in the consultation process. One of the most significant changes was to put in place a condition that for GLA funding of regeneration schemes there had to be a residents' ballot in which the majority of the residents have to vote in favour of the regeneration. The mayor opened another consultation on this particular change in April 2018 and, in July 2018, the requirement that resident ballots must be held for redevelopment schemes that apply for GLA funding and involve demolition of any housing association or council-owned housing and the construction of at least 150 new homes was approved. However, this measure is seen as insufficient by many activists and resident groups since it is only a requirement for those that apply for GLA funding. A freedom of information request revealed that many redevelopment schemes that were already in the pipeline – such as the demolition of the social housing estate in the Borough of Lambeth, Cressingham Gardens – had been granted funding from the GLA just before making such consultations obligatory.

Just Space has coordinated and collated detailed and thorough responses from community groups to each of the consultation documents.[5] One of the most significant aspects of the responses is the method they used to formulate a collective response, ensuring that as many of its member organisations as possible are involved and represented. For each consultation process, Just Space organised a 'community conference' (two conferences in the case of the London Plan, one of them in collaboration with the GLA), in which the attendees worked in themed groups to address particular chapters of the policy document and conclude with key points to address. After that, a working group collected the responses and put together a collective response, which was sent to all Just Space members before its submission to the GLA. This collaborative process, in which diverse community activists representing different community groups' interests wrote a collective response to policy documents, is unique and demonstrates a strong engagement with wider issues across London, beyond the boundaries of each of these communities (of interest and of place). The engagement of Just Space with policy-making in London also included meeting with GLA staff to discuss policy directions before they were published.

At the time of writing (spring 2019), the results of the consultation processes were yet to be declared as the Examination in Public (EiP) of the Draft London Plan was ongoing and being led by the Planning Inspectorate (see Figure 18.2). However, certain important achievements and limitations can be identified. One of the main achievements of the London Plan in regulating the speculation of social housing is that redevelopment plans should demonstrate no net loss of floor space of social-rented housing and, when demolished, they should be replaced 'like-for-like'. This was already expressed in the draft before the consultation but responds to the advocacy of community organisations and housing groups in their attempts to prevent regeneration schemes such as Heygate. Another relative achievement of the consultation process has been incorporating the requirement that residents are balloted for redevelopment schemes in order to obtain GLA funding. However, one of the main limitations is that most of the policies do not give statutory power to the mayor to stop developments, but condition GLA funding on meeting a series of 'good practices', which may not be strong enough to stop redevelopment schemes.

Figure 18.2　London Plan Examination in Public, February 2019 (photograph by P. Sendra)

Just Space has also been particularly concerned with the vague language used in many instances,[6] giving flexibility to local authorities, housing associations and developers to interpret the policy. In addition to this, despite mentioning several times in the policy documents the need for a transparent consultation process, none of the policies consider that residents may want to take the lead on a regeneration scheme, as many of the campaigns are claiming.

Emerging cultures of housing activism in London: From campaigning to policy-making

The 'successes' presented here are not definite victories where residents have managed to gain full control of their housing at neighbourhood or borough levels, but they are important milestones that have impeded or delayed redevelopment, proposed alternative forms of regeneration, stopped temporarily a joint venture between local authority and private developers, and, at a wider scale, influenced policy. There are two main points that emerge from these case studies:

- The achievements as a result of campaigning can motivate other activist groups to resist and fight for their rights, as well as generate knowledge transfer between campaigns.
- The rise of activism and denouncing situations of injustice can influence policy-making and reverse or indeed find policy alternatives to a politics of austerity.

Regarding the first point, successes from campaigning have a double effect: they *motivate* other groups to keep fighting and they generate *knowledge transfer* between campaigns. Motivation is a key component of every campaign, particularly during long ones such as those that involve resisting demolition and proposing alternative plans. Campaigning requires a lot of time, emotional effort and unpaid labour. It is important to have moments of success or to achieve milestones so that campaigns are sustained and the participants remain motivated. It is also important for campaigners to see that other community groups, in similar situations, are achieving milestones and successes that indicate campaigning is effective and that their efforts may be rewarded. Networks and alliances of community groups are critical for this knowledge transfer and support between campaigns to happen. The creation of alliances between campaigns and different community-based organisations is increasingly becoming common in other cities, as Ostanel (Chapter 17) explains for the case of Parkdale in Toronto.

Another key driver of the motivation for campaigning is the social infrastructure it generates. Campaigns such as WKGGCH, which organised events such as the film screening, bringing together residents and campaign supporters, develop their strength from the social infrastructures built around the campaign.

The cases we have presented in this chapter are examples of campaigns that have had varying effects at the neighbourhood scale, the local authority scale and at the London-wide metropolitan strategic scale. Their effects can motivate communities to keep fighting at all levels. Ostanel (Chapter 17), when explaining the case study of Parkdale in Toronto, highlights that community activism becomes stronger when it jumps between different scales, from the micro scale of everyday resistance to the macro scale of influencing policy.

In addition to motivation, there is also knowledge transfer between campaigns. For example, WKGGCH learnt two main lessons from WECH's experience: (1) how to plan a strategy for community ownership and control of their homes; and (2) how to keep a community together for a collective aim. These are two important knowledge transfers that WKGGCH is further developing, and thanks to this work, other campaigns will be able to learn from this and take this knowledge even further. The same happened with borough-wide campaigns such as StopHDV and with the participation of community groups in the consultation on the Mayor of London's planning documents. In the latter case, Just Space has kept a record of the process on its website and has collected both the responses from many community groups and also criticism of the policies once they are approved.

Another important point for this knowledge transfer between communities is the collaboration between community groups, scholars, students and professionals. Both the cases of WKGGCH and of Just Space's work on responding to the consultation on the Mayor of London's planning documents have had engagement with scholars and students, thus contributing to recording the knowledge generated in each of these campaigns.

The cases we have explored also offer examples of the way in which forms of activism can not only organise people against particular forms of injustice, but also influence policy-making processes and shift, reverse or find alternative policies. This process can be seen as part of a politics of counter-austerity, with each case offering a particular spatial scale of emergent forms of contestation as a form of policy-making (Arampatzi 2017).

In West Ken and Gibbs Green, the sell-off of public land and demolition in order to create a new master-planned neighbourhood was partly prevented. However, the contestation at the neighbourhood scale went further as it sought to develop a response based on legislation used in similar circumstances by WECH: namely, the Right to Transfer. Testing this piece of legislation was important as it demonstrated the potential of a policy to increase resident control of housing, but it also highlighted the flaws in the legislation as the decision remained stuck for years at the secretary of state level. Although the campaign has been able to halt the development, and the Right to Transfer notice has finally been accepted by the council, the transfer has not been completed yet.

The StopHDV campaign was an important example of a borough-wide coalition of housing and regeneration activist groups working locally and across different existing interests and parties to stop the Haringey Development Vehicle. The judicial review, although it was lost, challenged the consultation process and the wider implications of an SPV set up by the council with a private entity where there would be less public accountability and oversight. The judgement, although not in favour of the plaintiff as activist organisation, may encourage councils in the future to consider more carefully specific decisions concerning regeneration proposals and policies.[7] It also offers a salutary story of electoral defeat for political parties, which could encourage councils to be more tentative or even risk averse. These are, of course, only hypotheses at this stage, but they do trace the emergence of some elements of influence that housing activism can have at the London borough scale in the context of austerity politics.

Finally, the case of the London Plan and the consultation process has involved particular forms of activism related to the policy-making process. Just Space, as well as other important community networks including activist groups, have been able to articulate specific demands indirectly by means of the comments and official responses to the different stages and documents, as well as forums, including the EiP. Throughout this process, responses have been considered and submissions analysed in a laborious process of consultation. However, this has also been an arena for activist groups to discuss and compare ideas regarding particular policy responses. One example was the briefing sessions that Just Space organised at UCL once a month during the EiP, which were opened to activists, community group representatives as well as researchers and students. These forums for discussion, learning and knowledge exchange become spaces for the development of policy contestation and also exploration of new policy ideas. Therefore, they become important emergent spaces for activists at both physical and spatial level, but also at a discursive and policy-forming level.

Acknowledgements

We would like to thank Just Space, for their support and collaboration in the research project titled 'Community-led social housing regeneration: between the formal and the informal', and the community groups interviewed for this project. We would like to thank the British Academy and the Leverhulme Trust for funding this project.

Notes

1. Interviews with community organiser, housing organiser and resident (2017).
2. This information comes from interviews and email exchanges with the community organiser Jonathan Rosenberg between 2017 and 2020 and from the determination of the Secretary of State available here: https://assets.publishing.service.gov.uk/government/uploads/system/uploads/attachment_data/file/816103/West_Ken_Gibbs_Green_determination_letter_Redacted.pdf.
3. This came out in the interviews with Jonathan Rosenberg in 2017 and from two reports he wrote on the legislation in 2012 and 2013.
4. In the case of Tangmere and Northolt, structural surveys had been carried out and revealed serious structural damage in the panel systems. Strengthening costs were reported to be estimated at £33.6 million and rebuilding was estimated at between £32 million and £54 million. The cabinet opted for demolition and rebuild (Hill 2018).
5. See links for consultation documents prepared by Just Space for Response to the Estate Regeneration Guide, to the Housing Strategy, London Plan and Resident Ballots at http://www.justspace.org.uk.
6. This has come out in various discussions around the London Plan consultation in Just Space conferences and meetings during 2018 and 2019.
7. See Sackman (2020) on the use of judicial reviews to contest regeneration.

References

Arampatzi, Althina. 2017. 'The Spatiality of Counter-austerity Politics in Athens, Greece: Emergent "Urban Solidarity Spaces"'. *Urban Studies* 54(9):2155–71. https://doi.org/10.1177/0042098016629311.

Baeten, Guy. 2000. 'From Community Planning to Partnership Planning: Urban Regeneration and Shifting Geometries on the South Bank, London'. *GeoJournal* 51(4):293–300.

Baeten, Guy. 2001. 'Urban Regeneration, Social Exclusion and Shifting Power Geometries on the South Bank, London'. *Geographische Zeitschrift* 89(2–3):104–13.

Bailey, Nick. 2012. 'The Role, Organisation and Contribution of Community Enterprise to Urban Regeneration Policy in the UK'. *Progress in Planning* 77(1):1–35. https://doi.org/10.1016/j.progress.2011.11.001.

Beswick, Joe and Penny, Joe. 2018. 'Demolishing the Present to Sell Off the Future: The Emergence of "Financialized Municipal Entrepreneurialism" in London'. *International Journal of Urban and Regional Research* 42(4):612–32. https://doi.org/10.1111/1468-2427.12612.

Brindley, Tim. 2000. 'Community Roles in Urban Regeneration: New Partnerships on London's South Bank'. *City* 4(3):363–77. https://doi.org/10.1080/713657033.

Bunce, Susannah. 2016. 'Pursuing Urban Commons: Politics and Alliances in Community Land Trust Activism in East London'. *Antipode* 48(1):134–50. https://doi.org/10.1111/anti.12168.

Chakraborty, Aditya. 2017a. 'A Labour Council Attacking its Own People? This Is Regeneration Gone Bad'. *The Guardian*, 25 October. Accessed 10 May 2019. https://www.theguardian.com/commentisfree/2017/oct/25/labour-council-regeneration-housing-crisis-high-court-judge.

Chakraborty, Aditya. 2017b. 'Haringey Council Taken Over by Momentum? It's Just Locals Taking Back Control'. *The Guardian*, 12 December. Accessed 10 May 2019. https://www.theguardian.com/commentisfree/2017/dec/12/haringey-council-taken-over-momentum-locals-taking-back-control.

Haringey. 2018. 'Statement from Leader Cllr Joseph Ejiofor', 20 July. Accessed 10 May 2019. https://www.haringey.gov.uk/regeneration/haringey-development-vehicle.

Hill, Dave. 2018. 'Haringey: Bid to Have No-ballot Demolition of Broadwater Farm Blocks Reconsidered Fails'. OnLondon blog. Accessed 10 May 2019. https://www.onlondon.co.uk/haringey-bid-to-have-no-ballot-demolition-of-broadwater-farm-blocks-reconsidered-fails.

Jesssel, Ella. 2018. 'Haringey Votes to Axe Controversial Homes Deal Despite Lendlease Warning'. *Architects Journal*, 19 July. Accessed 10 May 2019. https://www.architectsjournal.co.uk/news/haringey-votes-to-axe-controversial-homes-deal-despite-lendlease-warning/10033292.article.

Just Space. 2016. *Towards a Community Plan for London*. London: JustSpace. Accessed 10 May 2019. https://justspacelondon.files.wordpress.com/2013/09/just-space-a4-community-led-london-plan.pdf.

Kober, Claire. 2017. 'Article from Council Leader Cllr Claire Kober on the Haringey Development Vehicle'. Haringey London. Accessed 10 May 2019. http://www.haringey.gov.uk/news/article-council-leader-cllr-claire-kober-haringey-development-vehicle.

Lees, Loretta. 2014. 'The Urban Injustices of New Labour's "New Urban Renewal": The Case of the Aylesbury Estate in London'. *Antipode* 46(4):921–47. https://doi.org/10.1111/anti.12020.

Lees, Loretta and Ferreri, Mara. 2016. 'Resisting Gentrification on its Final Frontiers: Lessons from the Heygate Estate in London (1974–2013)'. *Cities* 57:14–24. https://doi.org/10.1016/j.cities.2015.12.005.

Lipietz, Barbara, Haywood, Sharon and Lee, Richard. 2014. 'Just Space: Building a Community-based Voice for London Planning'. *City: Analysis of Urban Trends, Culture, Theory, Policy, Action* 18(2):214–25. https://doi.org/10.1080/13604813.2014.896654.

London Assembly. 2018. 'Broadwater Farm Estate Ballot'. Question to the Mayor of London. Accessed 10 May 2019. https://www.london.gov.uk/questions/2018/3010.

London Tenants Federation, Lees, Loretta, Just Space and Southwark Notes Archive Group. 2014. *Staying Put! An Anti-gentrification Handbook for Council Estates in London*. Accessed 10 May 2019. https://justspace.org.uk/2014/06/19/staying-put-an-anti-gentrification-handbook-for-council-estates-in-london.

Prynn, Jonathan. 2019. 'Council May "Land-grab" in Row with Company behind £12bn Earl's Court Scheme'. *Evening Standard*, 20 February. Accessed 10 May 2019. https://www.standard.co.uk/news/london/council-may-landgrab-in-row-with-company-behind-12bn-earl-s-court-scheme-a4071621.html.Raco, Mike and de Souza, Tatiana. 2018. 'Urban Development, Small Business Communities and the Entrepreneurialisation of English Local Government'. *Town Planning Review* 89(2):145–65. https://doi.org/10.3828/tpr.2018.9.

Rosenberg, Jonathan. 2011. 'Social Housing, Community Empowerment and Well-being: Part One – Empowerment Practice in Social Housing'. *Housing, Care and Support* 14(4):113–22. https://doi.org/10.1108/14608791111220908.

Rosenberg, Jonathan. 2012. 'Social Housing, Community Empowerment and Well-being: Part Two – Measuring the Benefits of Empowerment through Community Ownership'. *Housing, Care and Support* 15(1):24–33. https://doi.org/10.1108/14608791211238403.

Sackman, Sarah. 2020. 'Using the law and challenging redevelopment through the courts'. In P. Sendra and D. Fitzpatrick. *Community-led Regeneration: A toolkit for residents and planners*. London: UCL Press, 111–24.

Sendra, Pablo. 2018. 'Assemblages for Community-led Social Housing Regeneration: Activism, Big Society and Localism'. *City* 22(5–6):738–62. https://doi.org/10.1080/13604813.2018.1549841.

Sendra, Pablo and Fitzpatrick, Daniel. 2020. *Community-led Regeneration: A Toolkit for Residents and Planners*. London: UCL Press

Shrubsole, Guy, 2017. 'Where Are the Empty Homes in Kensington?' Who Owns England, 18 June. Accessed 10 May 2019. https://whoownsengland.org/2017/06/18/where-are-the-empty-homes-in-kensington.

Transparency International UK. 2017. *Faulty Towers: Understanding the Impact of Overseas Corruption on the London Property Market*. Accessed 10 May 2019. https://www.transparency.org.uk/publications/faulty-towers-understanding-the-impact-of-overseas-corruption-on-the-london-property-market.

Tuckett, Ian. 1988. 'Coin Street: There Is Another Way …'. *Community Development Journal* 23(4):249–57. https://doi.org/10.1093/cdj/23.4.249.

Tunstall, Rebecca and Pleace, Nicholas. 2018. *Social Housing: Evidence Review*. Research Report. York: University of York.

Vasudevan, Alexander. 2017. *The Autonomous City*. London: Verso.

Wainwright, Oliver. 2015. 'Revealed: How Developers Exploit Flawed Planning System to Minimise Affordable Housing'. *The Guardian*, 25 June. Accessed 10 May 2019. https://www.theguardian.com/cities/2015/jun/25/london-developers-viability-planning-affordable-social-housing-regeneration-oliver-wainwright.

Watt, Paul and Minton, Anna. 2016. 'London's Housing Crisis and its Activisms: Introduction'. *City* 20(2):204–21. https://doi.org/10.1080/13604813.2016.1151707.

Watt, Paul and Smets, Peer. 2017. *Social Housing and Urban Renewal: A Cross-National Perspective*. Bingley: Emerald.

19

Engagement and activism in community land ownership: The emergence of community land trusts in London and Toronto

Susannah Bunce

London and Toronto are cities that face similar affordable housing pressures and, as such, are contexts for the pursuit of alternative and innovative solutions to the provision of affordable housing and for a deeper consideration of community-based affordable housing needs. As a model and mechanism that combines community-based planning and activist practices with community land ownership and affordable housing solutions, non-profit and non-governmental community land trust (CLT) organisations have been successful in forming in both cities at the neighbourhood level. Indeed, since the 2000s, London's CLT development has grown from initial land ownership negotiations for the creation of the East London Community Land Trust (ELCLT) in 2007 to the recent emergence of a pan-London CLT organisation that encompasses multiple neighbourhood-based and resident-led CLT groups. The formation of CLTs in Toronto, comparatively, has not followed the breadth and size of London's CLT activism since the 2000s but has emerged in localised ways through informal, relational associations between organisational actors within specific neighbourhood contexts. CLTs, in both cities, have formed in response to similar challenges, namely the impacts of market-driven urbanisation primarily identified through the encroachment of gentrification into traditionally affordable neighbourhoods, social displacement, and the difficulties of securing and retaining affordable housing in cities with soaring and increasingly elusive rental housing and homeownership costs.

In addition to seeking to address these issues in their work, CLT organisations in London and Toronto have underlined the CLT model as a community engagement approach that aims to galvanise public discussion about a need for the community ownership and stewardship of land, local solutions for affordable housing and the identification of community needs through participatory engagement. As a community engagement strategy that centres the role of community residents in the formation and maintenance of CLT practices, the proliferation of CLT organisations and community-based land ownership and stewardship in London and Toronto raises important questions regarding the role of community-based, non-governmental organisations in affordable housing provision. As non-state entities, CLTs are self-directed and fairly autonomous but strategically partner with government actors in various ways, particularly in relation to land acquisition, planning approvals and funding arrangements. In both Toronto and London, fairly cooperative relationships between CLT organisational structures and local government are observed that have been cultivated through advocacy on the part of CLT organisations as well as an emerging public interest in alternative models of land tenure in both cities.

In the UK, a more comprehensive approach to government support for CLT organisations has arisen since the 2000s, primarily as a result of the more direct national to local government relationship. A recent outcome of the direct connection between national and city-level governments for CLT growth has been the national government-initiated Community-Led Housing fund that seeks to foster local community-led housing efforts, including funding arrangements for CLT groups. CLT organising has also benefitted from the presence of a National CLT Network that represents CLTs across England and Wales and offers funding and technical expertise to emergent CLTs. In the Canadian context, as result of the jurisdictional arrangements of municipal governance, local governments are regulated and funded by provincial-level governments, and therefore there is an absence of a direct relationship between city-level politics and nationwide governance. The emergence of CLTs in Canada is contained in a localised way as a result, and they have more limited relationships with provincial government legislation and policies and more connectivity with local government structures.

Despite these differences in governance approaches, the emergence of CLTs in London and Toronto can be viewed in the light of a similar and growing movement towards community-based solutions to the ever increasing affordable housing challenges in both cities. It also reflects long-standing interest and activity in neighbourhood-based community engagement and activism in both cities. In this way, CLTs have a role in fostering participation by and between neighbourhood residents in decision-making over community needs for land to be acquired or owned by the CLT organisation. In relation to the emphasis placed on 'community', as underlined in the community land trust model, the participation in the creation of equitable decision-making structures and the preservation of the place-based connections of neighbourhood residents are integral aspects of CLT activism and mobilisation in London and Toronto, and both contexts offer informative examples for the study of CLT organising more broadly.

Defining community land trusts

Over the past several decades, there has been an increasing adoption of the community land trust model across the globe in countries such as the UK (Thompson

2015; Bunce 2016; Moore and McKee 2012), Canada (Bunce and Aslam 2016; Bunce 2018; Bunce and Barndt 2020), Australia (Crabtree 2010, 2014) and Kenya (Midheme and Mouleart 2013). CLT practices first emerged in the United States in the 1960s as a way for African-American tenant farmers in Georgia to acquire and own land and as a component of the larger civil rights struggle in the United States (Curtin and Bocarsly 2010; Davis 2010). The first urban CLT emerged in Cincinnati in the early 1980s, in a downtown neighbourhood with a large number of African-American residents. The CLT was used to protect neighbourhood land from real estate speculation and residents from displacement pressures, and as a method of advocating for community needs. The urban CLT model, largely geared towards these purposes as well as affordable housing provision, quickly took hold in American cities; by 2007 there were approximately 250 urban CLTs, primarily located in cities in the north-eastern United States (Greenstein and Sungu-Erylimaz, 2007).

The Champlain CLT, a community land trust in Burlington, Vermont, became known as a key organisation for defining the CLT model and, due to political interest in this particular CLT, its features were embedded in the official definition of a community land trust that is articulated in the United States' federal Housing and Community Development Act (Davis 2010). This legislation recognised the general characteristics of community land trusts, as non-governmental, non-profit organisations that mobilise to acquire land that is either donated or purchased with organisational funds. More specifically, CLTs hold land in trust for community purposes and place legal restrictions on the future resale of the land and buildings as ways to maintain long-term affordability and prevent profit-making from increased land value and building prices. Structures on CLT land, such as housing, can be owned or leased by members of the CLT organisation, but a firm separation between land ownership and the ownership or lease of structures by individuals is articulated in a ground lease. This ground lease is created by the CLT organisation and identifies the CLT as the landowner, and prevents profit gains from the resale of housing and limits or prohibits rent increases for rental housing owned by the CLT (Davis 2010). The characteristics of the American CLT model have largely been taken up by CLT networks and individual organisations in other countries. Writ large, the general directives of CLTs are to hold title to land for an indefinite period in order to retain affordability and to de-commodify land; separate land ownership from the ownership or lease of any structures on the land through legal contracts; prevent any resale profits; and work with community residents to identify land uses through collaborative decision-making (Aird 2010; Bunce 2016; Bunce et al. 2013; Crabtree 2010, 2014; Davis 2010; DeFilippis et al. 2018; Gray 2008; Meehan 2014; Moore and McKee 2012; Thompson 2015). The dominant focus and outcome of the collaborative practices of CLTs have been the provision of affordable housing for homeownership and/or lease, and more recently the development of social enterprises such as small business incubators, community kitchens, community gardens and urban farms (Yuen 2014; Yuen and Rosenberg 2013).

Community land trusts in Canada and the UK (England and Wales)

CLT organisations have emerged in rural and urban locations in the UK since the 1990s and have grown steadily in numbers since this time, as opposed to the development of CLTs in Canada, which have largely formed in Canadian cities in more ad hoc ways and in smaller numbers since the 1980s. While housing associations in the UK, such as Coin Street Community Builders and Poplar HARCA, both located in London, have been active in community-focused redevelopment and affordable housing provision, a particularly robust and concentrated emergence of CLTs occurred in the 2000s in the UK. This increase occurred through the efforts of Community Finance Solutions, a research centre based at the University of Salford, which had developed professional ties with American CLT organisations and the national CLT network in the United States and was inspired by the American CLT model. Community Finance Solutions, in conjunction with Carnegie UK Trust and Tudor Trust as funding bodies, created two 'incubator' programmes for CLT development in the UK between 2006 and 2010 (Community Finance Solutions 2009; Moore and McKee 2012). In addition to the provision of support to local CLT organisations, the first programme aimed to raise the profile and applicability of the CLT model more broadly and encourage political support for CLTs, the latter of which led to the establishment of a statutory definition of community land trusts in the Labour government's Housing and Regeneration Act of 2008. Both programmes were able to generate enough interest among community-based organisations in the CLT model and jump-start the emergence of CLT organisations. The establishment of the National CLT Network in 2010 marked a further interest in CLT organisational development across England and Wales. The National CLT Network's acquisition of charitable status in 2014 provided an increase in funding, technical and educational assistance to local CLT groups (Scotland, due to differences in land regulations, has its own community land trust umbrella called Community Land Scotland). The proliferation of CLTs in both rural and urban locations in England and Wales was demonstrated in the number of CLT organisations formed over the past decade. By 2013, there were 100 CLT groups across England and Wales (Moore, 2013) and a recent estimate suggests that there are now 290 CLT organisations (National CLT Network 2019). Of importance to this chapter, the formation of CLTs in cities since the mid-2000s, in London as well as in cities such as Bristol, Leeds, Liverpool and Newcastle, has demonstrated the use of the model as a way to alleviate affordable housing pressures, resist gentrification and displacement processes, and advocate for community needs at the neighbourhood scale (Bunce 2016; Thompson 2015).

The growth of CLTs in England and Wales over this period has largely been supported by the existence of amenable national and local political contexts and the existence of both governmental and private philanthropic funding for CLT formation. Yet, as a contradictory element of CLT formation, CLT organisations have also emerged within the context of neoliberal austerity policies that have withdrawn funding for community-based agencies, 'big society' ideas of volunteerism and civic engagement, and a discourse of 'localism' and the downloading of governmental responsibilities to community organisations – directives that have been under-lined and advanced by the recent succession of Conservative governments. It was Theresa May's Conservative government, in its support for 'community-led' initia-tives that rely less on public investment and more on partnership-oriented funding arrangements with private sector bodies, that created favourable legislative condi-tions and funding for community-led housing, primarily through the creation of the Community Housing Fund – a £163 million start-up fund, to be implemented over three years, intended for community-proposed and -led housing initiatives (UK Government 2020). This initiative began in 2018 with funding from the Ministry of Housing, Communities and Local Government (Cooperative Councils Innovation Network 2017; Interview with F. Toomey 2019). The Community Housing Fund is delivered by Community-Led Homes, a programme managed by a consortium of non-governmental organisations such as the National CLT Network, the Confederation of Co-operative Housing, and Locality. In keeping with the gov-ernmental emphasis on partnerships, the Community-Led Homes programme operates concurrently with another programme, Homes in Community Hands, that is managed by Power to Change, a trust that has received funds from the UK's National Lottery Community Fund to provide start-up funding to local community housing groups in areas that are not covered by the Community Housing Fund.

In London, the Community Housing Fund is administered by the Greater London Authority (GLA), which was given £38 million through the Fund until 2023 (more than the three-year time frame). Community-Led Housing London (CLHL) has been allocated £8 million to support new community-led housing groups, with the idea that once the group obtains a development site CLHL then transfers the project to the GLA to fund the development process (personal correspondence with F. Toomey, 12 February 2020). The funding is intended to be directed towards GLA-based community-led housing groups such as community land trusts, com-munity self-build projects and co-housing groups (Community Led Homes 2018; Interview with F. Toomey 2019). CLHL allocates small loans of approximately £40,000 to groups that submit proposals for community-led initiatives. In conjunc-tion with loan allocations, CLHL also provides technical resource information to emerging community-led housing groups.

It is important to note here that although the funding for the Community-Led Homes programme originates with the Ministry of Housing, Communities and Local Government under the directive of the Conservative government, the discourse of the community-led housing movement is socially progressive and focused on empowering communities to address affordable housing constraints and problems. The Community-Led Homes programme refers to 'continuing headlines of housing targets missed, dodgy landlords, Dickensian conditions, block after block of empty luxury apartments ...' (Community Led Homes 2018).

It suggests that community-led housing is 'borne [*sic*] out of people all over the country who have reached the limits of their own frustration with the housing situation (either their own, their children's or the community's) and have decided to take matters into their own hands' (Community Led Homes 2018). On the topic of community empowerment, the programme suggests that 'community led housing isn't about giving people power, it's a mechanism for people to take power and create something better' (Community Led Homes 2018). Setting the rationale for community-led housing within a context of inadequate housing environments, the consequences of luxury flat development and the problems caused by 'on-the-make' landlords points to a critical stance on the conditions set forth by the austerity agenda and neoliberal urban development. It also demonstrates the contradiction that is inherent in the Conservative government's support for community-led housing, where community-led housing projects are funded by the government to try to mitigate some of the social problems that have been created by the government's championing of austerity and other forms of neoliberalism. This contradiction, unfortunately, underwrites some of the narrative of CLT development in the UK. For example, the funding and proliferation of CLT projects have occurred at the same time as large-scale public disinvestment in council housing. In this way, the government's community-led housing policy aims to offload responsibility to community-led housing initiatives such as CLTs to augment this disinvestment but also to address the need for affordability. The size and scope of CLT projects, however, have been small and localised and are not intended to replace the same scale of affordable housing provision as council housing. This also raises a question of how effective CLTs (and other forms of community-led housing) are in meeting the wider quantity of need for affordable housing across the UK. However, the focus on CLTs as a method of community-led housing – which lends itself to local mobilisation around a common issue – offers an emphasis on community-based engagement and development that suggests a range of community benefits and new approaches to housing and land tenure. These tensions and contradictions point to the complexity of the community-led housing agenda.

In Canada, there is no policy or legislative directive for community-led housing, and CLTs primarily organise in a localised and ad hoc way, largely in relation to informal networks of information sharing between existing CLTs across the country. Several CLTs in Canada emerged in the 1980s–2000s to acquire land for affordable housing, some of which were cooperative housing communities that adopted the CLT land ownership approach as a way to protect cooperative housing land from potential resale. From the 2010s onwards there has been a notable increase in neighbourhood-based CLTs that have organised in relation to affordable housing problems and gentrification pressures, galvanised by multi-scalar neoliberal policies (see Chapter 9), in cities such as Vancouver, Hamilton and Toronto. Across Canada, as of 2019, there are approximately 14 CLT organisations in operation (Bunce and Barndt 2020). In the jurisdictional absence of federal government legislation, policy and funding to support CLTs, some provincial governments such as British Columbia have created community land trust legislation to support CLT development. As a result, CLT organisations operate very locally and are left to curate their own relationships with local governments and other community-based, non-governmental organisations that share their perspectives. This situation provides CLT organisations with a certain amount of flexibility in terms of being more autonomous and self-directed, but it also raises challenges in terms of building organisational capacity as well as securing funding. The absence of policy and legislative support, and government funding for CLTs, provides fewer options for the necessary acquisition of funding and also creates more piecemeal support for CLT development across Canada. CLT organisations are thus primarily left on their own to raise their local profile and advocate for public and/or private land donations.

The creation of a non-governmental, cross-Canada network of CLT organisations primarily based in cities, the Canadian CLT Network, in 2015 demonstrated the emergence of broader public interest in and support for the CLT model. The Canadian CLT Network provides educational and technical advice to CLT organisations in a cohesive way and has also started to develop connections with CLT networks in other countries, such as the National CLT Network in the United States. Importantly, the network is also galvanising necessary discussions on CLTs, community land ownership and their relationship in the Canadian context to issues of settler colonialism and the struggles of Indigenous First Nations communities over land rights and justice (Bunce and Barndt 2020).

Community land trusts in London

London-based CLTs have steadily grown in numbers since the formation of the ELCLT in 2007, which was the first CLT organisation in London. The ELCLT was created as a charitable organisation under the umbrella of London Citizens, a member of the UK-wide Citizens UK network which aims to address social justice issues through the development of organisational and activist networks. The development of the ELCLT was unique as it was the first time the CLT model had been considered for use in an urban setting in the UK, and the organisation largely formed to resist the gentrification of London's eastern boroughs (ELCLT 2010). Other localised issues that the ELCLT sought to redress were growing wait lists for council housing, a lack of new build affordable housing and overcrowding problems in existing affordable housing units in boroughs such as Hackney and Tower Hamlets (ELCLT 2010). Through the identification in 2008 of a vacant former National Health Service hospital site, St Clement's, in the Mile End neighbourhood of Tower Hamlets (see Figure 19.1), which was under the ownership of the Homes and Communities Agency (HCA), the ELCLT mobilised to raise public awareness about the CLT model. The organisation conducted extensive community engagement with community groups in the Mile End neighbourhood about potential

Figure 19.1 St Clement's Site, Mile End, London (photograph by S. Bunce)

community uses for the site. These processes were intended to convince the HCA to donate or sell the land at a below market value price to the ELCLT (ELCLT 2010). What followed in subsequent years were challenging practices of building alliances with political actors and raising public support for the CLT (Bunce 2016). A key part of the ELCLT's work was to pursue ownership of the St Clement's site through several public tender bids that were first submitted to the HCA and then to the GLA following the devolution of the HCA's portfolios after the introduction of the Localism Act in 2011. The ELCLT was able to secure a 'land trust arrangement' for the site with the GLA in 2012, as a result of negotiations with the GLA and agreements with Galliford Try, a London-based residential development firm, and Peabody Trust, a local housing association. This arrangement positioned Galliford Try as the primary developer, with the transfer of land title to a 'to-be-determined' community foundation upon completion of the site development. Galliford Try would develop 223 housing units on the site, with 35 per cent of the units for afford-able rental or affordable homeownership (GLA 2012). The ELCLT would own and arrange the sale of approximately 23 of the affordable units, while Peabody Trust would manage the affordable rental units (GLA 2012).

The continued advocacy efforts of the ELCLT (now London CLT) have signifi-cantly altered the shape of the St Clement's site and, in its most recent formation, all the privately developed, rental and CLT homes for purchase are managed by residents (through the St Clement's Resident Management Company) as a way to encourage community governance over the site (London CLT 2019). The freehold of the site will also be owned on an indefinite basis by the Ricardo Community Foundation, a charitable organisation that formed to meet the specifications of the original agreement with the GLA and to act as a CLT (London CLT 2019).

The complex arrangements that were negotiated and undertaken for the St Clement's site underline some of the land acquisition challenges faced by CLT groups in London in the light of high land values and a planning culture that generally supports the sale of public land to private developers. Yet the process of acquiring a land trust arrangement for the St Clement's site has also been pivotal in raising public awareness in London about the benefits of CLTs and the role of community activism in community-owned land and affordable housing. The ELCLT's efforts led to its name change to the London CLT in 2015, and the organisation now acts as an umbrella for newly emergent CLTs across London and the region. It also acts as a model for newly formed CLTs as to how CLT advocacy can work and the types of resources that are required for land acquisition (Interview with H. Emery-Wright 2019).

London CLT collaborates with several community-based organising chapters (groups) of the national social justice network Citizens UK across Greater London boroughs to facilitate land acquisition for CLT use. These groups are located in the boroughs of Lewisham, Lambeth, Croydon and Southwark in south London, Shadwell in the Borough of Tower Hamlets and the Borough of Redbridge in east London. Starting in 2014, the ELCLT began work with Lewisham Citizens to secure a small site on the Brasted Close estate in the Sydenham area of Lewisham (land owned by the Borough of Lewisham), with the political support of Lewisham's mayor (London CLT 2019). London CLT now acts as a direct developer of 11 units of affordable housing on land that was 'gifted' by the Borough of Lewisham to London CLT on a long-term lease for £1 (Interview with H. Emery-Wright 2019). In Lambeth and Shadwell, London CLT collaborates with community groups in each area to identify vacant lands owned by Transport for London (TfL) and the GLA as potential CLT sites. These efforts have involved requesting the GLA's Deputy Mayor for Housing's support in negotiating CLT agreements for three TfL sites in Lambeth. It has included London CLT's involvement in a public tender bid, in 2018, for one of the sites in Brixton Hill (London CLT 2019). As of late 2019, these agreements were not yet finalised but the lands had been 'promised' in principle, with London CLT attempting to acquire funding from the GLA's Small Sites Fund to embark on planning applications for the sites (Interview with H. Emery-Wright 2019). London CLT notes that organising efforts in Croydon, Southwark and Redbridge have been slightly different, with the borough councils taking the lead on affordable housing development on identified CLT lands and London CLT identified as the eventual landowners following development (Interview with H. Emery-Wright 2019).

London CLT has multiple roles in acting as the umbrella CLT organisation for a growing number of CLT projects across London. The organisation provides technical advice and works closely with each of the Citizens UK chapters in the planning and development phases of the individual CLT projects. It also emphasises resident-led social justice and community empowerment through a focus on 'community cohesion' and support for diverse resident representation in CLT initiatives (Interview with H. Emery-Wright 2019). London CLT's activities also emphasise political mobilisation to support community-based CLT work. This has involved utilising the existing localised structures of Citizens UK and connecting with the social justice organising of London Citizens and Citizens UK more broadly, as well as leveraging the public recognition of these organisations to build political alliances. An example of this is the public assemblies that are regularly held by London Citizens, which gather over 4,000 attendees and where CLT organising is discussed (Interview with H. Emery-Wright 2019). In this way, London-based CLTs are part of a larger network of social justice and community organising across the GLA and the UK. In relation to this activist and political engagement, London CLT also arranges funding for the individual CLT projects through connections with various funding sources. Funding for project development has been generated through seed funding given by philanthropic organisations such as the Oak Foundation, as well as by the National CLT Network. London CLT has also submitted a bid to Community-Led Housing London for a loan to support community cohesion in CLT organising efforts in Shadwell and Lambeth (Interview with H. Emery-Wright 2019). In addition to external grants and loans, London CLT allows its members to invest in community shares from £100 upwards. For the Lewisham CLT initiative, this method enabled London CLT to raise £500,000 (Interview with H. Emery-Wright 2019).

London CLT's role as a pan-city umbrella for smaller CLT initiatives provides the ability to connect with emergent CLT and community-led housing initiatives that are not formal projects of London CLT, such as the Rural-Urban Synthesis Society in Lewisham, St Ann's Regeneration Trust in Haringey and NW3 CLT in Hampstead (Interview with H. Emery-Wright 2019). These projects are independent but part of a relational network in which there is awareness of each group's work (Interview with NW3 CLT staff 2019). What is unique about CLT development in London is that there are strong, neighbourhood-based rationales for CLT formation that vary across the city in relation to a broader citywide CLT movement. While many CLTs emerge in relation to gentrification pressures and affordable housing constraints, there is a difference, for instance, in the forms of gentrification that CLT organisations are addressing. London CLT explicitly works with local groups that are highly diverse, with communities that experience racialisation and marginalisation, and in neighbourhoods that have traditionally served the needs of low-income residents. The impacts of gentrification in these areas have created less affordable housing options, a heavier reliance on shared accommodation and a poorly maintained private rental stock (Interview with H. Emery-Wright 2019). NW3 CLT has organised to resist the decline in affordable and social housing in Hampstead – an area that is already gentrified but primarily by affluent 'socially progressive' professionals – in the light of a new and increasing "Chelseafication" of the area (referring to London's affluent Chelsea area). NW3 CLT employs this term to describe the conversion of multi-unit houses into single-family homes with luxury basement space and gated walls, intended for the very wealthy. Further observed in this process is the rise of 'buy to leave' buildings, where luxury properties are increasingly being bought and left vacant – a strategy for 'parking' investment finances (see Chapter 9) (Interview with NW3 CLT staff 2019).

Community land trusts in Toronto

There are two neighbourhood-based CLT organisations in Toronto – Kensington Market CLT and Parkdale Neighbourhood Land Trust – that have also explicitly emerged in relation to gentrification pressures and increasing constraints on affordable housing in the city. Similar to CLT development in London, they have organised in relation to neighbourhood-based issues that are constituted by these broader challenges. Two other land trusts, the Toronto Island Residential Community Trust and the Co-operative Housing Land Trusts, are also active in the city but are not explicitly based on the CLT model and are used to protect public land for existent housing and cooperative housing assets, respectively (Co-operative Housing Federation of Toronto n.d.; Toronto Island Residential Trust Community Corporation 2019). The differences in focus and ad hoc configuration of land trust organisations in Toronto are due to a lessened reliance on the adoption of the American CLT model, by comparison with London and the wider UK, which has resulted in more land trust experimentations that meet different organisational and localised needs within the city. This is symptomatic of the aforementioned lack of structural support for CLT formation in Toronto and across Canada, in terms of the absence of governmental legislation, policy and funding provisions that would require a more official definition for CLT organisations and their practices. Apart from the formation of the Canadian CLT Network, there has not been a formal organisational body to represent CLT groups over time and there is not a Toronto-wide CLT organisation similar to London CLT. As noted, the less 'top-down' and more ad hoc nature of CLT formation in Canada has provided for more flexible and fluid interpretations and implementation of CLT approaches, and this is certainly observable in the Toronto context. The following section, however, will outline the Parkdale Neighbourhood Land Trust (PNLT) and Kensington Market CLT (KMCLT) organisations as Toronto-based initiatives most closely resembling the characteristics of the traditional CLT model.

The PNLT formed as a non-profit, non-governmental organisation in 2014, in the western downtown neighbourhood of Parkdale, as a response to increased residential and commercial gentrification. These processes have been largely visible through quickly rising rents and the conversion of single-room occupancy housing ('rooming houses') intended for lower-income tenants into single-family-owned housing (see Chapter 17). Two primary objectives of the PNLT's work are the acquisition of land to remove it from the speculative market and the fostering of community participation in governance and decision-making over the land (Bunce and Barndt 2020). In terms of land ownership, the PNLT has acquired two properties in Parkdale, the first being a community garden site that was purchased at lower than market value through organisational fundraising efforts. The community garden is actively used by newcomer residents and connected with local environmental and food justice organisations in the neighbourhood such as Greenest City, a Toronto-based environmental group (Bunce 2018). The second site, a 15-unit rooming house, was obtained with capital funding provided for by the City of Toronto government. The acquisition of this site was an outcome of a neighbourhood-wide planning study conducted by the PNLT regarding the significant loss of rooming house units, as well as several years of building political support for PNLT initiatives (Bunce and Barndt 2020). The rooming house property is owned by the Neighbourhood Land Trust (NLT), an organisational arm that is allowed to hold land for charitable purposes and lease land to other charities as prescribed through Canada's restrictive federal charity laws (Bunce and Barndt 2020). In this situation, the rooming house property will be leased by the NLT to the Parkdale Activity Recreation Centre to provide very affordable housing through their supportive housing programme.

The PNLT has explicitly followed the American CLT model by way of research on existing CLT organisations in cities such as Boston, New York City and San Francisco, and it has placed strong emphasis on the role of organisational and neighbourhood-wide governance in the CLT approach. This has involved the formation of a democratic organisational structure and community representation through membership to Parkdale residents, while at the same time holding a core focus on social justice in their work. The PNLT's work has broadened to taking the lead on community planning studies that focus on neighbourhood-wide issues, such as the aforementioned rooming house study, as well as on-the-ground activist events to address gentrification and affordable housing challenges more broadly. This multi-scalar, multi-issue approach has led the PNLT to be at the forefront of an emerging CLT movement in Canada, and the organisation has taken the lead in the formation of the Canadian CLT Network (Bunce and Barndt 2020).

The Kensington Market CLT, located in the residential and commercial market neighbourhood of Kensington in the downtown core of Toronto (see Figure 19.2), was formed in 2017 in response to residential and commercial gentrification pressures. The KMCLT emerged as an offshoot of the Friends of Kensington Market, a resident-led and neighbourhood-based committee that had been actively engaged in protesting the encroachment of 'big-box' retail outlets (a Walmart and a Loblaws supermarket, respectively) on the arterial roads adjacent to the street entrances of Kensington Market. This advocacy was viewed as a way to protect Kensington from corporations that would threaten the traditionally working-class, independent and counter-culture nature of the neighbourhood (Bunce and Barndt 2020). The adoption of the CLT model by Friends of Kensington Market has been utilised with a 'neighbourhood protection' approach and as a way to retrench neighbourhood boundaries in relation to external pressures that negatively impact the traditional character of Kensington. An increase in short-term rentals such as Airbnbs, rising commercial and residential rents, and displacement of long-term residents as a result of more affluent residents moving to the neighbourhood are noted as impetuses for the formation of the KMCLT (Russell in Bunce and Barndt 2020). Over the past several years, KMCLT has been developing an organisational structure, raising local awareness about CLT practices and identifying resident needs through

Figure 19.2   Kensington Market, Toronto (photograph by S. Bunce)

community meetings. This has also involved building alliances with local politicians in order to garner the support of local government. This approach, akin to the PNLT's organising practices, has allowed the KMCLT to build a stronger rationale and context for neighbourhood land acquisition with a focus on attaining land for the purpose of building affordable housing.

The PNLT and KMCLT, as two neighbourhood-based CLTs in Toronto with very similar purposes and approaches, and which regularly connect with one another, are organisations that provide contexts for the formation of other neighbourhood-based CLTs across Toronto and perhaps a Toronto-wide CLT network at some point. The social justice and anti-gentrification perspectives of both organisations are shared by other non-profit community and housing groups in Toronto, and the CLT model provides a community-based, resident-led practice for meeting local needs for community engagement and affordable housing.

Conclusion

London and Toronto share similar urban challenges of gentrification, rising rental and homeownership rates, and a constrained supply of affordable housing; thus the everyday contexts in both cities form a strong rationale for the existence of CLTs as a community-based and -led response to these problems. This is particularly relevant within the larger context of a problematic decrease in government support and funding for social housing in both cities, and a reconfiguration of government support towards community-led housing in the UK context as an outcome of localisation and downloading/offloading. CLTs have emerged as a necessary organisational solution to address these challenges in both cities but with differing scales and breadths of engagement and influence.

While the impacts of luxury property development and rising residential costs in London have exacerbated the need for CLT organisational responses, the representation and outlook of CLT engagement and activism across London appears to be optimistic and buoyed by a robust CLT structure (London CLT) and a network of local CLT projects. This is enhanced by a sufficient national network of organisational support through the National CLT Network, private and governmental funding sources such as the Community Housing Fund, and local political will for CLT land acquisition. The more ad hoc and informal existence of CLTs in Canada, without comprehensive policy and legislative support for CLTs, has resulted in more flexible and very localised adoptions of the CLT model across the country. The absence of comprehensive political support has impacted funding mechanisms for the creation and longevity of CLTs in Canadian cities. In Toronto, however, the PNLT and KMCLT have formed in the light of these deficiencies in public support, with an aim to redress some of these challenges through advocacy for a Canadian CLT Network and by building more public awareness about the benefits of the CLT model in the city.

Community land trust activism and engagement is robust in both London and Toronto, although London has a more geographically and organisationally expansive approach to CLT development aided by policy support, while Toronto's CLTs are distinctly neighbourhood-based in the absence of a Toronto-wide CLT coalition. CLTs in both cities have formed in response to the impacts of gentrification, a tight supply of affordable housing and inadequate public investment in affordable housing, and other policy and planning failures in both cities. In particular, the emergence of neighbourhood-based community land trusts in London and Toronto demonstrates how residents and activist organisations can collaborate to determine how land and affordable housing can be stewarded by and for communities as well as respond to larger city-wide issues.

References

Aird, Jennifer. 2010. 'Reviving Community Ownership in England: CLTs Are Ready to Take Over the Land'. In *The Community Land Trust Reader*, edited by John E. Davis, 449–65. Cambridge, MA: Lincoln Institute of Land Policy.

Bunce, Susannah. 2016. 'Pursuing Urban Commons: Politics and Alliances in Community Land Trust Activism in East London'. *Antipode* 48(1):134–50. https://doi.org/10.1111/anti.12168.

Bunce, Susannah. 2018. *Sustainability Policy, Planning, and Gentrification in Cities*. Abingdon: Routledge.

Bunce, Susannah and Aslam, Farrah Chanda. 2016. 'Land Trusts and the Protection and Stewardship of Land in Canada: Exploring Non-Governmental Land Trust Practices and the Role of Urban Community Land Trusts'. *Canadian Journal of Urban Research* 25(2):23–34. https://doi.org/10.4337/9781785361746.00036.

Bunce, Susannah and Barndt, Joshua. 2020. 'Origins and Evolution of Urban Community Land Trusts in Canada'. In *On Common Ground: International Perspectives on the Community Land Trust*, edited by John E. Davis, Line Algoed and Maria Hernandez-Torres, 93–114. Burlington, VT: Terra Nostra Press.

Bunce, Susannah, Khimani, Noreen, Sungu-Erylimaz, Yesim and Earle, Emily. 2013. *Urban Community Land Trusts: Experiences from Canada, the United States, and Britain*. Toronto: University of Toronto.

Community Finance Solutions. 2009. *Lessons from the First 150 Homes: Evaluation of the National Community Land Trust Demonstration Programme, 2006–2008*. Salford: Community Finance Solutions.

Community Led Homes. 2018. Accessed 23 February 2020. https://www.communityledhomes.org.uk.

Cooperative Councils Innovation Network. 2017. *Community-Led Housing: A Key Role for Local Authorities*. Oldham: Cooperative Councils Innovation Network.

Co-operative Housing Federation of Toronto. n.d. *Co-Op Housing Land Trusts*. Accessed 13 February 2020. https://co-ophousingtoronto.coop/co-op-housing-land-trusts.

Crabtree, Louise. 2010. 'Fertile Ground for CLT Development in Australia'. In *The Community Land Trust Reader*, edited by John E. Davis, 464–76. Cambridge, MA: Lincoln Institute for Land Policy.

Curtin, Julie and Bocarsly, Lance. 2010. 'CLTs: A Growing Trent in Affordable Home Ownership'. In *The Community Land Trust Reader*, edited by John E. Davis, 289–314. Cambridge, MA: Lincoln Institute of Land Policy.

Davis, John (ed.). 2010. *The Community Land Trust Reader*. Cambridge, MA: Lincoln Institute of Land Policy.

DeFilippis, James, Stromberg, Brian and Williams, Olivia. 2018. 'W(h)ither the *Community* in Community Land Trusts'. *Journal of Urban Affairs* 40(6):755–69. https://doi.org/10.1080/07352166.2017.1361302.

ELCLT (East London Community Land Trust). 2010. Interview with staff, London, 11 October.

GLA (Greater London Authority). 2012. 'Mayor Announces Major Step Forward for Capital's First Community Land Trust as Developer is Appointed'. Press Release, 16 July. Accessed 23 February 2020. https://www.london.gov.uk/press-releases-5190.

Gray, Karen. 2008. 'Community Land Trusts in the United States'. *Journal of Community Practice* 16(1):65–78. https://doi.org/10.1080/10705420801977999.

Greenstein, R. and Sungu-Erylimaz, Yesim. 2007. *Community Land Trusts: A Solution for Permanently Affordable Housing*. Cambridge, MA: Lincoln Institute of Land Policy.

London CLT. 2019. Accessed 14 February 2020. https://www.londonclt.org.

Meehan, James. 2014. 'Reinventing Real Estate: The Community Land Trust as a Social Intervention in Affordable Housing'. *Journal of Applied Social Science* 8(2):113–33. https://doi.org/10.1177/1936724414497480.

Midheme, Em and Mouleart, Frank. 2013. 'Pushing Back the Frontiers of Property: Community Land Trusts and Low-Income Housing in Kenya'. *Land Use Policy* 35:73–84. https://doi.org/10.1016/j.landusepol.2013.05.005.

Moore, Thomas. 2013. 'Community Land Trusts Across the Pond'. *Shelterforce: The Voice of Community Development*, August.

Moore, Thomas and McKee, Kim. 2012. 'Empowering Local Communities? An International Review of Community Land Trusts'. *Housing Studies* 27(2):280–90. https://doi.org/10.1080/02673037.2012.647306.

National CLT Network 2019. 'History of CLTs'. Accessed 16 February 2020. http://www.communitylandtrusts.org.uk

Thompson, Matthew. 2015. 'Between Boundaries: From Commoning and Guerilla Gardening to Community Land Trust Development in Liverpool'. *Antipode* 47(4):1021–42. https://doi.org/10.1111/anti.12154.

Toronto Island Residential Community Trust Corporation. 2019. Accessed 13 February 2020. http://torontoisland.org/trust.

UK Government. 2020. 'Community Housing Fund'. Accessed 23 February 2020. https://www.gov.uk/government/collections/community-housing-fund.

Yuen, Jeffrey. 2014. 'City Farms on CLTs'. *Land Lines*, April.

Yuen, Jeffrey and Rosenberg, Greg. 2013. 'Hanging on to the Land'. *Shelterforce: The Voice of Community Development*, February.

Community, activism and engagement: A commentary

Loren March and Susan Moore

Who indeed is activist now?

The chapters in Part III speak to the widening range of actor 'types' labelled as activist or participating in variegated forms and platforms of activism in Toronto and London. From the outlook presented here, the two cities seem to be converging with respect to the range of activisms across each city, coming from all walks of life. Some maintain their grassroots credentials in the traditional sense of community-based and -led mobilisation through protesting, campaigning and lobbying against real social inequities of the urban experience. But might we also consider some government bodies, such as local authorities (i.e. London boroughs), to be activists? It is a struggle in many ways to equate March's (Chapter 15) DIY artists, living and producing their outputs secretly in the shadows of the emblematic skyline of the 'Creative City' that is Toronto, with the special purpose development vehicles mobilising from within local London boroughs – the purpose of the latter being essentially to capture the market value portion of the 'affordable housing' offer in order to meet its social housing commitments and more generally sustain long-term fiscal integrity in the face of austerity-riven desperation in a zero-funding reality. And yet, as we see in these chapters, their motivations, structures, practices and ideologies are colliding – or at least 'rubbing along' (Watson 2017) – arguably out of pure necessity and pragmatism.

Pragmatism appears as a form of 'making-do' observed through the manifold tactics of resistance to the status quo or to the constant threat of displacement, the championing of alternative models of community planning through subversive and persistent social infrastructure development (as per Bunce's community land trusts, Ostanel's Parkdale, or Sendra and Fitzpatrick's West Ken and Gibbs Green) as well as through repurposing and rebranding neoliberal entrepreneurialism (Penny's local housing companies) under the dubious guise of a benevolent manager struggling to provide a local 'progressive fix' to the housing crisis. Indeed, there is evidence herein of the blurring or hybridising practices of public and private actors in the wake of government retrenchment driven by austerity and neoliberalism, as well as the evolving nature of activism and planning for long-term equity and local survival under such conditions. The advance of austerity-induced funding cutbacks and neoliberalism consolidated under the Conservative Ontario Provincial Government's so-called common sense revolution in the 1990s (noted in Ostanel and March) has dramatically propelled Toronto into the present, and its long-term consequences are still being navigated by local communities and activists on the ground even as new waves of provincial Conservative cutbacks begin to come into effect. Meanwhile, the post-crisis 'austerity urbanism' in London described by Penny (Chapter 16) and Sendra and Fitzpatrick (Chapter 18) has resulted in a wide range of policy and local governance experiments with repercussions, both positive and negative, at the neighbourhood scale but with the potential to impact citywide patterns in new housing provision, security of tenure and democratic accountability.

The chapters in Part III all emphasise the increasing pressure placed on community actors by the intensifying housing crises firmly embedded in both cities. Toronto has now, apparently, outstripped London and San Francisco as the sixth least affordable housing market in the world (16th Annual Demographia Ranking 2020 Survey). The grip of unaffordability in each city may have been fuelled by different governance mechanisms and development cultures (as discussed in Parts I and II) but with the ubiquity of this experience comes a type of collective enlightenment that seems to be reinforcing new patterns of mobilisation and activism in the name of affordable housing and anti-gentrification, in particular. One could argue there is a kind of 'ambient' knowledge of planning, development and housing concerns hitherto unseen among the general public.

Some of this knowledge has certainly emerged out of everyday lived realities, out of experiences of being evicted or of having to navigate bureaucracies and legal or planning frameworks. Tenant organising and coalition-building is an increasingly common phenomenon across both Toronto and London, rooted largely in collective experiences of housing precarity, with many more people acutely affected by this with the recent onset of the COVID-19 pandemic. Social networks and everyday practices contribute to the development of an elaborate 'human infrastructure' on the ground. While infrastructure is often understood in terms of physical systems of roads, pipes and wires, the human activities that serve to render life more liveable might also be thought of as important and invisibilised infrastructural developments (Simone 2004). Organisers learn from one another, as well as from the past, sharing knowledge, tactics and models for survival. Connections, solidarities and even interdependencies are formed. Activisms often depend upon the functioning of this infrastructure, upon its preparedness and adaptiveness, upon the ability and willingness of residents and allies to collaborate or cooperate with one another, and upon their adeptness at engaging with complex institutional arrangements. Housing becomes a site where such an infrastructure converges, formed out of a multitude of different experiences, skills and practices, and out of a shared need and desire to stay in place.

Housing has also arguably become a crisis increasingly impacting not just lower-income residents but also the middle classes. In part, then, this cognisance might also have something to do with the levels of educational attainment in both London and Toronto, the discourse of 'middle-class' sensibilities and a generational shift to digital literacy. Indeed, the instantaneous and asynchronous formation and dissemination of highly context-specific social media (including NextDoor, Twitter, Facebook, Instagram, etc.) has arguably changed who and how one is activist now, especially in relation to real-time experiences of locality and place. More than ever before society can take part in campaigns, protests and lobbying without leaving their homes, without interacting with anyone face to face. Digital petitions (e.g. change.org) are part of the daily passive diet of social media intake for most of us.

The understanding of social media platforms as experiential infrastructures of everyday urban communications (Rodgers and Moore 2020) suggests that we might look at the types of activism in London and Toronto as emergent forms of a new urban public life. Normally this prompts debates about the emancipatory properties of social media to encourage and promote public participation versus the ambiguities of the monopolistic algorithmic curation of user contributions and meta-data (van Dijck 2013). Beyond the ease of accessing, following or becoming part of a local debate by virtue of posting a comment or 'liking' a tweet, platform-mediated participation is essentially now normalised within the governance of urban life. The subtle urban power structures exhibited through social media discourse (i.e. some issues and concerns being hotly contested, antagonistic and divisive, others generating consensus and/or digitally mediated echo chambers or filter bubbles) appear to delineate what Margetts et al. (2016: 34) refer to as a new pace and reach of local urban affairs 'built around tiny acts of political participation':

> innumerable, publicly expressed – and often archived – claims, commentaries, anxieties, or bits of content relating to an urban neighbourhood and its transformation. These tiny acts particularly in conjunction with mobile technologies, subsist especially well when users react, comment and share with others in apparent 'real-time'.

But the aggregate impact of these multiple tiny acts of political participation or 'ambient participation' (Rodgers et al. forthcoming) can also build into forceful catalysts and emotional triggers for organised forms of protest and opposition. Thus the question emerges as to whether or not activism spurred by social media is only activism when it takes shape in face-to-face physical protest. Yet concurrently, one could argue, we are witnessing in both cities a resurgence in public contestation and physical protest in the traditional sense of rallies, marches and strikes. London's 2015 'March for Homes' at City Hall (see Townsend and Kelly 2015) drew thousands demanding a political response from then London Mayor Boris Johnson (Prime Minister at the time of writing) to the lack of affordable housing in the capital, out-of-control private rent increases and the planned demolition and redevelopment of approximately 70 housing estates across London, with a net loss in social units. Similar throngs converged on Westminster in March 2016 to oppose the controversial Housing Bill.

In Toronto (and other Canadian cities, such as Montreal) increasing public and media awareness of 'renoviction' (Mancini and Common 2019) practices, a neologism for a rent-gap model of gentrification but in high-demand areas (near-to-zero vacancy rates spur speculative redevelopment by landlords and severe rent increases for sitting tenants), led to tenant protests in late 2019. Rent strikes and direct action are tactics now commonly used by tenants against major property management firms seeking 'above-guideline' rent increases that go beyond limits imposed by provincial legislation (Goffin 2018; Isai 2018). Concurrently the release of the city's Housing NOW Initiative, which will produce 3,700 affordable housing units on 11 sites across the city, is being met with resistance and lobbying from the likes of ACORN (Association of Community Organizations for Reform Now), challenging the definition of 'affordable' based on average market rents. Extensive consultations for the newly released 10-year HousingTO Plan also raise the issue of how 'affordable' is defined and calculated, the result of which has been the city's stated commitment to adopting a new income-based definition in 2020. The definition of 'affordable housing' in the London context is equally controversial – at 80 per cent market rents, the irony of which Penny points out: these rents are further inflated by the very same developments being touted by local authorities as flagship regeneration schemes.

All the chapters in Part III mention the lack of affordable housing and the increasing threats of residential displacement due to perceived forms of state-led gentrification, particularly via large-scale urban redevelopment and regeneration schemes. The spectrum of activists and activisms addressed in these chapters all foreground the serious challenges faced by policy-makers, communities and activists alike. Ostanel (Chapter 17) and Sendra and Fitzpatrick (Chapter 18) suggest that 'successful' activism occurs when policy is influenced, changed or even reversed. In these chapters the social infrastructure development pathway is outlined, and Ostanel's timeline visually demonstrates the piecemeal but tenacious process in which policy and programmatic changes in city governance culminated in the community benefit impact and inclusionary zoning policy discourse. Sendra and Fitzpatrick demonstrate the increasing prevalence of more locally responsive policy, precipitating U-turns, rethinks and alternative regeneration strategies. For the land trusts discussed by Bunce (Chapter 19), success in the struggle can take many forms, from gaining legitimacy, public support and visibility, to successful coalition-building, to a community's acquisition of land. Bunce speaks to the importance of advocacy efforts in shaping community development, pointing to a variety of arrangements and agreements between community land trusts and state actors reached largely through the development of broad coalitional support and mounting pressure from activists. The cases presented are all high-profile and visible at the neighbourhood scale, speaking to the importance of public support. Yet the perpetuation of DIY activism described by March reminds us that beyond the headline-grabbing cases, there are countless others individually or collectively existing in precarity, hidden behind garage doors and in sound-proofed back rooms that are still out of the realm of policy influence, and some would prefer it stayed that way.

'Successful activism' often comes with costs. These chapters speak to the challenges activists face as they mitigate the effects of structural issues at the local level and attempt to build community capacity both in the absence of real local government action and in the face of top-down government initiatives that can sometimes serve to aggravate problems. Many speak to a kind of double-bind between the importance of community-based organising in this setting, and the resulting implications of this increased and sustained pressure put on communities and non-governmental organisations. The risks of depoliticisation, absorption or instrumentalisation of more radical activist communities are evident in many chapters. The activists in Ostanel's Parkdale negotiate a careful line between engaging the state and developers and maintaining the local community's control over development. For the community land trusts Bunce explores in both Toronto and London, different forms of collaboration and strategic partnerships with state actors are often necessary routes to achieving goals. In the case of Toronto's DIY creative communities, as explored in March, alternative scenes, largely occupied by creatives, are caught between the potential benefits and drawbacks of both visibility and invisibility and are deeply entangled in the very processes which put them at risk. Meanwhile, in Penny's exploration of the case of the financialisation of council housing in London, we see a very severe case of this, with borough councils shifting their very functions under intense housing pressures and dramatically transforming into entrepreneurial property developers – a step that some herald as localism at work and others critique as the end of the welfare state. Indeed, under current circumstances 'success' takes many forms and may sometimes seem to come up short, especially for those who are most affected.

It is important to underline the ways in which the struggles these chapters foreground are heavily tinged by compounded issues of race, class, gender, bodily ability, mental health and citizenship. In London, the tragedy of Grenfell Tower attests to how some of the city's most vulnerable residents, who are disproportionately racialised, are deemed disposable and funnelled into compromised living situations. Arguments for the redevelopment of social housing estates in London are entwined with racially charged narratives of places such as the Heygate or the Aylesbury as dangerous 'badlands' or 'no-go' zones that need to be torn down (Romyn 2019), just as accusations of 'social cleansing' have accompanied redevelopment schemes. Yet Bunce (Chapter 19) illustrates how some community land trusts in London are explicitly working with diverse, racialised and marginalised low-income communities in the struggle against displacement due to gentrification.

In Toronto's Parkdale, the activist community we find in Chapter 17 includes many psychiatric survivors (largely patients discharged from psychiatric hospitals following Ontario's provincial deinstitutionalisation in favour of 'community-based care') who have needed and used the local ecology of service providers, and who largely make up the tenancy of the neighbourhood's tiny 'bachelorette' apartments (akin to 'bedsits' in London) and rooming houses (see also Slater 2004). The needs of this community have heavily informed local organising around housing. We might also consider how, more broadly, Toronto's urban development is deeply entangled with settler colonialism, white supremacy and racism, and how the ripple effects of restructuring at the level of the city are always unevenly felt in this regard. High-profile local community activists such as Desmond Cole, Sandy Hudson, Robyn Maynard and Syrus Marcus Ware, just to name a few, all attest to the violence disproportionately suffered by Indigenous people, people of colour and especially Black communities in Toronto. Disinvestment, abandonment and gentrification in the city can and should be understood as ongoing 'racialized class projects' (Rankin and McLean 2015). As both Ostanel (Chapter 17) and March (Chapter 15) hint, the upscaling of the city's downtown increasingly pushes marginalised groups, including refugees, immigrants and people of colour, out to the peripheries or to the urban 'in-between' (Young and Keil 2014). Community organising and activism around rights to housing, space and place can be observed across many of the surrounding region's largely underserved suburban tower neighbourhoods (March and Lehrer 2019; Parlette and Cowen 2011). Meanwhile, both grassroots and individually taken initiatives are important ways to help downtown residents hang onto their neighbourhoods, their communities and their individual homes or spaces. Yet in the city's increasingly affluent centre, we might note the ways in which the advent of 'hipster urbanism' (Cowen 2006) has made activism itself highly gentrifiable and potentially consolidated a privileged and 'enlightened' white middle-class presence in many activist movements (Epstein 2018). Going forward, artist-led activism, community-led development and community land trusts might be prime sites of survival, resistance and emergence where we ought to also critically keep watch for such phenomena, which serve to exclude marginalised people.

The important roles of community activism, organising and mutual aid in situations of necessity have been brought to the fore amid the rapid spread of COVID-19. The pandemic itself and the deployed mitigation strategies (which largely include the demand to 'stay at home') have had serious impacts on residents in these cities, especially among the most marginalised communities. In Toronto, we can observe increased tenant organising and activism around the question of rent (e.g. the Keep Your Rent movement, led largely by Parkdale Organize), as well as the proliferation of mutual aid networks across the city, and heightened engagement with DIY practices. Established community organisations and informal networks have emerged to fill the gaps where government policy is falling short. In London, where homelessness is on the rise (with the number of persons considered homeless on any given night in 2019 having increased by more than 2,000 since 2018), growing concern for how to ensure safe accommodation and isolation zones for the most vulnerable in society has produced a series of emergency funding schemes and local campaigns to deliver temporary pop-up 'safe villages'. Local Gofundme campaigns such as 'Project Parker' in Walthamstow, east London, are occurring across the city to ensure homeless populations are safely housed, screened and cared for during the pandemic, to avoid further community transmission. But there are still thousands of Londoners living on the edge of the poverty line who will struggle to avoid debt arrears and the threat of eviction during and following the pandemic. For many, foodbanks and the generosity and compassion of neighbourhood networks and groups loosely mobilised via platforms such as WhatsApp are changing how localised issues of inequality are experienced, shared and addressed.

Global-scale processes of restructuring influence and sometimes outweigh the power of local policy in cities, undermining local power through trends of privatisation and capitalist market orientation. But local actors and socio-political logics are clearly also at play in urban processes, capable of producing new and emancipatory forms of urbanity. The chapters included here speak to activities taken up at the city, neighbourhood and even household level to wrestle with (near-universal) processes of restructuring. They speak to the very different forms and trajectories that agency, action and community activism can take, depending on local contexts, and reveal multi-scalar dynamics of power at work in both Toronto and London. Some of the examples drawn out in these chapters suggest strong forms of resistance and long-term alternative viability, if they can be given the right kind of sustained support, while others approach these new governance models with scepticism. The field of actors perceived as activists is diversifying, as are the types of actions we might perceive in this light. Multiple activisms are emerging in Toronto and London, indicative of a broader shift in public resistance to particular manifestations of social injustice, austerity and neoliberal governance.

References

Cowen, Deborah. 2006. 'Hipster Urbanism'. *Relay* 13:22–3.
Demographia. 2020. *16th Annual Demographia International Housing Affordability Survey: 2020*. St Louis, MO: Demographia.
Epstein, Griffin. 2018. 'A Kinder, Gentler Gentrification: Racial Identity, Social Mix and Multiculturalism in Toronto's Parkdale Neighbourhood'. *Social Identities: Journal for the Study of Race, Nation and Culture* 24(6):707–26. https://doi.org/10.1080/13504630.2017.1310039.
Goffin, Peter. 2018. 'Parkdale Tenant Strike Expected to End after Landlord Backs Down on Rent Increase'. *Toronto Star*, 26 March. Accessed 22 July 2020. https://www.thestar.com/news/gta/2018/03/26/parkdale-tenant-strike-expected-to-end-after-landlord-backs-down-on-rent-increase.html.
Isai, Vjosa. 2018. 'Are Rent-strikes the New War Plan for Priced-out Tenants?' *Toronto Star*, 27 March. Accessed 22 July 2020. https://www.thestar.com/news/gta/2018/03/27/are-rent-strikes-the-new-war-plan-for-priced-out-tenants.html.

Mancini, Melissa and Common, David. 2019. '"Renoviction" Rates Soar Due to Big-city Housing Crunch'. CBC News, 30 December. Accessed 22 July 2020. https://www.cbc.ca/news/canada/renovictions-housing-shortage-1.5400594.

March, Loren and Lehrer, Ute. 2019. 'Verticality and the Role of Resident Participation in Revitalizing Suburban High-rise Buildings'. *Canadian Journal of Urban Research* 28(1):65–85.

Margetts, Helen, John, Peter, Hale, Scott and Yasseri, Taha. 2016. *Political Turbulence: How Social Media Shape Collective Action*. Princeton, NJ: Princeton University Press.

Parlette, Vanessa and Cowen, Deborah. 2011. 'Dead Malls: Suburban Activism, Local Spaces, Global Logistics'. *International Journal of Urban and Regional Research* 35(4):794–811. https://doi.org/10.1111/j.1468-2427.2010.00992.x.

Rankin, Katharine and McLean, Heather. 2015. 'Governing the Commercial Streets of the City: New Terrains of Disinvestment and Gentrification in Toronto's Inner Suburbs'. *Antipode* 47(1):216–39. https://doi.org/10.1111/anti.12096.

Rodgers, Scott and Moore, Susan. 2020. 'Platform Phenomenologies: Social Media as Experiential Infrastructures of Urban Public Life'. Chapter 14 in *Urban Platforms and the Future City: Transformations in Infrastructure, Knowledge, Governance and Everyday Life*, edited by J. Stehlin, M. Hodson and J. Kasmire. London: Routledge, 209–22.

Rodgers, Scott, Moore, Susan and Ballatore, Andrea. Forthcoming. 'Ambient Participation: Social Media Temporalities and the Experience of Urban Transformation'. In preparation.

Romyn, Michael. 2019. '"London Badlands": The Inner City Represented, Regenerated'. *London Journal: A Review of Metropolitan Society Past and Present* 44(2):133–50. https://doi.org/10.1080/03058034.2019.1584483.

Simone, Abdoumaliq. 2004. 'People as Infrastructure: Intersecting Fragments in Johannesburg'. *Public Culture* 16(3):407–29. https://doi.org/10.1215/08992363-16-3-407.

Slater, Tom. 2004. 'Municipally Managed Gentrification in South Parkdale, Toronto'. *Canadian Geographer* 48(3):303–25. https://doi.org/10.1111/j.0008-3658.2004.00062.x.

Townsend, Mark and Kelly, Liam. 2015. 'Thousands Gather in London to Protest against Lack of Affordable Housing'. *The Guardian*, 31 January. Accessed 22 July 2020. https://www.theguardian.com/society/2015/jan/31/hundreds-gather-london-march-for-homes-protest-city-hall-affordable-housing.

van Dijck, Jose. 2013. *The Culture of Connectivity: A Critical History of Social Media*. Oxford: Oxford University Press.

Watson, Sophie. 2017. 'Making Multiculturalism'. *Ethnic and Racial Studies* 40(15):2635–52. https://doi.org/10.1080/01419870.2016.1262543.

Young, Douglas and Keil, Roger. 2014. 'Locating the Urban In-between: Tracking the Urban Politics of Infrastructure in Toronto'. *International Journal of Urban and Regional Research* 38(5):1589–608. https://doi.org/10.1111/1468-2427.12146.

Conclusion: Critical dialogues on urban governance, development and activism in London and Toronto

Alan Walks, Susannah Bunce, Nicola Livingstone, Loren March and Susan Moore

While comparison is always a fraught exercise, it can produce important insights when conducted in sensitive and nuanced ways. In the search for common patterns and shared experiences, differences matter as much as similarities. The studies represented in this volume, while not seeking to compare like for like in systematic fashion, through their focus on unique, locally important processes and practices in each urban region nonetheless shed considerable light on the ways in which trends in globalisation, neoliberalisation and financialisation have affected urban development patterns. Although differing in scale, history and position within global trade and financial networks, London and Toronto share many of the challenges and experiences associated with contemporary urban change in global cities of the developed world. What can be learned from the comparative case studies documented in this volume?

There are at least three key conclusions that might be gleaned from our analysis of the case studies. Firstly, while the details differ considerably, both the London and Toronto case studies demonstrate the fragmentation of urban governance under neoliberalism and its relationship to contemporary urban development processes, as well as the importance of a multi-scalar politics to the ways such fragmentation has evolved. Secondly, although again the details differ, both Toronto and London have experienced pressures on their land and housing markets related to their incorporation into global circuits of capital investment, and this might be additionally included as one of the criteria making each place a 'global' city, as might also the serious social and political challenges that result from this. London and Toronto are therefore exemplars of both the successes and the failures of what might be called global real estate capitalism. Thirdly, in both London and Toronto, radical ambiguities are involved in the political evolution of neoliberal policies, as well as the political implications of the relationships between the global, the national and local politics. Not only is each city at the cutting edge of global processes, but community development and activism in each place are at the cutting edge of contemporary urban social movements, making the outcomes of both globalisation and neoliberalism destabilised and uncertain in both cities. Below we discuss each of these, highlighting the importance of the case study findings for promoting critical dialogues on urban governance, development and activism.

The fragmented nature of neoliberal urban governance and the politics of scale

Although it has been articulated in different forms in each city, both London and Toronto have witnessed a shift in the ways that urban development and governance are understood under the process of neoliberalisation. In general, the latter has been implemented through policies that roll back welfare state protections and promote privatisation of public assets and services, and that roll out new market-based models which empower private sector actors to profit from taking over selected urban functions, including financial firms. Yet neoliberalism and neoliberalisation are not monolithic processes, nor a monolithic ideology. The implementation of neoliberal policies has had a number of different implications in each place, but these differences themselves reveal some general patterns. Regardless, one key outcome has been the jurisdictional and spatial fragmentation of planning and governance functions in both cities, with implications for the development of politics in global cities.

Within London, neoliberalisation has been driven in part by austerity agendas enacted by the state at the national level which then force local municipalities to search for budgetary savings, but also by the state's agenda to privatise public lands and to harness roll-out market-based solutions to traditional urban problems such as housing estate regeneration and transportation. There has in turn been a rise in private sector firms tasked with previously public sector activities, including parks maintenance, housing estate regeneration, transport planning, and hospital and school rebuilding, often via public–private partnerships which privilege the private actors in the process. The boroughs within Greater London have adopted different ways of relating to this larger process, often by creating different planning regulations and practices, as well as differing approaches to new infrastructure and housing development. Even at the scale of Greater London, as Chapters 3 and 5 (by De Souza and De Magalhães, respectively) make plain, a fragmented approach to issues that otherwise normally appear as universal and consistent (such as park maintenance and management, and/or private rental housing regulation) has arisen in an attempt to find local solutions – often in accordance with the needs of local private actors – to citywide problems. This is producing a new hybrid and fragmented form of the public realm, in which the degree of 'publicness' (to use the words of De Magalhães) varies in significant but often subtle ways, and where the possibility of public control is elusive and secondary to the security of profits ensconced in the long-term contracts given to private sector firms. At the same time, as Chapter 12 by Short and Livingstone demonstrates, larger common pressures remain, including challenges related to providing sympathetic and appropriate regeneration in increasingly obsolete housing estates, and building new housing at higher densities to improve housing supply and affordability.

In turn, many of the challenges of the contemporary global city, including high levels of inequality, the need for greater transport infrastructure and the shortage of affordable housing, become layered on top of fragmented governance systems that ultimately work to promote private interests and that continue to displace the poor from valuable land. Thus has arisen a politics of scale within London, in which local councils and the Greater London Authority devise local policies that attempt to walk a fine line between promoting urban development and countering the most visible and egregious outcomes of that development. It is somewhat ironic that in the ultimate 'global city' – dependent on its connections to the rest of the world for the livelihood of many of its residents – it helps politically to blame global actors for such challenges and to deflect attention from the actions and interests of local actors who profit from this development.

Neoliberalisation in Toronto has come with some different flavours than in London. Although public–private partnerships have been used in limited ways (to build a hospital and a toll highway, and to redevelop a social housing estate and a downtown park, for example), such forms of roll-out neoliberalism are less advanced in Toronto than in London, and many traditional urban functions (such as park maintenance and management, and public transport) remain in public hands (either at the local municipal level or at the provincial level). Austerity in Toronto has come in select waves, always as the result of the election of a right-wing Conservative Party government at the (Ontario) provincial level, which is the level of government with ultimate authority over municipalities in Canada. During the late 1990s, and more recently with the 2018 provincial election, Toronto faced 'roll-back' attacks on its governance institutions (including regional government in 1998) and cutbacks to its budget and/or ability to tax (municipalities in Ontario are only allowed to implement taxes with permission of the provincial government, which can also mandate what the rates must be and how they are calculated and collected). However, the unintended (or perhaps intended) negative effects of such roll-back agendas often have not been addressed, but instead have been allowed to fester, and this has helped produce more fragmented planning and governance systems, as has occurred in London.

For instance, cutbacks to City of Toronto budgets have meant that new funding for the repair, regeneration and maintenance of local city infrastructure (including parks) usually had to be negotiated through Section 37 agreements with developers, in which developers agree to make payments in return for permission to build (this is similar to Section 106 and the Community Infrastructure Levy in the UK). This incentivises municipalities to seek out and prioritise new development (often high-end condominium developments), making them boosters for local developers. However, as Chapter 13 by Biggar and Siemiatycki shows, developers often want to build in desirable downtown areas. The result is that infrastructure upgrades most often benefit gentrifying areas. This itself creates a fragmented governance landscape, in which planning negotiations take on very different tones in different neighbourhoods, which have increasingly different social compositions (with gentrifying neighbourhoods increasingly white, while less desirable neighbourhoods in the inner suburbs are increasingly racialised). Similarly, although all the former municipalities of the old Metropolitan Toronto regional structure were amalgamated into one single City of Toronto in 1998, many of the planning regulations and laws of those former municipalities remained on the books, creating a fragmented landscape of 'ghost' regulations that should no longer exist (given those former municipalities no longer exist) but which still 'haunt' urban development processes in negative ways (such as forbidding rooming houses and secondary rental suites in many neighbourhoods, despite a citywide planning regulation granting universal and consistent permission). Meanwhile, many of the suburban municipalities outside the boundaries of the new City of Toronto have been left untouched by such provincial government attacks and neoliberalisation processes, mostly because those suburban residents tend to vote for Conservative politicians.

Such fragmented governance landscapes produce a somewhat novel politics of scale around urban development. This politics of scale operates both laterally/horizontally between the central city and the suburbs, and globally/vertically between the local, the national and the global. Laterally, new dichotomies have arisen between the interests of suburban locales – both those within the central city and those beyond their boundaries – and the inner cores of the central cities. It is the latter in London and Toronto that are most targeted by developers for higher-end development, and where it is profitable to 'regenerate' older lower-income communities (including social/council housing estates) into mixed-income communities. Given global investors often have familiarity with the downtown, can gauge its value and even often want to live there, it is the inner cores that have benefitted the most from global flows of investment. National policies promoting neoliberalisation have also promoted gentrification of the inner cores by reducing regulations, making finance more accessible and, with the withdrawal of the welfare state, reducing the ability of low-income communities to remain in place. Suburban areas not witnessing such influxes of investment, and which often then remain 'left behind' and must absorb low-income households displaced from gentrifying neighbourhoods, come to resent such processes. Even middle-class suburban areas – including those outside the boundaries of the central city municipalities – resent the capacity of the inner core to attract development that in the past might have gone into new development at the edges, in housing but also retail, infrastructure and other amenities. One result is that suburban voters elect Conservative governments that promise to attack the so-called liberal elites of the central cities, without understanding it is usually Conservative (neoliberal) Party policies that have produced the outcomes they resent (see also Walks 2004).

Meanwhile, contemporary urban development processes also produce a new politics of scale between the local and the global (and to some extent national) levels. Global cities such as London and Toronto, as Chapter 11 by Hawes and Grisdale (and others) attest, have seen housing units taken off the long-term rental housing market over recent decades and shifted into the short-term market servicing tourists and visitors (often through prominent short-term rental sites such as Airbnb), at the same time that their rental markets have become severely unaffordable to local tenants. While the COVID-19 pandemic closed some borders and significantly reduced influxes of visitors looking for short-term rentals, the damage had already been done and the rental markets of both cities remain the most expensive in their respective nations.

Furthermore, global cities such as Toronto and London derive much of their national and global competitive advantage from hosting the largest concentrations of financial services firms in each country, financial firms which have increasingly made their profits through innovations in mortgage finance, including finance for buy-to-let investors purchasing units for the short-term (e.g. Airbnb) rental market. The contradictions involved in these dual processes have in turn produced a scalar politics that is equally contradictory. Municipal politicians (including those of the Greater London Authority), and even politicians at upper levels of the state (such as the provincial government in Ontario), have found it politically beneficial to take advantage of what Raco and Livingstone call 'knowledge gaps' about the planning process, allowing such politicians to make political claims, without evidence, but which deflect attention from wider institutional problems and processes. For instance, in the Toronto context, politicians have pointed the finger at foreign investors and buyers, often through (as discussed in Chapter 9 by Walks) special taxes on home purchase by foreign buyers, despite the evidence that foreign buyer demand has paled in relation to local demand and investment in housing, and despite the stated objective of these cities to court foreign investment (as noted for London in Chapter 1 by Raco and Livingstone). As cities with traditionally very high levels of immigration and racial diversity, it is not clear how a balance between promoting local interests versus global investment and cosmopolitanism might be attained within this politics of scale. As noted below, this is one reason why the fragmentation of governance in global cities such as London and Toronto contains such 'radical ambiguities' (Raco and Livingstone's term) in its potential political effects. The political effects of the COVID-19 pandemic, with borders closed and non-locals blamed for importing disease, adds additional layers of complexity to such radical ambiguities.

London and Toronto as exemplars of *global real estate capitalism* and its failures

A key commonality linking London and Toronto, often repeated in the chapters in this book, is that they are the financial centres of their respective nations. While true, it is important to inquire what this means within contemporary processes of globalisation and financialisation. Just what, exactly, has been most financialised? Which asset classes have received the most investment from the many new financial innovations centred in cities such as London and Toronto? While infrastructure such as toll bridges, sewer systems and railways (as noted in Chapters 4 and 6, by Enright and Durrant, respectively) have become assetised in the process, and while many financial derivatives and other securities were created to facilitate trade with nations of different currencies in the context of floating exchange rates (McNally 2009), by far the largest asset class benefitting from the global flows of capital made possible by innovations in finance since the early 2000s has been housing. It is housing – for owner occupation, for individual investors in the buy-to-let market, as well as increasingly purpose-built rental housing being bought by real estate investment trusts and other large-scale financial firms – that is the main recipient of the 'wall of money' that has flooded into financial markets (Aalbers 2016) and that provides investors across the globe with flows of interest payments (Fields 2019).

London and Toronto have attained prominence as global cities, therefore, in part because of their role as financial centres in creating *a contemporary global capitalism based on real estate investment*. If it were not for investment into, and appreciation of the value of, housing markets around the world, including (especially) their own local housing markets, London and Toronto would not have witnessed near the level of growth in employment, population and incomes that they have since at least the mid-1980s. Lefebvre (2003, orig. 1970) presciently suggested in 1970 that a new form of capitalism was following and supplanting the old one based on industrialisation. This new form is based on urbanisation, including real estate investment in the cities in what he called a new 'urban revolution'. London and Toronto are the outcome of this new form of capitalism. Indeed, as many of the chapter studies in this book reveal, problems related to real estate development are among the most cogent and contested planning issues facing both cities, as well as the source of struggles facing many of those who work and live in them. Even infrastructure development (as noted in Chapters 4 and 6 by Enright and Durrant, respectively) is contested mainly on the grounds of how it might affect the trade-off between property values and access. Housing investment and development are key features of contemporary global capitalism, and global cities are the command and control centres not just for global finance, but also (partly because of this) for investment in housing.

London and Toronto are not just the products of a global financial system promoting investment in housing, they are in turn exemplars and symbols of the successes, but also the failures, of such a form of capitalism based on global real estate investment. The chapters in this book lay out a number of these successes, as well as the many failures, of this system. Both London and Toronto are cosmopolitan, diverse urban regions in which much economic opportunity has existed for in-migrants, with lively and (until the COVID-19 pandemic hit) largely safe street life, night life and arts scenes. Both are (still) among the most tolerant places to live in each nation. These are successes, but they have come at a cost. Although London and Toronto have experienced deindustrialisation (see Chapter 8 by Ferm), they have prospered while many other cities in their respective nations have suffered from job loss, slow or declining investment, rapid economic change and outflows of migrants. Often it has been housing and real estate investment that have maintained employment in such non-global cities suffering disinvestment in other sectors, but one effect has been to inflate housing costs in those cities too, beyond local means (albeit from lower initial levels), and, in turn, debt levels among their residents (see Aalbers 2016; Walks 2013). Yet despite gaining significant portions of their livelihoods from the financing of housing, both London and Toronto, as many chapters in this volume attest, have seen housing costs rise far more rapidly than incomes. Very little rental housing has been built to meet demand from tenants, producing rising rents and rendering average incomes insufficient to afford average housing costs. Employment in the financial sector, coupled with rising employment in low-level services, has produced burgeoning inequality, including among those migrants who are unable to insert themselves into the few sectors with employment and income growth (such as finance, insurance or real estate), a problem that was clearly present early on in the process of global city formation (see Sassen 2001). Rising inequality has led to concerns for public safety as a result of shootings and mass murder (including murder via automobile) in both cities, raising the question of how long these cities will remain as largely safe spaces. And the COVID-19 pandemic has exposed the vulnerability of large, globally connected cities to the spread of disease. The arts scenes which have provided these cities with their reputations for tolerance and creativity are under threat of displacement, as noted in Chapter 15 by March, as a result of gentrification pressures (deriving from investment in housing), as well as by the closures compelled by the spread of COVID-19. The chapters in this book suggest that the limited success garnered by a finance-led, real estate-based form of capitalism, and evident in global cities such as London and Toronto, might not make up for their potential failures, weak spots and vulnerabilities, even within those global cities which have seemingly been its main beneficiaries.

Contestations, coalitions and political possibilities

A third conclusion deriving from the various chapters in this volume revolves around the emergence of contestation and coalitional politics in response to the effects of globalisation and financialisation in both London and Toronto. As the chapters by Penny (16), Ostanel (17), Sendra and Fitzpatrick (18) and Bunce (19) make clear, local residents and communities are contesting dominant real estate practices, including not only processes of gentrification and displacement, but also the planning apparatus that favours large-scale developers over community efforts, and the promotion of commodified housing and land markets that disempower local residents. Rising rents, the residualisation of rental housing, the fragmentation of local political processes and the rise of evictions by large-scale financial firms to take advantage of rising rental costs – all are being contested by a larger number of groups, and it is in global cities such as London and Toronto where the largest ecologies of such groups now exist. We see an increasingly broad range of political responses on the ground as residents push back against, navigate and mitigate the effects of global capitalism in both cities. Emergent practices range broadly from direct action against developers on the part of residents and community organisations, to the creation and proliferation of alternative economic development frameworks and forms of housing and land tenure at the neighbourhood level, to the development of elaborate everyday habits of dwelling that simply make it possible to stay in place in these cities.

As noted in the Introduction, both London and Toronto have a history of switching among ideological regimes, typically between those run by Conservative Party politicians advocating for reduced regulation, neoliberalisation and pro-market development, and by left-leaning regimes intent on dealing with the negative outcomes of that development, from transport congestion to lack of affordable housing. And politicians who come to power at national and upper levels of the state often cut their teeth in the local political realm, and sometimes through the promotion of local resentments, taking advantage of the politics of scale discussed above. As some of the most contested urban sites experiencing both heightened redevelopment pressures and some of the most severe urban challenges related to growth, the politics of global cities, with their large, diverse and racialised populations, could go in almost any direction. Organising and resistance emerge largely in response to a shifting range of intensifying pressures that are increasingly felt at the level of everyday life. Current mobilisations centre on building multiple understandings of and relationships to justice; we see organisations working for social, environmental and racial justice in both cities. In London and Toronto there is an awareness that activists and organisations must work together across boundaries and spaces to inform and galvanise intersectional forms of equity and justice, as well as an increasing awareness of the challenging nature of coalition-building under circumstances where individual sites for targeted activism seem to constantly multiply. It is under exactly such circumstances that the interconnection of these sites and the importance of working collectively become apparent.

Efforts to organise and seek out alternatives are evident in communities and neighbourhoods of both cities. Yet while there are activist groups committed to building community land trusts which would provide for secure, affordable housing and community participation in the development process (see Chapter 19 by Bunce), there are also groups aiming to prevent the building of much-needed public transport infrastructure in their neighbourhoods (see Chapter 6 by Durrant). Politics is always uncertain, but global cities – as exemplified by contemporary London and Toronto and their many marginalised spaces and left-behind suburbs – contain what Walks (2017) calls 'radically open fields of possibilities'. As crises in housing, labour and urban politics evolve, these spaces have the potential to give rise to new transformative urban movements. The COVID-19 pandemic and the many policy measures introduced to limit its spread have only made the future even more radically open. For example, the pandemic changed, almost overnight, the logic of investment in Toronto's prime waterfront land by Google affiliate company Sidewalk Labs. Of course, the future exists as a series of potentialities, and it is through political negotiation and contestation that urban politics produces new forms of identities and policies (Isin 2002). Given the evolution of politics in London and Toronto, one thing we do know is that, going forward, there will be a series of alternative perspectives, progressive models for provisioning housing and regulating land as well as other ideas that will be engaged with through a myriad of community-based political, environmental and social initiatives and actions.

This edited volume has produced critical dialogues about the contested and variegated built forms, formal and informal governmental mechanisms and practices, and policy and community-based responses to contemporary urban concerns in two key global cities – London and Toronto. The chapters have contributed localised examples to existing scholarly research in London and Toronto and to understandings of global city dynamics. By taking a comparative and dialogic approach, this volume provides a platform for a continuing dialogue and a basis for future research in both cities.

References

Aalbers, Manuel. 2016. *The Financialization of Housing: A Political Economy Approach*. London: Routledge.
Fields, Desiree. 2019. 'Automated Landlord: Digital Technologies and Post-crisis Financial Accumulation'. *Environment and Planning A*. https://doi.org/10.1177/0308518X19846514.
Isin, Engin. 2002. *Being Political: Genealogies of Citizenship*. Minneapolis: University of Minnesota Press.
Lefebvre, Henri. 2003 (orig. 1970). *The Urban Revolution* (trans. N. Bononno). Minneapolis: University of Minnesota Press.
McNally, David. 2009. 'From Financial Crisis to World-Slump: Accumulation, Financialisation, and the Global Slowdown'. *Historical Materialism* 17:35–83. https://doi.org/10.1163/156920609x436117.
Sassen, Saskia. 2001. *The Global City: New York, London, Tokyo* (2nd edition). Princeton, NJ: Princeton University Press.
Walks, Alan. 2004. 'Place of Residence, Party Preferences, and Political Attitudes in Canadian Cities and Suburbs'. *Journal of Urban Affairs* 26(3):269–95. https://doi.org/10.1111/j.0735-2166.2004.00200.x.
Walks, Alan. 2013. 'Mapping the Urban Debtscape: The Geography of Household Debt in Canadian Cities'. *Urban Geography* 34(2):153–87. https://doi.org/10.1080/02723638.2013.778647.
Walks, Alan. 2017. 'Suburbs and Suburbanisms: Socio-Spatial Technologies and Radically-Open Fields of Possibilities'. *Lo Squaderno: Explorations in Space and Society* 46:13–19.

Index

CPSIA information can be obtained
at www.ICGtesting.com
Printed in the USA
BVHW022115200621
609777BV00031B/450